Childhood's
Future

BOOKS BY RICHARD LOUV

America II

Childhood's Future

Childhood's Future

•

Richard Louv

A Marc Jaffe Book

HOUGHTON
MIFFLIN
COMPANY

BOSTON
1990

For information about permission to reproduce selections from
this book, write to Permissions, Houghton Mifflin Company,
2 Park Street, Boston, Massachusetts 02108.

Library of Congress Cataloging-in-Publication Data

Louv, Richard.
Childhood's future / Richard Louv.
p.   cm.
"A Marc Jaffe book."
Includes bibliographical references and index.
ISBN 0-395-46474-9
1. Children — United States — Social conditions.   2. Family —
United States.   I. Title.
HQ792.U5L68   1990   90-42288
305.23'0973 — dc20   CIP

Printed in the United States of America

BP 10 9 8 7 6 5 4 3 2 1

The author is grateful for permission to reprint material from the
following sources:

Excerpt from U.S. Cellular advertisement, used with permission from
U.S. Cellular Corporation. Excerpt from "A Report from Mothers:
'If I Could Do It Over Again' " by Sherrye Henry, reprinted from
Woman's Day with permission from the author. Excerpt from "The
Future of Public Library Services" by Linda Crismond, reprinted from
Library Journal, November 15, 1986. Copyright © 1986 by Reed
Publishing, USA. Excerpts from *An Imperiled Generation: Saving
Urban Schools* by the Carnegie Foundation for the Advancement of
Teaching, copyright © 1988 The Carnegie Foundation for the Ad-
vancement of Teaching, reprinted with permission. Excerpts from
Housing as If People Mattered, by Clare Cooper Marcus and Wendy
Sarkissian, copyright © 1986 The Regents of the University of Cali-
fornia. Excerpt from "A Primitive Prescription for Equality" by Hel-
en Fisher and Kathleen McAuliffe, reprinted with permission from
U.S. News and World Report. Excerpt from "Perils of Teenage Em-
ployment," reprinted with permission from *U.S. News and World
Report.* Excerpt from "Support Parental Leave" by Mark Satin, ed.,
reprinted with permission from *New Options* newsletter. Excerpt from
"The Economic Plight of America's Young Families: An Update of
CDF's Vanishing Dreams Report" by Clifford M. Johnson, Andred
M. Sum, and James D. Weill, reprinted with permission from the
Children's Defense Fund. Excerpt from *Second Chances: Men, Women,
and Children a Decade After Divorce* by Judith Wallerstein and San-
dra Blakeslee, copyright © 1989 by Judith S. Wallerstein and Sandra
Blakeslee, reprinted by permission of Ticknor & Fields, a Houghton
Mifflin company. Excerpt from *The New American Grandparent: A
Place in the Family, A Life Apart* by Andrew J. Cherlin and Frank
F. Furstenberg, Jr., copyright © 1986 by Basic Books, Inc. Excerpt

To my sons:
Jason, class of 2000, and
Matthew, class of 2006

ACKNOWLEDGMENTS

Just as no one raises a child alone, no one writes a book alone. I am deeply indebted for the time and care of the following individuals, who helped give this book life and direction: my wife, Kathy, for unstinting patience, editing, listening, and love; my sons, for educating me; my editor, Marc Jaffe, for his wisdom and guidance; and my assistant Dennis Woo for his hard work over a period of three years. My other assistants, Tina Kafka and Kathleen Whatley, along with Richard Kipling, David Boe, Ronald Zappone, Ralph Keyes, Marianne Felice, Ralph and Barbara Whitehead, Pauline Louv, Jon Funabiki, Ellen Duris, Roz and Bill Frederick, Millie Loeb, Larry Kessenich, and my agent, Mary Yost, all expressed early and ongoing support and perspective. Among the readers of the drafts, to whom I am enormously indebted for their good humor as well as their editing skills, are Leigh Fenly, Bill Stothers, Dean Stahl, and Karen Kerchelich, Lizanne Poppens, and Marilyn Montanez. Special thanks go to the *San Diego Union*, particularly to my editors, Peter Kaye (unfailingly supportive, wise, conceptual, and constructively contrarian), Gerald Warren, and Karin Winner, and to publisher Helen Copley, for supporting this project through their sponsorship of my newspaper column. Many of the ideas in this book were first expressed in my column, which proved to be an invaluable way to test my notions and to gather feedback. Sharon Reeves and the *Union* librarians were of enormous help. I am also indebted to Erika Mansourian, Rachel Davila, and Becky Saikia-Wilson. Among the many others who helped were Kurt Bell, John French, Brian Athey, and Patricia Chryst. My appreciation goes also to Tom Payzant for connecting me formally with school superintendents around the country, and to the many parents, principals, teachers, and students who welcomed me into their homes and schools and shared their thoughts and feelings with me; they, too, have parented this book.

A word about the research: I have not presumed to be scientific in this evaluation of childhood's future; rather, my method was personal and journalistic. As the child psychiatrist Robert Coles has written, when attempting to draw conclusions from personal interviews one risks, through subjectivity or bias, distorting "what the children have said or meant to say." Nonetheless, by listening closely to children and to parents, one can, as Coles puts it, get "a sense of things, a drift of things — mostly vague, but at moments as clear and resounding as a giant bell." To gather this material I visited schools and parent groups in San Diego, Los Angeles, Seattle, Boston, New York, Philadelphia, Swarthmore, Miami, Wichita, and Kansas City and its suburbs. In selecting and presenting the voices from these interviews, I have tried to adhere closely to the themes that emerged again and again. All of the groups were eloquent, but some carried these themes longer and to some conclusion, and I have therefore returned to these particular persons throughout the book. I have changed the names of most children mentioned in these pages; in a few appropriate instances I have not. Here and there, quotations have been trimmed or condensed, but always with the goal of preserving spirit and meaning.

CONTENTS

Introduction: The Web • 3

PART I: THE VANISHING WEB

1 • "I'll Play with You Tomorrow" • 11
2 • The Bogeyman • 25
3 • In Search of Beaver Cleaver • 42

PART II: GRASPING THE STRANDS

Listening • 69
4 • The Compassion of Children • 70
5 • The Children Who Own Themselves • 83
6 • If Day Care's the Answer, What's the Question? • 96
7 • The Programmed Generation • 109
8 • Computers Can't Dance • 117
9 • The Thief of Time • 130
10 • The Children of Sex, Drugs, and Rock 'n' Roll • 148
11 • Healing Emotions • 165
12 • The Nature of Childhood • 173

PART III: WEAVING A NEW WEB

Weaving • 191
13 • Hope in Hell's Romper Room • 194

14 · Reweaving the Family · 206
15 · The Weaving of New Parent Networks · 215
16 · Toward Fourth-Wave Child Care · 238
17 · The Family-Friendly Work Place · 254
18 · Heading Home · 275
19 · The Global Child · 286
20 · Bringing the Generations Together · 296
21 · Creating the Family-Friendly City · 311
22 · Schools and the Reweaving of Time · 333
Postscript: Toward a Family Liberation Movement · 370

Notes · 377

Bibliography · 409

Index · 411

When everything else has gone from my brain — the President's name, the state capitals, the neighborhoods where I lived, and then my own name and what it was on earth I sought, and then at length the faces of my friends, and finally the faces of my family — when all this has dissolved, what will be left, I believe, is topology: the dreaming memory of land as it lay this way and that.

— Annie Dillard, *An American Childhood*

A spider's web is stronger than it looks. Although it is made of thin, delicate strands, the web is not easily broken. However, a web gets torn every day by the insects that kick around in it, and a spider must rebuild it when it gets full of holes. . . .

— E. B. White, *Charlotte's Web*

Introduction
The Web

Here is the beginning of understanding: most parents are doing their best, and most children are doing their best, and they're doing pretty well, all things considered. When parents and children speak of the nature of childhood today, they seldom advocate or criticize specific government programs or child-rearing philosophies; mostly, they express their sense of isolation and disconnectedness, their feeling that something unnamed is unraveling around them. They speak as if they were foresters moving through tangled woods, marking sick trees for later harvest, but without much sense of the forest's dimensions or shape. The foresters can hear movement and voices and catch glimpses of others in the woods, but these contacts are fleeting, almost dreamlike. On those rare occasions when parents meet and converse at length about their lives as parents and about their children's lives, they attempt to measure the forest. Their hope: if only this strange environment can be understood, personal and public solutions will follow.

As a father first, and a journalist second, I embarked on the researching and writing of this book as a personal journey — an opportunity to do what many parents would like to do: travel the country through the new landscape of childhood, listening to parents and children and, on occasion, experts. By now, anyone who reads the newspaper understands that the news about childhood is statistically grim, but is the news enough? Like Diogenes, who searched for an honest man, I was looking for successful adaptations — for signs of health.

Over the course of three years I met with groups of parents, children, and teachers around the country. These conversations usually took place in classrooms or homes. Occasionally I sat alone with individuals. But group interactions of ten or twenty or thirty people often revealed more about the connections among people and the environment around them. Children were surprisingly open — sometimes embarrassingly so. After some of the sessions, teachers would comment that they had known kids today were more open than in previous generations, but they didn't know kids were *that* open. Again and again students would come up to me after class and say, in various ways, "We never really *talk* this way about these things." Parent sessions that had been scheduled to last one hour would almost invariably be extended — by the parents — to three or four hours. Often, late at night, mothers and fathers would linger outside under a porch light, and one or two of them would remark that they had seldom had such a chance to talk to other parents, to reveal their fears, to understand that they were not alone. Despite the ever-expanding supply of how-to-parent books and the general agreement among parenting experts that the most useful experts parents can turn to are other parents, parents today feel isolated from other parents. Their confusion is seldom shared in any deep way. There is no time, or appropriate place, or they have not realized their need to share these feelings until they actually begin to share them.

What emerged from these conversations was often stunning, sometimes terrifying, and ultimately hopeful. Clearly the subject matter was larger than the current narrow debates about child care or educational reform. Parents and children described an environment that no longer makes much sense — people are divorced from nature, their time is polluted, they live in sprawling cities with no centers and few natural meeting places, neighborhoods that can barely be called neighborhoods — an environment that no longer nurtures children and which drives family life deeper into itself. To speak of these things as "children's issues" is to consider them in their diminutive form and make them easier to dismiss. These are no more children's issues than they are solely women's issues. When I asked one father what he thought about the problem with children today, he responded: "Is there a problem with children? I don't think so. I think there's a problem with us. With the way everybody is being socialized. We need to look at ourselves. We need to figure out what we really want."

What is it that we want? The word that comes to mind is *liberation*.

How can families liberate themselves and their full potential? Could it be that, after twenty years of movements (all of which were appropriate for their time, all of which were based on the rights of the individual, on breaking connections with tradition, with families, with institutions), a new kind of liberation movement is germinating — one that recognizes the right of the family to be *connected*?

Quietly, mostly beyond the Washington, D.C., Beltway, a parents' movement — or, more broadly, a family liberation movement — is being born. To be effective, this movement, by defining *family* in the broadest possible way, will enlist the commitment of people who are not parents; it will be both personal and political; it will define *liberation* not as the act of breaking off from one another, but as the individual's ability, particularly the child's ability, to live to the fullest potential — precisely because of the supportive strands that connect us. The goal of the movement will be to improve family life and the lives of children *now*, as well as in the future. The movement's success will depend on four things: our ability, economically and socially, to look beyond the needs of our own individual families; our ability to listen carefully to parents and especially to children; our willingness to work at the grassroots level as well as in the larger political arena; and our ability to see the interconnectedness of the new environment of childhood.

Today's children are living a childhood of firsts. They are the first day-care generation; the first truly multicultural generation; the first generation to grow up in the electronic bubble, the environment defined by computers and new forms of television; the first post–sexual revolution generation; the first generation for which nature is more abstraction than reality; the first generation to grow up in new kinds of dispersed, deconcentrated cities, not quite urban, rural, or suburban.

The combined force of these changes produces a seemingly unstoppable dynamic process: childhood today is defined by the expansion of experience and the contraction of positive adult contact. Each part of this process feeds and speeds the other. The more of the manmade world that children experience, the more they assume they know (and as they become teenagers, the less they think they need adults). Because children seem to know more about the world, adults are more likely to assume, sometimes wishfully, that kids can take care of themselves. As a result, children and adults pass each other in the night at ever-accelerating speeds, and the American social environment becomes increasingly lonely for both.

The way to reverse this process is to find ways to increase positive contact between adults and children.

That prescription is deceptively simple. It demands not only a reworking of priorities within each family, but also a reweaving of the larger environment so that positive contact is even possible.

We have heard much in recent years of society's safety net. We have been assured by some politicians that it was intact and all was well, that anyone who fell through would be caught. But it is clear today that, given current trends, the safety net cannot hold. I have therefore come to think of the overall environmental pattern in this way: visualize, above the safety net, a great network, a supportive and intricate web. This web is far more important than the safety net, yet we pay much less attention to it, to patching it and simply respecting it. It is a wonderfully intricate and liberating web, and not easily described or quantified or fixed through fad legislation. One strand, the most important, is made of parents; another is the school system; another is the work place and how it treats parents; another is the neighborhood; another is how the city is shaped. . . .

The web is emotional as well as physical. As a boy growing up in a troubled family, I sensed that I could get much of what I needed from the web — neighbors to watch out for me on the street, schools that cared, and an understandable community in which to prove myself.

James Comer, director of the Yale Child Study Center, described this aspect of the web. According to Comer, children are willing to accept parental influence until they're eight or nine years old; then they begin to drift toward forces outside the home. In the past, kids might have turned to extended families, churches, healthy neighborhoods. "Between home and school, at least five close friends of my parents reported everything I did that was unacceptable," he said. "They're not there anymore for today's kids."

Once the web begins to unravel, the smallest bodies fall through first. That is what is happening today.

How we face the destruction of the old web and the weaving of a new one will shape not only America's future character, but our character as individuals as well. The nation is in the midst of what could be called, to extend psychoanalyst Erik Erikson's famous categories, a "generativity" crisis. In Erikson's theory of personality growth, the seventh of eight stages of growth is *generativity versus self-absorption.* To Erikson, involvement in the well-being and development of the next generation is the essence of generativity. This stage includes being a good parent, but it represents more than that. Adults — whether or not they themselves are parents — need to be needed by the young. Unless adults can be concerned about and can contribute to the next generation, they suffer from stagnation. In Erikson's view, these adults are barred from passage into the final stage of development: *ego integrity versus despair.* In this stage, a sense of integrity comes from satisfaction with one's own life cycle and its place in space and time; the individual feels that his or her relationships and actions and values are meaningful. Despair arises when a person is convinced that it is too late to try again.

Although it may not be academically pure to apply Erikson's theory of personal development to an entire generation, doing so allows our current national condition to be viewed through a particularly clear lens. Just as children are at risk, baby boomers, beginning to parent in large numbers, are also endangered. Ultimately their sense of who they are is at risk.

Will we be able to look back with pride on how we cared for our young? One thirty-three-year-old mother told me: "I just feel like we blew it somehow. All that sixties idealism has been lost. But we can get it back, and the key is our kids. In the sixties, we wanted to change the lives of our parents, change their moral values. And it didn't work, so we cut our losses and focused on ourselves. After all these years, we're no more gratified or satisfied than when we started. And all the good we wanted to get from our parents and for our parents, our kids are waiting to get from us. The solution to where we're at is to focus on our children." She did not mean that we should indulge our children in obsessive, guilt-induced materialism, but that we should connect to something bigger than ourselves, bigger even than our own individual families. I heard this theme frequently, this yearning for generational redemption. The topic of childhood seems to touch some deep chord in my generation: *here is a challenge to which our idealism can once again rise.*

Even in their darkest moments, the persons who speak in this book describe the liberating web that could be. They do this indirectly, obliquely. They intuitively understand that this web supports us all, and that attending to it will improve life for children and also for adults, whether or not they have children of their own. What we have lacked is a conceptual framework and a set of guiding principles that could unite liberals and conservatives, principles that could help us, within our families and communities, move beyond fragmented, programmatic, and often counterproductive approaches. I believe that framework and those principles emerge from the voices that speak in this book. A new web, more appropriate for the times and the economy, can surely be woven. It will be created through transformed public schools, family-friendly work places, new community designs, new ways of structuring family time, a new synthesis of traditional and modern family values. Parts of this web already exist; the imagining of the rest has already begun.

So in researching and writing this book, I have attempted to listen to those who have fallen through the web, those who are barely hanging on, and those who have begun to weave.

PART I

The Vanishing Web

●

I've decided to tell you the difference between literature and life: Literature is mostly about having sex and not much about having children. Life is the other way around.

    —John K. Van de Kamp, attorney general of California

"Excuse me, I'd like to buy an hour."
"I'm sorry, we're all out of hours. . . ."
"Excuse me, but have you got a minute?"
"No, but there's a shipment coming in next week."

    —Radio jingle for U.S. Cellular
    (a company specializing in portable phones)

My family wasn't the Cleavers.

    —Ron Prescott Reagan, son of the former president

1

"I'll Play with You Tomorrow"

●

When we raise our children, we relive our childhood. Forgotten memories, painful and pleasurable, rise to the surface. A lost ball recalls another lost ball twenty, thirty years ago; the smell of cedar brings forth the Christmas of '57; the burial of a hamster brings forth tears of another time for another pet — perhaps a turtle wrapped in tissue and buried beneath an elm tree. When we hear ourselves raise our voices at our children, or see or hear ourselves through their eyes and ears, we meet the ghosts of our own young parents. So each of us thinks, almost daily, of how our own childhood compares with our children's, and of what our children's future will hold. Parents would often say that these questions had haunted them long before I asked them, and that answering them could not be done simply.

Tina Kafka, divorced, a good and caring parent of one girl and two boys, described the trickiness of memory: "I remember climbing in my tree for hours, playing in the wash with my friends, in an old dried-up riverbed in the San Fernando Valley, and sliding down the sides on pieces of cardboard, and playing Three Flies Up with the neighborhood kids in the street. I remember doing all this stuff with my friends, always with my friends. And when I described these memories to my mother, she said: 'What are you talking about? I always had to *import* a friend for you to play with. You would never play with the kids on the street.' Her memories of my childhood are completely different from mine. Maybe certain things stand out in my mind, and didn't happen as much as I thought."

Tina, who is thirty-nine, still carries about her the air of the sixties: her brown hair is long and straight, and she wears long dresses or worn jeans. She lives in a San Diego neighborhood suddenly popular among young parents. I live in this neighborhood too, with my wife and two boys. The neighborhood is known for its small wooden frame houses with front porches, hardwood trees in the front yards, wide sidewalks, and a usable park. Most of the parents who move here work long hours at two careers in order to support this expensive and nostalgic vision, though most of us grew up in tract houses somewhere in suburban America. So many of us, as parents, wish to capture the image of what we have been told family life and childhood are supposed to be. We're able to touch this image sometimes, but then it pulls away and hovers, like a Disney hologram, just beyond reach.

"My son is going to junior high now," Tina continued. "He figures this is the end of his childhood. He was crying when he told me that. The bright kids in advanced classes feel they missed out, the pregnant kids feel they missed out — though I'm not sure they have an understanding of what a childhood is supposed to be."

I thought later about the mythology of my own childhood outside Kansas City, about my daydreams of Huckleberry Finn and Lassie. . . . I would go with my collie into the woods near the house at the far edge of suburbia and build my own world out of small mysteries: exploring near a farm hidden away next to a swamp, lost in those woods; climbing a poplar, one of the tall straight hedge trees overlooking the corn fields, clear to the top, until the trunk was three inches thick, until it began to bend and sway in the Missouri wind.

For the first few years of my parenthood, I felt heartsick that my sons would not likely know these pleasures, the pleasures of a "real" American boyhood, unless we moved back to the Midwest. So my wife and I often thought of moving, and still do. Surely without being able to experience a boyhood like mine, my boys would be deprived. But after a time I realized something about the boys that are my sons and the boy that was me. Although there was love in my childhood family, there was also unhappiness from which I needed to escape. The boy and his dog in the woods had a reason for being there. Now I realize that my sons do not have so much to escape. Surely there will come a time when they will want to hide some of their lives from me, and that will be natural; but it is not my right to insist that they have a childhood just like mine, or that I impose my boyhood escapism on them. I would have traded the woods and even the dog for some peace in my boyhood family. My sons are surrounded now with that peace. I do not need to push them toward escape, or to re-create my own childhood mythology anymore.

But this realization does not erase the discomforting sense that my sons face a childhood in which the choice to play simply and slowly, to grow naturally, is being overwhelmed by an environment defined too much by electronics and speed.

Certainly, some parents insist, childhood today is more interesting. "My child is always asking me if I had computers in my day, if my family had a microwave," said one mother. And one father and teacher described his ambivalence about today's childhood: "What bothers me is the values. Cheating wasn't a factor when I was a kid, not like it is now. I wonder what's happening with these kids, where they're going to end up. And yet — I look at my son Andy's yearbook and at mine and there's no comparison. His class looks alive, mine didn't." He laughed. "I keep thinking it's technology. Maybe the color plating of photography has improved. Whatever the reason, his class looks alive. And if I came from outer space and looked at these two yearbooks, and had a choice in which time I lived, I wouldn't hesitate for a minute. I'd choose Andy's time."

It isn't a simple question, whether childhood is better or worse. Perhaps the difference is more one of balance than of quality.

Tom Payzant, fifty, superintendent of the San Diego Unified School District, described his sense that childhood has somehow tilted. A few nights before our talk he had read Annie Dillard's autobiographical *An American Childhood.* When we spoke, it was eight-thirty in the evening, the windows of his office were darkened, and he was due home, but talking of Dillard's memoir of her childhood in the late forties and early fifties drew him back into that time. "What she described seemed utterly familiar to me, and yet absolutely alien to the experience of my own children. I was trying throughout that book to see whether my kids would relate to it in the same way," he said. "I don't think they could. Maybe it's not so different that kids hang around video parlors and malls for their social activity than it was for kids to gather at the corner drugstore or the church social on Saturday nights thirty years ago. But what's surely different is that kids are gathering at the video parlor Saturday night, Sunday night, Tuesday night, Thursday afternoon — and most of them aren't engaged in other activities. Something just seems out of balance, out of whack. I suppose kids have more choices today, but among what options? Some kids in San Diego, poor ones, have *never* been to the beach. Maybe this is the main difference: we're losing the middle class. In the Boston area, as a middle-class kid, I didn't have a great deal, but I had as much as I needed. In my neighborhood there were professional people and working-class people. There were wealthy people too, and poor people, but most of us were in the great middle, and for a kid, it was a pretty good place to be."

The middle was also a state of mind, a sense of balance between work and family. This older middle is being replaced by an expensive, pack-aged, sliding-scale center, in which the images and symbols of middle-class Americana can be bought for a high price in the right neighbor-hood, catalogue, or amusement park, but somehow do not live up to their advertising and labeling. The middle has become *muddle* in Pay-zant's new world. The conventional wisdom is that children today are suffering from information overload, but the real villain is information *underload*. Parents and children face choices, choices everywhere, but with less value placed on the meaning of so many of these choices.

One father spoke wistfully of what he called "the diminished capacity for wonder" in children. I asked him to elaborate. "You know, to be thrilled with things. When you've played in a soccer tournament at the age of seven in a professional indoor coliseum here in Wichita, what's going to be left when you're eighteen years old? It's infinitely more com-plicated today than it was for me when I was growing up. We expect more of the children, expect our children to do better in school, to be more responsible, to be more aware. But there's a kind of deflation of meaning."

A thirty-nine-year-old junior high teacher in San Diego, a single mother, spoke of the accelerating weirdness in her classroom. "When I was in the ninth grade, no student came to school with a beeper on his belt, waiting to make drug deals. I try to fight the feeling that childhood is just getting worse and worse. I tell myself each person can make his or her own life as positive as they want it to be. Our parents used to say, 'Kids are going to hell these days,' and *their* parents probably said, 'Kids are going to hell these days.' I find myself tugging between my fear and my intellect saying, Well, they said this all along — every generation is worse than the one before. Yet I'm not so sure that this time isn't worse. I just feel something's coming apart and I'm not sure I can describe how I feel, but I know a lot of other people feel it too."

In my interviews with parents and children the shape of this anxiety gradually began to take form. Two dominant themes stood out: first, time — the sense that time is a decreasing natural resource for both chil-dren and parents; and second, the lessening of trust. Powerful, often subliminal fear burns slowly beneath the surface of American cul-ture. One mother summed up her most intense feelings this way: "Child-hood today scares me. But I don't have time to do anything about the fear."

The clearest evidence that the supportive web for children and for par-ents has pulled apart is the lack of family time.

In the sixties and seventies, social scientists enthusiastically predicted the coming Age of Leisure. Computers and automation were going to unshackle us from the tyranny of work; our biggest problem would be all the extra time on our hands. Somehow, things haven't quite worked out that way.

Forget the 40-hour workweek. In 1988, according to Louis Harris's surveys, the average workweek rose to 46.8 hours. Professional people work a weekly average of 52.2 hours. And small-business people — entrepreneurs — work 57.3 hours. (At Apple Computer, in California's Silicon Valley, development teams wear T-shirts that read, WORKING 90 HOURS A WEEK AND LOVING IT.) According to Harris, leisure time shrank from 26.2 hours a week in 1973 to 16.6 hours in 1987 — a 37 percent drop in the amount of time we relax, recreate, or spend with our families. (Those studies that disagree with this conclusion focus on the general population, usually ignoring the fact that families with children face significantly different time problems.) How we spend our leisure time reveals the effects of a kind of time "pollution" that not only steals time but contaminates its quality. For many Americans, leisure time is more numbing than renewing. The top choices for leisure are television watching and resting. In 1938, according to pollster George Gallup, people were a lot more active in their leisure time; the most popular leisure pastimes were reading, going to movies, and dancing. Resting wasn't even considered as a form of recreation or leisure activity.[1]

We're exhausted and overbooked — particularly career women with children, who still do most of the cooking and cleaning at home. Despite a greater willingness among some husbands to pitch in, studies show that a typical working mother does only two hours' less housework than a mother who stays at home. According to a report published in 1989 by the Family Research Council of Washington, D.C., the amount of time parents spend with their children has dropped 40 percent during the last quarter century. In 1965, the average parent had roughly thirty hours' contact with his or her children each week. Today the average parent has just seventeen hours' contact with children a week. A study conducted by Pittsburgh's Priority Management Company in 1988 revealed that the average working couple spends four minutes a day in meaningful conversation with each other, and the average working parent spends thirty seconds in meaningful conversation with his or her children. "Increasingly, couples find that their scarcest resource is time, not money," says Peter Morrison, director of the Rand Corporation's Population Research Center.[2]

How do we compensate for our time poverty?

• We sacrifice family rituals. Families are moving away from home dining; according to Morrison, most people don't want to spend more
than twenty-five minutes cooking dinner. As a consequence, we see the
astonishing growth of take-out and fast-food chains. A Roper poll
showed that, between 1976 and 1990, the number of families that ate
evening meals together dropped 10 percent. *Newsweek* has reported
that the length of the average family vacation has declined 14 percent
since 1983.[3]

• We tend to bear fewer children. The time shortage may be partially
responsible for the falling fertility rate — the total number of births a
woman has during her lifetime — according to Rita Ricardo-Campbell, senior fellow at the Hoover Institution of Stanford University.
"That rate is still falling [as of 1986], even though the birth rate is
slightly higher." The number of women in their child-bearing years
remains relatively high, reflecting the post–World War II baby boom.
"Time is the scarcest resource a working woman has, and the easiest
way to contain demands on her time is to have fewer or no children
than women did in the past."[4]

• We buy more gadgets to close the time gap. But studies of life satisfaction suggest that there is little relationship between "time-saving" gadgets and the quality of life. Does the fax machine save us time all the
time? Or does it make it more difficult to quit work — do we tell ourselves that if we stay a few hours later we can still get that report to
the New York office by morning?

    What about all that hired help and those labor-saving devices in the
home — the kitchen equivalents of the office fax machine? Ruth
Schwartz Cowan's *More Work for Mother* is a fascinating study of
household work and technology. In 1914, Cowan points out, the wife
of a college professor typically had two different kinds of household
assistants: a laundress, who washed and did heavy cleaning; and a
student who cleared after meals, did light cleaning, and supervised children when the parents were away. Between 1940 and 1980, the number of households in the United States more than doubled, but the
number of domestic servants fell by nearly half. In 1957, Americans
reported a level of satisfaction with their lives that has yet to be surpassed. At that time, only 9.5 percent of American households had air
conditioning, about 4 percent had dishwashers, fewer than 15 percent had more than one car (and nobody had home computers or
VCRs).[5]

• We attempt to compress time (much as television technologists have
learned to do by speeding up the pace of commercials) into "quality"

time. An ad for Pioneer electronics shows a handsome young man, legs crossed, in his lap a baby he feeds with a bottle. In front of him is a Pioneer PD-M700 compact disc player, with stacks of jazz and rock CDs. The young father is wearing earphones. The ad copy reads, QUALITY TIME. YOUR MOMENTS TOGETHER ARE TOO PRE-CIOUS TO WASTE. (And apparently too precious to waste doing only one thing at a time.)

However, most of us, as parents, are deeply ambivalent about quality time. Some of us spit the phrase out as if the thing it stands for were some kind of foul-tasting medicine — a cure worse than the disease. And children often feel the same ambivalence.

The Children's Time Zone

A few months after I began the research for this book, I found myself standing in the midst of a class of third-graders at Van Asselt Early Childhood Center, an elementary school in Seattle. I was late, but the children were eager to talk. So, with ten minutes left in the school period, I asked a single question: What is childhood?

Only a few hands went up.

"How you live, when you're a baby to when you're grown."

"What you do when you're little and what you do with your life."

One little boy said simply, "What your life is."

The hands on the clock were moving. The room was growing warmer. An odor was rising in the classroom, the smell of poverty or neglect. Some of the children were from shelters for the homeless. Some were from affluent families. The classroom held a variety of hues and colors and dialects: the students at the school came from eighteen ethnic groups and spoke fourteen different languages.

I didn't think I was getting anywhere. I asked another question: How did their parents spend time with them?

The class exploded in chatter. Hands flew up. I moved from child to child, bending close to hear their soft-spoken answers.

"My parents say, 'I'll spend time with you tomorrow,'" said a little girl whose voice was as light and high as a sparrow's. She was wearing an expensive-looking dress. She twirled her fingers as she talked. "But they don't."

A boy looked up and said, "My dad works morning till night, and my mom works afternoons and nights, so they say, 'Tomorrow we're gonna do some things,' but tomorrow comes and they go to work."

Another little girl, this one with her hair braided in corn rows, said: "When I be gettin' home from school my mom is just leaving to go somewhere. That happens mostly all the time, when I be gettin' out of school."

And another boy whispered, "My dad says, 'I'll play with you tomorrow,' but tomorrow comes and he watches TV. . . ."

I stood up. The bell rang and desks were shoved and books gathered and dropped and the kids bumped and clattered and giggled, and the room emptied. *I'll play with you tomorrow* — I've said that to Jason, my own son. How often, interviewing children, have I heard that phrase, or some variation of it.

All parents have said it at one time or another. (One father told me the first phrase his child learned was "Not now, later.") But there was an urgency in these children's voices, a vacancy and yearning. A child's desire for more time with his or her parents is part of the natural order of things (at least until a child is a pre-teen). But the yearning has grown emphatic.

When Nickelodeon, a television network aimed at children, conducted its ongoing Nickelodeon/Yankelovich Youth Monitor study in 1987, children were asked to name the things they wanted more of in their lives. One response stood out: 76 percent said they wanted more time with their families.[6]

In a class at San Diego High School for at-risk students (the class was called Problem Solving), I asked whether kids thought their parents spent enough time with them. Several students (some of them wearing earrings and some leather) laughed cynically. "I see my parents occasionally," said one girl. "We kind of eat dinner together, watching TV. Sometimes we all eat dinner together like at Christmas and Thanksgiving." Only two of the kids said they ate regularly with their parents. "This is a new age," explained a boy. "You don't have time to do things like that like you used to in the old days, like traditional farm families that had plenty of time to eat together. Like, the mom is working overtime and the dad is in the bar drinking somewhere else and the kid if he works, he works for McDonald's — he gets out at twelve or something."

I asked kids how they defined quality time, and how they felt about it.

"Quality time sounds pretty vague," said one high school junior.

"I think quality time is time with the parent and child together, alone. Loving each other, talking to each other. Something in a productive way. The kid's learning something and gaining something new other than just sitting around."

One girl at Trinity School, an elite private school in Manhattan, said: "I think kids were receiving a lot more quality time before they started calling it quality time. Nowadays it's something you've got to do. It's an effort. It's not natural."

To whom do children turn when their parents do not have enough time for them? To other time givers, some benign, some not so benign. To peers, to gangs, to early sex partners, to the new electronic bubble of computers and video. Or, if they're lucky, to a wider web of kin, neighbors, and teachers. More often, given the condition of the wider web, they turn to a sibling.

"When I was young my parents would spend a lot of time with me," said one high school junior. "Most of the day I'd have my mom at home. She'd just always be there. Now my mom has a full-time career and I have a little brother. When I was in seventh grade I guess I was kind of out of hand. But my brother is *seriously* out of hand. I can tell he doesn't get that quality time. So I give him the quality time. My parents try to do that but my mother has to deal with all sorts of bureaucracy bullshit and she's too tired to do anything. My dad teaches out of state four days a week. He comes home and he tries to spend time with my brother, but my brother — I think he's really missing the part that I had. You can really tell the difference. My brother's morals and mine are different. Because my parents brought me up and my brother is getting brought up by a lot of his friends along with me."

As I delved deeper into the issue of family time, I realized that the reasons for our anxiety about time are more complex than simply our concern with the number of hours we spend with our kids, or even the quality of those hours. At the heart of the matter is how we perceive time. Most kids have an acute sense of the quickening pace of life. A boy at Baldi Middle School in Philadelphia, describing the music he listens to, said: "Have you ever heard like the music that is so fast you can't understand what they're saying? That's *speed metal*. I think this generation right here that we're in is more fast-moving than the generation before and I think each generation is going to get a little bit faster than the other one." Though parents and kids share this sense of being pushed forward a few extra nanoseconds, children and adults still live in entirely different time zones.

The adult time zone allows for delay, distraction, pushing away. *If not this year, next year; that's when we'll do it.* Academicians say, "Something is wrong with childhood; we'll do a five-year study." *We'll play with you tomorrow.* Politicians suggest legislation. "But be patient," they say; "these things take time." But no such luxury exists in the children's time zone because children, annoyingly, grow up. By the time their parents do have time for them, many kids don't have time for their parents. The time perceptions of a third-grader are quite different from those of an eleventh-grader. Said one teenager, "By the time you're a teenager, the parents, you know, care *too* much."

"I don't think they have time to care in the beginning because of their careers and all," said a handsome, lanky boy at Trinity. Moments earlier, he had pulled a chair out from under a girl as she sat down. She had hit the floor with a crack, and the class laughed. His face had barely registered emotion. So now as he spoke, I found his sensitivity surprising. "I see my dad about seven or eight hours per week. My dad comes home and I see him an hour a night. He eats and takes a shower and goes to bed. Then I see him Sunday afternoons. My mom is always busy. I think there are two sets of parent groups. One is the struggling parents. They really tried to get some money, get their careers going. And the others are ones who are thrilled with the idea of having kids, but once they do, they're just not too keen on bringing them up. When you're older and you want more independence versus the caring, they're more willing to care because they realize you're getting older. That's just the way it is."

I wondered, Will these kids have enough time for their own kids? Will they eventually become time rebels? In Shawnee Mission, Kansas, at Hocker Grove Middle School (a school I attended during the mid-sixties), one of the brightest students, a girl decked out in combat boots and orange hair (one side shaved), said: "If I had kids, like accidentally, I'd give them all my time. . . . But I don't have time to have kids. I've got too much stuff I want to do in my life. It's kind of scary to think about. You know, you end up with a good-paying job, you move to a nice house, you get married, you have kids. But then if your husband has a good job, too, your jobs take over your life, and then you forget you have kids." She laughed, cynically. "There's this great song by the Godfathers, called 'Birth, School, Work, Death.' And I think that says it all."

How Parents Feel About Time

Parents, like their children, feel victimized by the lack of family time. One parent, Kathleen Duschene, wrote in a letter to me about the sense of distorted priorities and vanishing time:

> I'm sitting here at work at Abbott Laboratories in North Chicago, Illinois.
> I'm plugged into a phone where I spend what seems like most of my life.

I have a 19-year-old still living at home, a 16-year-old and a 4-year-old. Back in the '60s and early '70s I stayed home with my boys until they went to school, then when I went to work our family time fell apart. Not being able to be home with my preschooler is horrible for me. I've tried to think of a million things to do to be at home, part-time work (not enough money — no benefits), work at home (same reasons as above), own company where I can take my daughter (no money, no benefits etc., no education, no time and on and on). My company is really slow moving on day care, job sharing, part-time work (they want to give it to you but without benefits, vacation pay, medical insurance, etc.). I work for a very large, very wealthy health-care company, and this is what makes it even more frustrating. . . .

I might mention that I am working to help support my family in a middle-income house, in a middle- to low-income neighborhood. We own one extremely old car and one new one. We go out to eat *maybe* once a month. We have old furniture and appliances that are falling apart. We do go on one nice week-long vacation a year to a fishing spot in the car, and have elaborate Christmases, but we are not able to save much and seem to need everything. So you see, I feel I have to work!

What I've noticed is that more young women I work with seem to be choosing to have wardrobes instead of children, or choosing not to get married at all. I have felt for years that everything is gearing away from family time. Even the schools are making it difficult. Football practice starts right after school and goes on 'til dark, which means that from August through December there is no evening meal all together. The kids work, and have sports activities — everything interferes with family time. It ends up that we aren't as close to our children as we would like to be. We don't know as much as we would like to about what they are doing and about their friends. We don't have enough control, we just aren't there for them. Then we read about the crime rate and about "other people's children" and the trouble they are in, and we wonder if tomorrow the news will be about us, when all we want is to be able to give them a few things, a decent home in a half-way decent neighborhood and a few luxuries. How far should we go? I want to be there for them yet I want them to have what's good, too.

Particularly for single parents, the connection between time and money creates an almost unbearable challenge. In a group of single parents I interviewed at Dewey Elementary School in San Diego, one mother, a thirty-six-year-old woman who works as a hairdresser, spoke with intensity: "Sometimes you don't feel like a real person, you don't feel like you're doing your job as a parent no matter how much you love them, because of money. You don't have any time with them because you're working all the time. It's going so fast. Suddenly your child is walking and talking, and you've missed it. But then there's the child-care bill, and you have to put it off with excuses, and your child runs a fever for three days and you haven't the money to pay for a doctor's visit. When they get sick, you stay home with them, and you miss work, which means you don't get paid, and *aaaahhhhhh* . . . it's like a chain reaction."

Like all working parents, but with more intensity and inventiveness, single parents devise time tricks. First comes time shifting. "I do everything at night," said Sophia, another single mother in the group. "Wait till they're in bed and then clean all I can until late at night and then get up early and start all over again." Then comes time compacting. One of the younger single mothers said she never does just one thing at a time around the house. "When I'm cooking dinner, my daughter sits on the counter next to the microwave and we talk. When she's in the tub, I'll jump in and join her. And when I vacuum the house, I put her on the vacuum. She likes to ride the vacuum, and that's a time when we can talk."

"But once they get past five years old," said still another single mother, smiling, "you can't ride them on the vacuum anymore."

Yet even relatively affluent parents can't seem to buy enough time.

On a flight to Miami I met Steve Stein, a professor of Latin American history at the University of Miami. "I remember my parents saying they didn't have enough time, but I never felt they didn't have enough time for *me*," he said. "But I hear myself saying that too much to my own kids. Today, ask your colleagues, 'How are you?' The typical answer is 'I'm tired, I'm working too hard, and I don't have any time for anything.' When that happens with academicians we're really in trouble." He laughed. "Time is power, time and space. Space, because I had to fight like hell to get a new office. As I move up the hierarchy I have less time and I apportion that more carefully. I subconsciously realize who to ask for time and how much to ask for, and to apologize: 'I need to talk to so and so, but I'll only take fifteen minutes.' Do we start to see our kids in the same way we see subordinates, as people who are making demands on our time? I hope I don't. But it could happen. The other thing is our kids don't always see any serious external evidence that we're getting something out of all this time pressure. My kids say to me, 'Why are you working so hard?' I say, 'For the freedom.' They seem to accept it as an answer, but it's hard to say how they really feel about it. Maybe we're creating a new generation of flower children, who pull out of the rat race so they can have more personal time, more family time. But of course, that's what we said *we* were going to do."

He looked out the window of the jet at the clouds below. His hair was longish, thin, graying. He wore rimless glasses. "Remember that time? Time seemed — suspended then." He settled into his seat and looked down at his tray of food. "The other scenario is that the kids see their father and mother doing exciting things, and maybe the kids follow that path with some joy." He poked at the food in front of him. "There's this school in Miami. It's in the best neighborhood, with high-income families. This school doesn't give the kids recess! They have to spend the time improving their test scores. *There's no time for recess.* One thing that youth is supposed to have is time, but now what we're telling kids is not just that *we* don't have time anymore, but that *they* don't have time."

Many parents spoke of time in tones of rebellion — or, more precisely, retrenchment, withdrawal, disgust at the tempo and quality of life, both in the work place and in the family. Something is wrong, they said — we're on a fast track to nowhere. Through all this frantic running around some zenith has been reached, a point at which people have begun to say, This is crazy; we're not living, we're doing lunch. The rebellion is not against feminism; nor does it particularly support traditional roles. The rebellion is against time pollution, the feeling that the essence of what makes life worth living — the small moments, the special family getaways, the cookies in the oven, the night fishing with the kids asleep next to the lantern, the weekend drives, the long dreamlike summers — so much of this has been taken from us, or we have given it up. For what? Hitachi stereos? Club Med? Company cars? Racquetball? For fifteen-hour days and lousy day care?

When *Woman's Day* asked three hundred of its readers what they would do over again in raising their children, only a small minority said they believed that they had been with their children too much. "In fact, the lament heard most often was not enough time spent with the children. Most (95 percent) would opt for as much time *or more,* just as they wish, overwhelmingly, that their children had spent the same or more time with grandparents, other members of their families and, most poignantly (61 percent), with their fathers." This sense of time-slipped-away is felt both by those who had worked and by those who didn't. Six out of ten women who worked when their children were small now wish they had been home more. But 79 percent of mothers who stayed at home, though they never worked, express the same sense of loss. Lost time alone is not the major regret. What they mourn — even with vivid memories of noisy, whiny, sometimes obnoxious little people who blocked where they wanted to walk, seldom entered a room without leaving it in tatters, and never closed their mouths except to chew — is that they did not spend enough time "savoring" their children. What do they regret? Six out of ten regret not doing the simplest things — as one woman put it, the "picnics, silly sports, wiener roasts, camping out together." At the top of the list of regrets: not taking more vacations, followed by not going to church as a family more, attending movies and sporting events more, and visiting relatives more often.[7]

In Miami, one mother told me: "My daughter is only eleven. There's still time. But she has grown up faster than I was ready for. She is so much more mature at eleven than I was, and I now sometimes sit back and think, Her youth is gone. I've got a little girl here now, and she's not little. She's becoming a young lady much sooner than I want. Parents always feel that. I can remember my parents saying things like that — 'You're growing up so fast.' But these children *are* growing up faster. I mean, they actually reach puberty sooner than our generation did. When I think of my son, he's now ten, on the average I've got eight more years of him living in my house as my child. He'll be off to college. Most of the life that he'll live with me he has already finished. That's a good way to think about it because by thinking about it it gives me more patience and more time with them. Otherwise, you forget, you're thinking you've got tomorrow, but you don't. My husband and I hunger for more family time, but we're not sure how to do it — so much is beyond our immediate control. But we're *determined*."

This sense of rebellion among parents, if it grows, will be the most important element in weaving the new web. We yearn so deeply for time — not quality time but free time, dream time, time to *be* with our families and ourselves. Time to face the bogeyman.

2

The Bogeyman

•

The fear . . .

An old Volvo sat cockeyed in the driveway, in front of an old barn, and Tom Fitzsimons was wiping his hands on a rag and walking across the back yard toward his family's Victorian house. The porch swing in front was creaking slightly in the wind. The house was in Swarthmore, Pennsylvania, an idyllic town filled with old trees and young children and wide sidewalks, where, as Beth Fitzsimons told me later, there is one rule: nobody can hurt trees or children. It was, in short, the last place one would expect parents to express fear.

It was Sunday morning. Beth was cooking pancakes, and Tom came in to take turns with her at the skillet. The kitchen was filled with kids: Devin, nine, quizzical and impish, and haphazardly dressed Elizabeth ("Biz" for short), twelve, who describes herself as a "scummie," the opposite of a "trendie," and Biz's friends, Katie and Becky. Their oldest child, Justin, fourteen, had not yet appeared. The house is often filled with the clatter of neighborhood kids who feel welcome and safe here.

Tom and Beth were talking about fear. And freedom.

"I think childhood's a lot more dangerous today," said Tom, a big, balding man whose eyes, usually glinting with humor, now turned flat. "The frustrations that kids feel are not that much different from the frustrations that we felt as kids, but what causes them has changed, I think. The level of technology . . . it's a lot more impersonal world to be in." He turned to put a plate on the butcher-block table. "My father used to tell me stories about growing up on the East Side of New York, about the beat cop who knew every kid's name. If the kid did something wrong, the kid first had to deal with the beat cop and then the cop would take him to his parents and then he had to deal with his parents. The world just isn't organized like that anymore. You know, the proliferation of guns and drugs . . ."

Beth added: "Guns and drugs are the reasons that we say no to things that our kids would probably like to do. There are a lot of lunatics out there." She sighed. "It's so different. Even if Elizabeth goes down to Crum Creek behind the college, I want her to take the dog and make sure she's with at least one friend. When I was a little kid, there were woods at the foot of my street and I would get up at six o'clock in the morning and go down there for two or three hours and pick blueberries by myself and nobody ever had to worry about it. But Tom and I just had this discussion. The kids had half a day off and we talked about letting them take the train into Philadelphia. Tom was more comfortable with it than I was. And it wasn't because I thought they would do something stupid. It was that I was concerned about the people around them."

"When I was in the fifth grade, I would get on the train and go into New York City and go to the Boys' Club," said Tom. "It wasn't anything for me to take a thirty-five-minute subway ride to go to a swimming pool. So I'm more comfortable with the kids' going places than Beth is." But it's not just the parents who are less comfortable with these things. It's the kids, too. "None of these kids ever does anything alone. There's a change in the social behavior of children in that regard. It's amazing to me."

Biz agreed. "My friends and I are always together or — I just feel strange when I go up to the store and get candy all by myself. You're usually with people. You get used to it. Actually, I think it's better to be in a big group. Like with three or four people. Because if you're trying to decide what to do, there's usually someone who agrees with you. So you don't feel all alone. And also, I remember going to the library by myself, two years ago. And it's like, unheard-of now."

"People think you're weird," said Katie, Biz's friend, "if you go to the movies by yourself or you go walking in the woods."

Beth looked at the girls, one finger on her lower lip. "I travel and I love going to dinner by myself sometimes. I like the idea of being able to do things alone and independently, and I don't think Katie should feel worried about that. That should be fun for her."

She paused, wiped a plate, then added: "Did you follow the story in the *Philadelphia Inquirer* about that twelve-year-old girl whose parents went out to work and whose brother apparently went to school and forgot to lock the door behind him? Some fourteen-year-old kid who lived just three houses down walked in and stabbed her ninety-six times. A nice family neighborhood, you know. A neighborhood like this."

Biz knocked something over, making a loud thud. It gave everyone a start.

"We tell these kids all the time that when we're not home, to lock the door," said Tom. "They baby-sit for each other on Saturday night, if we go out someplace. We get them a video. They're not allowed to have friends over then, and they're good about that. But we've had to remind them about locking the doors.

"The thing is, you get this unreal, misleading feeling living in Swarthmore. You think you're safer than perhaps you really are."

Then Biz and Katie and Becky enthusiastically launched into a story about going down to the woods.

"The three of us were really bored and we went near the back of the Acme [supermarket] in Swarthmore," said Biz with enthusiasm, her eyes wide. "And we found these woods —"

"And so we went into these woods."

"And we had to walk our bikes through."

"And then these two guys with . . . *guns* —"

"One was a rifle and one was a shotgun," said Biz. "They were BB guns. But we didn't know that."

Becky continued: "We went down into Crum Creek and we were hiding under the trestle and this guy came. And he had, like, a machine gun! And we didn't know what it was. And we were like, '*Omigod!*' And then they threw this body off the top of the trestle, and it landed on our bikes. *Oh, no* . . . And we saw this guy with a video camera, and we're like, *hunh-uh — hunh-uh — hunh-uh* . . . They were making a movie!"

"Katie is saying, 'Oh, gosh, I wish we were at Dunkin' Donuts!' "

"And we come up and we go up this hill and we're a block away from Dunkin' Donuts!"

"So we got six Dunkin' Donuts and we sat there and then we ate doughnuts in front of the statue of the Blessed Mother."

"The end result of this adventure," said Biz's mother, "was that we talked to them about their boundaries."

"I think the only thing I do by myself anymore," Becky added, "is ride my bike."

Katie sighed. "It's worth getting grounded if you can ride your bike to Philly, because you've been to *Philly* on your *bike*."

"Yeah," said Becky. There was a pause. "Well, it depends on how long you get grounded for."

Tom smiled and sat down to his own plate of pancakes. The bogeyman could wait until after breakfast.

The Bogeyman Syndrome

✓Parents and, to a lesser extent, children speak often of a generalized fear. This fear, one of the defining characteristics of today's family life, is a complicated thing, having to do with television and AIDS, pesticides and homicides, Alar on the apples and pins in the candy. It has to do also with the diminishing amount of family time and the growing distances within the web. I was surprised to find the fear nearly as intense in Kansas as it was in Pennsylvania and New York.

"I have a rule," said Mike Tuel, one of several parents sitting around a dining room table one evening in Overland Park, Kansas. "I want to know where my kid is twenty-four hours a day, seven days a week. I want to know where that kid is. Which house. Which square foot. Which telephone number." He grinned. "That's just my way of dealing with it. Both of my kids have heard my preachings that the world is full of crazy people. And it is. There's nuts running loose. People that need to go through years of therapy and need to be incarcerated. They're out there driving around in cars and they've got guns on their seats. They're out there! And you have to deal with that situation. I'd be hesitant to let my kids go over to the park alone. Everyone tells you to never leave your kids alone. Always be after them. But you don't want to do that — you don't want to stand right in their face watching them. And you sure don't want to pass it on to your kids."

Then there's Halloween. I can still feel the paper bag in my hand, the smell of burnt pumpkin in the air; I can feel the dents in my shins from when I went over the hedge, bag shooting in front of me, Baby Ruths flying like bats in the darkness, the *thrump, thromp, thrump* of my feet and the whisking of my costume; the feel of the bag getting heavier, getting soft and crinkly up around the top, and the pace of the running: *one more house, one more house, one more . . .* What a feeling that was.

Now we're adults and the doorbell doesn't ring much anymore. Somebody stole Halloween, took it away in a plain brown paper bag and won't give it back. As it fades for children, it's becoming a national holiday for adults.

One mother at the table described how Halloween had been transformed: "When we were young we went through the whole city, I mean we'd leave at dark and we'd come back and get grocery sacks and go for more. But we never allowed our kids to go out of our neighborhood until recently, and then they go to a neighborhood that's controlled. We live a *controlled* life — we always know where they are — which makes it difficult to teach independence, doesn't it?" She paused, and a look of doubt came into her eyes. "As a parent, I know a lot of instances of what crazy people have done to children. When I grew up those were only rumors. You might have heard of somebody's uncle that lived three states away. But now, it's closer to home and we know about it more. A man in the neighborhood was going around naked in front of people. He's gone now, but it happened. It's not just there in the newspaper, it's in your neighborhood. But how did we really know that the kind of terrible things we know about now weren't going on when we were kids, even on Halloween?"

Good question.

Joel Best, professor and chairman of the sociology department at Cal State–Fresno, is considered the best authority on what he calls Halloween sadism. In 1985, Best conducted a study of Halloween terrorism — candy laced with drugs or pins, razor blades or poison. He reviewed seventy-six specific stories and rumors reported from 1958 to 1984 in the *New York Times,* the *Chicago Tribune,* the *Los Angeles Times,* and the *Fresno Bee.* "We couldn't find a single case of any child killed or seriously injured by candy contamination," he said. "The Halloween sadist is an urban myth."

Studies like Best's invite skepticism. Like most parents I interviewed, I'm not ready to let my sons eat Halloween candy that has not been scrutinized. Yet it's important to realize that our concern with "stranger danger" may be misplaced — may, in fact, be a way for us to deal with larger doubts about the future and our own sense of vulnerability.

Best pointed out that, in one particularly notorious case, a five-year-old Detroit boy died in 1970 after eating heroin supposedly hidden in his Halloween candy. Following widespread publicity, police discovered that the boy had eaten some of his uncle's heroin; it had not been placed in his Halloween candy. In a similar 1974 case, an eight-year-old boy died after eating cyanide-laced candy. His father was later arrested for poisoning his son's Halloween candy. Sometimes children have contaminated their own candy as a way of getting attention, or as a Halloween "trick." Since Best completed the study, he has seen no further evidence of anyone being killed or seriously injured.

The nation's missing-children anxiety rises and falls with a rhythm similar to that of the Halloween sadist myth. After the broadcast of the television movie *Adam* in 1983, commercial and government agencies began printing millions of images on milk cartons and utility bills. Fueled by this fear, a whole new industry has sprung up. The participants call it "people searching." The guidebooks of this industry, which has broadened even beyond missing children, include such magazines as *Family*

Protection, a pulpy tabloid. The cover headlines scream, DIARY OF A TEEN-AGE RUNAWAY . . . SHOULD YOU TEACH YOUR CHILD SELF-DEFENSE? . . . 22 PAGES OF LOST CHILDREN. One of the articles suggests that runaways can turn out fine — after all, Neil Diamond and columnist Hedda Hopper were runaways. One article on runaways is illustrated with a staged photograph of a voluptuous, miniskirted teenager being attacked. Then there's the Missing Child of the Month: "Whatever Happened to Bobby Jo Fritz?" A banner headline over another article proclaims, AMERICA'S MOST FAMOUS LOST CHILDREN. Reading *Family Protection,* one gets the feeling that there are a lot of people out there who find the missing-children phenomenon somehow titillating.

But as with the myth of the Halloween sadist, the threat of stranger danger in most neighborhoods is less than it might seem.

David Finklehor, co-director of the Family Research Laboratory at the University of New Hampshire, is conducting the National Incidents Study of Missing Children, which will likely be considered the most comprehensive and accurate report on the subject. As of this writing, the final report has yet to be published.

However, an analysis of FBI statistics done by the Family Research Laboratory for the Department of Justice suggests that a relatively small number of children are killed in the course of stranger abductions. Said Finklehor, "Some organizations have claimed that 4,000 children a year have been killed by strangers in the course of abduction. The actual figure is only about 150 — if that many." Also, there is no evidence that the number has increased since 1976, when the FBI began to categorize its statistics more accurately. Unfortunately, the data on this issue have only recently become available from the FBI. "You can look at time trends in terms of the number of children who are victims of homicides," said Finklehor, "but information about the perpetrator is not available for earlier periods because the FBI didn't keep it." Most parents believe that it is mostly small children who are snatched by strangers, "but it turns out that children who are killed in the course of abduction are most likely to be adolescent females — not the seven-year-old kid you see on the milk carton." This is not to minimize the grievous nature of these crimes; but the point is that the perception of danger to children is different from the reality.[1]

Why do we so fear the bogeyman in the form of strangers?

Several trends have converged:

• General crime rates have gone up, particularly violence committed on adolescents. Crime is also more generalized today than in previous decades. It used to be a more strictly urban phenomenon — in the fifties there were still many places in the country where crime was relatively uncommon. But now the borders of crime, like the borders of mass communication, have dissipated. Crime is everywhere.

- The risk of being criminally victimized has increased for parents themselves, and they often translate this fear into increased anxiety for their kids.
- Expanded and more interdependent media amplify our awareness of crime; people hear more about crimes that have occurred in other places, they hear about these crimes quicker, and they hear about the same crimes over and over — through television, through the newspaper, on the car radio on the way to work. Studies by the Annenberg School for Communication in Pennsylvania suggest that television heightens our level of apprehension. According to George Gerbner, all other things being equal, those who frequently watch television exhibit far more anxiety about crime than those who watch television infrequently.[2]
- The less time we spend with our children, the more we worry about them. As Finklehor pointed out, "Kids are in day care all day, they go to school further away than they used to — the neighborhood school is gone — the family doctor is gone, and so the kids travel further to get medical care from an impersonal medical center." As society becomes more heterogeneous, and as parents have less direct control over their children, the bogeyman grows. We project our parental fears of kids' taking drugs, becoming sexually active, falling away from traditional values onto the bogeyman.

All of these trends add to the sense of losing control. Symbolically, children represent two things to us. They are, as Best put it, "the walking, talking future," and they represent vulnerability and innocence. He pointed out that the frequency of the various bogeyman reports seems to rise during years of particularly intense economic and social tensions. "People are not as confident about the future as they were twenty years ago, and worrying about children is a way of expressing those fears — fears which are terribly frightening to express." And these fears are projected onto the stranger who's going to snatch our kids. It is the old theme of Dr. Frankenstein's monster who cannot be killed; frozen, burned, drowned, the monster yet survived from movie to movie, expressing our unconscious understanding that we cannot squash evil permanently. But in recent monster movies, particularly the outrageously successful *Halloween, Friday the Thirteenth,* and *Nightmare on Elm Street* series, the bogeyman theme has a new twist; the monster is destroyed and revived again and again, even within a single film. Also, the new movie monsters seem to present a generational threat. For example, *Nightmare on Elm Street*'s Freddy takes the form of an old man, the product of all the accumulated evil of an earlier generation.[3]

The effect of the bogeyman syndrome is four-fold. First, the bogeyman distracts us from larger social dangers about which we should be concerned. An overemphasis on stranger danger makes it easier to turn away from a myriad of other very real threats to children, including the often unseen violence of emotional and social neglect. Of course, to say that much of our anxiety is misdirected is not to imply that children are not endangered or subject to violence. Quite the contrary; teenagers are twice as likely as adults to be victims of violent crimes. For children, however, the greatest danger of violence is not from strangers but from family members.[4] The 150 children abducted and murdered each year are still far too many, but that figure needs to be put in perspective: by contrast, 1,100 children are killed each year by their own parents; 75 to 80 percent of sexual child molesting is by people the victims know. We just don't see most family violence as a crime because our image of crime is of something "out there." "Curiously, the Halloween sadist only comes out once a year," said Joel Best. "This makes the fear manageable. Parents can pour a year's fear into that night and then the next morning count the toes and heads and say, 'Whew, we made it through another year.' And then we ignore more important childhood safety issues, like the fact that nobody wants to pay to put seat belts in school buses or that nearly ten thousand children are killed in automobile accidents each year while auto manufacturers neglect safety."

A second effect is that the bogeyman changes the texture of family life — particularly American conceptions of freedom.

This issue is tricky. Many parents mourn what they perceive as their children's loss of physical freedom; but other parents point to new childhood freedoms that did not exist thirty years ago.

"When I was a kid, I would leave the house at seven in the morning — I'd be out in the woods playing," said a father in the Overland Park group, Jack Hughes, who grew up on a farm in Michigan. "My stomach would get to where I had to come home and get lunch and then I'd be gone again until my dad whistled for me when he got home from work and it was time for supper. If my daughters were gone like that I would be — I wouldn't know what was going on."

"The cops would be here," said Mike Tuel.

"The thing I wonder about is, What's going to happen to these kids' sense of adventure? Will they have less, or will they rebel?" said one mother, Laura Beth Clark. The group fell silent. She turned to her husband, Steve. "Tell them about the trips you took as a kid. I love the stories he tells me about those wonderful times. I can't believe it! His folks would give these wild, crazy kids a car —"

Steve grinned at the memory and said, "As soon as we had our driver's licenses we were allowed to take trips, camping trips mainly, by ourselves. Sixteen-year-old kids. And there would be four, five, six of us at a time."

"Tell them how far you'd go," said Laura Beth.

"Well, we started out just going on short trips, but we ended up going to the Black Hills of South Dakota. And we ended up going to Yellowstone National Park. But we weren't that crazy. We developed our parents' trust and we never abused it."

"Do you think we'll ever let our kids do that?" Laura Beth asked.

"I don't know yet," said Steve.

Another father said: "When I was in high school and college, kids were always thinking about putting on a knapsack and hitchhiking someplace. When I was growing up I was always looking ahead to the next adventure. But my daughter has a little bit of skepticism about leaving home. She's a relatively brave kid, but she doesn't have unbridled enthusiasm about venturing out there. And I'm not sure I'd let her."

Curiously, children are not nearly as worried as their parents about their loss of physical freedom. I was often struck by parents' sense of grief, which I share; their perception of loss, as adults, of their own innocence and freedom, adventure and passion. So much of what we perceive, in the next generation, may be a projection of our own disappointment and frustration. We must take some care with our grief and our perceptions. They are more powerful than we know.

"I can't relate to any of this talk about freedom," said one woman in the Overland Park group. She had remained silent through most of the discussion about freedom and now she spoke suddenly, vehemently. "I think of my kids having *much* more freedom than I did. I don't know if it's being raised in the South or if it was my particular parents, but it was like pulling teeth to get my parents to let me go to someone's house or to have someone come over. When I think of my kids' freedom to call somebody, to be invited someplace, and me saying, 'Sure you can go' — that's the kind of freedom I think is being allowed. And I wasn't allowed that freedom."

Mike, the contrarian of the group, took her side. "I don't feel saddened, I don't feel bad at all that my kids are missing out on the kind of freedom I had. When I was a youngster I never had the rush, the adrenal pleasure of doing some of the things that my kids have participated in in their young lives. Performing, dancing, doing something in front of five hundred, a thousand people. Throwing, pitching, hitting, playing soccer. Doing these — being a hero. Gaining that self-esteem that we didn't have. I mean, we may have had different freedoms, but so many more kids have so many more opportunities to experience that feeling of 'Wow, I did something and it was good!' "

When I mentioned to several teachers the perception of many parents that their children have less freedom today, the teachers were surprised. Yes, they said, they could see that some children have fewer of some freedoms; many of the children in their classes are overstructured by their parents. But so many other children have a freedom closer to abandonment — the freedom to spend hours alone in an empty house, the freedom from role models. For many children, physical freedom is decreasing as their mental, psychological, and moral freedoms are increasing. Children's physical boundaries may have shrunk, but their electronic and ethical boundaries are often more distant than their parents can imagine.

Third, the bogeyman syndrome decreases the strength of the best safeguard against crime: community.

Children who do not feel physically free within a city surely have less opportunity to know it, feel a part of it, feel wanted by it, or eventually, to feel a need to protect it.

Richard Nagely, a government teacher at Franklin High School in Seattle, said: "This generation of kids has more psychological freedom, more options in life, than we did. But at the same time, they don't have the bonds, the bonding to the community, to society, or to family. And so freedom for them is double-edged."

"For blacks of my generation there was less freedom, a lot less," said a physical education teacher at Franklin, an African American in his fifties. "There's more freedom now, but there were more attachments then, to the community. I admit I'm a fifties person, so a lot of my philosophy is dated. But I believe that all of the drugs, all of the stuff that we're going through now is because we allowed a lot of kids to have the freedom to make decisions that they're not capable of making, but they don't have the experience of living in a real community. I think where it's going to hit us the most is when these kids are in their late thirties and early forties when a lot of pressure falls on them. I think they're going to have a real problem handling it alone."

Fear is reshaping the physical environment in which we live. Most developers no longer sell community but instead offer a packaged security of socially controlled environments — condominiums and planned developments surrounded with walls and electronic surveillance systems (where residents have no choice about the color of their curtain liners or whether or not they can hang an American flag on their balcony). One wonders how children growing up in such an environment of fear and control will define freedom as adults — and whether the forces creating this environment can be countered and eventually reversed.

"It's relatively safe to be in the world," said Richard Farson, head of the Western Behavioral Sciences Institute in La Jolla, California. "But people are so afraid that they've let their communities erode. Fear is circular. In La Jolla, we no longer have a downtown community because we avoid the very thing that creates community — regular contact with friends *and* strangers. All of a sudden we have boutiques and iron bars. We don't need another dainty boutique, we need a family hardware store. That's what we need to run a community. Every time we lose community, other costs rise — for prisons, for psychological help. We should be going in the opposite direction: instead of putting kids on the milk cartons and giving them fear, we should be building community."

Finally, the bogeyman syndrome perpetuates itself. Most Americans believe that crime is a problem in somebody else's neighborhood, not their own; still, many parents are modifying their behavior based on their perception that crime is generally getting worse. Forty-one percent of parents avoid talking to strangers.[5]

As trust diminishes, we find it more and more difficult to ascertain what is a valid fear and what is not; what is effective protection and what is not.

Indeed, the bogeyman is creating a Guns-R-Us society, a children's arms race. *Barron's* reports that the latest gun-marketing effort is directed at women and young Americans. The shooting programs of the 4-H Club attracted at least one hundred thousand youths in the late eighties, a tenfold increase in five years. Students are carrying more guns to school. Interestingly, although the California Department of Education reported a 12 percent increase in the number of weapons confiscated from students in schools during the 1987–88 school year, drug abuse declined 17 percent, sex offenses 6 percent, and assaults with deadly weapons 17 percent. These statistics suggest three possible explanations: one (highly unlikely) is that an armed school population somehow decreases crime; a second reason is that fear, aggressiveness, anxiety, and the sense of helplessness among children (reinforced by parents and television) causes them to react by arming themselves even though crime has decreased slightly; the third is that guns are trendy, like Reeboks. In all three cases, the bogeyman wins.[6]

In the Midwest, one teacher, a pleasant middle-aged woman, told me: "I was standing in line the other day at the airport and a little kid was going around to look behind the counter and his mother said to him: 'Do you want somebody to snatch you? Don't walk away from me like that.' And here I'm standing behind them in line and I'm saying to myself, Well, I really didn't *look* like a child snatcher." There was laughter and disbelief in her voice. "But we teach our kids so young to be aware of everything. They lose their time to be innocent. My seventh-graders have had to deal with situations that we didn't know about until we were adults. Teaching kids intelligent caution around strangers is certainly important, how to say no to potential child abusers is essential. But we need to create a balanced view of danger. The damage that has been caused when you have families teaching their kids never to talk to another adult in a society where you desperately need more communication — what does that do to the kid?"

Ultimately, the bogeyman drives family life deeper into itself, reduces public trust, replaces real community with walls and gates, and isolates children. Ironically and tragically, the reduction of community and personal and public trust creates the conditions that produce real-life people like Freddy, the psychopathic slasher in *Nightmare on Elm Street*. A black seventh-grader in Philadelphia who made a show of being streetwise (though his desk was stacked with library books) offered this wonderful analysis of the power of the bogeyman: "I say if you worry about it too much that maybe you will lean towards it, like let's say, if you owe the mob money, and you walking down the street and you constantly looking over your shoulder to make sure nobody's behind you with a gun, and you never turn around, you constantly looking over your shoulder, they going to be in front of you while your head is turned that way. And then you going to run into 'em. So it's just like that."

Time to Face the Bogeyman

How do we appropriately confront our fears about childhood's future? One truth that emerged from my interviews is that family time and family fear are directly related. Another is that the best antidote to fear is action.

First, we can confront the fear psychologically within our own families. Second, we can do something within our homes, neighborhoods, and communities to lessen the danger. The place to start is to recognize that we should be concerned for our children's safety, but that the bogeyman — at least in the form of stranger danger — should not, in the hierarchy of fears, be at the top of the list. There are other dangers and forces that should consume our attention. Instead of projecting so many of these fears onto a bogeyman who is out of their control, some parents take action on those safety issues closest to home, which decreases their general anxiety.

One father, a psychiatrist, said: "Children don't have to participate in dangerous situations in order to develop self-reliance and autonomy. For example, my twelve-year-old wanted to ride his bike to school. I made an agreement with him. He had to wear his helmet — in fact, he's always had to wear his helmet when riding a bike, because I know too much about head injuries. I told my son, too, that he could ride to school only on a certain route, which I checked first, which was less trafficked. He told me he had checked out a couple alternative routes — and you know, he's growing, and separating, and those routes are okay. But still, I allow him to ride his bike to school only under these circumstances. Am I being too protective? Will he suffer some neurosis as an adult because his father made him wear a helmet? Maybe, maybe not. But I would rather he be around to have a neurosis. All it takes is one fall and it's over, he's a vegetable, or he's dead. I have that knowledge. What am I supposed to do with it? Deny it? That's what many parents do. I know neurosurgeons who operate on head injuries every day and don't require their kids to wear bike helmets."

In his own parenting, this psychiatrist tries to find the balance between overprotectiveness and abandonment. "So much of the child rearing in the past bordered on abandonment in the guise of teaching independence. At the other extreme, I see kids all the time who are spoiled in the sense that their parents, who have real hostility toward them, have made them seem so precious that they can do nothing wrong. But the spoiled child is a very depressed child. My twelve-year-old daughter is not allowed to go unsupervised to the beach with her friends. But I let her make up her own mind about whether or not she wants to baby-sit for friends of ours — though we would very much like her to do that, she resists, and we acquiesce to that resistance, because she is making her own decision. That's an appropriate form of freedom. I encourage my kids to make their own decisions in many ways, but risking their lives is not one of them."

Some families face the bogeyman by moving to those places that still retain some sense of community. Though small towns are not immune from drugs and violence, these threats seem more controllable. Michelle Dodge of Worthington, Massachusetts, described why her family had moved to a rural area. "A lot of families are moving out to this partic- ular area because they don't want their kids endangered as much, and also because they don't want their kids growing up as quick. Out here, I can find a sixteen-year-old baby sitter, but in the city, by the time they're twelve, they're dating. Also everyone is family-oriented here. When I go to the closest city I can't believe all the nine-year-olds are wearing long, dangly earrings. Kids aren't into the hippest fashions, but that's fine with me; I'd rather they go down to the lake with their families. I'd rather keep them kids. A friend of mine in Washington, D.C., said, 'Watch out for your kids — they go off to college and they might be too trusting of this world.' I don't know if that's true. But I like the idea that they are not brought up on fear."

Amy Stillman, of Rowaton, Connecticut (and president of Mothers at Home More, a support group for at-home parents), described how she deals with the bogeyman: "Fear didn't directly have anything to do with my decision to stay home. However, I do believe we are living in difficult times for children. I could not bear to have my children, when they hit their teens, run into serious trouble, in part because I was not home. I would rather risk my own professional standing than risk the happiness or safety of my children. And that's not to say that women who go back to work are necessarily risking their children's safety. Maybe I'm just increasing the odds that my kids will be safe and that they'll turn out fine. Everybody's fingerprinting their kids. But that's supposed to work *after* something happens. Sometimes the fear becomes over- whelming. I have this feeling that things are so good in my life that some- thing horrible must be about to happen. The speed at which you have to go, the missed enjoyment in the daily pleasures of family life, leads to this gnawing sense of dissatisfaction and fear. You begin to worry about child abuse at day care, because you don't know exactly what's going on. It's a very scary thing when you start thinking about it."

She stopped for a moment.

"I must have dealt with this, because I no longer find myself over- whelmingly fearful. My children are four and six, and I am with them almost all the time except when they are at school. Something could happen to them at school. But I have done my best to pick a good school for them. And I take the time, as all good parents do, to stay alert to what is going on with them in the school. Something could still happen to one of my kids. Just the fact that I'm around them a lot doesn't mean I can prevent it; but I'm as alert as I can be to it, and if something happens, hopefully I will be calm enough and have the time to try to work with it. I'm going to worry more when my kids are ten and twelve — they say it only gets worse."

As Stillman pointed out, she has the choice to stay home, and she lives in a fairly insulated environment, a relatively affluent suburb of New York. "I'm not sure we're representative, because I do have the flexibility. It's human nature to try to ignore fear and depression, to sweep it aside. I'm a believer that depression serves a very valuable function: if people are working too many hours and they're depressed because they're worried about their kids — or if they're at home and depressed because they're worried about their careers, and they're taking it out on their kids and themselves, then I think depression serves a purpose. Many people go on for years trying to ignore the depression. You only change if you're in pain. And I know a lot of parents who are in pain."

When I asked missing-children expert David Finklehor what he considered the most important thing parents could do to protect their children, he touched the core of the bogeyman syndrome. "There are an awful lot of programs out there today trying to teach personal safety to children," he said. "But I honestly think the most important thing a parent can do is to have a good relationship with the child, a good, supportive relationship, because a child who has good self-esteem, good self-confidence, a closer relationship with the parents, is much less likely to be victimized. Our studies show that. Predatory people are not as likely to mess with them, because the predator senses that these are kids who will tell, who can't be fooled or conned. The studies show that most kids who are victimized are emotionally neglected, have unhappy families or other deprivations."

There was the key. By focusing on building self-esteem and self-confidence in our kids — by spending the time with them that this goal demands — we give them an armor they take with them wherever they go, through their childhood and adolescence and into adulthood. An internalized armor.

The most important thing we can give them is our time.

To capture time, some families arrange for one parent to be home, often intentionally forgoing home ownership. But assuming that no mass exodus from the work force is about to take place, other remedies are called for. A few companies, for example, are looking more seriously at flexible working hours, part-time jobs, and job sharing, which would allow parents more control over their personal lives. A movement is building for such change. We cannot reclaim time and the quality of family life entirely on our own; much of this book is concerned with the wider paradigm. But some of the most important immediate decisions are the small ones made within each family.

At a PTA meeting in Shawnee Mission, Kansas, several mothers talked about the small ways — the time tricks — they have learned to reclaim time.

One woman said her family has made a rule that they all eat one meal together each day. "The one meal we know we can eat together is breakfast, because that's the only time anyone was home. And we eat at four-thirty A.M. nowadays." She laughed. "But it is a priority." Another woman said her family makes a point of playing board games, even though she hates playing games, "because board games force us to stay at the table for more than ten minutes." Even those parents who did not work full-time outside the home said that they felt the time deficit and had devised time tricks. One mother said that she had quit car-pooling the neighbor kids because she had found that "the time when I have my own kids in the car is the only time I have any decent one-on-one contact with them, so I make the best of that." Several parents said they make sure that they are at home right after school. "That's when the kids are really ready to talk," said one mother. "Mine come home at different times, so that gives me maybe a half hour with the high-schooler before the elementary student comes home. That's when my fifteen-year-old will sit down and have something to eat, and he'll talk. After that he's *gone*."

Linda Hoover, a PTA officer, spoke of "taking those steps backwards to where your family can sit out on the front porch and watch the sunset. Maybe none of us alone is totally capable of putting on the brakes and saying, Wait a minute, let's back up. But my husband and I are trying to show our son that we're valuable to one another in small but visible ways. Hopefully, he's learning that it's wonderful being an adult. But we're also trying to emphasize the importance he has of contributing to the family as a child. Not through wonderful grades, not through the soccer scores or anything other than being a valuable person — just being who he is, and being part of a family. I grew up on a farm, and looking back I think I had the best of everything. I just didn't realize it. I knew that I was helping my family. When we would go fishing at the creek, I knew that I was putting a meal on the table one night a week.

"My family fell into the high-achievement trap," Hoover continued. "We're having to reevaluate our values. Our son was overstressed, we were overstressed. This realization came to us on one of those nights when all of our voices had risen an octave and all of our eyes were open just a little wider than normal and we all were just — it was just too much. We all reached this level at the same time; we peaked out. And we said, 'This is not what we had in mind when we brought a child into the world.' We realized that we were giving our son the message that he had to achieve in order to be lovable. That sounds terrible for a parent to say, but it's true. My husband and I were doing it, too: he was working long hours to be lovable and I was doing all these extracurricular activities to be lovable in the community, and it was just crazy. We were getting less lovable."

So Hoover's family backed up, and made lists.

"Each of us took a piece of paper. We drew a line down the center, listed things we like, things we don't like, things we enjoy doing, things we don't enjoy doing. And then on the second column we listed things that we did that we really didn't want to do anymore. It was very simple — because we didn't have much time." Hoover laughed. "I think we all saw where we were headed, and where we didn't really want to be. So we started deleting some of the activities we didn't need in our lives. I was working full-time but not for pay. I was a volunteer. Very dedicated, very committed, highly structured. It was easier when I worked for *money*. When I stopped to really think about it, I realized I didn't really enjoy much of it. It was just insane. I needed to learn to say no."

Her son surprised them.

"Our son hated organized sports. We had never realized that. And we said, 'What would you like to replace sports with?' And he said, 'Playing with the neighborhood kids in the back yard.' It was an eye-opener for us. Soccer had more to do with social acceptability, and our expectations, than fun for my son. So he withdrew from soccer. He started working in the back yard vegetable garden. Both grandpas are farmers. He loves to do that, and we didn't know that."

Then there were the activities that the members of the Hoover family learned they all wanted to do. "Just to walk through the park. Or bike it or just to spend some time outside. That may not sound like a big deal, but that is what we found we wanted the most. And we didn't need to be talking to one another, either. It was just having that wonderful physical closeness. That was one thing we all put down. That we all wanted to be outside. We all like to camp. But we knew we couldn't just haul out the camper every time we all had some free time together, so now we walk.

"It's been almost a year. We still struggle with outside pressures. Every day, we have to consciously make the decisions, the small decisions. And I still find myself saying yes too often and having to call back and say 'Whoops, I changed my mind.' It's not easy, but it *is* worth it."

They made their separate peace: her husband cut his overtime, Hoover cut her social activities, their son quit soccer, and now they go on long, meandering walks together through the trees, listening to the Kansas wind.

And, for a while, they've bought some time.

3

In Search of Beaver Cleaver

•

We do not raise our children alone.

Private family decisions about time and fear are the most important adjustments that many of us can immediately make, but directly and indirectly, our children are also raised by every peer, institution, and family with which they come in contact. Yet parents today expect to be blamed for whatever results occur with their children, and they expect to do their parenting alone.

"We [parents] no longer speak with the strong voice of the working majority," writes social historian Barbara Whitehead. "The consumer culture is now driven by the individual — child-free, career-primary, with a wallet full of credit cards." Parents, she says, aren't valued as parents. In much of the national debate about childhood, parents have been shoved aside. Increasingly, the nation's policymakers view kids as capital, little economic soldiers to be crammed full of facts and statistics and sent out onto the economic battlefield against German and Japanese children. But this picture is false, "for the little workers of Germany and Japan have parents too. The difference is that their parents are strongly valued and supported by the society for their contribution *as parents*. We won't be facing up to reality until we are ready to pit our parents against their parents, and thus our family policy against theirs." [1]

A successful family policy will not be shaped primarily by committees and lobbyists in Washington, D.C., but by parents themselves, who come to see their need for each other, and for the interconnectedness of a new childhood ecology.

The standard approach to viewing childhood's future reduces social, economic, and moral problems to simple cause and effect. Parents are immoral, for example, and therefore children are destroyed; or the cuts in social services during the Reagan administration ruined the family; or the problem is not enough quality day care. Such reductionism is especially popular among political leaders. But just as in the natural sciences one no longer speaks of the food chain but of an intricate food web, so the strands of childhood are interwoven; pull one, and all the others loosen or unravel. To strengthen one strand, those attached to it must be strengthened as well.

Let's take a look at some of the strands that are being stretched to the breaking point, at some of the interconnected stresses buffeting the American family.

The Strands of Family

First, what *is* the American family?

As parents, many of us dream about the past, about what families are supposed to be. But we cannot quite remember what we dreamed, as when lying half awake in the morning we catch and assemble the trails of mist from disappearing dreams. We attempt to remember our collective American childhood, the way it was, but what we often remember is a combination of the real past, pieces reshaped by bitterness and love, and, of course, the video past — the portrayals of family life on such television programs as "Leave It to Beaver" and "Father Knows Best" and all the rest. For many of the baby boomers I interviewed, the illusory Cleaver family came the closest to encapsulating what they felt they had lost, even if they had never had it. These television images drilled the myth of the American family into our minds and our culture even as the majority of families took on quite different shapes and characteristics. American family life has never been particularly idyllic. In the nineteenth century, nearly a quarter of all children experienced the death of one of their parents. (No wonder the plots of so many Disney tales, psychologically rooted in the nineteenth century and earlier, were centered on the death of a parent.) Not until the sixties did the chief cause of separation of parents shift from death to divorce. The twentieth-century trend toward a widening variety of family definitions was interrupted only by the post–World War II boom in large families and early marriage.

That period, however, may have been the real aberration. In the fifties, about 55 percent of American families were configured along the lines of the Cleavers. Today only three out of ten American families fits the "traditional" pattern of a homemaker mother and breadwinner father. Families today are more diverse and less stable. As Peter Morrison, director of the Rand Corporation's Population Research Center, told a congressional committee: "People think they are seeing departures from the norm, but departures now are the norm." [2]

Among the current realities of the American family:

- The family is shrinking. There are now fewer parents, children, and other members per family than ever before in our nation's history. [3]
- Younger couples divorce more readily and earlier in their marriages, which means that young children are more likely to be involved.
- The level and nature of divorce today foreshadow a future in which most first marriages will end in divorce. [4]
- Stepparents are entering the social mainstream. Many schools now publish directories cross-referenced to two sets of parents with different last names.
- More children are born and raised out of wedlock. According to the Census Bureau, nearly two out of ten of the women in the United States who gave birth in 1988 were unmarried. [5]
- More families are headed by single parents — and children are spending more of their lives with single parents. [6] Soon a quarter of white children and close to half of black children may lose regular contact with a parent at some point during their childhood.

How Kids Feel About New Family Forms

Just about everyone these days seems to have an opinion about what the right kind of family should be, but children — especially younger ones — define *family* in a much looser and a much more open and forgiving way than do many of their parents. Valeria Lovelace, the director of research for "Sesame Street," studied how children define family in the late eighties. "We asked children about all kinds of configurations, whether a 'real' family is a nuclear family, or a mother and child, or a number of other possibilities," said Lovelace. "And what we learned from them is that children are very open in what they're calling family."

For example, children were most likely to identify "Mr. and Mrs. Brown and Billy" as a family. The nuclear family is still the most readily accepted. "However, later on in our interview, we said Mr. and Mrs. Brown and Billy live together but they don't love each other. Are they a family? And half the children who had earlier identified Mr. and Mrs.

Brown and Billy as a family now said no, they were not a family. In the minds of three- to five-year-olds, when you say 'family,' they don't just think about a configuration, but an expectation of love and caring that goes along with it. When they talk about family, they talk about love. They talk about caring. As adults, we don't necessarily give children credit for thinking in these terms."

In the interviews that I conducted, the younger the children were, the more open they were to new family forms. At Jerabek Elementary School in San Diego, I asked a classroom of third- and fourth-graders to define a "normal family." Was a single-parent family normal? Or did a normal family need two parents? Among the comments:

"I think a normal family is a dad and a mom and then two kids who live in the same house and like each other."

"A normal family is sort of like the 'Donna Reed Show,' a sister and brother same age, a wife and husband, and maybe a little baby, and they do the normal stuff and the wife stays home and cooks and stuff, the dad goes out to work, and the children go to school in the morning."

"A bad thing is if you have two parents in one house, there's more of a chance of big arguments, and of roughing it out on the kids."

"Well, I don't think a normal family has to have two parents living in the same house, but a normal family is like, a mom and a dad — they don't have to live together though — and the kids — they know that their parents love them and know that it's not their fault that they got a divorce."

"I don't think a normal family has to have two parents because all the family really has to have is people who care about each other."

Ironically, as the average size of families becomes smaller, stepfamilies — or "blended" families (mine, yours, ours) — give some kids a greater sense of family and belonging. At Franklin High School in Seattle, one eleventh-grader told me that she felt her stepfamily was more normal than her birth family because she now had siblings: "My father was the oldest of seven in a real big, real family-oriented family, and I missed having brothers and stepsisters to get in trouble with and go with on vacations and whatever. I was an only child until I was ten. It was a clean divorce, you know. And now I have such a big family, I have stepbrothers and stepsisters and people that I would never have had. I treasure it. It's not always perfect. There's problems. My father was married three times, so I have these stepbrothers and stepsisters all over the place. But, I mean, I just have one big family. I always used to think when I was little, I'll never be an aunt, I'll never have those little kids around. And now I'll be sixteen years older than one of my stepbrothers, and I love it. But it probably makes a big difference that my parents get along."

Despite younger children's flexibility in defining family, I often came away saddened by how older children described the wounds of divorce, and by the yearning and rage within so many of them about the absence of positive adult contact within their families, regardless of their form.

Rachel, a girl with long dark hair at Franklin, a mature and popular young woman, described her vision of family. "I just assume anybody I meet, their parents are divorced," she said.

"I was in the third grade when my parents got a divorce. My first reaction was, I was sad and I wanted them to stay together. Even though I knew they didn't really get along, I just wanted my family. I cried for a straight three hours, and after that I just blanked it out and I really can't remember anything before then. I mean, any vivid things. Like, I only remember the things that my mom or dad told me that I did or what happened to me. I lived in [another city, in the East] until I was six and then we moved here, and there was a custody fight and a divorce. So I just want some stability in my life.

"A couple of weeks ago I asked a new friend of mine if he lived with his mom or his dad. And he kind of went, 'What?' I was embarrassed. To me, it was just a given that he lived with one of them, and he said, 'I live with both my parents.' And it was like, 'Oh, oh, I forgot.' People can still be *married,* you know. It never even crosses my mind that somebody's parents might still be married."

Only a handful of the kids in this class — a typical class — still lived with both of their natural parents. To them, watching the Cleavers is like watching Martians.

"It seems like a dream world to me," said Rachel. A pinched and puzzled expression came into her eyes. "But I would love it, actually. To have a life like that." She said this low and clear.

"I want to be a teacher, 'cause teachers have stable jobs. I want" — she paused, laughing — "a husband and kids and I just want to own a house and just never have to have any kind of big changes in my life anymore." Her voice became low again and tense. "But I know that's not very realistic."

A kid with spiked hair wearing a MINOR THREAT T-shirt spoke up. "I'd watch those shows, like 'Leave It to Beaver,' and I can't imagine life being so simplistic. Like the Beave, he's growing up with a demented conception of life where everything is really, really trivial."

The girl spoke in defense of the Beaver. "Well, my family is basically like the Cleavers. My sister's Wally. I'm the Beaver." She laughed. "It's not exactly like that, but it's nice and it's stable. I have something to go home to."

She said she sometimes lies awake at night thinking about the fact that her family is so unusual. "I think — no, my parents could never divorce. I mean, they love each other, and —"

Rachel interrupted. Her voice was bitter; she directed her question to me. "Your generation didn't want to be stable, did you?"

No. A lot of us didn't.

"Well, to me, stability is just a dream," said Rachel. "I think it's just gonna get worse and worse. I think family is just gonna be gone. I don't have the slightest idea how a family works. How can I know what to do if I've never experienced it?"

The girl who had compared her own family to the Beaver's said, "You can sleep over at my house." Everybody laughed.

"Let's assume for a moment," I said, "that what Rachel said is correct, that family — the nuclear family — is going to fade. What replaces it? Any theories?"

"Independence," said one boy. "I think the family'll still exist as more of an — outline. There might be two people and they might be married or living together and they'll have a child and maybe they'll get divorced and people will come and go and the unit will look about the same, but the people themselves will behave more as separate entities, especially the children." He visualized this image of the future as a kind of family portrait, with a lot of dotted lines and empty spots. "It seems more empty, more — people out for themselves, mostly."

The school bell was echoing down the hallway.

"I think it would be good for the children," he continued. "I personally prefer to be independent. Mostly adults will be oblivious to it. They'll either ignore it deliberately or they won't notice that people are just drifting away emotionally. That's basically the way it is now, anyway, among my friends."

The Strand of Money and the Children's Depression

Any family form, as these children suggested, can function quite well, given enough love, but love is sometimes not enough. New economic realities for families have replaced the expanding middle class of the fifties and sixties with a new "divergent middle class," according to Ralph Whitehead, a professor of journalism at the University of Massachusetts. The previous middle class, once sure of its shared economic and cultural values, is diverging into three quite separate groups: an expanding number of "bright-collar workers," the twenty million "knowledge workers" born since 1945; "new-collar" workers, primarily in the service industries; and a shrinking pool of blue-collar workers. The new economy has not been kind to new-collar and blue-collar families — or, of course, to the poor.[7] In the aftermath of the stock market crash in 1987, many Americans were puzzled that a serious recession or even a depression did not follow immediately. Some folks assumed that the next depression would be announced with media banners and flourishes and choruses of "Brother, can you spare a dime?" But the next depression is coming quietly — among America's young families.

During the boom times of the fifties and sixties, family income soared almost effortlessly; according to one study, the average thirty-year-old man at the beginning of the fifties watched his income (adjusted for inflation) rise 58 percent during the decade, and an average thirty-year-old man at the beginning of the sixties saw his income jump 52 percent by the end of that decade. But a thirty-year-old man in 1973 would see his real income fall by 1 percent over the next decade. Of course, during this same period women improved their real income substantially, though it still lags far behind men's income.[8] Even with women working, during the eighties a generation of young families — much like the farmers and steelworkers who had already suffered their own market-sector depressions — began to sense that the American dream was slipping away.

Between 1973 and 1986, according to a study by the Children's Defense Fund and the Center for Labor Market Studies at Northeastern University, the median income of young American families with children headed by persons under age thirty fell by 26 percent — a decrease virtually identical to the per capita income loss of 27 percent which Americans suffered between 1929 and 1933. If the family's increased childcare costs are also taken into account, the net income losses were even greater. The news was even worse for *very* young families with children, those headed by persons under age twenty-five. Of all the generations, they suffered the greatest declines in earnings and income since 1973. The median earnings of very young family heads with children plunged by 60 percent, so that by 1986 more than half of all children living in such families were poor.

The poverty rate for young married-couple families with children has doubled since 1973, leaving one in every eight such families poor in 1986. Thirty-five percent of all children — one out of every three children — in young families lived in poverty in 1986, a generational condition comparable to President Roosevelt's description a half century earlier of "one-third of a nation ill-housed, ill-clad, ill-nourished."[9]

The economic break with the past was linked to a number of factors. Baby boomers, facing stiff job competition with each other, began their careers just as the economy entered an eleven-year stagnation of living standards. Between 1973 and 1986, the share of income a young family with children needed to carry a mortgage on a newly purchased, average-priced home more than doubled — from 23 to 51 percent. Unemployment fell during the eighties, but the nation's economic shift from manufacturing to service meant lower income. Though Reagan administration officials disputed the numbers, Lester Thurow, dean of the Sloan School of Management at the Massachusetts Institute of Technology, maintained in 1988 that the bottom 60 percent of the population had had the lowest income since the Census Bureau started collecting such figures in 1947. Bennett Harrison, a professor of political economy at MIT, estimates that, in 1979, 31 percent of all jobs paid less than $12,000. After 1979, however, 56 percent of the new jobs counted paid less than $12,000.[10] All this occurred at the very moment when the number of parents not receiving adequate child support was multiplying.

"The best thing about being a single parent is that there's no interference, or at least less interference, from the other parent in raising the child," said Joan, who at forty-five was the oldest of several single parents I spoke with at Dewey Elementary School in San Diego. She said she was proud of making it alone, with a child, proud of the engine grease beneath her polished fingernails — grease from fixing her own car. "But sometimes you don't think you're going to make it. There's the child-care payments, you have to put them off until the end of the month, the excuses you have to make up."

Another single mother, a hairdresser, said she considered herself lucky. Her children go free to the elementary school's sliding-scale day-care program, which is sponsored by the school district and the state. The list of parents waiting to get their children into the program is long. For her two children, she might pay $500 to $800 a month for private day care, which illustrates one reason so many single mothers remain on welfare: she brings home just $800 a month.

Only four of the twelve parents in the room were covered by any kind of health insurance. They consider day care, unlike health insurance, a necessity if they're going to stay off welfare. According to a study by the sociologist Lenore Weitzman, the average divorced woman in California is awarded no alimony, less than $10,000 in property, and child support (if it can be collected) averaging $200 a month for two children. The reason: California's no-fault divorce laws, which do not take into account differences in earning power acquired during marriage. Divorced women thus suffer an average 73 percent decline in their standard of living in the first year after divorce, whereas former husbands experience a 42 percent gain.[11]

For many families in the near future, the strand of economic support will be strained even further. Families who expect to help their children with college costs now face what might be called "eduflation": rising costs, rising expectations, and tougher entrance requirements. By the year 2000 (the year my older son will graduate from high school), four years of education at an average public institution in America could cost close to $50,000 — or over $100,000 for four years at a private institution. This College Board projection includes fees, tuition, room and board, and expenses. Though the rate slowed slightly in 1990, for nearly a decade tuitions have risen far faster than the nation's inflation rate.[12]

"The college entrance mania has outpaced anything I've ever seen," said Jim McClure, director of guidance at T. C. Williams High School in Alexandria, Virginia. "Parents are coming into my office with their kids saying, 'I don't know how I'm going to pay twenty thousand dollars a year.' People are mortgaging their homes a second and third time. They're frightened."[13]

This dismal portrait of young families and childhood's economic future may yet reverse if the job market becomes a seller's market as the so-called baby-bust generation comes of age. But the psychological effect of the new economic realities for families — the broken strand of faith in the economic future — cannot be overstated. For example, the Children's Defense Fund reports that young men who do not earn enough to support a family are three to four times more likely to remain single than those with adequate earnings. As the income of young men fell sharply between 1973 and 1986, their marriage rates also dropped by one-third. During that same period, the proportion of out-of-wedlock births nearly doubled. The fragmentation of American families is linked to the economy; it is not simply a question of personal morality or individual fidelity.[14]

The children's depression has also helped shape the psychology of families that have prospered economically in recent years. Parents today may own an array of electronic gadgets, but the families of the fifties and sixties generally had more time, less fear, and greater economic hope.

Karl Zinsmeister estimates that under prevailing standards it will cost $200,000 to raise a child to adulthood.

Further, it will require enormous amounts of time devoted to Suzuki music lessons, computer camp, gymnastics training and challenging play groups. Being a parent has always been a difficult, time-consuming undertaking, but in a world that includes French lessons and classical music at pre-school for 3-year-olds, the standards of successful parenthood seem to have risen today. Our children, as much as our electronic devices, must be programmed. "Parenting" has become not only a new word but a newly serious, even grim, responsibility, full of crushing demands, competitiveness, and guilt.

Parents feel compelled to make more money to buy more electronic gadgets, to fit their kids with the latest Reeboks, to get them into the most prestigious colleges. They must do all these things, they somehow feel, in order to be adequate parents — especially because they have so little family time.

Not surprisingly, an increasing number of Americans see kids as expensive burdens. A majority of Americans will, within the next few years, live in childless households. Considering decreasing economic support, rising economic expectations, and the growing feeling that children are a luxury, should it be any surprise that so many young people have rejected teaching and other helping professions in favor of high-paying specialties in computer science, medicine, business, and law? Ironically, this trend away from the helping professions has further weakened the supportive web.[15]

How Kids Feel About Money, Family, and the Future

I was curious how children who have grown up during the children's depression felt about money and their future. Were they as materialistic as the media have made them seem?

After a Parent-Teacher-Student Association meeting at Hamilton Middle School in Seattle, a group of parents and a few student members sat around a large old oak table and talked about money. Josh, a thirteen-year-old, was the student representative at the meeting. Self-assured, precocious, Josh seemed like the kind of kid who would start a software company at nineteen. But he didn't feel optimistic about his economic future.

"My prospects are bleak, basically," he said. "I mean, it costs so much to go to college and then you have to pay it back, and I mean, I don't know if it's worth it."

Mike, a drama teacher at Hamilton who appeared to be in his thirties, cut in. "I work with Josh here in the classroom," he said. "We surveyed the kids last year in the drama classes — kids eleven, twelve, thirteen — and their number-one interest was bucks. I sometimes wonder how what Josh says compares to my generation. When I went to school, there was no question that I was going to go to college and get a job. We *ran* from jobs and security, knowing we could come back anytime we decided to."

One of the parents, a well-dressed man in his late thirties, described himself as naturally optimistic. "How much of this fixation on money do kids pick up from listening to their parents' financial insecurity? I suspect that my kids think that we're the poorest people in the world, and we're not!" The others laughed. "We're well off. My wife is a nurse and works in research at the University of Washington. I'm an attorney. We're very comfortable, and yet my wife and I seem to talk an awful lot about how much things cost and how much college is going to cost, and it does preoccupy us. Our kids are really worried about college because they think it's going to cost so much. How much of this money anxiety do they pick up from parents? How much of it do they just get out of the environment, because they see homeless people, families on the street?"

At several schools I asked kids this question: How much money did they think they would need to make in the future, as adults, to be successful? I was continually surprised at the answers.

At New York's exclusive Trinity School, a classroom of uniformed fifth-graders offered definition of monetary success. The figures students volunteered ranged from $100,000 to $200,000. I asked how many thought that they could be successful making under $100,000 a year. Nobody raised a hand — not surprising, perhaps, given the wealthy backgrounds of most of them.

What was surprising was how close some of the kids in middle-class schools came to that figure. The average family income in America today is about $31,000, yet the students estimated, on average, that they would need to make more than twice that amount as adults in order to view themselves as successful. When I asked this question at a gathering of parents and children at the private, upper-middle-class Wichita Collegiate School, first came the usual flippant answer, from a ten-year-old: "Oh, about a million dollars." Then "thirty thousand dollars"; "fifty thousand"; "a hundred thousand." Most of the kids agreed that $50,000 would be enough to be successful.

What about defining success itself?

"Well," said a nine-year-old boy, "I think you should be able to help all your friends and support your family and have a good security system."

In a class of seniors at T. C. Williams High School, the answers ranged from $40,000 to $100,000; most kids said $75,000. A few agreed with one young man who said, "Success translates into six figures for me." I mentioned that his teacher, Pat Welsh (who frequently contributes opinion pieces on education to the *Washington Post*), was a success, but that I doubted that he made six figures. "Right. But he's a success in a different way. He really likes to be here and is happy about telling you what he knows. My idea is to do something I like and still make six figures. Not like screw somebody over." He paused. "Did you ever see *Wall Street,* with Michael Douglas? Do you remember when he was talking in the limousine and he said, 'I'm talking hundreds of thousands of dollars in liquid cash — so much money that you don't have to waste time, you'll have your own *Lear jet.*' That was awesome." Moments before, this same young man had expressed anger and cynicism about the nation's failure to help the homeless.

At Baldi Middle School, in a racially mixed working- and middle-class neighborhood in Philadelphia, a class of seventh- and eighth-graders assured me that they weren't all that worried about nuclear war. What they were worried about was money — money and personal issues. "Let's put it this way, the first million is always the hardest," said one boy. I asked the class how many believed they would be millionaires someday. Eleven students held up their hands. One boy said his image of the future was "four kids and a wife and to be successful." I asked him how he defined success. "If I had to pick it would be money, because with the money you can do what you want. Have like a nice house, a nice car, and a wife." In that order? "Maybe. A lot of money. Live in the nicer part of town."

I asked the kids at Baldi how much money they thought they would have to make to be successful. "Per year?" asked the first boy. More answers came.

"A hundred thousand dollars."

"A hundred thousand isn't a lot."

"A hundred thousand would maybe be enough if you lived alone."

One girl offered, "If you had a family you'd need a hundred and fifty thousand." I asked her what she based that on. "My family." Did her parents both work? "Yes." And they made over $150,000? She laughed. "No. Far from that." I assumed, then, that what she heard from her parents was that they wished they could make $150,000; then everything would be okay. "No, they say it's okay the way it is."

One boy grew increasingly agitated. His hand shot up. He was wearing a gray sweat shirt and his blond hair was cut in a flattop. "I don't think money's the most important thing in being successful. Being happy in what you're doing is first. And probably your family would come before money. Success really depends on what you set out to do, like if you set out to live on the streets and hang out on the corner and you grow up and be a bum, then you're successful. If you want to take over a certain country when you're young, like Castro, then he's a success if he wanted to do that. It all depends on what goals you have." He turned and looked at a quiet, trendily dressed girl. He explained, in front of the class, that he planned to marry this girl someday. He said, very seriously, "I'd like to be happy, and if you're happy then I'll be happy."

The class laughed, and she answered demurely, "Okay, well, I'm a very material person." She turned to me. "I'd still like to have, like, a home and hearth and kids. I won't want to be so fast-paced like a yuppie that I wouldn't have time and I'd have to shove my kids in boarding school. But I'd still like to do something as me, you know." She thought for a moment. "It would be nice to have seventy-five thousand dollars. That way you could take nice vacations, send your kids to a good school, stuff like that. But I wouldn't want to be a super yuppie if it meant having a kid that's real lonely or screwed up. I wouldn't be happy making a thousand dollars a year either because you can't afford a house on a thousand bucks a year. I'd wake up on a grate instead of on a bed."

A boy who had not spoken till then said quietly, "Sometimes I worry, like, that if I try too hard and like try to do everything that's best, like people won't like me and maybe I'll like lose a job, and I won't be able to get a job and maybe I'd like have to live with my parents if the worst came to worst."

Then one girl expressed the curious compassion I was to hear often from kids of her generation. She explained why she wanted to be a millionaire. "Because my parents work really hard now to give me everything that I want and I'd like to give it back to them if I'm able to."

"That's wrong!" called out an earringed boy dressed in black. "Your parents didn't *lend* you all the money and all the care that you got. They gave that to you, and you shouldn't have to pay them back."

The girl answered softly, "I'm not giving my parents back the money. I want to give them some joy, I guess. That I was a success. See, my mother never had it as a kid, so I'd like to give that to her."

Had she told her mother that? I asked.

"No."

What did she think her mother would say if she told her that?

She laughed a little nervously and said, "She'd cry."

Lost in Time: The Strands of the Generations

Just as time and money are disappearing family resources, so is our sense of *place in time*. Just as there is comfort in knowing intimately the land on which one lives, there is comfort in knowing one's place in the fabric of time.

Tom Hilleary is a parent in Overland Park whose mother was murdered (she had been a volunteer in a Christian Science Reading Room; a thief had walked in one day and, when she produced no money, shot her). He described how he had found solace, after the murder, in spending time with his small children, in watching them grow from one long week to the next. "It's all a continuum, isn't it?" he said to me one evening, alluding to the childhood we had shared, as neighbors and good friends. Now, as he watched his daughter play on the carpet — his daughter with the blond hair and blue eyes of his mother — he saw clearly that his children offered him a link to the past as well as to the future; they were a bridge over tragedy, an assurance that life goes on and that the future can often heal the past.

Yet most parents seldom talked about the future except in a fearful way. The present seems disconnected from the past and from the future. One reason is that the old distinctions between life periods are blurring. Today marriage, childbearing, and serious career choices are often delayed until people are in their thirties. Through the centuries, the period of a person's life considered childhood (adolescence being a twentieth-century invention) has been gradually extended, to the point that the difference between children and adults is unclear.

The good news is that age stereotypes are rapidly disappearing; the not-so-good news is that we're not quite sure anymore who, generationally, owes what to whom. We may find it difficult to know what, of ourselves, we can appropriately be expected to give to people who are older or younger than we are. Without generally agreed-on generational markers, we feel lost in time.

More and more, adults and children dress and talk alike. As the distinctions between life stages disappear, so does some of the richness of life. For adults and increasingly for children, how far one has been in life is beginning to matter less than how fast one can run. But the growing outward similarities between children and adults only serve to push them apart emotionally. Given the fuzzy distinctions of age, children may find it more difficult to find adult role models; if there is nothing particularly special about adulthood, then there is nothing particularly worthy of graduating to, and a child's peers may appear to have (and often do have) as much authority and expertise at giving advice and guidance as adults.

As Americans live longer, the proportion of their lives that they spend in the company of their children decreases. White American women born in the 1880s could expect to live about 21.3 years after their youngest child reached age eighteen. By contrast, those born in the 1950s will survive approximately 34.1 years after their last-born reaches adulthood. So the average baby boomer mother will spend nearly twice as many years free of children as she spends devoted to them.

"The way we see the future can tell us much about ourselves. And if we can judge from recent science fiction, our plans for the future will have little place for children," writes historian John Sommerville. "The family is a major element in most novels, but is almost absent from futuristic ones." This fact may be related, he suggests, to the increased longevity which we expect in the future. "Caring for children has always been our main opportunity to be generous and altruistic," he writes, adding that science fiction writers "seem to sense that longer life will involve our becoming more selfish."[16]

Yet people who live longer, healthier lives will be better able to care for following generations in indirect ways — as employees or volunteers in day-care centers or schools, for example — if society places more value on such work.

Certainly, without a more positive age consciousness, the political clout of families diminishes as the population ages. Without clear signals as to what each generation needs from the others, older people drift further and further away from any sense of connection to the young.

In 1983, for the first time in our nation's history, the over-sixty-five group outnumbered those under twenty-five. According to projections by the Bureau of the Census, by the year 2000 there will be more persons aged fifty-five and over than children fourteen and under.[17] Society's resources are following that curve:

• In 1972, the United States spent approximately equal shares of the gross national product on health and on education. By the mid-eighties, health expenditures were 50 percent greater than education spending — mostly for the treatment of diseases associated with advanced age.[18]

• A study conducted for the Congressional Joint Economic Committee

revealed that the share of national income going to families with children has dropped 19 percent between 1973 and 1985. In 1987 the percentage of children living in families in extreme poverty surpassed the percentage of poor elderly.[19]
• The federal government spends only one-tenth as much on each child as it does on the average senior citizen.

In increasing numbers, older Americans are cut off from children and young families. As a child, I adopted older couples in my neighborhood as surrogate grandparents, from whom I would gain a sense of warmth and security and continuity. Today in that same neighborhood, the ranks of the mentoring old have thinned. In what is nearly a generational exodus, many seniors are moving into seniors-only housing complexes and communities. The tragedy of this movement — which is expanding out of the Sunbelt states and into the upper Midwest — is the psychology that it promotes: the unstated assumption that the old and the young do not need each other anymore. In the context of the vanishing web, nothing could be further from the truth.

Rather than accepting the drifting separation of the generations, we might begin to define a more complex and interesting set of life stages and parenting passages, each emphasizing the connections to the generations ahead and behind. As I grow older, for example, I might first see my role as a parent in need of older, mentoring parents, and then become a mentoring parent myself. When I become a grandparent, I might expect to seek out older, mentoring grandparents, and then later become a mentoring grandparent.

Such a set of age markers would be associated with generational *service*. For instance, recruiting the young-old (people in their fifties and sixties who are vital and active) as volunteer or paid learning aides in public schools would signal a new age marker to society and help all of us find our place in time.

The Strand of Shared Values

Without real linkage to the past or to the future, many of us romanticize what was and dread what could be. As a result, many parents say they have difficulty focusing on the present in their family life. One father put it this way: "I'm so nostalgic for the past, and so obsessed with the future — you know, with making money to take care of the future — that I have to *work* to focus on my kid today. What's more, I have to work at it to remember that I have some kind of meaningful connection to kids who aren't my own, especially kids who are younger than mine — the kids coming up. Do you know what I mean? It's a weird feeling. When I stop to think about it, I realize that I should feel an attachment to them, and to *their* future. This feeling should be natural, like breathing, but it's not for me. I feel like I have to have some kind of excuse to care about them, so I pay attention when people talk about how we've got to educate them to compete with the Japanese. But you know, I shouldn't need to *find* a reason to care."

Historians of childhood point out that, for at least four centuries, adults have been aware of children and their needs and have increasingly seen children as symbols of the future, of hope. Immigrants who came to America often did so not with the assumption that their lives would be better, but that surely their children's lives would be. Children would lead the lives that parents could not, and parents, by God, would help them do it.

During recent decades a number of liberation movements have transformed Western society, and these movements were pursued in the name of future generations. Yet that positive association of children with the future has been declining for at least two decades. In the seventies, children began to represent overpopulation, a drain on future energy, food, and employment resources that would compound pollution, crowding, and environmental degradation. As Karl Zinsmeister points out, the choice of childlessness is even more pronounced in many parts of Europe. In Germany there is actually a word, *Kinderfeindlichkeit,* that means "hostility to children." A poll in Bonn's *Die Welt* found that "90 percent of West Germans considered careers and possessions more important than children." Tour guides advise that in some areas of Europe children are less welcome in restaurants and other public places than pets.

"Babies are the enemy," writes John Sommerville. "Not your baby or mine, of course. Individually they are all cute. But together they are a menace." In recent decades, a frightening number of movies have portrayed children not as innocent and idealized but unpredictable, even evil. *Lolita* suggested that the young corrupt adults. *The Exorcist* implied that children are the devil's doorway. An ad for *It's Alive* read: "It was born three days ago. It has killed seven people. Its parents are human beings. Whatever it is . . . It's Alive." As Sommerville points out, in no other age has folklore projected such fiendish hostility onto children. He infers we may well be experiencing a historic break from the past, a turning point in the history of childhood.[20]

Our children feel this break. When I asked one class of high school students what they most feared about the future, several said, "Kids." I asked why. A tough-looking junior answered, "Because kids will just keep getting worse."

The Fundamental Divide

As a result of the lost linkage of the generations, the divergence of the middle class, the children's depression, and the rapidly changing definitions of family, two radically different views of childhood are emerging. One is fixated on idealized images of the past, and the other is focused on rationalized visions of the future.

Some academic visionaries, for example, see family change "moving in a direction that should be highly compatible with our ancient human spirit." So writes Helen Fisher, an anthropologist for the American Museum of Natural History, in an article for *U.S. News and World Report.* "Men and women," she believes, "are moving toward the kind of roles they once had on the grasslands of Africa millions of years ago." This is no backward trend, but a "thrilling" step forward.

The trend seems novel to us, Fisher argues, because we're only now emerging from a male-dominated agricultural tradition, in which families lived in isolated units. But we're no longer so dependent on each other; today anyone can "hunt and gather" information. Worried about rising divorce rates? Don't be, says Fisher. The statistics may seem bleak "until we recall that the vast majority of couples who split up remarry. The constant making and breaking of marital ties is a hallmark of hunting-gathering communities." We're returning to the extended family of past communities, so don't "equate divorce with failure," she advises. Children are going to grow up "with more adult role models and a larger network of relatives, increasing their range of power and influence within society."[21]

But the web we should be weaving, unlike Fisher's hunting and gathering model, should help families stay together, not encourage or romanticize their wanderings.

A view of childhood's future notably different from Fisher's comes from psychoanalyst Judith Wallerstein, co-author with Sandra Blakeslee of *Second Chances: Men, Women, and Children a Decade After Divorce,* who conducted the first long-term study of the effects of divorce. She contends that a lot of recent professional advice to parents has been based on the false assumption that divorce is a short-term crisis, that the effects of divorce on children last only two or three years. Not so, writes Wallerstein. She describes what she calls the "sleeper effect" that can hamper children of divorce in forming loving relationships and in achieving educational and working goals a decade and more after their parents' divorce. Unless the parents are extraordinary in their civility and attention, the sense of abandonment is almost unbearable for many children.

Wallerstein's study tracked sixty families, most of them white, for ten to fifteen years after divorce. Looking at children twelve to eighteen months after their parents' divorce, she and her fellow researchers were stunned to find that an unexpectedly large number (37 percent) were in a downward psychological spiral. Their symptoms were worse than those recorded immediately after the divorce. In a ten-year follow-up, 41 percent were doing poorly; they were entering adulthood as worried, underachieving, and often angry young men and women. Wallerstein also found that a quarter of the mothers and a fifth of the fathers had not repaired their lives a decade after divorce. As adults, they often exhibited a "diminished capacity to parent." The "overburdened child," as she calls many of the children of divorce, feels compelled to rescue the troubled parent. Wallerstein suggests that it would be "hard to find any other group of children — except, perhaps, the victims of a natural disaster — who suffered such a rate of sudden serious psychological problems."[22]

Not all offspring of divorce are overburdened children. And certainly some young lives are improved by the divorce of their parents. But many of us cannot help but feel repelled by a society that, by breaking so many supportive strands, practically guarantees that divorce will be the norm.

As society moves toward a family life quite unlike that experienced by our parents' and grandparents' generations, many parents and children feel a sense of dislocation. The anxiety created by social change is becoming an increasingly powerful force in our political and religious life.

Today just about every politician wraps him- or herself in "family values," the latest catch phrase in the political firmament. The devil is in the details.

During the 1988 presidential primaries and election campaigning, the Republican party, extolling family values, was dominated on this issue by the New Right, particularly Pat Robertson and activists Paul Wyrich and Phyllis Schlafly. This faction wished to abolish legalized abortion, return prayer to the public schools, support private schools, make divorce more difficult, and repeal the child-care tax credit because it offers women an incentive to take jobs outside the home. Their unlikely agenda: to use government to reverse basic cultural trends of the past twenty years — including changes brought by the women's movement.

The Democrats, also selling family values, expressed their desire to manage the results of cultural trends, focusing on children rather than the family per se. They advocated federal health care for children, national family-leave laws, federal day care, and an overhauled welfare program focusing more specifically on children.

Like divorced parents locked in a custody battle, the two major cultural and political groups continue to fight over America's kids. A third group is emerging, but the dominant groups can be roughly characterized as high-tech modernists and nostalgic traditionalists:

- High-tech modernists, absorbed by the technological future (though generally fearful of the human future), are relatively tolerant of divorce and of family forms other than the nuclear family. Modernists also tend to favor government or corporate day care and greater spending on schools. Chief values (at least professed): individualism, careerism, equality.
- Nostalgic traditionalists believe that government has no role in the family — that the family's only salvation is to "go home" again, with husband working, wife at home, and the kids held in check by religious values and stern parenting. Chief values (at least professed): duty, parental authority, sacrifice.

What has the custody battle between nostalgic traditionalists and high-tech modernists produced for the American family so far? Mainly cultural and political paralysis. On the issue of family, nostalgic traditionalists have shown little interest in seeking common ground with modernists. While members of the religious Right fight abortion and the dispensing of birth-control information in school clinics, they do little to create new adoption agencies or homes for unwed mothers. Though family-leave legislation would allow parents more time with their infants, the religious Right has consistently opposed it. And though nostalgic traditionalists say they believe one parent should stay at home with the kids, they obstruct efforts to equalize pay between the sexes — which would allow more fathers to stay home. For their part, high-tech modernists have often reduced the debate about childhood to simplistic, programmatic approaches while ignoring the underlying spiritual issues shaping childhood's future.

Both groups — and their children — would profit from listening more to each other. There is some evidence, in fact, that a new synthesis of values is beginning to take place. Beyond nostalgic traditionalists and high-tech modernists, a third group is emerging: what some observers have called neotraditionalists (though this term may be too limiting).

The new political obsession with family values is part of a general shift toward "a politics of values, not issues," according to the Daniel Yankelovich Group, one of the nation's premier social research organizations. "In the sixties and early seventies, family values didn't strike at the heart of the American psyche," said Lawrence Kaagan, previously senior vice president of the Yankelovich Group and now president of Kaagan Research. "In the fifties, America valued the centrality of the family — white picket fences, 'Leave It to Beaver.' Then, with the metamorphosis of the sixties, traditional family life was perceived to be more of a trap for individuals. People wanted to explore their potential for personal growth. Birthrates went down, divorce rates went up. People indulged — if that is the right word — in their individualism." Kaagan described the emerging social and political mood: "A lot of people — who in the sixties believed in complete personal freedom — used to say, 'Let a thousand flowers bloom.' Now they're saying, 'Make that six hundred and fifty flowers.' Many of these people are having children later in life, and they're beginning to recognize that maybe it's not such a great idea to have the magazine racks covered with images of naked people. A lot of these people, to whom Jerry Falwell is anathema, now recognize that what he has said about pornography and permissiveness has truth to it — though they would rather slit their throats than admit it."

The problem with using the term *neotraditional,* or *new traditionalist* — though either of these phrases may stick — is that it suggests a pendulum swinging away from liberal values, back to traditional ones. "This isn't happening," said Kaagan. What is emerging, he suggested, is a new synthesis — a tenuous mixture of liberal and conservative values. The trend toward neotraditional values is primarily a movement of high-tech modernists toward an accommodation with traditional values and toward a rejection of some of the materialism and the fast pace of modern life. Unlike nostalgic traditionalists, neotraditionalists tend to reject the sexism inherent in traditional family life. And they reject religious or family isolationism. They sense the need for the web.

In recent years, leading feminists have laid the groundwork for such a movement by moderating their ideas about the family, pulling well back from some of the more radical repudiations of marriage and family life by the women's movement of two or three decades ago. Neotraditional parents also express a growing sense of unease about the gradual shift of child care away from the family and to institutions.

The alternative to finding and planting and stewarding this common ground? More political and cultural paralysis, and another generation growing up in the vacuum.

The Strand of Dreams

All of the strands of the web, including the ones I have not named, depend on the strand of dreams — our ability to envision a better future for childhood.

I have employed the ecological image of a web, but the general image of the circular, interconnected structure of social, psychological, and spiritual health appears in nearly every culture's mythology. For example, Black Elk, an Oglala Sioux holy man who witnessed the destruction of his tribe during the mid-1880s, described his vision of what he called the nation's "hoop" this way:

> I was standing on the highest mountain of them all, and round about beneath me was the whole hoop of the world. . . . And I saw that the sacred hoop of my people was one of many hoops that made one circle, wide as daylight and starlight, and in the center grew one mighty flowering tree to shelter all the children of one mother and one father. And I saw that it was holy.

Later, Black Elk described the loss of his nation's hoop — how "all the marching animals grew restless and afraid that they were not what they had been, and began sending forth voices of trouble, calling to their chiefs," how he looked down and saw "that the leaves were falling from the holy tree . . . all the animals and fowls that were the people ran here and there, for each one seemed to have his own little vision that he followed and his own rules; and all over the universe I could hear the winds at war like wild beasts fighting." The nation's hoop was "broken like a ring of smoke that spreads and scatters and the holy tree seemed dying and all its birds were gone."[23]

Another image of the web appears in the prophet Deutero-Isaiah, 540 B.C., who wrote, "There is One Who is dwelling above the circle of the earth, the dwellers of which are as grasshoppers, the One Who is stretching out the heavens just as a fine gauze, Who spreads them out like a tent in which to dwell" (Isaiah 40:22).

The social environment is unraveling around us partly because we fail to imagine it otherwise. The ability to dream, to connect the past with the future, is as nourishing to an adult or a people as it is natural to a child; the strength of all the other strands depends on our ability to imagine how our environment can be woven anew. To mend our hoop — our web — we must envision the whole ecology and not only the parts.

If we desire a kinder nation, seeing it through the eyes of children is an eminently sensible endeavor: A city that is pro-child, for example, is also a more humane place for adults. Parks, wide sidewalks, access to nature, decent health care, safety — adults desire these cultural attributes for themselves as much as for their children. It may be easier, and politically more practical, to gain these life enhancements for ourselves by first obtaining them for our children. As adults, we may become jaded over time, unable to imagine what changes would create a more humane urban environment. What makes a city or a nation most livable are those attributes that cannot be measured immediately on the balance sheet.

Can we begin again to imagine the whole?

To do so will demand a degree of trust in institutions, a trust that many of us have not felt for a long time. Creating supportive institutions that deserve our trust will be no easy task, but the new web demands strong, new institutions if it is to hold.

What the Left began in the sixties with its wholesale rejection of the culture's family structure and public institutions, the Right continued in the eighties with its promotion of slash-and-burn, laissez-faire development and its virtually indiscriminate attacks on educational and social programs for children and families. In the nineties, some of us who so fervently attacked modern institutions (often with good, if overly wrought, reasons) are now coming to understand how essential to healthy family life those institutions can be.

We may have, in Paul Goodman's phrase, grown up absurd; the public school systems by which most of us were educated may have been riddled with hypocrisy, but in the expanding economy of the fifties and sixties, public education enjoyed plenty of public support and, in turn, offered a modicum of social support for children. Though overly rigid and tangled here and there, the American educational system at the very least exerted a democratic influence on our culture. Yet this is the first generation since the advent of public schooling in which middle-class parents are showing a preference for private schools or other forms of education. The number of children being kept out of public *or* private schools and educated in home schools was a handful ten years ago, a few thousand five years ago, and as many as twenty thousand today — and the number is growing. Much of our faith in the vision of democratic education has been lost.

Similarly, many people began to view the traditional family structure as riddled with absurdities, inequities, and hypocrisy. But at least a logistically workable support system for children was in place.

Many of us have long since disconnected ourselves from these structures, but we have yet to design institutions, work places, and neighborhoods to give meaning and support to the loose improvisations that followed. During the twenties, for example, pre-Levittown suburban planners assembled livable, pedestrian-oriented hometowns, with neighborhood commercial centers, wide sidewalks, front porches, defensible space — decent places for families and children to live. Halted by the Great Depression, this progress was virtually forgotten in later decades as sterile, mass-produced housing tracts and strip developments spread over the land.

I do not mean to imply that the good old days were perfect. But the institutions and structure — the web — of society needed reform, not demolition. To have cut the institutional and community strands without replacing them with new ones proved to be a form of abuse to our own generation and to the next. For so many Americans, the tragedy was not in dreaming that life could be better; the tragedy was that the dreaming ended.

It is not too late to dream again.

PART II

Grasping the Strands

●

Condescension is a constant danger to people bent on finding things out, wrapping the world up in wordy formulations, explanations. A clever mind, stuffed with facts and buttressed by theoretical underpinnings, can miss the very essence of a people's situation, their sense, quite well known by children, of what must at all costs be done.

—Robert Coles, *The Political Life of Children*

Listening

●

As a spider begins to build a web, it comes to understand, by whatever mysterious sensing devices it possesses, its environment — how distant the branches are, how wet the leaves, how stiff the wind.

As a parent, I am reminded each day of how different my own sons' childhood is from my own. The physical, social, and technological environment for children and parents continues to change at a rate that leaves parents and institutions grasping for some sense of stability. The branches have separated; some are gone entirely; electrical wires have replaced others; the wind is up. Strands of a new tensile strength are called for, but how strong? From what properties will they be made?

There is hope for a new web, and in later chapters I will describe some of the exciting strands that are beginning to emerge. But to create a better life for children and families, we must first closely examine the realities of family life today — not the way we wish it were, but the way it is.

Rather than assuming, with nostalgia and yearning, that the old web will suffice — even if it could be restored — we must weave a web *appropriate* to the new environment. To do this, we first need to listen closely to how children, and parents and teachers too, describe the new environment of childhood and the possibilities within it.

4

The Compassion of Children

•

One truth emerges immediately from these voices: the central aspect of the environment of childhood is the emotional health of parents and children. The new landscape of childhood is increasingly threatening to emotional health; yet there is much raw material with which to work — some of it unexpected. Many children I interviewed, for example, were surprisingly compassionate toward their parents and their parents' generation. Their compassion amazed me all the more because of the lack of empathy that many baby boomers had for their parents' generation. In San Diego, I asked a class of tenth-graders to think about what their parents had told them about their childhood. I asked, Which childhood would they rather have, their parents' or their own? As in many other classrooms, most of these kids voted for their own childhood.

"No way would I want my mom's childhood," said one boy, who is black. He elaborated: "My mom says she had about three brothers and six sisters. It was hard, one kid taking care of the other kids. One is fifteen, the other thirteen, go down the line. She had to be the mother to those children, comb their hair, get 'em dressed for school, cook, clean the house. She told me, 'I wouldn't want this to happen to you, to grow up without a mother or a father around to let you know that someone loves you.' "

This boy, speaking in a matter-of-fact tone of voice, mentioned the racism his mother had encountered as a girl. "She got called bad names, people used to throw rocks and stuff. She grew up down South and that's where prejudice really started, back in Mississippi down there. It was hard being chased home by kids throwing bricks through the windows, doing everything that she wouldn't like them to do."

The boy pointed to his chest.

"I'd rather have my childhood now, 'cause my mom's around, I do got that. I go spend the summer with my dad sometimes, but my mom's always around when I need someone to talk to."

I asked a related question: How did they view their parents' lives? Did they respect their parents?

A girl, brow knitted, looking oddly at me through thick glasses, a slight edge to her voice, said: "You *have* to respect your parents. My father, he was smuggled from Puerto Rico to Miami when he was thirteen, and he came here and he started out with nothing. They used to treat him bad. They used to treat Puerto Ricans bad, they used to do them wrong, when my father was young. But now he's a district attorney in New York —"

Her voice broke. She was struggling to maintain control. She said, "A lot of people in here are seventeen, and eighteen, and maybe as you get older, you find out more about your parents. As you grow closer, you respect them more. You know how when you're young, you wonder, Why she want to make me do that? I can't stand her. As you grow older, you understand they're just trying to protect you. . . ." She stopped, unable to continue. Behind the glasses, tears gleamed.

Another girl spoke up, without raising her hand, relieving the Puerto Rican girl. From the style of her clothing, she seemed to come from an affluent family. "A lot of parents had to start from dirt poor, and now you are so proud of where they are. My mother did, 'cause she ran away when she was fifteen, and now she has her own business so I'm very proud of her."

In classroom after classroom, this was the pattern: first, kids maintained that they would rather have their own childhood than their parents'; then in a sudden shift of tone, the kids would begin to list all the elements of their childhood that they thought were worse than their parents'. At the top of their list: drugs, crime, and fear.

One third-grader said, "Probably parents might have a lot of stress on them too because they worry about kids when they're playing outside, that they might just get mugged, or stolen, or drug dealers might come up and give coke to kids."

Even in north Philadelphia, in the midst of the most devastating drug culture, some children were remarkably forgiving of their parents' generation.

Often the feelings of empathy were associated with their parents' anxiety about money. A girl at Crawford High School in San Diego said: "When my parents first got married, they lived overseas, and then my mom had to get a job 'cause my dad wasn't making enough and so my mom started off working at McDonald's 'cause we didn't have enough money. Now she has to work too. It's gotten to the point where the field my dad's in [shipbuilding], you're not always sure you're going to have a job tomorrow 'cause they've been laying off and on, so we have to save. We don't get a lot of stuff." She added that she wished her parents didn't have to work so hard, but that she understood why they had to.

The concern for money and the future is heard even in the lower grades. At Kenwood Elementary in Miami, a fourth-grader said: "I think parents are worried about the pressure because if we don't work in school, they think when we grow up, it's going to be harder for us to take charge of the world and stuff. My mom, she has to work from seven until five and I'm happy because she's so important to me."

I heard this generational compassion again and again, in every geographic and economic area that I visited. I thought often of how different this tone was from how we baby boomers often spoke of our parents' generation: they were squares; they were the materialistic over-thirty establishment that was not worth trusting; they were irrelevant, laughable. Today, children are thrown into battle alongside their parents, compatriots on the field.

In Seattle, at Franklin High School, a tenth-grader told this story: "My mother grew up with only her father. Her mother died from a cerebral aneurysm when she was thirteen. And my parents were divorced when I was two and a half. So I grew up with my parents across the country, one the farthest east you can get and one the farthest west you can get. I think my mom had a lot harder time than me when she was a girl, 'cause she never got to know her mom. I regret not having such a good relationship with my dad as I do with my mom. But you know, I have the chance whereas she didn't. I still have time and she didn't have time."

At Bell Junior High in San Diego, a teacher in charge of a peer counseling class said: "I get mad when people say this generation is totally selfish. So many of them have such a strong sense of compassion for their parents, and for other kids. They see a kid looking really depressed and immediately want to help him."

At first, hearing children express such sensitivity, I was heartened, encouraged, and this feeling persisted. Yet I also began to sense a vague, grating discomfort emanating from beneath the compassion. For a generation of kids who don't see a lot of their parents because of work and

divorce, maybe absence makes the heart grow fonder. After the class at Crawford High I asked Robin Visconti, the teacher who had been listening in, what she thought about the fact that these kids did not want to trade their childhood for their parents'.

"I can't imagine that they really believe that," she said, with a hard edge in her voice. "Perhaps their parents have told them stories to justify the way they behave. The children want to believe that their parents are doing all these things that they're doing for the right reason. Even abused children protect their parents. I resent this idea that some of them express that they have grown up to be more responsible people because they've been put out on their own. That's completely erroneous. Most of them have not had the nurturing that they've needed. They wouldn't know what it's like to have two people at home caring about them, wondering what went on today, talking things over at the dinner. These children have learned to rationalize what has happened to them."

A Paradox of the New Childhood: More Isolation, More Openness

Think of the child of the nineties: shuttled between Mommy and Daddy (divorced); coming home from school to wait alone for hours until a parent appears on the scene; propped in front of a television or conducting an intimate conversation with a voice-simulating Teddy Ruxpin stuffed bear; being sent off to school the next day, where he or she will spend part of the day in front of a cathode-ray tube, alone, plunking away at spelling drills while the teacher does paperwork.

I was often struck by the contrast between the openness of children, their willingness to talk about virtually anything, and the isolation described by teachers, principals, and other adults who observe children away from their families. Children too described this isolation, but in more circumspect ways.

At the East Harlem Performing Arts School in New York, a public school for middle school kids talented in the performing arts, principal Jon Drescher spoke of parents' lack of involvement with students. "We have a rule here — or rather, we had a rule. No matter whether you passed or failed a test, you had to get it signed. Kids who got a hundred on the test would come back without the test signed. Many of them certainly love going home with a good report card. But too many of them weren't that interested in showing it to their parents. It just didn't mean that much to them. Perhaps they knew, deep down inside, that their parents were not that involved in their lives anymore. And that's very different from twenty, thirty years ago. I mean, you couldn't wait to get home with that hundred, and you certainly didn't want to go home with an F. And now, for some kids, it just doesn't make that much of a difference."

Educators, more than most parents, witness how children react in a wider social setting, and one theme emerged immediately: children may spend more time in groups, but they often seem oddly alone in those groups.

Asked to name the characteristic among students that has changed most in his nearly two decades of teaching, Drescher said, "Kids today are more group-oriented, they take their direction from the group; they're very *me*-oriented, but within the group."

Nancy Shelburne, principal of Crawford High, gave another view of this change in group interaction: "I see kids desperately in need of more human contact. Ten years ago you would see a much higher proportion of kids horsing around at lunchtime, laughing and joking in little groups. It's far more fragmented today. As the kids leave school, instead of walking by twos and threes and talking, you see them going off individually with their ears plugged into their Walkmen. They cut out all other human contact, place themselves in their own little worlds. You'll see a kid sitting against the wall reading a book, or you'll see a kid sitting all by himself eating lunch, maybe with one friend. They're more open, but just don't seem to have the kind of close long-term friendships with other people. They still have groups, cliques, but fewer real friends."

One evening at my local library a group of library volunteers, most of them elderly, told me in no uncertain terms what they thought was wrong with my generation. A retired schoolteacher in her late sixties, who had taught for thirty years and now worked part-time with emotionally disturbed teenagers, summed up the verdict: "Parents your age have been sold a bill of goods. You think you're failing if you don't get your kid into some kind of fancy nursery school or educational day care. Well, a child can learn to read in three weeks. What they *can't* get in three weeks is enough adult contact. Children should apprentice themselves to adults; they need to be apprentices to life. They don't need to count little plastic pieces. There's enough time for that. They should be out with adults. In day care, you don't learn much about life from a two-year-old, except how to fight."

Indeed, what children miss most of all isn't contact with their peers, but positive adult contact.

The Boy with Dead Men's Clothes

An affable and eloquent boy at Franklin High spoke of his sense of being cut off from the adult world, and his need to hold on to some part of it. He contrasted his father's childhood with his own: "It seems as though my father had a much better childhood than I do, because he had a lot of brothers and sisters, and I was an only child till I was like eight or nine. They were really poor. I don't remember what you call that game — where you throw the cards into the corner of the wall and try to get them to stick into the crack between the wall and the floor. My father used to win and my uncle would beat him up and steal his money." He laughed. "I think in general my father's childhood was better than mine. Or maybe worse than mine, I don't know. He was basically ignored. His mother was crazy, but it brought him closer to his father — my grandfather. The strange thing, though, is although my father and grandfather were really good friends with each other, my grandfather never cared about my dad's opinion on anything, just because my father was a kid, a child, and not an adult. But my grandmother, being crazy, did bring the two closer and they were really good friends throughout my grandfather's life until he died about two years ago.

"During my childhood, my parents split up. I was a real happy kid, I guess, until then. There's a lot of weird stuff involving the divorce. They did a lot of drinking and fought a lot, and I was about six. And I remember being really happy until the divorce and then I went to live with my mother and didn't like that very much, and then I went to live with my father, and because we didn't have any unifying force to bring my father and me together — my mother not being a horrible person or crazy or irrational or anything — basically we're still on the basis of an authority figure and a child and it kind of alienates me from him. And I'm not on very good terms with my mother either, but that's just because we don't happen to get along. But with my father, we like each other okay, but mostly it seems like I'm obligated to live with him because there's no place else I can go until I'm legally of age to move out."

I asked him what he would do to change that, to make it better. If he could go back and fix the situation, what would he do?

"I'd probably want to live with my father straight away. I think that would have worked. I was on really good terms with him up until the time that I was thirteen and then . . . my ideas changed. It's not a battle of ideals between us; I mean we basically have the same ideals, but we do less stuff together, we are less interested in the specific things that the other person is doing."

Such as?

"Well, writing. He has written, and I want to write, but mostly it's just different lives. He didn't have much of a social life when he was younger and I do, and so he doesn't think that certain things that I think are necessary *are* necessary. Like I like to go out and have coffee after school and he just didn't do that because he was sort of an outcast when he was a child and a teenager. There are just things that he doesn't understand because he never went through them himself, or because he never wanted to. But we're basically the same person.

"I think it just has to do with the difference in society between then and now. For instance, the schools and the way they were conducted were different than they are now. Like dress codes and long hair and stuff. He used to be kicked out of school for stuff like that when he was going to school in the fifties and early sixties. I think that there's less conformity now."

I told him I liked his clothes. He was wearing quite an outfit. I asked him how he would describe the style.

"Everything else is pretty dirty." He laughed.

What kind of boots were those? Combat boots, right?

"Yeah."

And the pants?

"These are, I guess, paratrooper pants, they have little tabs all over so that you can tie them to your parachute and they don't rip off."

He was also wearing bright suspenders and a loud purple shirt, and a little white cap with a short brim turned upright.

"I'm glad you asked me about this hat," he said, laughing again. "This is a gas station attendant's hat. A dead person's hat. I get a lot of my clothes from dead people."

I asked him to explain.

"Well, my granddad died, and I liked him a lot, and this was his hat. If I like somebody then I adopt their clothing. Like my stepfather, I liked him so I took his field jacket. And I like looking dopey because a lot of girls think it's real sexy."

His classmates laughed.

He described his haircut as "white sidewalls." "I went to Jim the Barber on Fifteenth, he's the Republican barber of Capitol Hill." He grinned. "I like this haircut because George Orwell had one and Dashiell Hammett and T. S. Eliot, and girls like it. It's nice to look dumb. Spencer Tracy looked like a sack of potatoes, but everybody liked him. I kind of have to utilize my dumbness and strange traits to be more — likable. You know?"

I was struck by this boy's sense of proportion.

He had expressed such deep understanding of and compassion for his father and grandfather. Like many other childhood survivors I had spoken with, he had created his own small web in a group of friends, and he clung to pieces of fabric from the past. As do so many kids, he wore the artifacts not of his own past or even his own experience, but of previous generations.

Baby boomers dabbled in nostalgic dress for a time — granny glasses, bib overalls, back-to-the-earth beards. But the context of our teenage nostalgia was different: we were going to remake the world. We were rejecting (or so we thought) the gray flannel sameness of our parents' generation, and our minds were set on the future.

These kids seldom express the kind of political or social hope about the future that we did. Their nostalgia is more pure: they feel they have lost something, and they do not know how to create it again. When they wear the clothes of dead people, they mean to do just that. This boy did not blame his father for his father's isolation. He intended to survive it.

The New Openness

The sheer openness of kids is extraordinary, a counterpoint — or perhaps a companion — to their isolation.

At Baldi Middle School in Philadelphia I asked Max Ehrlich, a principal for twenty-six years, to characterize how he thought kids have changed since he began teaching. He said that children have become "more worldly wise." They're less inhibited, he said, and "very open." Years ago a principal would walk down the hall and no student would say a word to him. Today, said Ehrlich, "a youngster will stop you and think nothing of asking you a question that's off the wall."

I asked him when he first noticed this new openness.

"I would say in the seventies. Kids began to use language we would have shuddered at earlier. One morning about ten years ago I was standing inside the school as the buses were pulling in, with one of the boys who had offered to count children who came off the bus. We happened to look across the street and there was a huge German shepherd dog over there barking, and I said, 'Boy, that really looks like a mean dog,' and the youngster said to me: 'You know, Mr. Ehrlich, the other day that dog came out and chased two of our kids down the street. You should have seen those little fuckers run.' " Ehrlich laughed. "He didn't blink an eye, he didn't hesitate. And my immediate response was, Boy, I guess they *were* scared. And at that point it hits you, how open and uninhibited the kids have become. And they're even more open today. I think it's kind of refreshing."

Refreshing for some, discomforting for others. During one particularly grueling classroom session, when students had talked about their ambivalent yearning for the world of Beaver Cleaver, one especially bitter girl said that she hoped her parents would divorce. Richard Nagely, the teacher of that class, commented that he was unnerved at this openness. When Nagely graduated from high school in 1960, he said, "We wouldn't spill our personal business out the way these students do, and there's something — and I'm not sure what it is — but there's something that really bothers me about that." He described how kids who seek his counsel will unload the kind of intimate details that, at that age, he would never have considered sharing outside his family.

We had moved to the cafeteria, and I was sitting at a table with Nagely and several other teachers, eating Sloppy Joes.

"That openness goes back to overall self-worth, self-pride," said one of the other teachers. "You think it's openness but it's really a quasi openness. Kids are modeling themselves off television. If the Cosbys are open, they're open."

I thought, Is that a bad thing? I had to admit that much of the openness that I had heard expressed by children and teenagers had been a kind of rhetorical openness, statements into the ether, electronic signals sent out with no expectation of response: Is there life out there? This new openness hangs like a moon above the children's landscape: one side bright with possibility, the other dark with portent.

In Alexandria, T. C. Williams High School's Pat Welsh, an outspoken teacher and writer who is clearly loved by his students, told me: "If parents knew what kids said about them, in front of classes, they'd probably keep them home and lock them up. When you're a teacher, it gets to the point where you want to cut it off. Kids embarrass me. If one kid starts ripping apart his old man, you just cut it off."

What about the compassion I had detected?

"One side compassion, the other side rage," said Welsh.

How Kids Feel About the New Openness

Most kids, particularly teenagers, said they felt good about being able to talk openly to their parents. A high school senior in San Diego said: "In the old days, if you didn't like the way you were being treated, you couldn't talk back to your parents, but now you can. And sometimes they feel bad because they weren't friends with their parents. We're friends with our parents. We have a lot more freedom of speech within our homes." A hint of resistance crept into her voice. "One of the things that's kind of interesting is that my mom was a hippie, so she is a lot more liberal than I am." The girl said she was a Republican, and laughed.

I asked her how her mother dealt with the fact that she had a Republican for a daughter. "She pretty much lets me go my own way. But when we do come into conflict, it's like, *backwards* almost."

John, a black tenth-grader, described how he perceived the relationship between generations: "Teenagers need to get more closer with they parents and get to know much more about them. Like communicate with them. 'Cause most kids come home, go home, don't do nothing, go home, get high, drink and do whatever, go out and hit the streets, run the streets all night. Mom be worried they don't come home. 'Mom, I had a nice day at school, you know, I got a little girlfriend, talking, got a job, working, trying to help you out.' My mom tell me anything, anything that's on your mind to the point where you have to go to school and think about it. I can talk to anybody in my family, really, but my mom is the only thing that I can grab on to right now that would make me stronger."

Those children who expressed the most appreciation of their parents' openness were those whose parents gently but firmly guided their values. But some children, particularly younger ones, expressed a certain hesitancy about all this openness, a feeling of not being prepared for it. "I probably think the feelings were better back in the old days," said a third-grader at Southwood Elementary School in Raytown, Missouri, "because back then if your mom asked you to do something, you wouldn't argue with her like you do now. You'd just do it. And then you go out and go for walk and you're just happy. You'd have two choices. You could have a red hiney or you could agree. But now, if you don't get to do what you want, you're all mad, and you argue with your mom."

This boy, like other children who expressed similar sentiments, was not, it seemed to me, particularly interested in parental strictness; what such children were suggesting was that they felt burdened with too many choices too early. They wanted openness from their parents, but what they really craved was gentle leadership.

Tom Cottle, host of the teen talk show "Soapbox," has said: "I am absolutely struck — and studies bear me out on this — that overwhelmingly the No. 1 concern of these kids is the well-being of their parents. You always find the need for good moms and dads who will love you and demonstrate it. It supersedes almost anything else. The families may change, but they still want a mom and a dad to love them." In any discussion of teenagers' values, he has found, the critical question is, What are *parents'* values? He suggests that teenagers and adults today seem to be moving toward a cultural understanding that, a decade ago, would have been unthinkable: first, that parents — not peers — are the primary establishers of values; second, that when parents err, they usually do so on the side of being tentative in their leadership.[1]

How Parents Feel About the New Openness

Among the parents I spoke with, most held generally positive feelings about this openness — more positive feelings, certainly, than did many of the teachers. Parents said that kids were more open within the family, as well as in the school, than they themselves had been.

"My mother always acted like she knew everything," said one mother in her late thirties. "My son is raised with much more grayness and innuendo, which at times makes it more difficult for him to be a child. These kids are gradually being given the awareness that there are no easy solutions, that parents don't know everything. I try to treat my children as individuals who need to know the truth. Sometimes I think that allowing this grayness makes for more anxiety for everyone. But then I remember how I felt as a child. My mother considered any show of fallibility on her part as a sign of weakness. I remember going on a train trip with her, and looking out the window at the landscape going by and asking, 'What are those flowers?' She said they were rhododendrons. Now, I knew they weren't rhododendrons and said so, and she looked at me like I was nuts — to question her judgment. That moment always stuck with me. I remember thinking, Why is it so important to always be right?"

One cause (and one of the results) of the new openness — a kind of age confusion — is disconcerting to some parents.

"I didn't know what any of my friends' parents first names were," said Jack Hughes, in the Overland Park parent group. "They were just Mr. and Mrs. Tanner or Mr. and Mrs. Smith. When we were growing up all adults were authorities who, we thought, had great power. You didn't joke with them, you just obeyed them. They were not friends, they were not peers, they lived on a completely different level. Like most of the other fathers in the neighborhood, my father would come home from work and he'd take his tie off and that was it. *Very* seldom, he'd come home from work and change into some shorts and say, 'Let's go into the back yard and play catch,' or 'Let's ride bicycles.' That just never happened.

"One of the really great changes for kids and parents today is that they share more interests, they can do more things together," Jack continued. "But the trouble is that isn't what often happens. A lot of the families that we see are so busy keeping up with finances that they don't spend any time with their kids, but the bigger problem is that so many of the parents I know are so emotionally — I don't know if the word is *immature* or what — but they're so busy just keeping up with their own emotional needs that they don't have time to provide for their children's emotional needs. It's like kids taking care of kids."

Several parents in the Overland Park group attributed children's openness to new parenting styles. Their own parents, they said, hadn't been expected to be particularly open with their children. Also, parents of baby boomers usually had more children, so they weren't as focused on each child.

Parents of the fifties and sixties tended to rely on — or at least trust — institutions for the conveyance of values. Some of the people I spoke with described how as children they had attended church with their families or been sent to Sunday school, but at home religion was seldom discussed. "I never debated the existence of God with my parents, and they certainly never tried to impart religious values aside from those that I was supposed to learn in church," said one mother. "My kids are small now, but I would hope they would come to me and talk about religion. I don't plan on ramming religion down their throats or making them believe just exactly the same way I do. But I intend to have talking together be a normal part of their growing up."

Mike, who expressed bitterness at the lack of family openness he had experienced as a child, viewed the conversation as overgeneralized and too optimistic. "I'm sure that within two square miles of where we sit, there's a lot of parents out there that treat their kids just like we all were treated, in terms of intimacy. There's a lot of people out there that don't get involved with their kids. So maybe a few of us want to do it differently. Maybe my kids, when they get older, when they start raising their own kids, they'll say, 'God, I'm going to stay out of my kids' face and let them grow up and leave them alone.' "

Probably not coincidentally, the new openness and the heightened compassion among children coincide with more understanding of the need for help. One mother said: "In our generation, you were thought to be really tippy if you needed therapy. You didn't even admit that your family had problems. When I was a kid, nobody talked about abuse, nobody talked about sex. My father used to say you don't tell your children anything because they'll tell the neighbors. But, now the kids come home and tell *you*. Billy came home one day and told us about one kid in the class whose parents were separated, and how the father was going out with another kid's mother who *wasn't* divorced. And everybody is either in therapy or knows someone who is in therapy."

The main reason for today's openness, she suggested, is that "there is so much more for kids to cope with on a daily basis, and even with all this openness I don't think most adults are even aware of what kids are really going through. And I admire them tremendously, because they do share with each other."

The isolation from adults that many children feel is acute, painful, and ultimately numbing. Logically, children turn for comfort to the most available people, their peers, but they do this in an environment that discourages long-term friendships, just as it discourages any long-term emotional investment in a place — a city, a neighborhood, a street, a woods. Consequently much of their openness, whether with peers or with parents, is fleeting but intense, with a vague sense of desperation attached to it — but they still reach out.

The isolation of childhood reflects the isolation of adults: our withdrawal into our homes, into adults-only, electronically protected condo complexes, into computers, into headphones, into electronic entertainment systems, into cars, into drugs. Our new housing developments isolate singles and the elderly from families, and families from other families. Ultimately, this environmental isolation can promote the pathologies of family alcoholism, mental illness, incest, child abuse. All of these family conditions are marked by secretiveness and isolation from the larger world.

To acknowledge and change the isolation of our children, we must acknowledge and change our own isolation. We already have some of the tools necessary to make that change.

Many members of the contemporary generation of parents are keenly and freshly aware that a child should be treated with respect, as an individual — not as something that just happens as a result of marriage or plain sex, but as a choice. We may also, paradoxically, be the first generation for whom time has become such a diminishing resource; and we recognize, at least subconsciously, that time is love. As a consequence, many of the parents I spoke with expressed a vague sense of failure. Yet these feelings of helplessness and slippage need not be inevitable.

For many children, the new openness is a cry for help, a response to stress, a by-product of the vanishing web; the faster the web unravels, the more kids reach out verbally — at least for a while. The same is true of parents. By reaching out in this way, we give ourselves the first strands of a new web, should we choose to weave it.

5

The Children
Who Own Themselves

●

Oddly, we expect our children to be more independent — even as we overstructure their free time and fear for their safety in the neighborhood or in the woods. Childhood is moving in two seemingly contradictory directions at once: self-care and controlled care. On the one hand, children spend more of their lives on their own and are given increasing autonomy in many of their personal decisions. On the other hand, children — often the same children — spend an increasing proportion of their time under controlled, institutional supervision, by day cares, schools, even libraries — and also by parents who overprogram them.

This paradox is dizzying, noteworthy not because it is entirely new but because of its growing intensity, and because of the confusion it causes when we seek balance in our personal lives and in the political life of the nation.

The Self-Care Generation

Coming home from school to an empty house is one form of self-care.

An editorial in the *Journal of Home Economics* five decades ago warned of "door-key children": "boys and girls who run loose on the streets at all hours of the day. They get the name from the key each wears hung on a string around the neck." In the year the editorial was published, 1941, the existence of door-key children was blamed on the women who would soon be stereotyped in the image of Rosie the Riveter — like women today, they were squeezed between contradictory social expectations.

> These children of working mothers are of all ages and are to be found in practically every community where there is a defense industry. Wherever they are, they present a grave problem. Day nurseries and other child care agencies geared to normal times can no more handle such a situation than can a boy with a peashooter put to rout a charging bull . . . home life and family relationships must be safeguarded while America is engaged in the present titanic struggle, else more will be lost behind the lines than can be gained at the front. . . . America's children must not be sacrificed on the altar of national defense." [1]

Of course, children have always taken care of themselves for part of the day or assumed household responsibilities at an early age. But several factors have changed since 1941: supportive neighborhood life has all but disappeared; advertisers, who understand that early autonomy in kids means a bigger consumer market, have increasingly targeted self-care kids; and the sheer number of "latchkey kids," as they are called now, has become prodigious because so many parents are working.

Available studies give contradictory figures on precisely how many latchkey kids there are. Estimates of the number of children who care for themselves during some part of the day range as high as seven to fifteen million. A poll conducted by Louis Harris in 1987 found that 41 percent of parents surveyed said they leave their children on their own between the end of school and five-thirty in the evening at least once a week, and almost 25 percent said they leave them alone every day. In 1988, the Census Bureau report "After-School Care of Children" noted that 7.2 percent of children aged five to thirteen were left unsupervised after school, including five hundred thousand children without adult supervision *before* school.

Studies of latchkey kids reveal some surprises. The report by the Census Bureau, for example, estimates that a higher percentage of white children (15 percent) than black children (7 percent) have no adult care after school — despite the fact that black mothers are more likely to be employed full-time than white mothers. Another unexpected finding was that children in higher-income households — and children whose mothers were better educated or in white-collar occupations — were more likely than others to be unsupervised after school than children of families with less income and education. Two possible explanations: higher-income families are more mobile and therefore have fewer relatives available to care for youngsters (though they do have more money to hire baby sitters), and upper-income parents may feel more confident about their children's ability to take care of themselves. A third possibility could involve the priorities that many parents establish in their lives in the relative ranking of things and kids.[2]

Although after-school self-care works for some families, too often the outcome is tragic. When Elizabeth Rhodes of the *Seattle Times* investigated latchkey kids in her city, she found that children as young as three were being left to fend for themselves and sometimes their younger siblings for days and nights at a time.[3] Of course, the Seattle example is an extreme case. The parents of most latchkey kids are decent, caring people who think they have no choice but to leave their children without adequate adult supervision. Society and economics have changed, but most institutions — particularly the work place — have failed to accommodate those changes fully.

So far, the kindliest and most flexible public institutions, libraries, have taken up much of the slack, but not without resistance. Particularly during the summer months, libraries become informal day-care centers. Several librarians told me that latchkey kids seldom read when they go to the library after school. "They can't," said one librarian. "They've been in school for six hours. They really need a place to run and jump, and it's not the library."

In Philadelphia, one librarian, a single mother herself, told this story: "I see kids go from three P.M. to eight P.M. with no money for food. These are not welfare kids, necessarily. Some are upper-middle-class. We see the kid whose mother has her sometimes, and the grandmother has her other times; the mother and the grandmother are feuding and they use the kid to make points against each other — who picks her up and who doesn't. We have kids waiting out front at eight at night. As a librarian, you're told you're not supposed to wait for somebody to pick them up because you could get sued. You're not supposed to go out with the kid and wait.

"But what if the mother forgets that the library closes early that day? What if something happens to the kid? This is a high-crime corner. A couple of us will not let a kid wait like that, outside a closed building alone. So we wait with them. Then we have to rush to pick up our own kids, and we're late ourselves. A few times, we've called the police and asked them to escort these kids home. But then the mother always drives up. We explain to her why we called the police, but that's very touchy because no one wants to be told as a parent that they didn't do something right; none of us likes to hear that. My bottom line is I won't leave that kid out on the corner. It comes down to me — doesn't it? — to

wait with that kid. No matter what happens. Because if I go away and
then something happens to that kid, then it is my fault. And I don't
mean my fault legally. I mean ultimate liability. All this legal mumbo-
jumbo doesn't mean a damn thing when it's five o'clock and the library's
closed and nobody's there and the kid's standing on the corner. I've got
to act. But if our staff is cut any more than it already has been, we won't
be able to wait with them anymore."

Getting "Clock-Wise": How Kids Feel About Self-Care

In past decades, children would have been more likely to go home to a
neighborhood still populated with adults — other parents, aunts, uncles, friends. But latchkey children today find adult contact, such as it is,
only in public libraries or relatively rare after-school programs. Going
home becomes an excursion into isolation, or (from a teenager's point
of view) into a child's wonderland, a separate world free of adult restrictions.

For reasons that range from the sublime to the subversive, some kids
feel surprisingly good about being latchkey kids, and for taking more
adult responsibilities. In general, the older the children, the better they
feel about their independence.

And to be fair, some children do make good use of the time — and
their use of it is associated with the compassion of this extraordinary
generation. Cheryl, a tenth-grader at Crawford High School in San Diego,
said she had been a latchkey kid for most of her childhood. "It makes
you more responsible. I know my parents are going to be too tired when
they get home 'cause they've been working all day long. So I just take
on the responsibility of the chores and the house. I make sure stuff gets
done so they don't have to do it. It's a good thing, because if you have
the type of parents that's always doing things for you, then when you
do come of age you will never want to take on the responsi bility."

John, a black tenth-grader, spoke also of responsibility in a kind of
wonderfully empathetic rap: "Like Cheryl said, you have to take the
responsibility. Soon, you be a man or a lady, have a family, you don't
want to be letting them do everything, you want to do things too, get to
feel that you could do whatever, clean the house, listen to music. Take
on your own responsibility. I don't stay with my dad, it's just me and
my mom stay at home. My dad stay in Indiana. My mom be tired 'cause
she go to school, she come home tired, I go in there and wash dishes,
clean the bathroom, do something so she won't have to tell me what to
do, make her proud of me. I know most parents don't let their kids go

home now and try to clean the house. Probably get electrocuted or killed. But me, everything is *clock-wise.* I go home, come in, put my books down, look around the house, see what needs to be cleaned up, clean up, do my homework, turn on the radio, and kick it. It's just like a routine, *clock-wise.* Everything goes, come home, do whatever you're going to do, take your time, do it right, water the plants, watch TV, do whatever. My mom gets home at three-thirty, it depends on what she has to do. Sometimes I come home, I be there by myself for a while so I do what I got to do. She come home, 'Well, you cleaned the house, that's good!' "

After the kids had filed out of the classroom, the teacher remarked that John's little speech was the most he had said in class all year.

Among the comments in other high school and junior high school classes:

"There are the pros and cons to it," said one tenth-grader. "It's good not getting bugged, especially at my age. But if a person were to think back about how it was when they were younger, then they would re- member times when they had these feelings of not being thought about — Maybe Mom doesn't care about me 'cause I'm here by myself. You know — She likes to work better than she likes to be home."

"My mom works and my dad works. And I kind of raised myself. So my parents really didn't have to worry about parenting."

"I still think it was better, 'cause I mean, my family never got along when they were together at all. I never sat around and dwelled on it but I liked it more than when people were home 'cause they were always yelling."

"I'd rather for my mom be at work 'cause my mom, she don't do nothing anyway 'cause when I come home she leaves everything dirty so I can clean it up so I still have the responsibility whether she's there or not. She cleans up her room and leaves the rest for me. When I was younger and my parents weren't home, all my friends would come over and we'd just party at my house until they got home and they'd all leave."

"It was hard when you were in grade school and your teacher maybe praised you about something and you come home to an empty house and nobody's there. It was like, 'Hey Mom, guess what happened?' If you had a bad day and you needed to talk with somebody about it there was nobody there. I mean, even if you couldn't find an adult to talk to, you could always get on the phone and call a friend. But then by the time your parents got home you're on the phone and you get yelled at for that. So either way you were in a losing situation."

"How well do kids really know their parents when they just let them stay at home and do whatever they want? Our house is large. I have seven brothers, one sister. We do whatever we want. My mom and dad, they just kind of like work, and we do just whatever we want. I handle everything myself. I cook my own food. I never really knew my parents too well, or my grandparents or any of my relatives. So it's kind of like a separate world of mine."

How Parents Feel About Child Self-Care

Rather than pooling their political resources in support of workable alternatives for latchkey kids, parents often view each other with suspicion across the fundamental divide. For example, some parents who stay home become surrogate or mentor parents to the children of working parents. But many of these resent being depended on, informally, to take care of other parents' kids after school. One parent called it the "four o'clock dump."

At Kenwood Elementary in Miami, a mother said: "I know when the empty-house kids come home, because my phone begins to ring off the hook about five minutes after the bus goes by. Those are kids calling my daughter. My daughter feels that some of the other children have it easier because their parent is at work; they go home to an empty house, whereas Jennifer comes home to me — and here is Mom nagging her. I'm sure this is how she sees it: 'Get your work done, do this, Jennifer, do that.' But the children from split homes are at home by themselves with all this freedom — eating Fritos and watching MTV. I don't think the kids are all that comfortable with the freedom. They're lonely, unhappy. But in Jennifer's eyes, they're free. And she wonders why she can't be that free."

Parents of latchkey kids often view themselves with embarrassment, which only serves to deepen their sense of isolation.

"I can't express the embarrassment and pain I feel when I go to the library to get my kids after work," said one single mother. "I can feel the librarian's eyes on me. She kind of straightens up the books and turns her back and I know I must look like this terrible parent, but there isn't any after-school program at our school, so what am I supposed to do? Where am I supposed to have them wait for me, the street corner? The video parlor? Why is it a sin to have them spend time in the library? Of *course* it would be better if all the moms were still around in the neighborhood, and my kids were at home. But what am I supposed to do, go on welfare?"

Not all parents see self-care as negative, however. Some believe that self-care makes kids more responsible — given the proper circumstances and enough guidance, that it builds character.

In a group of middle-class black parents, one woman gave an illustration of the thin line between what is enough autonomy and what is too much: "I grew up in Pittsburgh in a single-parent family. My mother died when I was quite young. There were thirteen children in my family. We all had responsibilities before and after school. Now, I knew if I didn't do it, not only would I suffer, but my brothers and sisters would suffer too. Also, we didn't have all these extra clothes. As a consequence, if we didn't do the laundry, somebody didn't have clothes to wear that day, and that somebody might take *your* clothes. I had far more physical responsiblities for my own self than I can ever badger my kids into asuming. If they don't want to do it, it won't get done. So today, I don't think it's whether the kid has more independence, but what he's taught to do with the independence. If it's learning to take responsibility, that kind of growing up fast is fine with me."

The Self-Care Struggle: Mixed Messages from Society

Parents receive mixed messages from the experts on the issue of self-care.

Some experts advise against leaving children under the age of twelve on their own, but others suggest that some children under twelve may do fine for several hours alone in the house. Location seems to make a difference. The self-care experienced by the farm kid who comes home and starts his chores in the late afternoon is far different from that of the inner-city child.

But the professionals who see kids on a daily basis, librarians and teachers, are unequivocal: a Harris poll in 1987 revealed that 51 percent of public school teachers said leaving children on their own after school was the biggest cause of youngsters' difficulties in the classroom. A study by researchers at the University of Southern California revealed that latchkey children who must care for themselves after school are more likely to use alcohol, tobacco, and marijuana. The study of eight thousand eighth-graders in the Los Angeles and San Diego areas showed that latchkey kids spending eleven or more hours a week on their own were twice as likely to use alcohol, 2.1 times as likely to smoke cigarettes, and 1.7 times as likely to use marijuana as were children with a parent awaiting them at home after school. "It is possible," said the USC researchers, "that a lack of parental involvement in the child's activities is an underlying problem that becomes most pronounced in the self-care situation, leading eighth-grade students to express autonomy by use of drugs."[4]

The latchkey phenomenon needs to be viewed, by parents and professionals alike, in the context of the general drift toward earlier autonomy among children.[5] When Sanford M. Dornbusch, director of the Stanford Center of Family, Children and Youth, addresses parent groups, he asks them, Is it good to give kids early responsibility for their actions? "When I ask this question, everybody nods. But I believe one of the most crucial things we can do is to encourage parents *not* to give early autonomy to their children on such decisions as how to spend their money, their choice of clothes, and so forth. Giving kids very early autonomy exposes them to more of the power of the peer group. It's a loss of parental control and community control. Smoking, early dating, truancy, running away from home, contacts with the police, arrests — every one of those is associated with early autonomy of the kid."

Yet our culture continues to push children toward earlier autonomy. The almost overwhelming commercial message being sent to parents and kids is, It's fine for children to assume adult responsibilities early — because it's good for business.

"Who is the advertiser's dream? Today's latchkey kids, that's who," advises Joan King, an advertising executive at J. K. Communications in Glen Ellyn, Illinois, in a bimonthly newsletter published by the Retail Advertising Conference in Chicago. "They're buying much more than clothes, bubble gum and electronics gadgets. . . . You'll see them doing the family grocery shopping. They do much of the household cooking, laundry and cleaning and they have a lot to say about which microwave they'd prefer and which vacuum cleaner they can handle. They have a major influence in buying television sets, computers, washing machines — even cars." Teen-age Research Unlimited in Lake Forest, Illinois, calls the youngest consumers *skippies,* "school kids with income and purchasing power."[6]

The New York advertising agency Backer Spielvogel Bates, reporting the results of its nationwide Teen Scan survey in 1989, reports: "Rising from the ashes are truly awesome adolescents — the Proto-Adults — who are materialistic, savvy, cynical and old beyond their years." The survey found that 68 percent of teenagers already think of themselves as adults.[7] As more marketers realize the buying potential of young people, they place even greater pressure on children to become early consumers of adult products. In Denver, the Young Americans Bank offers credit cards to twelve-year-olds.

Because of commercial pressure and the consequent hunger for money, and because of deep shifts in the labor market, children and teens are moving into the work force in larger numbers. During the transition to the industrial age, children were an exploited source of unskilled labor. Today, children are swept up in a similar transition. Because of the aging of America and the reduction in the fertility rate, the pool of new workers is growing slower than at any time since the thirties. In the post-industrial economy, children and young people are increasingly able to fill the types of entry-level service jobs available in the new labor market.[8]

Though the definition of exploitative child labor is tricky, government enforcement agencies are showing increased interest in young workers. In 1989 and 1990, a five-hundred-member Labor Department strike force charged thousands of businesses around the country with violating child labor laws, including working children long hours on school days and hiring them to operate hazardous machines such as meat slicers. In 1989, more children were found working in violation of the Fair Labor Standards Act than in any year since the law was enacted in 1938.[9]

Some school officials who a few years ago worried about teenage unemployment now worry that the emphasis of childhood has swung too much toward working to support the consumer habit. Among the reasons high school administrators give for declining attendance at football games: everybody works. One educator described "McDonald's time," that time of day when students stream into fast-food restaurants to work.[10]

I asked a parent group in Seattle if kids in their neighborhoods ever came to the door to ask for lawn work. "They don't need to do that kind of work," answered one father, "because McDonald's will snap them up like *that!*" Another parent complained that this newly stimulated work ethic even changes children's attitude about chores at home. "I ask my daughter to do something at home and she'll say, 'How much are you going to pay?' " And in New York, a middle school principal complained: "Some of the kids in my school are working in banks. These kids are fifteen-year-old workaholics. They don't have time to be kids." The similarity is striking: working parents, particularly working mothers, and children now face some of the same conflicting pressures of balancing the demands of home, work, and school.

"Extensive part-time employment takes a toll on the growth and development of youngsters," says Ellen Greenberger, professor of social ecology at the University of California–Irvine. "Kids who work long hours beginning at an early point in their high-school careers are at greater risk for dropping out. When teachers look into a classroom and see tired faces and know that everybody has been at work the night before and is going back that afternoon, they often cut back on their expectations because it's hopeless to do otherwise."

In many cases, work was found to have a negative effect on students' values. Kids "become more cynical about the potential satisfactions of work, and some show an increased tolerance of unethical business practices. In our studies of middle-class Orange County, California, students, we find evidence that working increases things like copying other people's homework, cheating, skipping school and buying alcohol and marijuana." Greenberger says also that studies found the availability of a paycheck in some instances prompts working children to use more alcohol and drugs. Moreover, job stress from performing dull and routine tasks contributes to substance abuse.[11]

A University of Michigan survey found that more than 80 percent of high school seniors spend all or nearly all of their earnings on daily needs and entertainment. They don't save their money; they consume.[12]

Laurence Steinberg, a researcher with the University of Wisconsin's department of child and family studies, suggests that teens become accustomed to large amounts of discretionary income given to them by parents (to pay for family groceries as well as their own self-care) or earned in their jobs, to be spent on the latest clothes, cars, and entertainment. The long-term effect: raised expectations for a lifestyle they might not be able to afford as adults.[13]

Still, working may give some children and teens the contact with adults they so desperately need, and that they have not received from workaholic parents.

We may be moving toward a society that views childhood employment as a reasonable alternative to neighborhood play and family time. If so, such a future is at the expense of childhood itself — at least the childhood we think we know. By pressuring children to accommodate to our own work schedules and to the demands of the marketplace, we force them to grow up too fast, and as parents, we lose them too soon.

What's Being Done About Self-Care?

What is being done to maximize the benefits and minimize the detriments of self-care? Not much.

While child-welfare officials and lawmakers puzzle over where to draw the line between self-care and child neglect, marketers and advice-givers offer commercial products as palliatives. Barr Films in Pasadena, California, for example, markets a video called "Home Alone: You're in Charge," which according to promotional literature is the story of "Tracy, a latchkey kid whose house comes alive one day to teach her everything she needs to know about being home alone." A chilling image indeed.

> One day, Tracy arrives at her quiet and lonely house, telephones her mother, throws a hot dog on the stove, and wishes for someone to talk with. She remembers a lady in a TV commercial whose house talks back. Feeling down and alone, Tracy jokingly asks the kitchen drain, "Are you clogged?" Amazingly, the drain answers her in a clear booming voice. . . . The bread box springs to life and gives Tracy suggestions on protecting her house key. The telephone's buttons do a little dance and its musical tones sing a song praising Tracy after she wisely eludes a suspicious caller's questions. . . . Meanwhile, Tracy's hot dog has been frying for so long, it sets off the smoke alarm [which] gives her a crash course on fire safety.

The home lesson continues with a box of bandages showing Tracy how to bandage her cut finger; then the lights go out. "As the exhausting afternoon ends, Tracy receives a boisterous chorus of approval from her lively friends in the house." Mom arrives home and Tracy tells her that she can take care of herself.

Another way portions of society are reacting to excessive self-care is by becoming more punitive. Some states and municipalities are adopting laws or ordinances spelling out at what age children can be left by themselves or can baby-sit younger siblings.

In 1988, Flagstaff, Arizona, prohibited parents from leaving children under the age of ten unattended in public libraries. In Atlanta, parents are warned by signs posted in the libraries that they could face criminal charges of child abandonment. And a policy statement in the headquarters of the Montgomery County, Maryland, public library system warns that it considers leaving children unattended at a library to be a "form of child neglect." However, the American Library Association warned librarians in 1988 not to adopt "hasty and punitive" policies intended to protect libraries from liability, but which tend to discourage all children from using the library.[14] Some library leaders believe that libraries, redesigned and reimagined, could serve as a new kind of community center. But they cannot fulfill this function by themselves.

If the detrimental effects of self-care are to be ameliorated:

• Many of us, as parents, need to reevaluate our values about autonomy. We are living through a period of transition in how society weighs independence and autonomy. Over the last half century parental attitudes have virtually reversed. In a famous Middletown study of Muncie, Indiana, in 1924, mothers were asked to rank the qualities they most desired in their children. At the top of the list were conformity and strict obedience. More than fifty years later, when the Middletown survey was replicated, mothers placed autonomy and independence first. The healthiest parenting probably promotes a balance of these qualities in children, but finding that balance is made more difficult because of the sheer force of social expectation and commercial interests. Parents need to reclaim this territory as their own, and define their family's appropriate balance between independence and autonomy. Finding that balance is a highly individual matter, but we do need to allow our children to be children. For many parents, this will demand a substantial rearrangement of home and work time.[15]

• Employers must offer flexible work schedules for their employees. Ellen Guggenheimer, president of the Child Care Action Committee, described the "three o'clock syndrome." The chief symptom: parents at work start watching the clock because they know their kids are getting out of school. The chief results: anxiety for parents, lower productivity for workers. "School hours are geared to a rural society. At three o'clock kids go home and till the crops. We don't have many crops in New York."

• Institutions such as schools, libraries, and community centers should open new child-care services, as some have already done, to target the hours of the day when children are most likely to be on their own. Though more family time is preferable to more institutional time for kids, not all parents will be able to arrange fewer or more flexible work hours, so such support is essential to them. Many schools are beginning to provide after-school programs, but in some areas of the country after-school provisions are actually decreasing. One New York teacher complained: "There's no supervised center, no after-school program, no parents at home. There is just this big block of time that nobody seems to care about."

One alternative to depending on the availability of after-school programs is to reweave work and school time.

Steve, a Seattle parent, spoke of the poor timing of school schedules. "A major issue that comes up over and over and over again is that kids here start school at seven-forty-five A.M. and they get out at two-fifteen P.M. So then there are two or three hours when a parent often cannot be in the home." If school were to start later and let out later, kids might still be on their own for an hour or so, but the length of autonomous time would at least be lessened. But Hamilton Middle School, like so many others, runs not on kid or parent time but on *bus time*. As the principal of Hamilton said, "Because our system doubles up on buses, our buses run to the secondary schools, drop off the kids, then go and pick up the elementary schools." Increase the number of buses, and some of the autonomous time would vanish.

Instead of revolving around the availability of buses, said the principal, "the schools need to revolve around the working household. If parents would rather have kids in school from ten A.M. to six P.M. to match their work schedules, why couldn't they? We have adult learners coming to school during the evening; why couldn't we have kids coming then, too?"

As part of a family liberation movement, parents ought to demand more freedom in choosing their own work hours *and* their children's school hours, thereby creating larger windows of family time. Our goal should be to help parents care for their children, and to have the time to do it. The alternative: a society in which children spend most of their waking hours taking care of themselves, watching television, or being watched and shaped by institutions.

6

If Day Care's the Answer,
What's the Question?

●

Many parents express anger at the lack of help from institutions, particularly the scarcity of quality day care and the inflexibility of school hours, but they also describe their sense of growing discomfort at the fact that children are spending more and more time under the control of institutions, from six to ten hours a day at day care, then to school — sometimes with year-round classes, or after-school care — then later to work at McDonald's or Burger King or some other job. Parents want supportive institutions but sense something dramatically wrong with the work–family time equation, and the gradual drift toward the institutionalization of childhood (the companion trend to self-care). Their ambivalence about day care — and the feelings of children toward day care — are intense, and these feelings often rush out suddenly.

In Wichita, a secretary wearing a plain polyester dress had listened to just about enough. Inside, she was fuming. These people just weren't seeing the whole picture, they didn't understand.

Around the table, some of the workers and volunteers of the Kansas Children's Service League were criticizing parents who, as one of them put it, "choose to dump their kids in day care." One social worker had said with disdain: "I know this one married couple. They're mental health professionals at the top of their careers, and they put their child into an abusive day-care center, and they let it go on for a year. They just overlooked it because their careers were so important to them."

Another man, a program administrator, huffed, "The value is on the career, the BMW, the nice home — not on the kids, not on staying home."

But now the secretary, who had been silent for an hour, sat straight up.

"You've got to be able to pay your electricity," she said. She was speaking with great intensity. "I have an eight-month-old baby. I hated going to work, I hated putting her in day care, but I have to if we're going to maintain our house payments and the car payment and the dental bills and insurance. I'm talking just about the basics. *Not everybody makes a good salary.*"

She looked at them, and the room fell silent. There were tears in her eyes, tears of tension and embarrassment and anger.

"I have to work! And I get pissed when I hear people saying I have a choice. And I feel like sometimes you think people have a choice. Do you think people *choose* to be on AFDC [Aid to Families with Dependent Children]? That's how the world is."

This woman speaks for millions of Americans for whom life is a day-to-day struggle to make ends meet, to pick up the kids on time, to withstand the pressure of the economic vise slowly tightening around young American families.

The tightening vise has placed the highest-quality child care out of the reach of most families. Today the average price, per child, per year, of child care is $3,000, and it is hard to imagine most low- or middle-income families being able to pay much more than that — particularly if they have more than one child.

At least for the foreseeable future, demand for child care will be intense. Although the supply of child care is probably meeting current demand, the supply of *good* day care, particularly infant care, is not. In many cities the waiting lists for infant day care, private or public, are over a year long. "Parents used to joke that the minute you got pregnant, you got yourself on a day-care list," said Jacquie Swaback, childcare coordinator for the city of Sacramento, California. "Things are worse now. The joke is, 'Not tonight, dear, we're not on the waiting list.' "[1]

The transformation of child care is among the key elements in the new childhood environment. Just as baby boomers were the first generation raised with television, children today represent the first day-care generation. Yet surprisingly little is known about how children, parents, or even child-care providers feel about day care, although these perceptions will shape the future of child care more than any legislation or commission reports.

When I spoke with parents, children, and day-care providers, several shared themes, and some quite divergent viewpoints, emerged.

How Parents Feel About Day Care

The degree of ambivalence toward day care among parents may partially explain the difficulty of achieving political support for child-care legislation.

"I can't stand the idea of leaving my child at a place I'm not totally certain about," said one mother, a secretary. "And I'm angry — and I feel guilty at the same time — that there isn't someplace I trust, like it's my fault somehow. So I've quit work a few times, but then the bills begin to mount up. . . ."

Besides, she added, the neighborhood had changed. Like other parents, she described the empty neighborhood syndrome: how few children were at home in the neighborhood, available for play time — partly because the baby boom is over, partly because most of the kids are being taken care of somewhere else.

One of the themes that came up often among parents — among those who supported government child-care support as well as those who did not — was the concern that institutions are gradually taking over childhood. Do we, they asked, really want a country in which the majority of children spend most of their lives growing up in some kind of group or institutional care?

One single mother who had struggled to succeed in the business world said: "We've gone from the extended family to the nuclear family, now we're going from the nuclear family to the single-parent family and the extended day-care family. When is this going to end? Every twenty years, we seem to take another in a series of progressing steps. I don't know whether we're really capable of stopping at this point. We live in an age where our children spend a majority of their waking time with somebody else. So since we've already arrived at this point in history I think the issue now becomes, How can we provide *quality* institutions?"

Parents do not want to be replaced by institutions, but they do want to be helped out. The line, many of them admitted, is thin.

Some parents eloquently described day care as an extension of their families. Day-care workers, they said, provided them with the kind of advice that grandparents and older uncles and aunts once gave. Tom Fitzsimons said: "If anything, day care should be a place where values are transferred. The nuclear families are a relatively new phenomenon. What the hell is day care if it's not an extended family?" In Swarthmore, parents spoke with near reverence of the main day care in the town, which, they said, provided them and their children with a central community focus — and served parents by helping them with parenting issues, connecting them with other parents, and guiding families through their child's transition into public school.

Ralph Keyes, whose older son had been in day care in Swarthmore since he was three months old, begrudgingly described day care as an enrichment of his son's life. "I remember feeling that it was too bad that we didn't have other kids, that my son had to go to day care. I work at home, and a lot of the time when he was with me I would be looking for ways I could occupy him so I could get some work done. Whereas at day care, the teachers spend time with him. The kids are there to play with. So I hate to admit it, but he's had a richer, more natural experience at day care than he probably would have if he had stayed home with me all the time."

Most parents, however, did not feel their lives or their children's lives were particularly enhanced by their day-care providers. Some parents described how they frequently felt dehumanized by day-care centers, which often (and sometimes with good reason) treat the parents like children. One father joked: "If a father shows up five minutes late at my day care, they take him out back and shoot him. They just want me in and out. I'm just a weekly fee to them."

In Miami, a mother complained that the operators of her day care made her feel guilty for checking on her child. "If you want to visit your kid, you have to call ahead of time. That always bothered me. You can envision them taking the chains off your kids." She laughed a little nervously. "Why should I have to call a school to tell them that I'm going to pick up my child early or that I'm going to pop in for a visit? That makes no sense to me. Makes me feel uneasy. I mean if I feel like going in and feeding my kid lunch, why shouldn't I be able to? At least till he's old enough to defend himself and say no if someone tries something strange with him."

Perhaps the most telling statement was made by a father in Wichita: "We haven't yet figured out how to measure the quality of what we're getting."

How Day-Care Workers Feel About Day Care — and About Parents

I spent an evening with a class of day-care workers at Grossmont Community College in San Diego. There thirty or so women were attending an infant/toddler class in child development to fulfill part of their California child-care credential requirements. These were women already working in child-care centers — not the owners of the day cares, but the front-line workers. Their ages ranged from early twenties to late forties. For the most part, they were economically lower-middle-class women, and their opinions on the matter of day care and parents were razor sharp.

Karen Shelby, a woman in her thirties with a teenage son and an enveloping personality, described why she had become a day-care worker: "It's in your gut. I can't remember when I didn't want to work with kids. I can remember being about nine and how all the 'bad boy' four-year-olds in the neighborhood would come to my yard and we'd easel-paint. I used to wind my dolls up and read and do storytime with them. It's something that's in your heart. You're loved all day long by these little people. You have these moments. The other day, we came out of the staff room and all the three-year-olds were laying out on the patio and they were all lying there as if they were frozen. I said, 'What are you guys doing?' And Charlotte lifts her head and goes, 'We're not done dying yet.' And she puts her head back down. Another day, there were three little girls sitting in the quiet area on the couch and they were all going like this." She made the motions of brushing her hair. "I said, 'What are you guys doing?' They said, 'We're playing parlor beauties.' I must have laughed for a half an hour. Someone could say to me, 'Gee, you only have one kid? I say, Are you kidding? I take twelve home in my heart at night. The money is just not the object."

"We'd like it to be," said another woman. The women laughed.

Surprisingly, only a third of the women in the class who had small children said they could afford to send their children to the very centers where they worked. Most of the woman had relatives or neighborhood women who took care of their children. Sometimes this was a matter of choice. "We may take care of other people's kids," said one woman, "but that doesn't mean we necessarily want our kids in day care."

The women in the class thought that much of the parenting they had seen in the past few years had improved, and continued to improve, and that more parents were coming to realize the effect on their children of too many hours away from home. "Parents are paying more attention, particularly the younger parents," said one day-care worker. "The ones who have the toughest time cutting back their child's day-care hours are the older parents who have been working for a long time and can't take the time off."

Another woman, who had been working in child care since the early seventies, said: "I've begun to see more parents consciously arranging for a night shift for the dad and a day shift for the mom so that each parent could spend more time with the kid. After a few months, they'll reverse shifts. So it's almost like single parenting. But at least there's somebody there with the kids more. Also, we have several parents who have begun to work out of their homes so they can spend more time with their child. They'll bring the child in for three four-hour days or three six-hour days because they can't get all their work done with their child always underfoot. But they do have two full days and three half days when they're at home. They make a conscious effort to avoid the situation where the child is just dropped in at seven o'clock in the morning and picked up at four or five."

One day-care worker explained the logistical problems faced by parents. "Sure, eight or ten hours is too long, but we have parents who live forty miles away. They lived closer when their children were infants and toddlers, but then they moved and they bought a house, but they continue to come to the center because they trust it. They don't want to give up the trust." Still, the women complained that too many parents leave their children in child-care centers too many hours. One day-care worker said (and her eyes opened wide as she spoke): "It gets dark, and the kids are all saying, 'Is my mom coming? Could you call her?' Maybe the time changed and it's dark now at five-thirty instead of six-thirty, and the look on some of the little ones, the look in their eyes. We're in a wealthier area of town. A lot of the parents have their nannies bring them because they have appointments and tennis club. We see the parents whenever we have special programs. But that's about it."

Here is an uncomfortable truth: for many children, day care is more like family than home. "I've got kids in my room that, when their moms and dads come, introduce all the children in the room as their brothers and sisters," said one woman. "And there are times when the kids will come up to me and they'll go, 'Mom!'"

Karen Shelby said that her center consciously includes many of the activities that kids usually miss if they're not at home during the day. "The children load and unload the dishwasher and help with the laundry. They take a part in preparing the meals. We're not trying to supersede what the mother or father would do when they're not home. We want a family atmosphere, particularly because these children are away from home such long hours. Some of them are here ten hours a day. When they go home, they eat dinner, have a bath and storytime, and they go to bed, then they get up the next morning and head right back. Some of them are just awakened, dressed, and brought in. They've only been up for twenty minutes and they're already at the center. It's like, 'Oh, I'm awake now.' And then we serve them breakfast."

The day-care workers expressed a mixture of respect and frustration about parents, reserving their special ire for the parents' employers. Among the comments:

"We had an infant yesterday that needed to go home and her mother was not afraid to take off work to do it. Of course those are the parents we really like. But some employers, particularly the banks, are really picky about letting them get off early — or at all — to come and get their sick kids. So we've had to put the child in a crib, because they need to be isolated if they have a fever."

"I've known parents who have lost their job for staying home for three days with a child who has chicken pox. The parents have no support system."

How Kids Feel About Day Care

Kids are seldom asked in formal studies how they feel about day care. So I asked informally.

I found a distinct difference between older kids and younger children. The younger children were generally more positive about their day-care experiences (just as they are more open to a wider definition of family). Several factors could be responsible for this: day care a decade ago was more of an exception than it is today. Consequently, younger children may be more accepting of day care because their parents are more accepting of it, or at least more accustomed to it. A second reason could be that day care, generally, has improved. A third reason could be that small children are by nature more accepting than older children.

In a class of thirty or so third-graders at Jerabek Elementary in San Diego, all of the children except three had been in day care or preschool. And most of them said they felt good about it:

"I'm glad I went to preschool 'cause my dad would be at work and my mom would have to care for my little sister and I would have nothing to do but sit in my room."

"Me and my friend Aaron used to go to preschool together all the time. We're still best friends, so that was a good memory."

A handful of the third-graders reported negative feelings:

"I didn't like day care 'cause I didn't get to play with my baby brother."

"I like staying home by myself better 'cause then I can do what I want to do, but when you're in day care they don't let you do anything there, always making you go outside at this time, or making you do work at this time, and not letting you have your own time. I go after school."

"I didn't like to go to preschool 'cause I always missed my parents."

Down the hall, a class of fifth- and sixth-graders at Jerabek, nearly all of whom had gone to day care when they were younger, recounted their memories.

One boy said he liked day care because "it was where I met my first friends."

I mentioned that many parents with whom I had spoken had said day care was a kind of "neighborhood" for their kids, and that this was a good thing. Several kids shook their heads in disagreement. Among the comments:

"At day care all your friends are always coming and going and leaving."

"I think you can have friends better in your neighborhood because you can go to their house and there's different things to do than just at day care. And when you go to day care there's a lot of napping."

One boy, who still attended an after-school day care, said: "It's kind of hard to find something to do because you don't have many things that you like to do at day care, just what they think you like to do. And most of the time when you go to day care there's usually a lot younger kids than kids your age, so they have little toys for littler kids."

A class of seventh-graders at Hocker Grove Middle School in Shawnee Mission, Kansas, described more sharply negative memories of day care. The school draws children from lower-middle-class neighborhoods. Among the Hocker kids' comments:

"We had these cots we had to sleep on and they were plastic and they were in rooms called the blue and the green room and I didn't like 'em."

"Before I went to day care I stayed with my aunt and then I was in third grade and I stayed by myself till fifth. Then I stayed in day care for fifth and sixth grade after school. Mostly I was on my own, but day care, it was okay, it just got a little dull sometimes because there wasn't much to do. So my mom took me out of it 'cause I didn't enjoy it and I was on my own again."

Another girl, wearing black and with a punk hair style, spoke. "I was in day care from when I was two to when I was five, I think. I couldn't sleep in the daytime, but we'd take naps and I would just lay there and talk to kids and they moved me out because I was keeping everyone awake, I guess." She laughed. "They moved me into their office and I smeared vaseline all over my face." She laughed again. "So they moved me into a closet. It was like — a toy closet. So I had fun." Again, the laugh. "It was fun there because I had toys everywhere — and got to play."

Sometimes after the groups would leave the room one or two kids would stay to express an opinion in private. No child ever related any personal experience to me regarding child abuse at day care. At the Wichita Collegiate School session in which both parents and children were present, however, one family spoke of the residual stories about day care which had seeped out over the years. These parents, like most, rock back and forth between their positive and their negative feelings about day care.

The mother said: "I went back to work when my oldest was three and the youngest was eighteen months and they went to a day care. It was very hard for the eighteen-month-old to leave home, and for me to watch him leave home. But overall I feel that they socialized and became a part of the peer group a lot faster than being home with me. And my working out of the home brought my husband and me close together because he had to share the responsibilities at home and with the kids."

Her husband added, "Even so, we were never completely satisfied with the care that our children were receiving."

"Not that they were really horrible," said the mother.

"Well, some of them were horrible!" The father laughed.

"Especially one," said their teenage boy. He continued: "I really hated it. The only time that I was really with my parents was like, at night for dinner during the week. On the weekends we were too busy. We had to do a lot of things around the house because we were never there during the week. I really hated the day-care center. Some of the things that I remember were really stupid that these people did. Like, if you didn't go to sleep at nap time they came by with a flyswatter. They told you to roll over on your belly. And they hit you with a flyswatter. I mean, that is the stupidest thing I could think of. And you could get in trouble for really stupid things like not cleaning up after yourself and they'd really yell at you and make you feel like you were a felon if you didn't pick up a crayon or something."

I turned to the boy's parents and asked whether their son had ever come home and told them about that.

"The flyswatter?" said his mother, with a grim laugh. "Well, we've heard lots of stories, yeah. It's upsetting to us that we never heard those stories when they were little. These day cares were not places that any of us would have been concerned about, at the time."

The Preparation Gap

The future of childhood will be written less by today's parents than by tomorrow's. How will the first day-care generation decide to care for their own children? Will they use day care? As I ranged through the schools, I wondered if children were talking about this among themselves. Is the topic of child care and family life discussed in the schools? During this epochal transformation of gender and work roles, the topic must come up. Surely it must.

But mainly it doesn't. Today, in many schools, the topic of family roles is a subject more taboo than sex.

I began to ask kids in classrooms around the country a series of related questions.

"How many of you will have kids?" Nearly all of the hands would go up.

"How many of you are going to have careers?" Again, most hands would go up.

And then: "How many of you will put your kids in day care?" Only a few hands would rise, hesitantly.

What's wrong with this picture? "What are you going to do with your kids?" I would ask. In response came blank stares, giggles, snorting jokes from the boys and from a few girls. "Give them to our parents!" ". . . to my brother!" "Leave them with Grandma!" There would be lots of laughter. "Seriously, who's going to take care of your kids?" I pressed. "Nobody," said a girl at Crawford High. "Our children will disappear for eight hours a day!"

Adolescents enjoy shocking adults, of course, but in classroom after classroom seriousness seeped from beneath the jokes, and then the jokes were replaced by kids' memories of day care. What this first day-care generation remembers isn't particularly dramatic; mainly, just that day care was boring. Children said, in so many words, that they felt warehoused, pushed away from their parents.

"If I had to send them to day care," said a high school junior, a girl, "I would find one that was a benefit of my job, like the hospitals have day-care centers. But I wouldn't want to have my kid in full-time day care." By full-time she meant eight to ten hours a day, five days a week. Kids were clear about full-time day care. They didn't like it for themselves and they didn't want it for their own kids. I wondered, If these kids didn't want full-time day care for their own children, how were they going to work out the logistics? Among the comments of fifth- and sixth-graders:

"I'm hoping for a family member to take care of the kids. Like maybe my little brother. Or my mom. She would be a great grandmother." "I'd go out and find a nanny. I'm going to be rich." "I'd hire a person like a maid, 'cause they'd get more attention than at day care." "I'd hire a housekeeper until the child's in fourth grade and then they can stay home alone."

I asked, "Is that what you do?"

"Yeah."

"How do you like that?"

"It's okay."

More than a third of the kids were open to one of the parents' staying home part-time — especially the husband. Surprisingly, boys were as likely as girls to view this favorably. Or so they said.

"I can't see having my kids call someone else 'Daddy' or 'Mommy,' " said one boy at T. C. Williams High School. "I'd definitely like to be with my kid as much as I can, at least till he gets into kindergarten and then my wife and I could trade."

"It'd be great," said another boy. "You could watch ESPN all day. You could experience what it's like not to go to work and make money. And raising kids — well, that's your benefit. Like, once that kid is off to college, you know you were a part of that." Another boy theorized that staying home with the kids would be fine as long as he had a pool table. "And maybe an abdominal exerciser so I wouldn't get fat and lazy."

Some of the girls said they would work at home. "I sort of have thought about — if I have kids, I don't want to put them in day care 'cause I'd like to spend the time with them to get to know them, 'cause I didn't spend a lot of time with my mother. So if I ever have kids I would try to work out of my home. I'm going into such a field that I could probably do that. Graphic design."

A few students said with conviction that they were not going to have kids. "I'm not going to have them. I'm going to take responsibility and not have kids. That's my answer to day care," said one girl.

At Hocker Grove Middle School, the seventh-grade girl dressed in black and with the punk hair said: "I don't intend to have kids, but if by chance I do I'll have a problem with that, because if I have kids I'm going to want to give up just about everything for them. Because my mom, I hardly ever saw her, and I don't want my kids to be like that. I don't know how they would fit in to my life if I didn't work. Maybe I'd be living with a bunch of hippies. Maybe that would work."

During these class sessions, it occurred to me that kids lacked much real understanding of the logistics of parenthood. But after some reflection — and some comparison of their comments with the views of parents — I decided that kids were neither less nor more informed than adults. It seemed to me that their emotional grasp of child-care logistics was somewhat clearer than that of adults. Kids are closer to the reality. Yet they seldom discuss it.

I asked the kids in each of these classes if, in their whole school career, they had ever spent a class period discussing the tensions created by parents' choices involving careers and having children?

"No," the groups would answer, almost in unison.

When I mentioned this curious gap later to Bob Hartman, director of the Kansas Children's League, he coined an apt phrase: "People our age had a generation gap. Kids today have a *preparation* gap."

These kids, it seemed to me, had done a surprising amount of thinking about their roles as future parents, but the thinking had been done in isolation. In each classroom, I asked, Had students ever, in their years in school, taken part in an extended classroom discussion on the subject of parenting — on, for example, the pros and cons of day care or staying home or hiring nannies?

"No," the groups answered.

Of course, my generation wasn't prepared for parenthood either. Still, we grew up with a set of largely unquestioned expectations about work and family structure. Right or wrong, a social contract existed. Kids today face an almost overwhelming choice of roles. More than ever, the options should be examined, hashed out. Yet with the exception of scattered elective courses (which most kids don't take), parenting just isn't considered an important topic in most schools.

A girl spoke up: "I don't constantly think about it and worry about it. But I think the people that are having kids now are the ones who are not thinking about *anything* in the future. I do think kind of vaguely, sort of — sometimes you wonder, you hear so much about day care and the need for it is increasing. I don't know. . . ."

Several teachers remarked that the issue of family roles is touchy because of pressure from religious conservatives and, to a lesser extent, extreme feminists. "Plus, we're just as confused as anybody else," said one teacher. "So we leave it up to the parents."

But parents aren't talking much about parenting either, according to the kids I spoke with. A boy at T. C. Williams offered this explanation: "They're real open with us. But they talk about careers, not kids."

I asked the class, As they prepared for college and chose careers, should the possibility of bearing children be part of career planning?

The boy answered: "You have to remember that when you ask people of this generation about having kids and futures and stuff, that you're looking at people whose parents have gotten divorced and . . . nuclear war. All kinds of stuff. The future is just so uncertain."

I pointed to a book on a student's desk, and asked whether he thought the subject of parenting wasn't at least as important as William Faulkner.

"Probably, but right now it's not affecting us," said the boy. "The furthest that I've really gotten, not like planning, but seriously talking to a girl about it is like, 'Do you want to have kids?' That sort of thing. It's not like, 'What are you going to *do* with your kids?' That's a hypothetical question. I don't even know what I'm majoring in in college. And then you ask me who's going to take care of my kids — I don't know. It's like asking, Who's going to win the World Series?"

Day care can work. But we should cherish our ambivalence. This ambivalence, if acknowledged and respected, will enable us to see that day care is part of the web, not the final goal, and in no sense a panacea. We do need more and better day care. But gradually, almost imperceptibly, the role of the family in raising children is being assumed by day-care providers and schools operating in near isolation from parents. The shift from family-based to institutional child care amounts to an almost accidental revolution in family life. This revolution has few leaders and fewer long-term philosophical goals, except the paean that more is better and better quality is desirable — though a definition of the quality we want is exceedingly difficult to pin down. Day care can work, but it must be a different kind of system than the one currently taking shape. Parents, children, and day-care workers hinted at the system that could be: parents must have more time off work to participate in their children's day care; and the hours many children spend in day care need to be shortened. The most important long-term question isn't how to encourage more companies and government to provide day care but how to decrease the need for day care.

How can we make it easier for parents to spend more time with their families, and thereby decrease the number of hours children spend in institutional care? Both liberals and conservatives committed to family liberation should be asking why America seems to be moving toward a future in which parents find it increasingly difficult to balance family life with work. The country seems bent on creating a kind of family life that few people ever intended. We should question the inevitability of that future.

7

The Programmed Generation

●

O ne afternoon I picked my son up from school and we stopped at a neighborhood park to play catch. The park was filling up with children's soccer teams. Coaches were marking off their territories with orange cones. Jason and I found a patch of park with no soccer players, and we began to toss a ball back and forth.

The mother of one of Jason's classmates approached. She is an athletic woman, very committed to her children's schooling and athletic achievements.

"Whatcha doing? Waiting for a team?" she said with a friendly smile.

"Nope. Just playing catch," I answered, tossing the ball to Jason.

"Killing time, eh?" she said.

I stopped for a moment.

When did playing catch with your son become a form of killing time?

Why do so many of us feel that we must fill every second of our available family time with structured, programmed activities?

One explanation for this inclination is that the less time we have with our children, the more we feel required to pack into their lives. Another aspect is the general devaluing of parenting. One programming message sent commercially, politically, and personally is that everyday parenting is somehow not enough, that quiet time spent with a child is somehow not as valuable as the time spent with the child by an expert (a soccer coach, a violin teacher). This mythology also suggests that a child's free-flowing dream time is less valuable than a planned activity, and that a child is not capable of planning.

Another reason for overprogramming is fear — fear of the environment, fear of falling behind. The more we feel out of control of our children's physical, emotional, and economic environment, the more we try to control their time. The absence of a neighborhood web for families and children creates an atmosphere in which we interpret free, wandering, unsupervised time as danger time.

How Kids Feel About Their Programmed Time

I asked a class of fifth- and sixth-graders at Jerabek Elementary to describe their schedules. I was particularly interested in their play time. Some children are expected to be more responsible for self-care when their parents aren't around, but find their lives highly scheduled when their parents are off work.

The comment of one girl was typical: "I get home first, and I have a lot of time to myself, and then my mom gets home, and right when she gets home she says, 'You have to get a snack, you have to do your homework, and then you have forty-five minutes to play.' But you can't really do anything in forty-five minutes."

"Weekends are when I don't have to be bothered by all that stuff," said one fifth-grader. He added a qualification. "Saturday's the only day I have extra time, because on Sunday I'm at my dad's and we always go to church and we're always doing stuff and I never have time to play. You have all these extra things to do like baseball and swimming. I don't really have much time to play."

Another comment: "I don't really have much time to play at all because I have piano lessons. My mom makes me practice for about an hour every day, and then I have my homework, and that's about an hour's worth, and then I got soccer practice, and that's from five-thirty to seven, and then there's no time left over to play. On weekends we usually have soccer games, and I have to practice piano and then I have to do yard work, and then I have the chores, and then I'm free to play — which is only about two hours, three hours, something like that."

I was intrigued with the way these children were defining play: it did not include soccer or piano lessons.

I wondered, How did these kids feel when they did have extra, unscheduled time?

"I sort of feel free, like I can do anything in the world that I want to," one boy answered. "It's a good feeling. I know I don't have homework and I know I don't have soccer practice or anything like that, and it's just a really good feeling that you can get out and go hike or bike-ride."

Increasing educational pressure is part of the reason children feel so programmed. After a classroom session, one teacher said she was amazed at what the children in her class had said. "We never get a chance to talk freely like that. Teachers *and* kids have to meet so many new educational requirements that every moment of classroom time is programmed. The programming of these kids doesn't only happen at home."

In a classroom of fourth-graders at Kenwood Elementary School, I asked on a whim if anybody worried about getting into a good college or getting a good job in the future. More than half of the children raised their hands.

I told them I was surprised at this, that when I was a kid nobody worried about those things. A very serious little girl, eyebrows scrunched up behind her thick glasses, explained: "Well, you should not stare out the window or dream. You should get your mind on your work 'cause you can never get a college education if you don't."

"I'd kill to go to Yale," said one high school junior in New York. "It's all-consuming. All I think about is college entrance exams. My parents are going to be frightening during this." At T. C. Williams, Pat Welsh told of a prestigious Quaker nursery school in Washington, D.C., which "is supposed to feed into prestigious elementary and high schools" that in turn feed into the Ivy League. Said Welsh: "Some people — even Irish Catholics — literally convert to Quakerism to get their kids into that school. It's crazy. The more expensive prestige colleges get, the more pressure and scheduling you see parents putting on these kids at an earlier age."

How Parents Feel About Their Children's Programming

Most parents I spoke with were concerned about overprogramming their children, but did not necessarily know what to do about it.

One response to overprogramming is to schedule programs on the subject. The Parents' League of New York, for example, a private organization that helps parents cope with the intricacies of private schooling, also helps parents come to terms with overscheduling — by scheduling workshops for parents, sessions with titles like "The Hurried Child," "The Pressured Parent," and "Super Baby Grows Up."

"Of course," one of the league's officers said, "you're always talking to the converted anyway." She described the ritual of "play dates," the elaborate scheduling of play time. "You make a specific date and a time to visit with a friend. Depending upon that friend's schedule, you may be booking two weeks in advance rather than just planning a pickup in the back yard. Everybody gets their respective calendars in front of them. Sometimes the negotiations are quite long. Ultimately you arrive at a date that's unscheduled. And on that day both children probably take a note to school telling the teacher instead of their normal routine, that they'll be going home with so and so's mommy."

The sense of leading breathless, overscheduled family lives is true even for parents who enjoy the luxury of on-site company child care. A woman who works for Bankers Insurance Company in Miami, which operates its own on-site day care and elementary school, described her tightly wound schedule: "I bring my kids to school in the morning, I pick them up in the afternoon, they play for an hour outside, they come in, they take a bath, they do their homework, they eat, they watch TV for another hour, and they go to bed at nine. That's Monday through Thursday. Fridays, on the way home from work, we stop at McDonald's. That's marked. We don't forget that around my house. It's got to be *the* McDonald's, the one that has a playground on the outside too. And boy, they do *not* forget that it's Friday."

Parents in Kansas were as concerned about overprogramming their children as parents in New York City. And families with an at-home parent were also worried.

In the Overland Park group, Tom Hilleary suggested that one reason the current generation of children is overscheduled is that families are smaller now. Tom grew up in a family of six boys. He laughed out loud at the idea that his parents would have had the time, energy, or finances to overschedule their kids' lives.

Jack Hughes talked about what he called the Catch-22 of having an active, programmed child. "You're running your kid to all the events, you're the shuttle. And you get home and you have things to do at home and the kids want you to play with them. But you've already spent all your extra time moving them around and you've got to attend to the house duties. When I was growing up, I would be out running around while my mother was cleaning the house or fixing supper, and then when I was ready to play with my parents, they had their housework taken care of, and they could spend time with me."

"There are no car pools anymore," said Sherry Hilleary, who stays home with her three children. "It's not just because there are fewer parents at home, but because everyone is going in too many directions. So it's hard to take several neighborhood kids to one thing, because there isn't any one thing that the kids are all doing."

Many parents wondered if all this scheduling was worth it, for the kids or the parents. Tina Kafka of San Diego wondered if her children will remember much of what she has scheduled into their lives. "I am often amazed how some activity that I have carefully planned pales in their long-term memories compared to another activity that was completely spontaneous and hardly memorable to me. As adults, we can plan a million things to take up our kids' time in a 'meaningful' way, but what really clicks into their inner being is beyond our control. Sometimes I wonder why we think we need so much control."

Certainly anxiety about the economic future, as well as flat-out materialism, drives many parents, too, but most of the parents I spoke with felt victimized — and overscheduled themselves — by the economic and psychological realities of work.

Some of these parents, for example, expressed near panic about weekends. They described how the panic sets in on Saturday morning — the spasm of unreleased pressure, of guilt, the feeling that someone, somehow, was gaining on them. One working mother told how free-time weekend panic had led her back to religion: "I couldn't stand the lack of scheduling on Sunday morning. Sunday night, I think, Thank God it's Monday."

Both overtly and subliminally pushed and shoved to compete, to race, many parents feel compelled to keep up with the multitude of commercial activities that will, they assume, allow their children to be successful. In decades past, parents might have hoped that their children would have better lives than they did — lives of less drudgery and more pleasure. Today, consciously or not, we ask ourselves, Will our children be able to compete? Surely soccer will help, or high-intensity music lessons. . . .

Holding On to Childhood

With all these lessons, children may appear to be prodigiously creative, but how long does this kind of trained creativity last if dream time is diminished? How long does childhood itself last?

As I listened to children, two keys to their emotional health emerged:

• To deprogram our children, we need to deprogram ourselves. The overprogramming and isolation of children are intimately linked to the overprogramming and isolation of parents.
• We need to do everything possible to allow children to hang on to their childhood for as long as possible, even into their teens. The steady drip

of economic pressure, commercial greed, parental absence, and over-programming eventually robs children of their innocence and, later, their maturity. Encouraging children to be children allows them to mature at a steadier, more natural pace, as opposed to imposing whatever commercial facsimile of maturity is in vogue at the moment.

Given half a chance, children, even teenagers, are quite good at holding on to their childhood.

I spent a morning with a class of high school seniors. They were nearing graduation and weren't particularly thrilled with the idea of becoming adults. These kids were highly gifted, placed for much of their school careers in a special class, cut off from the rest of the kids.

They were hanging on hard to their childhood.

"We're programmed to go to college, we're programmed to succeed," said Karen. Her hair was long and dark and she wore a black denim shirt in the new bohemian style. "We're, like, the special kids."

Her voice sounded flat, fatalistic.

Was she glad, I asked, that she'd been treated as special?

"Sometimes." She added: "We've always been separated from other kids. Our teachers even refer to them as 'the *other* kids.' But we're probably the same kids as they are, but with above-average parents. My mom didn't work when I was a child, and I had every kind of lesson in the world. When my parents were growing up, there were a lot more people like us, a whole class of kids that had two parents at home, went to college. All of us in this class are bright, but I don't think we're *that* bright."

She looked out the window, at the kids out on the asphalt. Their voices were drifting in with the sounds of bouncing basketballs. "Sometimes I think, see, that *they're* the normal ones. And we're the remnants."

Remnants?

"We're the remnants of the way kids used to be. We haven't changed." She pointed to the playground. *"They've* changed."

Paul, the natural leader of the class, large-boned, athletic, pointed out that not everybody in the class came from intact nuclear families. "When my parents were divorced, I was the mom in my family, 'cause I had to raise my little brother. So I feel like I missed out on a lot of my childhood."

He paused for a moment, and then pushed ahead.

"I had a big talk with my mom and stepfather last night. I get real scared of conflict. So last night, before I had this big talk with my parents, I just pulled down my Legos from the closet and started playing with them again."

Why Legos?

"See, my aunt and uncle have been the happiest family that I've known for a long time, except they didn't have kids. Now they're separated and that just drew up a lot of hurt feelings I had about my mom leaving like she did. My uncle left the same way, without trying to work anything out.

"Anyhow, my parents wanted to talk about my future last night, and I started thinking about how I'm going off to college and that's the end of my childhood. Always in the past, you think, I can't wait. But I've got two babies in my house now, my half sisters, and I don't want to leave and not see them grow up. So I guess that's the reason that I pulled down my Legos from the closet last night and started playing with them. I wanted to see if I still had that little creative knack that you get when you're a kid."

Did he?

"Well, I built a pretty good Lego ship, but it took me a long time, and at the end of it I wanted to put more stuff on it, and I couldn't think of what to put on it. Maybe when you lose your childhood, you lose your creativity."

Karen wasn't buying this. "Paul, remember the day you were yelling at me and you said, 'This is the way we are, we're not *supposed* to be children.' I wanted to say to you then, but I didn't know you well enough, that there are thousands of adults who keep the child in them alive."

I mentioned that one of the ways to hold on to childhood is to have children of your own. All parents are forced to relive their childhood (and their parents' parenting) whether they want to or not. One way or another, everybody gets a second chance at childhood.

David hobbled into class late, on crutches, his leg in a cast. He was an ebullient, dark-haired seventeen-year-old. His chest was festooned with Batman buttons, and his notebook was decorated with an elaborate drawing of the Caped Crusader. (This was a year before the Batman craze of 1989.) I asked him about the buttons.

"Batman's my hero. I'm sentimental. I like what's in the past. A lot of the music I listen to, the sixties stuff and early seventies stuff, the reason I listen to that is because if I listen to the eighties music, I feel like I have to keep up with it. If I listen to the new stuff, I have to grow up more."

David (as his teacher pointed out) was a do-gooder, like Batman. He worked as a volunteer at an elementary school latchkey kids program.

"I've had a good childhood. But I see a lot of kids are growing up too fast. There's this one kid, his mom is on welfare, she doesn't bother to have a job, yet she spends all the money she gets in bars, flirting with everybody. And the kid, who's twelve years old, has to take care of three of his younger siblings. The kid has no life of his own. I gave him some juggling balls. . . ."

Then David launched, with pride and enthusiasm, into his personal Batman philosophy. "Batman is not really the cream puff portrayed in the TV series. Batman is a criminal, actually. He's a vigilante. He's a human being, not like Superman. Batman is somebody I admire because he is willing to take a stand." He grinned. "I suppose I really go overboard sometimes. About a month and a half ago, on a Friday night, it was incredibly foggy out, and I have this Batman costume, see, and at midnight I put on my costume and snuck out of my house. I was riding along this dark street in the fog on my bicycle, my cape was flowing, and this guy was walking along and he saw me and he says, 'Yo, Batmaannnnn.' " Then I came to the high school and I decided that I wanted to prowl around on the roof, and I did, and I was up there for an hour. I really felt pretty good. It was something that I wanted to do, and I don't really care what anybody else thinks. It was just me."

The rest of the class sat quietly through the story. I looked around at their faces. No one was laughing or smirking at David. They were listening with recognition and respect. They were up on that roof with him.

8

Computers Can't Dance

•

Not too many years ago, a child's experience was limited by how far he or she could ride a bicycle or by the physical boundaries that parents set. Today the physical boundaries may be drawn closer to home, but the real boundaries of a child's life are set more by the number of available cable channels and videotapes, by the simulated reality of videogames, by the number of megabytes of memory in the home computer. Now kids can go just about anywhere, as long as they stay inside the electronic bubble.

In the Company of Machines

Out there in the night, the lonely electrons beep with ecstasy; young shoulders hunker over keyboards, and faces glimmer in the green light; hackers and syscrashers, pirates and worms upload, download, make contact — through computer bulletin boards. These electronic messaging centers (often a computer left on, and connected to a phone line, in some hobbyist's back bedroom) allow the user to send private messages to specific persons, or leave public messages for anyone to answer.

I connected to several electronic bulletin boards, including many used almost exclusively by kids, left public messages asking a series of questions, then turned off my computer and waited. A week later, and at intervals thereafter, I called the bulletin board systems (which computerphiles call BBS's) and typed in my name. Scores of messages were waiting for me.

Here are a few from teenagers: "You can get all kinds of information on a BBS, from software reviews to movie reviews, from newsletters to love letters. Anything! If you ask a question, somebody is bound to answer! I have asked many questions! I have received many answers!" From Xandor Xet (real name and whereabouts unknown): "Hi, I've been looking in on some of your conversations and I would just like to throw in a word or two myself. For one, I'm getting sick and tired of reading magazine and newspaper articles that misuse the word 'HACKER'!!!!! A hacker is not — I REPEAT — a hacker is not a 'THIEF' or a 'PIRATE' and especially not a 'CRIMINAL.' " And from Xandor Xet a few days later: "Hi, it's me again. I just wanted to say that I am a full-fledged HACKER!!! Just look at the times my messages are posted! I don't know the meaning of the word 'sleep'! I faithfully call up at least 10 local BBS's three times a day. Face it, I'm hooked."

Some boards are sexually oriented, and though many now have established elaborate screening procedures, some are open forums for precocious kids.

I called up one of the sexually oriented bulletin boards and browsed through the public message section of the board. Considering the content of the messages, it was fortunate that my computer had a cooling fan. And right in the middle of all this electronic sex was this message: "Do any of you girls want to talk? I am not interested in sex. I am looking for a girl to have a mail-phone relationship with. I am a 13-year-old boy. If you are interested leave me mail."

In the literature of those who have studied computers, little attention has been paid to how children feel about this medium. So I asked that question, and discovered a surprising intimacy between children and the machines. In a class of gifted children at Dewey Elementary in San Diego, which included kids in grades three to six, I asked kids how they felt about computers and about their new, digitized environment.

"I feel good when I play on the computer because it's neat to watch the things move around the screen and you can control them," one girl explained. She said that sometimes she felt that she was moving all around — "like, inside the screen."

Nearly half of the fifteen or so kids in the classroom said that they would rather play with their computers than talk with people. "Sometimes when I'm not real happy and I play on the computer, it makes me feel better," said Paul, a little boy with thick glasses who wore a T-shirt that read, THE GOOD, THE BAD AND THE GNARLY. He said his future plans included "being single and living in a two-bedroom apartment and being a programmer."

"When you're on a computer, the computer doesn't get hostile if you win. Like, if you say something, it doesn't jump back at you like other people."

A girl next to him added: "You just ask the computer to do something, and it will do it unless it's not in its word-command box. The computer gets me away from my sister, instead of talking to her and letting her scream at me." The computer also made her feel creative. "I can do things all by myself and I don't need help." She looked up, chin up, proud.

Paul spoke again. "In one of my games, he [the computer] will say a lot of mean things, and I get to say mean things right back to him, and certain words he can't say back." He grinned. "I say the bad words he can't say back."

Why would children identify their computers by gender?

One boy explained: "I think of it as a 'he' because boys don't yell a lot like girls. And because it helps me through my homework, and it's kind of like a companion through my school and it helps me do spelling, and so forth." Another boy said his computer was a he "because he's powerful." One girl, with absolute certainty and an edge in her voice, said: "Well, I think of it as a he 'cause it's kind of stupid. Like in a word game, I typed in all the words and it came out wrong. So it's stupid."

A few girls in the class called their computers "she." One girl said, "I call it a she 'cause it doesn't fall asleep like my dad." Another said she thought of her computer as a she because "it stays home and it never goes out and that's how it used to be with she's. The woman would stay home and the man would go out to work." And a third girl added: "Sometimes I think of it as a she or a he. I think of it as a she when it obeys the commands." She laughed. "I think girls are more receptive to obeying commands. And I think of it as a he when it messes up, so then I pound on the keys."

Her classmates giggled; I could hear whispers of "sexist" in the background.

Paul, the good, the bad, and the gnarly, waved his hand frantically, then described how, when he played games on the computer, he could "feel the thoughts" of "the person who programmed the computer's thoughts." I asked him what they felt like.

"When you're doing something on the computer, it makes you know that you can say whatever you want to the computer and the computer is just like another person saying something back. Except through a program."

A few kids argued that real people are more interesting than computers. A girl named Carli said: "When you talk with people, you can learn about what's going on. Your computer doesn't know what's going on. It doesn't read the newspaper every day unless someone puts it into the computer's mind."

Ben, one of the oldest boys, very serious, leaned over, his elbows on his knees, and said: "I'm real pro-computer. Maybe it gives me a feeling of power, but also it's 'cause of how many people we've heard say and how many articles we've read in the newspaper that say the future is going to be strictly computer, everything is going to be run by computer, and so much is done that way already. Like when I go to my dad's office, everything is kept on a computer and at the hospital where he works there's a billion-dollar computer with millions of megabytes just sitting down there which keeps track of everything. So I'm obsessed with computers. But when you really get down to the rock bottom, it's people who have the emotions, and the computer really doesn't *give* you anything. You don't get emotion from a computer, you don't get feelings."

I asked, How many students thought they spent too much time on their computers? No hands were raised.

Five of the children did not have computers at home. They live on the periphery of the bubble. One girl said, "I feel kind of sad because sometimes I have to use an electric typewriter and I don't get things fully typed." And one boy, physically much smaller than the other boys, said in the faintest of voices, "I'm sad because my mom said she's going to buy a computer, and then I waited for a month, and then she said, 'Wait till Christmas.' " He paused. "Most of my friends have computers at home and they got games and sometimes they invite me to the house and play some of the games. I feel sad because if I had a computer I would let them come in my house and play some of my games."

I asked, In school, did they ever talk about their feelings about computers — their feelings about talking to computers compared to talking to people? Did they talk about this at home?

Several shook their heads, and only one boy answered. "Usually at dinner when we're talking," he said, "my mom gets upset at my dad because he spends four or five hours on a computer a day and she's upset 'cause she doesn't really get any time with him." He added, matter-of-factly: "I think computers have really revolutionized homes because now everybody's got a computer, everybody's spending time on it. And time is money."

The truth is that, despite the ardor of computerphiles or the antipathy of computerphobes, we simply do not yet know this medium's true social powers.

The most important question we should ask about computers and children is, Are we creating an environment healthy for children or healthy for computers?

Parents are of at least two minds on this issue.

Most parents, while mourning some of the lost reality of their own childhood, think that their children are capable of understanding what is real and what is simulated, what healthy interaction with a machine is and what borders on pathology.

Ben's mother, Tina Kafka, expressed the worry felt by many parents of children with a special aptitude for computers: "My concern about Ben's development as a human being goes beyond whether he will think too linearly or that somehow his computer literacy will affect his approach to other problems. I want him to interact with other people in a positive way, to stay in touch with his own needs as a human being — needs for warmth and caring; to be able to reach out to other people and feel good about himself — because no matter what he does in his life, these are the sources of happiness. Ben has an amazing intelligence and sense of humor. Adults always respond to him in a positive way, but his own peers sometimes don't quite know what to make of him. He's twelve and will read for hours, and yet he still goes to bed at the same time as Simon, who's six, just so he can be tucked in and get his goodnight hug and kiss. He even snuggles up and listens to me read bedtimes stories to his younger brother and sister, and *that* is what makes me feel best about Ben."

Juliette Mondot, who described herself as "very high tech," operates a desktop publishing company in San Diego. For Mondot, the electronic bubble isn't threatening at all. "For our daughter, Misha, who is five, it's a new frontier. It's positive, not all prepackaged like television. We own Macintosh computers. When my daughter works with the Superpaint program, she's simply using electronic drawing tools. She creates her own environment."

What about the isolating nature of learning on a computer?

"If dealing with other people is anything like it is at Misha's school, I can understand that children would want to deal more with computers. Maybe we're blaming computers for something that isn't the computer's fault. Misha goes to an elementary school in one of the lowest socioeconomic areas of the county. The school is overcrowded, overenrolled, and there's not really enough supervision. The atmosphere among children is very abusive — they hit each other, pull at each other. At least the machine doesn't call you names or call you stupid." She laughed suddenly. "I must add, though, that I've never felt so stupid as I did learning to operate a computer. That has to do with my adult fear of failure. Kids don't have that fear with computers.

"I watch my daughter using the Mac's mouse to overlay texture on texture on texture with the painting program. She has figured out a way to do this that I never would have thought of in a million years. I've electronically catalogued her computer artwork — her fantasy life, animal designs, her rich internal environment. Crayons are the tools she uses when the power goes out. I joke that the most important thing kids can learn now is how to push a button.

"People who criticize computer nerds forget that our environment is so hostile to children. The computer environment is a sanctuary, a safe place for Misha to be. I know she is not going to be hurt. I know where she is."

In 1985, early in the personal computer age, one study suggested that home computers had a positive influence on family time. And some computer experts have even recommended that the computer be centrally located (like a kind of electronic potbellied stove) so that all family members would have easy access to it and so that two or more people could use it at once.

Still, many parents report a gnawing sense of unease about the use or misuse of computers in the home and in school. Tina talked, with a tone of puzzlement in her voice, about "screens, all these screens" in her children's lives. She said, "Sometimes I think all this computer mania is happening not because kids are so into computers, but because the parents have found a new toy for themselves and they're imposing that toy on the kids." Nonetheless, children are spending more of their childhood in the company of machines.

Not all of these machines are desktop computers. For example, whereas board games and puzzles have been employed as teaching aids for centuries, now comes "edu-play" — toys that listen and talk and respond to instructions, teaching toys such as Speak and Spell, introduced by Texas Instruments in 1978. ("That's correct," says Speak and Spell, or "Wrong. Try again.") Newer games combine voice, music, and visuals to teach object recognition, math concepts, even reading. Some machines reproduce simulated conversations with synthetic tutors. Supplying a child with these educational toys can, according to columnist Vic Sussman, "help fend off guilt ('Am I doing all I can for my child?') and fear. The popular wisdom is that only children who can spell and count earlier and better and faster than other kids on the block are going to survive the competition for kindergarten in the best schools."

Research shows that the machines, though controversial among educators, can accelerate learning, at a price. Judy Frank, a partner in the Park Center, a private social work practice in Bethesda, Maryland, which treats family developmental problems, asked: "Is my child more educated at five because he can spell all the words that the Speak and Spell has? Or is he more educated because he's mastered certain skills in terms of frustration levels and interpersonal relationships, the basic skills he needs to get through a day? What we hear over and over from the kids is, 'I want someone to play it with me.' We see kids who are hungry for personal interaction, somebody to really sit and play with them. Playing with a machine, no matter how brilliant its responses, still leaves a child essentially alone."[1] These electronic tutors are only going to get smarter, making them increasingly seductive surrogates for flesh-and-blood parents, playmates, and teachers.

In an almost religious rush of requisitions, schools are making computers a standard and expected centerpiece in American classrooms. Hardware sales alone, to schools, are increasing by nearly a billion dollars each year. In 1988, fifteen million students were using two million computers. Most school systems assume that the ideal would be to have a computer on every desk — though many districts cannot afford textbooks, let alone teachers.[2]

Some futurists envision what would amount to computer shrines in the schools. In the classroom of tomorrow, according to Harold F. O'Neil, professor of educational psychology and technology at the University of Southern California, "computers will replace desks, wall-size computer displays will replace overhead projectors, and students will be able to use the Library of Congress at the touch of a button." By 2013, O'Neil predicts, each student will carry a three-by-five-inch "smart card," a battery-operated computer that will contain in its memory the student's educational history as well as a list of all the skills the student has mastered. To do homework, the student will insert the card into a home computer, which will later update the smart card's records to show what the student has completed. Back at school, the student will insert the smart card into his or her desk, which will be equipped with more powerful voice-input computers, and whose entire surface will serve as the screen. New desks will "solve the problem of students and teachers not speaking the same language in the classroom. Thanks to the voice input and output on these computers, there will be an instant translation on the computer screen from English into any other language, or vice versa, as a student or teacher speaks." In the classroom of twenty-five years from now, he says, the walls, ceiling, and floor will be "giant computer displays, much like the kind we see today at football games."[3]

Well, maybe. But somehow all of this seems like an awful lot of trouble.

In several specific educational areas, though, computers do seem to make a difference. Computers in schools can help individualize instruction for individual students or for small teams of students. They can make complex ideas understandable through the use of graphics. Computers can also help children with special needs or communication handicaps, particularly in situations where children cannot be mainstreamed. In 1988, Stanford University researchers studied the use of computers with thirty patients in a children's psychiatric ward. These children had behavioral problems ranging from conduct disorders to schizophrenia; many had been hospitalized for years.

According to the chief psychologist in the children's and adolescents' ward, computers are successful in giving individual attention to patients who are easily frustrated. He said: "We can't have a thousand staff members there. This computer talks to them." Also, children with abnormally short attention spans are able to concentrate longer. And some children who have had trouble relating to their peers now play with them regularly. The computer offers these children what the researchers called a "shield" from both criticism and failure, and allowed them to develop new patience with learning.[4]

Another area in which computers have made a difference is in helping children learn to write through the use of word-processing software, which seems to let kids worry less about making mistakes. As desktop publishing gains popularity, elaborate school newspapers and literary magazines, even in elementary grades, could help produce a generation of self-confident writers.[5]

In rare cases, too, computers with modems can be used to break down isolation by connecting students with other students. The National Geographic Kids Network, for example, is a telecommunications-based science program that links two hundred schools in the United States and abroad. Fourth-, fifth-, and sixth-graders use telecommunications to send the results of their local science experiments to a central computer in Washington; there data are analyzed and the results sent back, sometimes in the form of a map or tables. According to a participating teacher, "The kids are getting a great sense of geography from all of this — a feeling of how where someone lives affects their pets, their games and after-school activities."[6]

But have computers made any measurable overall difference in children's academic skills? Not so far, at least not that has been detected.

The second "National Survey of Instructional Uses of School Computers," which was commissioned by the U.S. Department of Education and released in 1987, found no evidence to indicate that school-wide test scores had been affected by the kind of computer use that occurs in most elementary school settings. Also, according to the survey, despite the widespread use of computers for drill and practice in the lower grades, they had not markedly affected most student learning in language and arithmetic. The study found lots of computers in schools, but that they were used very little in high school mathematics classes, including algebra — and even less in the highest-level math courses. Though word processing had become a large component of the high school business education program, most students did not write their English compositions with word processors. Among the most telling findings of the report: for elementary schools, the function of computers was primarily to acquaint students and teachers with "a new cultural object."

In the late eighties Henry M. Levin, a professor of education at Stanford University, studied how computer use affects test scores among grade school students. He found the use of computers to be more cost-effective than reducing class size or extending the school day by an hour. However, Levin also found that tutoring by older children produced much larger gains in math and reading, at much less cost. Flash cards, his studies suggested, might have accomplished as much as computers.[7]

The failure of computers to make much of a dent in education as yet is due to the brief experience and limited training provided students and teachers (only a third of public school teachers have had as many as ten hours of computer training); the generally unsystematic use of software at the lower grades; and the subtle, usually unspoken myth that computers can replace what kids need most — positive adult contact.[8]

What values get lost in the rush toward the technological classroom?

"I could see where a computer could someday be useful, possibly, for choreographing," said Jon Drescher of the East Harlem Performing Arts School. "Computers can help you compose music. But we don't have any computers here. That's our version of 'back to basics.' Somebody asked me why we don't, and you know what I told him? Computers can't dance."

Tom Snyder, considered by his peers to be one of the best educational software developers in the country, believes schools are imposing computers on children and teachers — and driving both deeper into isolation. When I visited him at his Cambridge, Massachusetts, office, he rocked in his early American rocking chair as he described one developer of educational software, "pants up over his belly, who says this sweet thing, says teachers are a dying breed. This guy writes software to replace teachers. He's just thrilled that teachers are disappearing. If teachers will only disappear, there's gonna be a great market for his software!" Snyder hit his fist on the table next to him and a computer keyboard hopped. "Sweet deal!"

Snyder, thirty-seven, a former grade school teacher and rock 'n' roll recording artist, rocked faster. He's angry at education (not at teachers), enraged at the vast majority of software developers busy designing software to replace teachers, software to isolate kids, software destined to fail. He contends that the computer, so far, has done little that is educationally significant. "What it has done," he writes in his book *In Search of the Most Amazing Thing,* "is capture our imagination and prompt us to finance possibly the biggest unfocused research effort in the world."

The current educational software (eighty-five hundred packages are now available for schools) is selling well enough. "Sixty percent of the software used in education is drill and practice, and most of it is never used once it gets into the classroom," said Snyder. When software is used, it's by one child, sitting in front of one screen, nerded out, alone.

Snyder designs a different kind of software.

He practically whispered his radical theories: teachers are most valuable when they are teaching an entire class of children; the best way to use a computer in the classroom is for creating group learning experiences. His goal: don't screw up traditional ways of teaching. The teacher should come first, not the computer.

Take one of his first games — baseball.

"Check this out." He called it up on the screen. "Tommy's at bat. I've got two teams: Sox and Reds. Every kid in the classroom gets to play a role. Pitcher. Shortstop." Up on the screen pops a history question. Tommy answers the question, the computer asks the teacher if the answer was correct, the teacher answers by tapping on the keyboard, Y-e-s. The computer says, "A single!" Tommy moves to first base. The teacher remains in control of the computer, not the kids.

"When I was a teacher, I told the kids, I'm thirty, you're seven, keep your hands off!"

Snyder also offers more sophisticated classroom simulation games, including a series called "Decisions Decisions," which allows groups of children, led by the teacher, to grapple with problems as wide-ranging as urban growth, immigration, media ethics, and revolutionary wars. ("Rebels seek to overthrow an unjust government. Your students take on the role of a governor caught in the middle.")

All of this software is aimed at the group.

No other educational software developer is creating anything like

Snyder's software. Why? "Because software is designed by people who hate people, and because software developers don't understand that homes and classrooms are supposed to be *human* places.

"We don't listen to teachers, we don't ask them what the kids need, because teachers are considered low-life," he added. "I don't care if my kid ever touches a computer in school. If my kid loves his teacher and the teacher loves my kid, that's what counts." He rocked. His voice softened. "You know, today is my kid's first day at school. This morning I'm walking him down the hall to his classroom. His little hand is wrapped around my finger, and he's singing, real soft, *'Somewhere . . . over the rainbow,'* and I'm thinking, Who — or what — am I handing him over to?"

The Electric Father

Of course, the way computers are often being used now in the home and in the classroom does not mean they cannot be used in another way.

One can go too far in resisting the electronic bubble. As they evolve, computers will enrich childhood's environment if their communicative nature is favored over their isolating aspects. The work of Apple Fellow Alan Kay, for example, suggests one possibility: students working together, using artificial intelligence to create simulated natural environments to solve ecological problems. The computer and modem can, indeed, open up a world of new connections both for children and for parents. My own son surprises me with his computer creations — which he assembles next to me, and shares with me, in my office. Tom Snyder movingly described his desire for parents to use his software as "lapware," with parent and child using a computer together.

Though Snyder had said software is designed by people who hate people, I came to believe something different while interviewing programmers about computers and kids. I came to believe, in fact, that much of the reason so many of us today spend so much time in the company of machines is because the true company of people is becoming harder to come by.

"When I was in high school," said one former college major in computer science, "I spent long hours in the computer lab working with other students on programs. I had a computer at home, but I chose to go to the lab with the other computer geeks because I wanted the company. Of course our talk was pretty superficial. We didn't talk about ourselves much; we talked about our computers, our programs."

Robert Hecht-Nielsen, whose company, HNC, topped a *Business Week* list of five "companies to watch in the neural-net race," told me he thinks programming is dehumanizing for kids. "One requirement of traditional computer programming is you have to think in linear terms," he said. "The person who sits down to write a computer program first of all has to immediately think in procedural terms, take the problem and break it down to a sequence of steps. There is no room for error. Think of the computer as a parent. Browbeat your kid, expect perfection from him day after day, and you'll wear him down, kill his spirit. Kids need all the abilities that they can get to deal with society, and computers can be a way of avoiding getting those abilities. I know this because I lived it as a kid, and have spent much of my adult life undoing that isolation. For a lot of kids, programming quickly becomes an obsession and an excuse for not dealing with life. But if your kid learns how to use a word-processing program and a modem, that could be a real advantage. If they're word processing, they're integrating themselves into a very ancient human tradition — writing."[9]

Like Hecht-Nielsen, software developer Frank Boosman, a rising young star in the hothouse of West Coast software development, wondered about the future relationship between machines and children — especially his own infant son. At the end of a long conversation about computers we were standing next to his car in a parking lot, and Boosman's thoughts turned to his father. "When I was a kid I was absolutely voracious about the acquisition of knowledge. I probably annoyed my dad. I'd always be asking something: 'Why is the grass green? Who is Cabrillo?' But he always answered my questions. Then my parents were divorced when I was five. My mom and I didn't interact like that. And I had no contact with my dad for quite a while.

"Not every kid has a dad who calls him Chief and Sport and answers his questions. So I'd like to help make it possible for kids to have something like that in a computer form, maybe notebook size. The kid could ask the computer, 'Why is the grass green?' And it would answer. It wouldn't just be an information resource, but a friend. I'd like for the child to say to the computer, 'I'm doing a report on Cortez,' and for the computer to know enough about Cortez to say, 'I can help you with that.' I missed having my dad answer my questions. It would be neat to give kids a tool to ensure that that doesn't happen again to any other kid. But I don't know. . . ."

He looked out at the stretch of asphalt, and an odd look came into his eyes.

"A few years ago I was in the army, stationed in Germany. One time

I was out on the base, walking along, and I saw a man with a young son who was maybe five years old. It was great. This was right after one of the *Star Wars* movies came out. I heard the kid ask his father, 'How big was Darth Vader's ship?' His father got down on one knee and pointed to the airstrip and said, 'See, from *that* end to *that* end, that's how big.' The kid said, 'Wow!' And I thought to myself, 'That's it. *That's it.*' That's the pinnacle for a father-child relationship: for the child to make informational queries about the world around him and for the parent not just to respond with a simple answer, but to put the answer in perspective. It's not enough for the father to answer, 'Two miles long.' That's meaningless. But the father should point out physical landmarks and phrase the answer in terms the child can understand. That's the pinnacle.

"I don't know how well computers will ever be able to do that." He paused. "Kind of interesting, isn't it? You and I can make use of computers that have horrible interfaces and are kind of stupid, but as you go down the scale in age, the computer has to be smarter and smarter."

9

The Thief of Time

●

In the classroom at Chesterton Elementary School in San Diego, the top of the blackboard was rimmed with traditional alphabet cards. I turned and looked at the fifth- and sixth-graders and was impressed by the mixture: Vietnamese, Filipinos, white kids, black kids, in-between kids.

I asked them about television. What did they like? What didn't they like? What did they want changed?

"Soap operas should be put on weekends instead of school days," offered a girl with thick black hair. Saturday morning cartoons were popular. One girl said: "I watch them every Saturday. But first I go and say good morning to my mom and then good morning to my dog and then go to the bathroom and wash my Bionator."

Her what?

"My Bionator." She blushed. "It's like a retainer for my teeth."

I asked students about violence in cartoons.

"Sometimes the cartoons are more violent than they used to be," said the girl with the Bionator. Several kids agreed.

"What's *violent* mean?" asked a boy at the back of the room. The class laughed.

"That's a good question," I said. "What do you think it means? Are the Transformers violent? Are the Roadrunner cartoons violent? Can you tell me?" Nobody raised a hand. "How about wrestling? Is wrestling violent?"

The heads began to nod. I asked for a show of hands. How many watched wrestling on television? Every hand went up except two. The class loved wrestling. I asked the students whether they liked wrestling better than superhero cartoons. Wrestling won, hands down. Why?

"Because wrestling is real," said a boy.

Now wait a minute. . . .

"It's real people doing fake things," he continued. He was the boy who had asked what violence was. "There's more action in wrestling than in cartoons. It's real but it's fake. It's neat, especially women's wrestling. Their suits are pretty neat."

The classroom broke into laughter.

A girl with curly brown hair who was wearing a flowered dress jabbed her hand into the air and said enthusiastically, "I like GLOW — you know, Gorgeous Ladies of Wrestling. GLOWmania. The girls fight. Like Americana and Jungle Woman and the California Doll. They show how strong women are."

"Some of them break their ribs and stuff when people push them against the ropes," said another girl. She shrugged. "I think they waste their lives." Several kids in the class disagreed with her.

Why, I asked, would people want to fake hurting each other?

"Money," said a voice in the class. "I don't like the Million Dollar Man," said the girl with the Bionator. "He thinks he can buy everything." A boy to her left agreed. "He always makes fun of people. The Million Dollar Man says everyone has a price."

I was impressed with the distinctions these kids made. They knew what was violent and what was not. And what bothered them most wasn't the broken ribs but the verbalized values, what the wrestlers said to each other and to them. I asked the kids if their parents approved of their watching wrestling.

"They watch it too."

Of the thirty or so kids, sixteen said their parents approved. The same number said their parents watch wrestling with them. Only four said their parents actually talked with them about the wrestling.

"Some parents watch it with you and at the end of the match or something they body-slam you on the couch," said a boy with a blond flattop.

I continued my informal poll. I asked them about violence on other television shows and in the movies.

All but one of the children had watched at least one of the *Friday the Thirteenth* horror films. "I've watched all of them," said the girl with the flowered dress. "And all the *Nightmare on Elm Street* series and *Bloody Valentine*." She added authoritatively, "All those are fake."

I asked the class if there should be more or less gore in the movies. "More," someone said. Two-thirds of the class agreed.

Did these movies teach them anything?

They answered: "Don't go to sleep at night." "Don't go out in forests where there have been murders." "Not to get killed." "Not to live on a farm." "When they say there's a burglar on the loose, don't ignore it."

Did any of them believe in the bogeyman?

Two kids raised their hands. "There are just maniacs like them," said the girl with the Bionator.

"Let me ask you," I said: "What is it in your real lives that scares you the most?"

"My dad," said one boy. There was nervous laughter. Then the kids reeled off a list of horrors — real horrors from the real world.

One boy, from Vietnam, described "robbers" who came into his village. "They went to beat up me and my sister. We ran. We hid behind these things. They were going around and had these guns, they were shooting the people."

The boy with the blond flattop said he feared his father "because this train came by and he got up and shot the train signal lights and he said not to tell anybody about it and I told him, 'Why not?' And he said for a certain reason and I said that's fine with me." The boy looked down at his desk.

"Last year was my first Halloween here," said a pretty Filipino girl. "Someone came along in a truck and said he'd give me one hundred bucks if I'd go with him and he would do something to me."

She said the word "something" very softly.

"I faked him out and got away from him. Then he starts calling me at home. He wants to know what I'm wearing that night and I go, um, like I'm wearing pajamas and I told him my dad will get mad at me if I stay on the phone. And he asked if anyone was there with me and I said, 'My dad.' I faked it, because no one was there."

A tiny girl with a single pigtail said she feared the family that lived behind her "because there was this guy who was raping the kids and it was an ex-husband and the kids . . ."

Did she mean he was beating them up?

"Yeah, raping them. He was holding one of the kids by her neck and goin' like that." She shook and choked someone in the air. "And then the next day he came back and punched his ex-wife who was pregnant and then he went away in his Volkswagen."

Somehow, in this context, Hulk Hogan and GLOWmania make sense.

I asked the kids what they did, in their real lives, to be less afraid. They said: "I pray." "I lock the doors." "My dad teaches me to use his gun." "Just keep saying it's not true." "Think about Disneyland." "I watch TV to take my mind off things."

I had one last question: What could adults do to make them feel less afraid?

"Stay home and give us protection." "Talk with us."
Be with us, they said.

The New Television Environment

Despite the ascendancy of computers, Walkmen, videogames, pocket Nintendos, and a host of other electronic gizmos, television — in all its mutated new forms — remains the most powerful force shaping the electronic bubble of childhood.

The parents, grandparents, teachers, and some children I spoke with felt in their souls that television disfigures childhood, but many of them sensed that its effects are more complex than merely children's daily exposure to the medium's depiction of violence. Indeed, television's most pernicious quality may be its power to decrease creativity in children, and to serve as a poor substitute for the web.

And television, they said, has *changed*.

In Seattle, a group of senior citizens, members of the first generation of television-era parents and now volunteers at a grade school reading program, remembered how innocently television had begun. One woman recalled "standing in front of Gerke's down in Ballard. We took our kids down there to listen; they had speakers outside. We were fascinated by it. But I was the last person on earth to buy a TV for my children. The meanest mom on the block. The programs were decent then. It wasn't all this terrible violence. And there were fewer channels."

An elderly man, his voice faint and insistent, said: "It's a devil. That's what it is. A demon. You couldn't feel it right away, but that's what it became."

Young parents today also point out that the nature of television, even within the past ten years, has changed. They describe television as an inescapable environment: go to the mall, to friends' houses, anywhere, and televisions are there. One company, Whittle Communications of Knoxville, Tennessee, offers sophisticated television systems to schools — as long as the schools run the company's educational programs with commercials for Head and Shoulders shampoo, Wrigley's gum, Gillette shaving products, and Levi's jeans. (Teachers report that children are more likely to watch educational programs if they contain commercials.) As John Condry of Cornell University has said: "Television is a kind of uncontrolled part of the culture. Parents are worried about the effect it's having, but they don't know what to do about it."[1]

• Television technology has created a moving target. Roughly half of all American homes are now wired for cable. Many other homes that do not receive cable can receive the same special channels using rooftop microwave antennas or the larger, more powerful satellite antennas. Videocassette players, as every thankful parent will tell you, have become the new babysitters.

• The debate over children's programming is stalled largely because the debate is irrelevant: there is little if any dividing line today between children's television and adult television, just as there is little if any dividing line between Saturday morning children's entertainment and commercials. As Joanmarie Kalter points out in an article in *TV Guide*, in the era of cable, market segmentation has created a new prime-time audience: children, especially the self-care kids who do so much of the family's shopping. Between eight and nine in the evening in most homes, television watching is dominated by children, who usually make the program selections — programs such as "Family Ties" and "Growing Pains." Adult characters are included in these shows so that adults will join to watch with the child, but the primary target is children. And, as Kalter points out, the adult characters on many shows are more child-like than the children.[2]

The parents I spoke with weren't worried about the family comedies; they were worried about "sexandviolence." As Peggy Charren, long-time director of Action for Children's Television, pointed out, that's how parents say it — *sexandviolence*: one word, no pause, no dashes.

"When I was growing up, the June Taylor Dancers would come on TV and my mother would tell me to close my eyes," said Mary Hubbard, who owns a clipping service in La Mesa, California. Hubbard spoke of growing up black in the South and of participating in civil rights marches in Birmingham. It was "a different time and place," characterized, paradoxically, by its mature innocence. Television, she emphasized, has taken innocence from her children but gives them nothing from which to construct maturity.

"Today, I sit there and look at the commercials and I cringe and I want to get up and go out of the room and my kids say, 'What's wrong with you? It's nothing!' They've become numb to everything. I watch the Disney movies and they watch *Friday the Thirteenth* when I'm not around. They can't get enough of the gore, and they're just numb. It means nothing to them to see a head cut off. Maybe there was all this gore when I was growing up, but I didn't know about it."

At Jerabek, I asked a class of third- and fourth-graders to describe their favorite shows on television. Jerabek is in a relatively affluent neighborhood, so I expected children to name the programs on, say, the Disney Channel or Nickelodeon, cable networks dedicated to children.

But only five or six kids said they liked Disney or Nickelodeon shows best. To my surprise, when I asked them which channel or network they preferred, two-thirds of the class immediately answered, "HBO!"

One boy explained: "Nickelodeon has some good stuff, like specials, but they have all these little cartoons like 'Pinwheel,' which I hate. I like HBO because it shows some of my favorite movies. Like *The Golden Child* and *Rocky IV* and *American Ninja,* all those."

I asked the kids to yell out the names of some programs or movies that they had seen recently on television and liked. A few titles were reassuring: the "Cosby Show," *Charlotte's Web.* But the other third- and fourth-graders yelled, "*Over the Top!*" "*Back to the Beach!*" "*Space Balls!*"

A few minutes later, a class of fifth- and sixth-graders voted MTV the favorite network. "Nickelodeon is dumb, childish," said one boy. "MTV has all these cool songs. It's the music authority. You get, like, staring into the TV and you can think about anything. You can relax when you're watching it."

In earlier generations, children learned first about childhood and then about adulthood, first about the neighborhood and then about the city, first about the nation and then about the world. And we learned about sex a little at a time. One mother said: "My six-year-old is fixated on the rating system. He looks at the movie ratings in the newspaper and uses pencils and crayons to make lists of movies, with the ratings next to them. We go to the video store and he picks up the boxes and looks at the ratings, and comes home and adds to his lists. It's not so much the movies he's interested in as the ratings. He wants to know how old he has to be before he can see an R-rated movie."

By one industry insider's estimate, 60 percent of the satellite dishes sold in 1988 were delivered with illegally modified decoders, which offer no way of locking out X-rated material. One major distributor of satellite antennas told me that when dishes are sold with legal boxes to decode pay channels, parents are often confused by the sex-censoring technology of the controls. "Anyway, usually the kids are more computer knowledgeable than their parents, which means the parents are locking themselves out and can't get back in, but their kids can."

"Now these kids come into my classroom talking about R-rated movies and X-rated movies," said a teacher at Bell Junior High in San Diego. "It bothers me that they have such easy access. With some of them, an older brother or sister in high school, that's all it takes. And they aren't embarrassed about saying they watched an X-rated movie last night. It's like a little trophy."

Madeline Cartwright, principal of Blaine Elementary School in vio-

lent and poor North Philadelphia, told me that some of the neighborhood residents steal rooftop receivers to pick up cable porno movies.

In a class of fifth- and sixth-graders, with Cartwright standing to one
side of the room, I asked kids about the sexual messages they received
from television, and how they interpreted those messages. All but three
of the thirty or so children said they had seen a hard-core X-rated movie.
All but eight had seen one by the time they were in the third grade. A
very serious young girl, with her initials imprinted on the frames of her
glasses, said: "Back in the old days they didn't have much HBO or tapes
that had X-rated and sexual movies and in today's world they have
more sexual things that go more deep down into it and a lot of people
see it. A lot of children know about it so they say if they're doing that
and they get to be movie stars too maybe it's okay for me and I should
do it and stuff."

"I went to my uncle's house and he had a VCR," said one boy. "I was
in the third grade. I looked at it and my eyes popped out." There were
lots of giggles in the background. "It was terrible. I looked at it and then
I went to sleep on the sofa. I looked at most of it."

A girl next to him said: "When I went down South for the summer
that just passed, to my cousins', I knew that they had rented a movie,
but I didn't know they had rented an X-rated movie, and they had put
it in and I didn't know but everybody was asleep, and when it first came
on, I went in the bathroom because we had just ate, I went in the bathroom and I started throwing up."

And a boy told this story: "One time I just happened to glance at the
movie that my mother had because she was borrowing it from a friend
so she could tape it for another friend, and I said, 'Oh, my goodness,'
because it seemed like the lady was getting hurt the way he was doing it
to her, you could just hear the noises coming from her saying, 'Stop,
you're hurting me,' and stuff like that. And, I don't think the women
should do pornography movies because what if the man had AIDS or
something."

Children growing up in the electronic bubble probably have more
ability than we give them credit for to discriminate between what is real
and what is fake, between prophecy and reality. The amazing thing is
that so many children express such strong moral values in spite of their
early exposure to pornography and other sexual influences. This is not
to suggest that early media exposure to "sexandviolence" is a good thing,
but that children are morally resilient, if given half a chance. Even in the
midst of the most violent and abusive sexual *reality*, the child senses the
existence of some higher rating system. But I wonder: at what point does

video prophecy become reality? At what point does the brutal sensibility that confronts children on television begin to shape their perception of reality?

One child at Blaine said: "When I go places most of the time, I see like people's clothes separately all over the ground like at school and on Kelley Drive, it looked like people have been raped or something and you always are hearing about people being raped, or sexually abused like Oprah Winfrey said her nineteen-year-old cousin did it to her. And that makes you feel uncomfortable in life."

A very strong and confident girl described how she resisted the force of sex media. "I really don't have any sexual environments 'cause I just live with my mother and my brother. But I have a role model like Ma, and she didn't have any kids till she was about twenty-two, and she had another kid when she was twenty-eight. But when I be watching TV or I be walking down the street, and I see all these magazines and stuff, that doesn't really do anything for me because I just keep on walking, I just keep on thinking to myself that I don't need those and none of that junk like that. I can live on myself, I don't need no sex, don't need no boyfriends, stuff like that, I just depend on myself, I don't need anybody except my mother and my father."

In a sense, for children, television has turned the world inside out.

The latest word in children's television is "interactive." Now children can shoot at encoded video images with special electronic guns. Lionel has introduced a model train with a miniature black-and-white video camera mounted in the engine's nose. Hooked up to a video player, Rail Scope can display an "engineer's view" of tracks and surrounding scenes.

Remember when you used to put your face right up to the train table and squint at the train and the little lichen trees and *imagine*?

I thought of this peculiar way of viewing a child's world when I sat with a group of migrant children in Florida. One nine-year-old girl whose father was a foreman (and relatively affluent, as migrants go), and who was very intelligent, seemed a little sad and lonely. What this little girl wanted most of all was for her family to stop moving around, to find a home, to go to the same school year after year.

"My dad, he has this camera like the people in the news use," she told me, "and he takes pictures with it of the places we go, like when we went to California, or to the Big Apple — that's New York. We got a VCR in the trailer and I can watch where we've been." She was not particularly enthusiastic about the videotapes; she simply accepted that this was a way of looking at the world as it passed.

In the electronic bubble, nothing is real unless it's on videotape.

What's Really Wrong with Television:
Information Underload

Surely a child who grows up witnessing a brutalizing video world may, while still being able to determine wrestling from real violence, gradually come to believe that the world is a place where the unreal is real, where everyone has a price, where murder and rape are the norm, where one should not go to sleep at night. How many generations can be raised with this brutality without our culture's being shaped by the fictional distortions that television tolerates and encourages?

One current running through some of the most recent research is not necessarily that television makes children, and society, more vicious, but that it makes all of us more fearful, creating what researchers at the University of Pennsylvania's Annenberg School for Communication describe as the "mean-world syndrome." Kids and adults who watch a lot of television do not necessarily behave more violently, but they do express more apprehension about society and are more likely to feel they are victims. Young girls who watch several soap operas daily, for example, express an exaggerated sense of the frequency of extramarital affairs, premarital sex, and rape. "This is deeper than fear," said George Gerbner, dean emeritus of the Annenberg School and professor of communication. "The use of the word *fear* suggests that it's conscious. These people are not conscious that they're afraid. They feel more apprehension, more mistrust of people, are less likely to say they are willing to go out at night in their own neighborhood. So this is not necessarily conscious fear, but a heightened sense of apprehension of danger and meanness in the world." This apprehension can lead to greater conscious fear and also to more feelings of "gloom and doom," added Gerbner.[3]

This mean-world hypothesis can be tested. Spend an hour flipping through the television channels. Flip quickly. Then write down how you feel — not what you think about television, but how you feel. Chances are you won't list words like *warmth* or *love*. More likely, you'll write down such words as *anger, anxiety, frustration, fear*. Now think about the collective influence of television — of these programmed feelings — on children. Think about growing up with this wall of visual noise. Think about spending more hours with television than in school, more hours with television than reading (22.4 hours a week of television compared with 5.1 hours of reading outside of school), more hours with television than with friends, and most important, more hours with television, in many cases, than with parents.

Each day children and parents are thrown against this wall of sound and sight. And yet, in a society based on information, we seem able to do less and less with that information. We like to tell ourselves that we suffer from information overload, but perhaps a more precise term is information *underload*: the assault of a narrow, repetitive band of negative information. Little nonfiction video programming is produced specifically for children. Though current books for children contain some of the most imaginative, intricate, and beautiful illustrations produced for any age group, television cartoons are dominated by crude, uninspired animation.[4] Neither cable channels nor video stores offer much fresh material. One major video-rental company president told me, "If you want educational tapes for your kids, go to the public library."

The assault of empty information grinds down, suppresses a generation's creativity.

University of California sociologist David Phillips has described what he calls the "imitation society," in which individual creativity fades and mass-produced culture dominates. As the nation's most knowledgeable expert on the relationship between the media and copycat suicides, Phillips studies imitation, the opposite of creativity. In the late eighties, dismayed by the lack of individuality in his college students, Phillips began to tell them a lie once a week in his lectures. He would not identify what the lie was. At the end of the week he would tell them what the lie was — but one out of four times he would by lying about that too.

"As a consequence, I believed that my students would really think critically; they wouldn't just swallow what I was saying." The experiment failed. "The students were too uncomfortable with the process. They said, 'It's not right for you to make us guess; we want to know what is true and write it down.' It's part of their inability to deal with uncertainty."

He holds television responsible.

"For example, the conventional goal of TV news programming is to present both sides of the issue, as if there are only two sides to every issue," he said. "Consequently, most people today believe that objectivity is presenting two sides to an issue, although this approach is simply the artifice of a compressed medium. I also notice that when I lecture to students, they get restless after twelve minutes of talk. They grew up watching TV programs that never ran for more than twelve minutes between commercials. I have come to believe that the most deleterious effect of mass culture is not that it produces deviance, but that children become more and more imitative of *nondeviant* behavior, less and less capable of creating their own ideas."

That theme — the loss of creativity because of television — came up again and again among the parents and teachers. Jon Drescher of the East Harlem Performing Arts School remarked: "In a peculiar way, children seem overstimulated and understimulated at the same time. During the last ten years they've been bombarded with television, computers, Walkmen. Their senses are being overwhelmed. They're left very little room to use their own imaginations. As a consequence, many kids I see don't have much appreciation of the arts. They go home and all the technology keeps them busy. It's not just television doing this to children, but the multiplying forms of media and information."

He thought about this phenomenon for a moment.

"Of course, many of the new technological forms offer wonderfully creative possibilities. But I don't see too many of my students taking creative advantage of the new technologies, just as I don't see these kids getting into the theater, going to concerts. I don't know how many of them really read for pleasure any more. They have no time to be bored, let alone creative."

Surely time and creativity are related; surely, children need those unallotted, unassigned moments to understand, interpret, and embellish incoming information.

Any parent who has ever punished a child by taking away television privileges and then watched the child play — slowly at first, then imaginatively, freely — will recognize the connection between time, boredom, and creativity.

"Though TV is a visual medium, I find visualization has to be a taught skill now," said Monica Roberts, a veteran teacher and reading specialist in Seattle. "Kids are accustomed to having their visualization done for them. I'll describe to my students some wild story about, say, a black panther trying to climb up a flagpole — and I ask, 'Do you see the picture?' They look blankly at me, but then I say, 'Make your own TV picture in your mind,' and *bam*! they have it, they understand. I ask parents to put a black cloth over the television and sit their children in front of the tube to *listen* to a favorite program. In effect, I teach parents to teach their kids to visualize."

Recent research supports the notion that television does stifle creativity.

• Dorothy Singer, co-director of the Family Television Research and Consultation Center at Yale University, studied how children watch "Mister Rogers' Neighborhood," one of the few programs that attempts to encourage kids to use their imagination. Singer found that the kids who watched no television and played with an adult scored the highest on standard creativity tests, followed by children who watched "Mr. Rogers" with an adult. Those who scored the lowest were children who watched the show alone.[5]

• Child's play is becoming more scripted. At its best, play is a process in which the child is in control, say the authors of a study published by Teachers College Press at Columbia University. For example, a child invents a story and characters and improvises props. But many children no longer seem to be inventing their own play. Children assume the role and behavior of characters they have seen on television and play out scenes that resemble a television script. There's nothing new here, except that children, particularly when playing with television-based toys, exhibit "little evidence that they're discovering any meaning of their own from the play."[6] The results of another study, also published by Teachers College Press, suggest that the video emphasis on vaporizing, blasting, or smashing adversaries has made it difficult for many children to tell the difference between pretend assaults and real ones, especially when playing with toy copies of television characters.

• The University of British Columbia studied an otherwise typical Canadian town (dubbed, in the study, "Notel") that did not receive television service because of isolating geography. The researchers compared kids in that town with children in two other towns that did receive television. The children in Notel did significantly better on tests of creativity. The director of the study concluded that television "displaces other activities. . . . We had an impression," she said, "that one of the reasons the kids in the town without TV scored higher was because they'd been bored more often and had had to figure out more things to do."[7]

Aletha Shuston, co-director of the Center for Research on the Influence of Television on Children at the University of Kansas, remarks that "there's something about television — maybe that it provides so much in the way of audio and visual stimulations that children don't have to generate very much on their own."[8]

Television hijacks so many of our senses, so many parts of the brain, that it leaves little room for self-generated images and ideas; more important, television is simply a thief of time — of creative time, of family time.

Rewiring the Television Environment

What can parents do about television?

First, they can admit some of their own complicity. Consider the results of a survey by *Parents* magazine. The adults surveyed watched 2.3 hours of television each evening — more than their children, who watched 2.0 hours. Forty percent thought their children watched too much television, but only 28 percent of these adults thought they themselves watched too much television.[9] One San Diego mother admitted her own unconscious alliance with the tube: "Every once in a while I go on my rampage and I round up the televisions. The last time I did this I was shocked. I didn't know I had as many televisions as I have in this house. I have *six*. And the biggest one I can't move."

Parents can lobby for more variety in cable and broadcast television. Another pressure point in the video culture is the video store. Parents can ask owners to carry a wider variety of children's tapes.

Programmers of children's programs, watching their dominance of children's viewing habits slip away (as they are upstaged by prime-time programmers), are actually offering *more* violence to children. While prime-time violence has leveled off, violence on children's programs has increased, from 18.6 violent acts per hour before 1980, to 26.4 acts per hour after 1980 — the year Federal Communications Commission codes pertaining to violence were scrapped.[10]

Peggy Charren believes passionately that the goal should be variety, not censorship. "A number of nifty people got hired by the networks in the seventies, through two Republican and one Democratic administrations," said Charren. "They were producing 'Thirty Minutes,' a news magazine for kids, a series of specials called 'What's It All About?' (what's Congress all about, for instance) and 'In the News,' short news spots between shows on Saturday morning. These shows were breathtaking. But when Reagan took office, the good people all got fired, the decent programs they had created were canceled. They've never seen the light of day again. The FCC, dominated by Reagan appointees, refused to enforce the public interest obligation in the Federal Communications Act — the law which requires that, in return for using the broadcast spectrum, television promises to serve the public interest, convenience, and necessity. That law is what makes TV broadcast different from the shoe business.

What parents don't understand is that TV has an obligation to serve the public. I didn't know that when I started out — that the broadcast spectrum belonged to *me*. Trying to ban programs, however, is an inappropriate way to fight TV too. You don't need a First Amendment for speech that everyone likes. We're talking about increasing choice, not limiting it. If a network does away with 'Garbage Pail Kids' [a controversial CBS cartoon show prevented from airing because of public protest], there's no reason that network wouldn't respond the same way to public pressure directed at afternoon children's specials that deal with AIDS and teenage pregnancy. Petition for *increasing options.*"

One goal of a family liberation movement, then, should be to reverse the political trend that has encouraged narrow, brutalizing programming.

In fairness, some children's programmers are attempting to offer more diversity.

A few years ago Gerry Laybourne, executive vice president and general manager of Nickelodeon, set out to discover just what kids did want. (She remembered the power of television when she was little: "When I was three, the TV installer came in, plugged our first TV in, turned it on, and my mother said to the television, 'Well, hello, Television!' And the person on television said, 'Hello out there in Television-land!' And I thought, 'Oh, my goodness! This is *something!*' After that I would get dressed up every time I watched TV. I would watch 'Hopalong Cassidy' with my best dress on.") During the early days of Nickelodeon, the cable network failed to listen to children directly; Laybourne says she mainly listened to experts. "We began with a lot of great of intentions, a lot of lofty goals," said Laybourne. Nickelodeon ran a show about "superkids," for instance, children who had accomplished great things. "Our audience said, 'Well, that's something *I'll* never be able to do.' Instead of being motivating to kids, this show was discouraging to them, so we took it off the air." Her next approach was to listen to real kids in focus groups. "We had four groups of eleven-year-olds. When we first started asking them questions, the kids said they didn't want a kids' network because they didn't associate anything positive with being a kid. They felt uncomfortable even with the fact that we were calling ourselves a kids' network. So we began asking kids what it was they liked about being kids. We received some answers that just jarred us. For example: 'We like being kids 'cause we're worried about being teenagers.' They would mention drunk driving, AIDS, and on and on. One kid said, 'We're not sure about this, but we think teen-agers' brains shrink.'

"That told us that kids want an environment in which a kid can be a *kid* — with a kid's humor and fun and without the pressure to deliver."

The stunning popularity of Nickelodeon's "Double Dare" — a kids' quiz show with slime — and the spinoffs and copies that have followed suggest that Laybourne has a handle on the future of children's television.

I attended a taping of "Double Dare" at WHYY-TV in Philadelphia. Inside the studio kids were crammed on bleachers, screaming and wiggling, as the two teams of children on the stage — one called Wet Paints and the other Ghastly Goobers — wallowed in the slime, or "gak," as the show's staff calls it.

Tom Beaman, the Gak Master, wearing an iridescent yellow fright wig, grappled behind a curtain with what appeared to be a giant blender.

"This is pretty much the standard gak," he said. "We put some pudding in it, oatmeal, flour, some egg whites to thicken it up. Gak is kind of what it sounds like when you land in it — *gak*!"

Robert Smythe designs the "physical challenges" on the show. "We like to spice things up," he said. "Yesterday we created the La Brea Tar Pits by filling a horse trough with chocolate pudding. The kids had to find dinosaurs stuck in the chocolate pudding. We call it 'rubber yucky dunk.' Kids who really watch the show know that the slime can help them get through the obstacle course faster. And they're not self-conscious about the cameras. Most of them have been operating VCRs or video cameras since they were one year old!

"Remember when you were a kid and you'd get home at three-thirty and start watching the reruns drift by — 'Gilligan's Island,' 'Mr. Ed' — and by the end of the day you were drained? But this show is physical — it's cathartic."

"We have a theory: everyone looks at kids and either talks down to them or treats them like they're another species," said the show's producer, Mike Klinghoffer, thirty-two, who was walking around with a clipboard. Klinghoffer is tall, with a thin red beard and jeans, a bullrider straw hat, and a subversive grin.

"We talk to them. We say, 'It's you against the world.' And that's often the way seven-year-olds feel. 'Why can't I do this?' 'Because we said so.' What kind of an answer is that? No one loves school, and we tell them, 'We know you don't like school, but you have to go, and it's okay not to like it.' That helps a kid realize he's not the only strange kid who doesn't like it. We make kids feel good about themselves. We're saying, 'For this half hour, it's okay to play with your food.' "

Perhaps part of the show's popularity (and the popularity of its sister show, "Family Double Dare," which invites parents to participate) stems from the fact that childhood's environment has become so overcontrolled.

I asked Klinghoffer to describe the dream show he would like to make someday.

"Probably combining the talk show with the game show. If we had time to sit around and talk during this show, we'd serve two purposes: have fun, make a mess — and *talk*."

Back out on the stage, between taping sessions, I walked over to one of the bleachers and talked to the kids, who were mainly girls between seven and ten years old. I asked them why they liked "Double Dare" so much.

"It has kids." "Like the food and stuff." "Messy." "It's weird!"

What did they think about the messiness?

"It's *neat!*"

Did they get to be messy enough at home?

"*No!*" screeched a bunch of kids in unison.

I felt good about what I saw at the making of "Double Dare"; the youthful enthusiasm of the show's producers was contagious. But within a few months of my visit to the set of "Double Dare," the show had been revamped and renamed "Super Sloppy Double Dare" and was advertised as "beyond the power of normal kids." The producers, faced with a host of copycat shows, thought they had to up the ante. In fact, the success of the "Double Dare" challenge game and its clones led to the development of a crude adult program called "American Gladiators," in which grown men and women, in gladiator outfits, fight their way through a physically challenging obstacle course.

Once again, the line between adult programming and children's programming was blurred.

Petitioning for more variety in programming is no substitute for the creation of a wider, stronger web of reality outside the electronic bubble.

"The only good TV show is one that stimulates kids to turn off the TV and *do* something," said Shari Lewis, the multitalented ventriloquist most baby boomers grew up watching on television. She now produces her own children's videos. "I suggest in my videos to turn off the TV, that viewers turn into doers. Parents can't just be negative about TV, they've got to look for alternatives, be positive. If you don't like TV, sign your kid up in an art class or a Girl Scout troop for Saturday mornings. *Start* a Girl Scout troop. Go hiking on Saturday morning. I was listening to a farmer on TV the other day describe how he tried to control the quality of the seed, the quality of the soil, and the quality of the care. He said the more you can influence all three elements the closer you come to a superior product. You can't control the weather, he said, but you can control those things. So control what you can of your environment."

One way of controlling the environment within the home is to "talk over TV," as the director of research for "Sesame Street," Valeria Lovelace, put it. When I spoke with Lovelace in her New York office, I was impressed by the way of coping with television that she had worked out in her home. The subject came up when we were talking about, of all things, television wrestling. I told her of my surprise at its popularity.

"Well, there are a number of things that make it popular," she said. "It's visual, there's movement, there's suspense. Those elements exist in all good drama and good comedy. In cartoons, you have the same kind of back-and-forth action, falling down, bouncing around. I mean, it's not a *news* broadcast." She laughed. "And children are constantly searching for role models."

Why wrestlers as role models?

"I think strength, physical strength. As a child, you're trying to understand what it's like to be a really strong man or strong woman. Children see so much violence on TV, but then they watch wrestling and say, 'Oh, this is fake, no one is going to get hurt.' They're saying, 'Let me look at this closer. Let me see if I can figure out how they're faking it. . . .' "

I told her she sounded as though she watched wrestling.

She laughed and said, "I try to watch television."

Did her kids watch wrestling?

"Oh, yeah. They like it. I try to restrict television, but I let them watch a lot of different types of programming, and I usually use a technique called 'talking over television.' I intervene. I scream and holler. I say, 'This isn't right! . . . Look at this! Look at that! Now that man's not telling the truth there! Why is it that this cartoon doesn't have any females? Do you see how those people are laughing at this person? Do you think that this is right?' " Lovelace laughed. "I'm like one of those irritating folks in the movie theaters who narrates everything. What I'm trying to do is to impose my own values on top of the medium. I talk back to the newscaster, but I'm talking *to* my children. So what if I'm loud and noisy and distracting at times? I'm getting my viewpoints across. If I wait, it's too late. I find out what topics my kids are interested in on TV, and then I take them to the library and get books and follow up in more depth."

I asked Lovelace if she let her children watch the nightly news, with its very real violence.

"I do. My smallest watches the news. And we will talk — 'Those people died, those people lived, why do these people hate these people?' "[11]

Try to limit television violence without talking about that violence, and kids will still pick up images from their friends, from the electronic bubble outside the house. These images, like drought-resistant seeds, burrow deeply.

Watching television with my sons, the violence flashes and I'll reach for the remote control; I'll just see the blood and go *click*. But the image is already planted.

Lovelace agreed. "Even if I do not talk with them right away about what they have seen, I try to do it later, maybe riding in the car. The point is to talk."

Some parents had intuitively made the connection between television, violence, and creativity. One mother told how creativity may be a victim of television, but it can also be used as a weapon against it. She had become fed up with the violent toys, most of them connected to television programs, that her six-year-old had received over the years. She made a deal with her son.

"I told him we could go to Toys-R-Us and replace his violent toys with new toys — but they had to be creative. We came back with Play-Doh and games and art supplies and Legos and a giant box of new crayons. Later, I was listening to him sing as he played. Instead of singing cartoon superhero songs in that slightly mean-sounding, destructo-boy tone, he was singing something gentle: 'Put in the Play-Doh and out comes the fun.' He was still singing a TV-generated song, but it was about creation instead of destruction."

We need such antidotes to the mean-world syndrome.

By squelching creativity, television may well limit children's ability to imagine a world without violence. And if they cannot visualize such a world, they surely cannot create it — in their hearts or in the future. As parents, we need to reclaim the environment. For some of us, that may mean absolute rebellion.

"My husband and I haven't owned a TV for five years," said Charlene Goldman of San Diego. "We have a three-year-old. This year my husband started thinking he wanted to get a video monitor (without tuner so it wouldn't technically be a TV) to have 'controlled' viewing of films in our home. You can imagine the salespeople's reaction to someone looking for a TV without channels. He found a video monitor used for commercial purposes. I wasn't keen on the whole idea."

Then something happened.

"He spent one Saturday evening fireplace-gazing with his son, who fell asleep in his arms. It was an ultimately peaceful and quiet evening and one of hundreds we enjoy. My husband realized a TV, no matter what form, would threaten that peace."

And the Goldman household quietly survived.

10

The Children of Sex, Drugs, and Rock 'n' Roll

●

For so many children, the phosphor strands of video and computers, of street gangs and cults, and of course sex and drugs become a kind of false webbing, like scar tissue replacing healthy flesh. And so, even for healthy families, the world rushes in.

Tom and Beth Fitzsimons face their children's increasingly pressurized sexual environment straight on, as best they can. The trick, said Beth Fitzsimons, is to be direct and clear about the costs and limitations of sex. And that's not at all easy in the age of television and high-powered advertising. The important thing, said Beth, is to get *other* messages into their brains — though this approach has its shortcomings.

"We've tried to answer all their questions, and we're comfortable with one another, so that's helpful. But over the past couple of years, I've come to understand that you can answer all the questions right, you can educate them in a very modern way about the issues of sexuality, and they're going to screw it up anyway.

"I was cleaning the tub one day. Justin came in and said, 'Mom, I know all about the eggs and I know all about the sperms. And I know all about penises and I know all about vaginas. There's only one thing I don't understand. How does the sperm get through the two pairs of pants?' He was dead serious. He looked at me for a moment, and then realization dawned in his eyes. He went, '*Eeeeeeewwww* . . . unless you're *naked*! *Eeeeeeewwww*! That's *disgusting*!' And he was running around the second floor yelling this out and I was yelling at him, 'It *is not* disgusting! Your mother and father do it all the time!' And then I said, 'Oh, God . . . this is not good sex ed.'

"But you know, that phase went by and now he's very matter-of-fact.

Elizabeth says, 'I prefer not to discuss this with you. I'll just read a book.' " Beth laughed. "Our kids had a great sex ed course at school. And this year, they had a program for the eighth-graders, too. They invited parents to take a corresponding course at night. We went. It was one of the best things we've ever done. Six Monday nights in a row. The kids were hysterical. Justin said, '*What?* You're going to a sex course *now?*' Actually, the kids loved it. We had the same teacher that they had. We talked about what our kids were talking about. One of the comforting things was that the parents all had the same concerns, especially that we would not like our children to be sexually active real young."

"I don't really think kids were doing it all that much these days anyway," said Tom. "They're probably just like we were. They talk about it more than they do it."

Unfortunately, kids are doing it more, and at earlier ages.

And the stakes are greater.

Childhood's New Sexual Environment

Four main elements define childhood's new sexual environment: sexual activity at younger and younger ages, AIDS, teenage pregnancy, and adult hesitancy to act.

A poll conducted by Louis Harris for Planned Parenthood in 1986, which surveyed one thousand youngsters from twelve to seventeen, found that 4 percent of the twelve-year-olds, 10 percent of the thirteen-year-olds, and 20 percent of the fourteen-year-olds had already had sex. More than half the kids surveyed said they had had intercourse by the time they were seventeen. That rate was underscored by a study conducted by researchers at Brandeis University and Wheaton College, which showed that — even in the era of AIDS — more than two-thirds of U.S. male teenagers aged seventeen to nineteen reported having sexual intercourse in 1988, up 11 percent from 1979.[1]

"Most of the parents I meet aren't fully aware of how early and how intense the sexual pressure is for kids," said teacher Mary Olbersen, who conducts a peer-counseling program in San Diego. "Some of these kids have done really well standing up to pressure and just saying no and walking away with their chin up. Others fight it for a while, but come in one day and say, 'I blew it, now what?' And it's not just the girls who get pressured into sex. One ninth-grader in this class, a good-looking, nice, intelligent boy who just transferred here to live with his father, told me there were four different girls on this campus who wanted him to get them pregnant."

How do kids perceive the sexual pressure?

"There's more of a stress on sex being so *important* in life," said one girl, an eleventh-grader, with resentment in her voice. "Since ninth grade, it's just been sex, sex, *sex*. Sex is constantly thrown at us."

An exuberant letterman added: "My parents and a lot of my friends' parents, instead of sitting there and saying sex is something horrible, they say be safe about it. Instead of trying to ignore the problem, they're trying to face it. It's accepted. I know my parents think I have sex. A lot of parents would be really, like, *old-fashioned* I guess is the term if they didn't think that. I've seen movies about how if someone your age had sex when they were teenagers it was like *incredible*. Like really *strange*."

His classmates laughed.

"My parents know that I'm sexually active," he said, "and they can accept that and they're not trying to sit there and turn their backs on it and say it's not happening or anything, but I don't think it's exactly real to them."

Why, in the age of AIDS, is sexual activity among children increasing? Partly because of the sheer power of sexual images in the electronic bubble, which push them into sexual activity at younger and younger ages. Partly it's logistics. "Forget the back seat of the car," said Pat Welsh, the outspoken author and teacher at T. C. Williams. "During the days these houses are empty. There are kids here who leave school during their lunch hour, go home to get laid, and then rush back for their sixth-period class." And partly, it's naiveté, or worse, on the part of parents. "Parents don't connect drinking with sex," said Welsh. "The parents would rather have them drinking than doing drugs. But kids will tell you that the kids who are the heavy drinkers are often the most heavily into sex."

In this new sexual climate, kids are not only doing it a lot more, but they're disturbingly naive or fatalistic about the consequences, they're far more at risk than previous generations. The truth is that kids know everything about sex, but not much at all about getting pregnant or contracting AIDS. The *Detroit Free Press* reports that some girls think that they can't get pregnant if they wear high heels during intercourse, or that they can't get pregnant the first time, or that they can't get pregnant standing, or that they can't get pregnant if they don't kiss. Although condom use among the general teenage population is gradually increasing, condom use among teenagers in high-risk groups is *declin-*

ing.[2] Such ignorance is astonishing in a society so blanketed with sexual images.

I asked kids at San Diego High School, How had AIDS changed their lives?

Some of the boys were wearing fingerless gloves and earrings. The girls favored leather and killer stares. Others were decked out, fifties style, in bobby sox.

"You can't go out and have your little —"

"Flings," said a girl. There was laughter.

"Gang bangs," said a boy. There was lots of laughter.

"It used to be you'd worry about getting pregnant and stuff and now it's directed toward getting AIDS," said the girl. She was wearing a leather coat and had a soft voice.

What about all those warning ads on television? Weren't adolescents getting inundated with the message? *Nah,* they said, *we tune 'em out. Too depressing.*

I asked what proportion of kids were sexually active in that school.

"Two-thirds," someone at the back of the class said. "Three-fourths," a girl said. A boy topped her estimate. "Nine-tenths," he said.

How many of the guys knew somebody who used condoms? A few hands went up.

If most of them were sexually active, why didn't they use condoms?

Several of them answered at once. "Embarrassing." "It's not cool." "Some of them bust so it doesn't matter." A girl said: "I think boys are embarrassed to go buy them. I think they'd rather steal them than buy them."

I thought they would be smarter than this, I told them.

"Adults aren't," said a girl.

Should condoms be more available to kids? Would that help? I asked them to raise their hands if they agreed. Most of them raised their hands.

"They should have them in the boys' bathroom," said the boy with the earring. "Like they have pads in the girls' bathroom, they should have condoms in the boys' bathroom."

Was AIDS talked about much in school?

"No. Except in a joking sense." The class agreed with that.

"They give us pamphlets," somebody said sarcastically. "You see them piled up outside the class doors. You see them in the hallway at lunch. Like it's a joke. Everybody goes, 'Hey, books on AIDS, it'll never happen to me, see ya.' "

A serious, athletic-looking boy said: "It's a joke. We had a presentation last year, New Image Theater or something, 'How to Use Condoms.' They did it in a joking manner because maybe it was too personal or embarrassing to just get right down to how everything is done. They have to do it that way because they're too afraid to really be honest."

"They had a guy dressed like a condom."

"And a girl dressed like a diaphragm."

"I understand the reason they did that," said one of the girls. "People might joke about it on the outside, but when we're sitting alone in our room we might think to ourselves a lot more seriously than we do when we're with our friends."

After the bell rang and the class had thumped and rattled out of the room, their teacher, a small, gray-haired woman, came up to me and with urgency in her voice, said: "I'm supposed to talk to these kids about AIDS? These kids can't imagine me having sex, certainly not being *spontaneously* sexually active. I think they need to talk to young people, some young doctors. Someone they'll believe."

Walking to my car, I reached into my coat pocket for my keys. There was a note in my pocket, folded, written in pen on ruled notebook paper. Someone had slipped it in there.

It read: "There IS sufficient information about AIDS passed around in school! What can they do? Beat it into us?"

I stood in the parking lot looking at the note, wondering if its pessimistic author was correct, that nothing could be done, that teenagers would just be teenagers. No matter what the risk.

A few miles away, at Garfield High, I visited a class of pregnant teenagers. Protected by an armed security officer, the campus exuded an end-of-the-road atmosphere. This was where many of the city's problem students end up.

The innocence in the girls' eyes was surprising. They fidgeted and squirmed and pulled their legs up beneath them. One of them, wearing glasses, sat bolt upright and held on to her books as if, were she to let go, she would fly backward through the window and across the patched playground where nobody plays anymore, fly right up into the brown haze and disappear.

"I thought I knew myself good," said the squirmiest and least bashful of them. "Knew my body real good, but it played a game with me. It tricked me."

The girl with the books didn't say anything. Her hands were flat, fingers curled over the top edge of the books.

"That's what all of us thought," said one girl. "A lot of us start, you know, real early, so you think that since you weren't getting pregnant all those other times that you can't get pregnant. So you keep doing it."

Eighteen girls, aged fourteen and up, sat in this classroom. Some of the children who have attended the class at one time or another have been pregnant as young as eleven or twelve years old. All but one of the girls in this class were black or Hispanic. The exception was a Vietnamese girl who was perhaps four and a half feet tall, with a slash of red lipstick across her mouth. (This racial mix, I should add, does not reflect the national demographics of child pregnancy, which is increasing at a faster rate for whites than for blacks and Hispanics.)

Some of the girls had already given birth, and their babies were at home with their mothers, or with baby sitters, or in the school nursery. The rest of the girls were pregnant, their bellies still growing. But their arms and legs were still growing, too. They were still children. Perhaps that is what I could see in their eyes — not their innocence, but their childhood.

"Some of us really wanted babies so we went out and got 'em," one girl said defiantly. The girl at the back of the room, hair braided tight, said, "Some of us were forced to fool around." So they were, most of them. According to statistics collected by a California network of teen pregnancy programs, as many as nine out of ten pregnant teenagers who carry their babies to term have been sexually molested or raped during their childhood.

"After I had the baby I went sort of dingy for a few minutes," said a fourteen-year-old. "I tripped out because for nine months I had a little human inside me. It was weird. That's a baby! In a way it was a bad thing that I got pregnant because I'm still young. In a way it's good because it drawed me and my boyfriend closer, so it worked out pretty well. Except me and my boyfriend aren't talkin' right now. . . ."

I asked, How many of them were glad they had gotten pregnant?

Two girls raised their hands. One of them, in the back, said: "I wanted to see if I had a baby, How would I treat my baby? Would I beat my baby, or abuse my baby? I feel good. I love my baby."

One out of six babies in the United States is born to a teenager, a pregnancy rate that has plateaued. But the nature of teen pregnancy has changed: the pregnancy rate among younger teenagers is rising.

The tragedy is magnified in the next generation. Seventy percent of children born to mothers aged seventeen or younger — compared with 25 percent of children born to mothers in their twenties — will spend part of their lives in single-parent homes. Eighty percent of teenage mothers never finish high school. (Most were dropouts when they became pregnant, which suggests that keeping kids in school may help lower the teenage birthrate.) The likelihood of living a life of poverty is seven times greater for a teenage mother than for other teens. Sixty percent of the nation's total welfare budget is provided to women who first gave birth as a teenager. . . . These grim statistics are part of the price of the vanishing web.[3]

The future of teenage mothers does not have to be such a portrait of disappointment. Most experts on teen pregnancy agree that remedial education is the one factor that can improve the later lives of these young women and their children, and that the programs should extend beyond high school and well into the women's twenties.

"I wanted to be a cheerleader," said one of the fourteen-year-olds a little uncertainly. "I think I still be able to do that."

The Vietnamese girl said, in the smallest of voices: "This class gave us encouragement to go on with life. We're all a big family here."

"Sometimes when we go on our little walks," said a girl with cornrow braids, "we'll walk around the block here, 'cause they say walking's good, and everybody driving by instead of keeping their eye on the road, they slow down because there's twenty or forty people walking down the street and all of them pregnant."

She giggled at the image and hid her face.

"Ironically, a teenager often sees having a baby as a way to make something good in her life, to become a 'good girl' by becoming a mother," explained Judy Kirsten, who heads the Garfield Pregnant Minors Program. "Look at the need for status. Look at the fact that so many of these girls have been molested themselves, as children, and yet they insist on carrying their own babies to term, to create six pounds of self-esteem, to do something good in the world."

One of those good things is to make contact with an adult.

Among pregnant adolescent programs nationwide, there is a new awareness that men in their twenties, thirties, and forties — adults — are primarily the ones getting young girls pregnant. In San Diego County, for example, teenage boys father only 15 percent of the babies born to girls aged twelve to seventeen. "This used to be called statutory rape and was legally prosecuted. It is not being prosecuted anymore," said Kirsten. "The courts are too jammed with other things, the girls are not good witnesses, or they fear that the father will retaliate against them."

These kids live in a fairy tale; they believe that someday a prince will sweep them away to the Land of Cosby, where the father always comes home and the ratings are always high. But today, an unmarried pregnant black teen has a greater chance of miscarrying than she has of marrying;

only one in five premarital pregnancies is resolved through marriage. What about the girl's family; what about the baby's grandmother? Isn't the child-mother taken into those adult arms? In some cases, yes; but more often the girl's family does more harm than good.

"Typically, the girl takes the baby home and the girl's mother and grandmother help care for it — they compete for the baby while the girl goes on with her life," Kirsten said. "Meanwhile, the baby grows, isn't as cuddly and cute anymore, and then the girl's mother hands the baby back to the teenager and says, 'Okay, now it's your turn.' But the girl is unprepared to take the baby back, has never developed a sense of responsibility, hasn't bonded to the child, and has few parenting skills."

These children, particularly the African American ones, are far more culturally conservative about some aspects of the birth process than white kids. They wouldn't, for example, consider placing their babies up for adoption or aborting. Some of the girls, however, had considered suicide. One of them said she had considered taking sleeping pills. "Or like poison or something," she said. "I didn't want to have a slow, agonizing death. I like to get it done quick and over with." Fortunately, her parents had taken her back into their home, and the thoughts of suicide had drifted away.

Now, for the first time, the girl with the stack of books spoke up. "I didn't want to be pregnant," she said fiercely. "There was a lot of things that I wanted to do and I'm going to do them. I'm going to college."

"Who's gonna take care of your baby?" asked one of her classmates.

"My mom, or a baby sitter," said the girl with the books. "Or they got day-care centers at community colleges —"

"Ain't no baby sitter at four o'clock in the morning," said one of the other girls, her voice light and trilly, almost taunting.

"You got to deal with it," said the girl with the books, hanging on for dear life, her fierceness still there even as she began to cry. "You got to deal with it."

Sex and the Fundamental Divide

Most adults are not dealing with it — not with the threat of AIDS to teenagers, not with children having children, not with the fundamental divide.

First, unlike Tom and Beth Fitzsimons, most parents do not talk with their children about sex. Clinical research indicates that kids whose parents talk to them about sex are more likely to delay having sex, and when they do have sex, are more likely to be responsible. Yet former U.S. surgeon general C. Everett Koop has pointed out that the vast majority of parents of children under twelve have never discussed sex with their kids — despite all the openness of this generation of parents and kids on other topics.[4]

Second, most of our institutions are failing to confront the issue directly. As the kids with whom I spoke rightly suggested, our schools and other institutions have done relatively little to educate children about the danger of AIDS. In the late eighties, thirteen- to nineteen-year-olds accounted for less than 1 percent of individuals infected with the AIDS virus nationwide. Read that statistic cold and you might assume that teens are somehow insulated by their immune systems from the syndrome. But the next age group, aged twenty to twenty-nine, accounted for 21 percent of the individuals diagnosed with the virus. When were they likely to have been infected? *When they were teenagers.*[5]

During the year following this report, the U.S. Army tested about half a million teenage recruits and announced in May 1988 that results showed a higher than expected prevalence of the virus among teens. Recent studies also show that teenagers are more likely to have multiple sex partners than persons in other age groups. Gary Yates, director of a pilot medical and psychiatric clinic for teenagers at Children's Hospital in Los Angeles, reports that more than half of street kids barter their bodies to survive, and 35 percent of street kids are involved in intravenous drug use. They therefore constitute a prime group for the transmission of AIDS.[6]

Yet, trapped between dueling moralities, the schools are moving at a snail's pace. The San Diego Unified School District, for example, is using a "social concerns team," a group of about twenty teachers who go around to the schools and teach about drug abuse and AIDS. In 1988, the district's goal was to reach every student in grades six to twelve with at least one hour of AIDS instruction in a classroom setting. By the spring of that year, the district's director of health services estimated that only 50 to 60 percent of the students had been talked to.

For a relatively enlightened school district, this record is horrific, and all too typical of other school districts around the country.

Surprisingly, no study has ever proved or disproved that school sex education per se has any effect on the frequency of sexual activity among students.[7] What *has* been proved, at least in the prevention of pregnancy, is the effectiveness of classes in sexuality combined with school-based clinics offering birth control information or actual contraceptives. The success of this combination was first demonstrated when the Mechanic Arts High School in St. Paul, Minnesota, adopted such an approach in 1973 and cut the teenage birthrate nearly in half. The reason school-based clinics make headway is twofold: first, they offer more than talk; second, they offer follow-up. A nurse or nurse practitioner at a school clinic can establish continuing, first-name relationships with students, guiding them through the sexual minefield of adolescence.[8] School-based clinics can also diagnose serious health problems, identify children with inadequate immunizations, and offer prenatal care — all of which, in the long run, can reduce the nation's health expenditures, as well as the number of babies born to children.

Though few, if any, school clinics counsel abortion, these clinics have met determined resistance from some religious and socially conservative quarters.[9] Judy Kirsten spoke angrily of the fundamental political and religious divide that creates adult paralysis in the face of such a threat to children. Religious organizations, she said, have consistently opposed expanding programs for pregnant teens and health clinics in the schools. "I speak throughout the community. I'm on TV often. But in four years, only *one* church has asked me to speak. They're not interested. All they see is *this*." With a motion of her hand she described a pregnant abdomen.

One group of religious fundamentalists did, however, come to visit Kirsten's class. They came to promote something called "secondary virginity," the idea that whatever a girl's past, she could, with a little prayer, become a born-again virgin. "They did a very good job. I kept calling them to come back, but they never returned. Maybe they learned something when they were here. Maybe they learned that things are more complex than they thought."

But Kirsten's anger was not restricted to those on the conservative, religious side of the divide. She said she feels this anger toward liberals as well. "The welfare system is destroying children. I would like the laws tightened so that you don't get welfare unless your kid is attending school and getting good prenatal care."

There should also be more discussion in schools of the moral dimensions of sexual activity. But I was astonished to find how little teenagers in the classes I interviewed talked about the morality of sexual activity.

Ironically, the timidity of teachers to bring up such issues was due in part, I was told by teachers, to their fear of attack by religious parents who often do not want sex discussed in school, or by other parents who, for whatever reason, have resisted the introduction of religion or morality into the debate.

Yet the stark realities of AIDS are slowly opening up both sides of the divide to the discussion of previously taboo topics. C. Everett Koop —

known for his conservative views on birth control and abortion — was a forceful advocate of the use of condoms as AIDS protection. At the same time, many social liberals, to whom the word *abstinence* was in recent decades a joke, now advocate the teaching of this concept in schools.[10]

Unless this sense of common adult purpose can be nurtured, the fundamental divide will widen and children will continue to fall into the gap in ever-increasing numbers.

Drugs: From Rehabilitation to Habilitation

Each year during the eighties, the "National High School Senior Drug Abuse Survey" reported that drug abuse among high school seniors had decreased slightly. But while Americans in general appear to be slowly turning away from the use of illegal drugs, the people doing so tend to be the most educated and affluent, and drug abuse among the poorest and least educated continues to intensify.[11]

There are three especially troubling aspects to the trends in drug use among children and teenagers. First, a new wave may be on the way. Whereas drug use among other teenagers appears to have peaked by the end of the eighties, drug use among junior high and elementary school children is rising. Second, hard-core drug use continues to destroy inner-city neighborhoods, and the children in them. Third, alcohol abuse among children and teens is worsening. With drug and alcohol abuse, as with sex, what parents believe the kids are doing and what the kids are actually doing are often different.

A Louis Harris survey for the Metropolitan Life Foundation in 1988 pointed out "wide discrepancies between parental perception and what students report in the areas of alcohol and drug abuse." Five percent of the parents surveyed reported that their child had used drugs, whereas 17 percent of students said they had used drugs. Thirty-six percent of parents said their child had had at least one alcoholic drink; but 66 percent of students surveyed said they had used alcohol at least once or twice.[12]

I asked a class at San Diego High what they saw, in their lives, as the major drug trends. One boy offered: "We're in a state of flux. People are more extreme, on one side or another. You have the Say No to Drugs group over here and you have the group over here that's doing drugs and selling drugs, and there's nothing in the middle."

One girl said, "If you're in the middle, you're only in the middle for a while."

The kids spoke almost at once now. "It starts really early and that's pretty scary." "Elementary school." "I know someone who was doing heavy drugs in fifth grade. Acid."

"My brother's and sister's in elementary school and they come home and say they have friends who are into drugs right now." "I've seen a lot of people get scared away from drugs in elementary school and then seen them turn around and do them in junior high and then turn around and not do them in high school."

Most of the other kids said drugs started later, around eighth grade.

I asked, How did they feel about the Just Say No campaign?

"I think it might affect people in elementary school, but I don't think it affects people in high school. They're going to do what they want to do and no campaign about Say No to Drugs is going to stop them."

Most of the class agreed with that. One girl said, "I knew this guy who had a JUST SAY NO bumper sticker on his car and he's a cocaine addict."

Among these kids, alcohol was currently the drug of choice: "Easier to get." "Easy and inexpensive." "You go to a store that isn't afraid to sell to younger people, you get someone who looks twenty-one, you fish — ask someone out on the street who's over twenty-one." "Or you just get a friend you know who's over twenty-one." "It seems drinking is more acceptable and when you drink you can accept what you're doing 'cause your parents do it, it's not as bad." "I've been to a lot of parties where parents will get the alcohol, will sit there and will stay there, and they'll say it's because they don't want anything to get too rowdy, which might be OK — but then why did they get the alcohol in the first place?"

Some of the kids believed the Just Say No campaign had worked, but not exactly in the way it was intended.

"We say no to drugs, and *yes* to alcohol," said one boy. "It's made alcohol acceptable. A friend of mine was doing pot a lot and then he started forgetting things so he decided to quit. He's been clean from pot for a month, but he was telling me about all these alcohol drinks he's been tasting; every night he tries something different."

"Drink as much as you can as fast as you can. That's the goal."

What did adults tell them to say yes to?

"Milk: it does a body good," said one boy.

As with sex, drugs aren't the problem. The problem is adults and the messages they send to children.[13] Consider, for example, the messages sent by adults — the signals that saturate the electronic bubble — regarding alcohol.

The three most heavily promoted product groups in the United States today are, first, pharmaceuticals; second, tobacco; and third, alcohol.

A few years ago, Michelob ads rang with the jingle, "Weekends are made for Michelob." That message was consistent with what was then the prevailing American norm: drinking is for time out, for weekends. Then came "put a little weekend in your week." The most recent theme is "the night, the night, the night belongs to Michelob" — ads with a thumping rock beat aimed at a youth market.

In a matter of a few years, advertisers have worked to condition Americans — particularly young Americans — to think of drinking as an appropriate nightly habit rather than a weekend escape. Wine coolers, introduced in the past decade and targeted specifically at young women, are what one alcohol-abuse expert describes as the "alcoholic soft drink for girls." The alcohol industry's newest thrust is to increase the number of outlets for "off-sale premises" — gas stations and minimarts — where teenagers buy most of their alcohol. It's not unusual today to find beer priced more competitively than Pepsi.[14]

Not surprisingly, when the *Weekly Reader* and the National Council on Alcoholism and Drug Dependence conducted a survey of student attitudes in 1987, the survey revealed that alcohol is the only drug that children are *less* likely to identify as a drug as they grow older. In grades two and three, 33 percent of students called wine coolers a drug; by grades seven through twelve, the figure was 25 percent.

Meanwhile, alcohol-related problems are the leading cause of death among adolescents.

The problem, it seems to me, is not the drugs themselves, but the commercial exploitation of children and young people and the environment in which they live. In any effective war on drugs, the emphasis must shift from the drugs themselves to the environment in which children live. Specific drugs will come and go; stop cocaine smuggling tomorrow, and methamphetamine will burst into production in basements all over America — and children, of course, will still drink. But the commercial and social environment that encourages drug abuse will remain.

Researchers now find that crack is considered no more intrinsically addictive than other drugs, and that the difficulties faced in treating crack addiction have less to do with the biochemical reaction produced by crack than with the environment in which users live. "Crack addiction can be treated," Dr. Herbert Kleber, deputy to U.S. drug czar William Bennett, told the *New York Times*. But the key, as Kleber put it, is "habilitation more than rehabilitation." Drug users must be surrounded by family and social structures that they may never have experienced previously.[15]

When children spoke of alcohol or other drugs, they would often talk, almost in the same breath, about their sense of isolation within their neighborhoods or schools. This was true even in upper-middle-class neighborhoods.

Beth and Tom Fitzsimons's son Justin, for example, a ninth-grader, talked about how he feared entering high school: "There's really a big drug problem at Strath Haven. It's pretty scary because drugs are bad, of course. But you know they can do really nasty things to you and everything. It's weird to think about peer pressure and everything. I was talking to a tutor that I have from the college, and she said that sometimes people get so used to the fact that there's drugs around, they sort of think that drugs are normal. And the teachers aren't going to be there. They're not all going to know your names or anything. And it's just a lot bigger place. They won't know me."

It's Not Only Rock 'n' Roll

One of the best ways to understand how children and teenagers perceive their environment, and the need to change it, is through their music — not through the music itself, or its packaging, but through what kids say about their music.

At Baldi Middle School in Philadelphia I asked a class, What about all the people who say heavy metal music causes kids to take drugs?

One boy who listened to heavy metal said: "People who are going to take drugs are going to take drugs anyway, and if a lot of people like to blame the music — I mean, if someone says, 'Go jump off of the Empire State Building,' or 'Go jump off a bridge,' or 'Shoot your mother,' are you going to do it? The only people that are saying, 'If you play a record backwards you get a Satanic message and it's going to harm your child,' the only people that are saying that are the ones trying to find an excuse why their daughter or son did drugs, 'cause they're scared it's just going to come down to their kid had emotional problems."

A boy who favored rap music explained why he likes to turn his boom box up loud. He likes to create an *environment*: "Since we like it so much, we get into the illusion that a lot of people must like it, so we go around playing it loud and we have this feeling that we're bringing them the music — so we can make everybody dance, make everybody say *ho*, and it's like a symbol of power, just making you believe that you can bring the music that everybody likes to them, like you're the supplier of what they want."

One tall, lanky student wearing a *Sesame Street* yarmulke said: "I can sometimes listen to a song, and I'll be having a problem with something that I want to do or that I don't want to do, and I'll hear the music and it'll click, and I'll know what I want to do and it's sort of an answer. It does match with something inside my head."

I asked him what kind of music he listened to for guidance.

"Groups like Suicidal Tendencies and Black Flag and Dead Milkmen. They're sort of a parody group, but you listen to it and you know what they're trying to say. It's sort of a parody on life, I mean there's something wrong with the world and they know it. But they're trying to find a little bit of solution and you hear it and you're pretty sure of yourself after you listen for a while."

A Baldi counselor later told me that this boy was one of the few kids in the school to outwardly display any manifestation of his religion, but that he wore the yarmulke with pictures of Bert and Ernie and Big Bird on it as a joking camouflage. Listening to our conversation, Baldi's principal said: "I would hope he would have someone else to turn to other than the Dead Milkmen. Has he tried prayer?"

Baby boomers grew up thinking of rock 'n' roll, the music of defiance and rebellion, as their personal sound track. *Tsk, tsk,* they cluck today. Look at all the teenagers listening to all that imitation rock. No meaning, no context.

In fact, today's children may be the first generation since the advent of vinyl and radio to embrace its parents' music; in that sense, teenagers today are more unusual, musically, than the boomers.[16]

Francis Thumm, forty, is a musician, a contributor to the albums of singer-songwriter Tom Waits, and a music teacher at Point Loma High School in San Diego. He says teenage music today is as rich and diverse as it was in the sixties.

"But young people today have a sense of history about the music. A kid who listens to heavy metal knows instinctively that the guitar solos he hears had roots in Jimmy Page and Eric Clapton." The Beatles are popular. (One of the Baldi girls said she liked the Beatles because "some of their music sounds like hard rock, and some of it sounds like Easy One-Oh-One music, and some of it like sounds like elevator music and that's why I like it, because whatever I feel like, I can listen to.") Thumm continued: "Jimi Hendrix is a god to these kids. They don't know much about him personally. But musically, he's a symbol of fiery virtuosity."

Revealingly, Jim Morrison, dark prince of the Doors, is a bigger star today than he was in the sixties—bigger than the Beatles. "Kids love the gothic quality of his songs, the preoccupation with death, the sense of isolation and waywardness, and the fact that he died young." The Jim Morrison biography *No One Here Gets Out Alive* is the current teen generation's corollary to what *The Autobiography of Malcolm X* meant to baby boomers.

Why does this generation of children and teenagers hold so tightly to rock and other artifacts of their parents' past? I thought of my theory of openness: absence makes the heart grow fonder. I remembered the boy with dead men's clothes in Seattle, who wore clothing that had belonged to some adult in his life who had either left him or died. And so it is, perhaps, that kids wrap themselves in old rock 'n' roll.

Of course, rock's survival has to do, too, with reasons other than a generational yearning for adult contact. Baby boomers program MTV. Classic rock stations chase after baby boomers, still the biggest market slice, so kids are exposed to it more than we were to, for instance, Benny Goodman.

But hearing certain rock songs can carry bittersweet associations for these teenagers. Some of Thumm's kids describe how, say, "Let It Be" reminds them of being four or five years old — back when Mom and Dad were still together.

In Thumm's songwriting class, students stand or sit under the light of a single lamp and sing or simply read their songs or poetry. A frequent subject of these songs is their painful home life.

What impresses Thumm most is how closely the kids listen to one another. "When they sing, you can hear a pin drop. Unlike most of us baby boomers at that age, these kids listen to each other with absolute respect."

Sometimes they write about suicide. A few years ago, one girl, "tall and stunning, like a model," killed herself. Thumm pulled one of her poems from a manila folder. It read, "The air gets warm / and thinner by the breath / when will be the mercy / of the coming of my death. . . ." The lines, written so neatly, nearly disappear on the page.

When Thumm showed me this poem, his face filled with pain. "I have learned over time to pay close attention to these songs and poems."

Despite the inherent sadness of rock 'n' roll nostalgia, many teenagers display strong survival instincts. For every sad song, there's a song of hope. Thumm is moved by his students' reverence for nature. And some things never change. "Quality music always wins," he says. "For example, they love gospel music. Just today, when I asked the members of the chorus what they wanted to sing, most of them held up 'Ave Maria,' a thirteenth-century motet. We had a school assembly that began with six students singing an a cappella rendition of Leadbelly's 'Sylvie,' a southern work song. Suddenly this chaotic auditorium became as quiet as a church. I attribute that to the surprising peer respect among these young people and to the simple, noble power of the music."

For teenagers, the need for approval and love from parents and peers has never changed. Teenagers are insecure and scared to death. That hasn't changed either.

Joan Baez has complained that youth music today has no context — no Vietnam War or civil rights movement for which to serve as sound track. But the affinity for classic rock suggests a context. And surely heavy metal and rap music have their own context. Some of this music glorifies destruction, but much of it criticizes what drugs, advertising, environmental ignorance, and divorce have done to our society. Of *course* there's hysteria in much of today's music, and *sure,* it lacks grace and joy. But the context is kids growing up with single parents trying to make ends meet, growing up with divorce, growing up with disintegration.

"There's a sense now, in the music, of a people about to slide over a cultural waterfall," said Thumm. "My response to Joan is, Wake up, honey, it's a different world."

11

Healing Emotions

●

Today's childhood environment holds within it the seeds of a gentler future: the openness and compassion of children, the suggestion in their voices of the human connections that could be made. But too much of the new childhood environment conspires against the emotional health of children and families: the absence of neighbors and kin; the twin trends of early autonomy and overinstitutionalization; the overprogramming of family time; the technologizing of childhood and the powerful seductiveness of the electronic bubble; and the destructiveness of the fundamental divide.

It also becomes clear that public perception of the new environment is largely out of focus or even delusionary. This perception is fixated on symptomatic bogeymen rather than on more primary threats — especially the emotional neglect of children.

When it comes to the emotional health of children, I've come to think of our current culture as a kind of giant General Motors, a big, self-satisfied, undercapitalized child-production industry. This industry is staffed with distracted, stressed-out workers and poorly trained managers. It emphasizes production quotas, not quality. The industry's one-size-fits-all approach ignores market needs. As a result, the industry is spending more and more on recalls, on removing life-threatening products from the road, on fixing what should never have been broken in the first place.

Between 12 and 22 percent of the nation's children are suffering from some type of mental or emotional disorder, such as depression, hyperactivity, chronic drug use, anorexia, and so on, according to the National Academy of Sciences' Institute of Medicine. It's unclear whether there is more mental illness among children than in the past, or whether diagnosis and reporting have improved. What is clear is that as kids come down the line, they aren't getting the help they need from parents, schools, and mental health professionals. Only about a third of kids suffering some kind of mental disorder are receiving professional treatment.[1]

This is true even though our ability to understand, prevent, and treat many of the mental diseases of youngsters has greatly improved in the past twenty years. As a result of this neglect, an increasing number of kids simply self-destruct. Suicide among children aged ten to fourteen rose 112 percent from 1980 to 1985, according to a study published this year by researchers at Johns Hopkins University. One out of every three eighth- and tenth-graders (25 percent of the boys and 52 percent of the girls) surveyed in twenty states said they had seriously considered killing themselves, according to the national Centers for Disease Control.[2]

Why aren't these children getting help?

First, as a society we don't place much of a premium on the mental or emotional health of children. Most school counseling programs focus more on academic achievement than on the emotional well-being of the child. Second, outpatient mental health care is too expensive or unavailable. Fourteen million children in this country are not covered by private health insurance. And private insurance often fails to cover outpatient treatment and family counseling.

What private insurance does cover is hospitalizations. So some of the damaged kids roll off the assembly line and directly into the shop for an overhaul — even if they don't need it. Adolescent psychiatric care is the fastest-growing segment of the hospital industry. Nationally, total psychiatric admissions of patients under eighteen have more than quadrupled since the early seventies.[3] The average age of admission to state psychiatric hospitals for children is declining. Turn on the radio these days and you'll hear commercials for some of these hospitals that go something like this: "Is your teenager acting like a jerk? Bring him on in; we'll fix him!" According to a study by researchers at the University of Michigan, two-thirds of children in private mental hospitals are hospitalized for relatively minor personality disorders and nonaddictive drug use.

"We have at least one or two calls a week from families that are having difficulty with their children," said Jim Lanez, director of the Maude Carpenter Children's Home in Wichita. "A lot of them are wanting to get the child into our residential program. In many cases, we advise family counseling rather than placement of the child. But a lot of families don't want to go through the counseling themselves. They just want to place their kid with us and have us fix their kid."

Nearly 500,000 American children now live in hospitals, detention facilities, and foster homes; that number is expected to climb to more than 840,000 by 1995.[4]

The institutionalization of so many children, however, does not mean that the children who most need help are necessarily getting it. Many of the children from uninsured or underinsured families who most need care are being deinstitutionalized because there's no room at hospitals. For children under twelve, state psychiatric wards are suffering from what some mental health professionals call "kidlock" — too many children, too few beds, and no place to put the kids after they have received treatment. Some states are attempting to shift child psychiatric care from the hospital to community-based residential treatment centers. However, few such treatment centers are actually being built. Many mental health officials suggest the establishment of community day-treatment centers for children, but this support system is not being built either.

One mother told me of her frustration and anger at her health insurance company. Like most, it pays for temporary hospitalization for a child in a mental health crisis, but not for long-term residential care.

"At the end of this month, the hospital is going to kick my fifteen-year-old out," she said. "He's suicidal and borderline psychotic. The insurance only covers him in the hospital for sixty days." What happens after her son is discharged from the hospital? "The insurance company tells me that in order to get readmitted, he has to get in trouble again — maybe attempt suicide." In a letter of denial, the insurance company suggested that if "intensive parental supervision" couldn't handle the problem, the legal system could. "We've been in intensive family counseling and private therapy for two years and eight months. How much more intensive parental supervision do they want? What they're saying is, 'We're washing our hands of your son.'"

What happens to the kids who should be getting serious help? Many of them are scrapped, pushed out of the home and onto the street as runaways or throwaways. Many children truly in need of care will likely receive no residential treatment — they'll be back home or out on the street in a pattern that is a sad echo of the fate of homeless adults who were deinstitutionalized from psychiatric wards during the seventies and eighties.

Other children are piled up in a juvenile justice system that serves a purpose similar to that of those vast automobile graveyards at the edges of cities. Each year about forty-nine thousand children and youths are held in public youth facilities, and thousands more end up in adult prisons. In California, although criminal activity among adolescents appears to have been on the decline since the early seventies, the state is incarcerating substantially more youths in state and county facilities.[5] Many of the youths in the juvenile justice system have diagnosable mental disorders, but receive no diagnosis or treatment.

In America, there are more college-age black men in jails than in school. The ultimate institutionalization of childhood is prison.

The larger issue, however, is the emotional well-being of children in general — their right to happiness, and the need to refocus on preventing so many emotional problems from occurring in the first place.

Increasingly, children themselves are being asked to take responsibility for the emotional health of their peers. For example, a handful of pioneering schools across the country are making real inroads in decreasing drug and alcohol abuse among children and teenagers. They target student leaders, especially athletes, and train them as role models and drug counselors. In these schools, abstinence from drugs is a requirement for extracurricular programs, and trained student leaders help enforce the rules, even to the point of turning in their fellow students. The peer programs are built around a process of getting kids to talk openly in a relaxed, student-controlled setting in the presence of a drug-abuse expert. When a student turns in another student, or turns himself in, the offender receives counseling, not punishment. At some high schools, as much as a 90 percent reduction in alcohol use by senior athletes was recorded in a six-year period. The drop was greater in lower grades: at one junior high, eighth-grade usage dropped from 38 percent to 2 percent.[6]

In San Diego, at Bell Junior High, I visited the peer-counseling program overseen by Mary Olbersen, a particularly dedicated and compassionate teacher.

"Kids often feel intimidated about approaching adults," she said, "especially if they have a teenage problem that they feel no adult is going to understand. But students can be trained to listen to other students." At Bell, students can take the counseling course taught by Olbersen as an elective, or they can be recommended to it by teachers. "We look for students who have leadership abilities," said Olbersen, "though they may not have been using those abilities in constructive ways." She motioned to her class. "This group, for instance. You would not want to say they are angels."

A wave of giggles went through the class.

"We wear badges," explained one of the boys, a ninth-grader. "Little I.D. badges in the school colors, blue and white."

A girl said: "Sometimes the kids come up to us in the hall and tell us their problems. Sometimes you're late to your class because you're standing there talking. Every day, at least one kid comes up with a problem."

What kinds of problems? I asked.

"Drug problems," said a girl wearing jeans. Thick eyeglasses were perched on her nose. "Boyfriend and girlfriend problems, sex problems, maybe they're thinkin' of killing themselves."

The teacher interjected: "There are a few issues which the peer counselor is required, by law, to report." Any evidence of child abuse, any talk of suicide, any signs on campus of drugs or alcohol influence must be reported.

"One of my friends stayed home from school because he was scared to come 'cause he was all beat up," said one of the girls. "He'd walk up to the top of the hill because he was scared of his father, and then he'd watch his father leave and then go back home. He didn't take out the trash so his father beat him up, punched him in the face and threw him against the wall. At first I felt I was really being mean to report my friend, but I thought, He could be killed from this, so I should report it now."

Did he know she was going to report it?

"Not till after I did it. A social worker went to his house and discussed it with his parents."

How did he feel after she had reported the abuse?

"He was mad at me. He started rumors about me. Every time I was around him: 'You're a liar, I hate you, I can't stand you, you're ugly.' But after a while he came to me and said he was sorry, because he knew I had to do it. He just keeps reminding me, saying, 'Thank you, I needed the help.' "

The training includes lessons in decision making, the effects of illegal drugs, basic counseling, role playing. Sometimes the kids bring a problem they have confronted back to class and seek the group's advice. The basic peer-counseling rule is this: When counseling other kids, don't tell them what to do; tell them their options.

One boy in the class was wearing a glove on one hand in the approximate style of Michael Jackson. It was a gray wool winter glove. He raised the gloved hand and said: "People in this class realize we have to set an example for the rest of the kids. Adults look up to us, too, to help them."

Adults?

"Sure. Sometimes a teacher might say, 'What do you think I should do about this kid? I can't stand him anymore, get him out of my face.' "

So now children, already overburdened with adult responsibilities, are asked to be their brothers' and their sisters' keepers. One way or another.

We watch the video images of the latest sniper and we say to ourselves, Where are all these crazy people coming from? Well, unlike automobiles, children always pass on abuse they've suffered, one way or another. From 1983 to 1987, according to FBI records, arrests of Americans under the age of eighteen for murder jumped 22.2 percent, for aggravated assault 18.6 percent, and for rape 14.6 percent — compared with a 2 percent decline in the total number of teenagers in the United States since 1983. On it goes, from generation to generation. According to a study by Johns Hopkins University, the leading cause of injury death among children under the age of one is homicide.[7]

The common-sense alternative to perpetuating abuse and violence would be to establish a supportive system that helps parents and children from one end of the line to the other. In the daily life of children, the most important goal should not be surround-care, but surround-love.

Preventive approaches do not work with every mental illness, but early intervention can make all the difference for some balanced on the razor's edge. In the absence of support, some kids try to fix themselves, often with disastrous results. Psychiatrists and psychologists sometimes characterize adult drug or alcohol abuse as self-medication, but one seldom hears this characterization applied to child or teenage drug or alcohol abuse. How much of the substance abuse among young people is actually self-medication?

Indeed, though school psychologists and counselors can't do all the healing, they could do more of it if someone would let them. "We have fifteen hundred gangs in San Diego. Why? Because gangs give the kids the feeling of belonging and acceptance that they crave," said Dr. Barry Worthington, president of the San Diego City Schools Psychologists Association. He suggested that schools offer kids "places where kids could talk about their feelings and be heard. We don't allow kids to talk. We tell them to sit down and shut up." Teachers often make the crucial difference in a child's emotional health, but teachers are too often overburdened. Said Worthington, "I've been in a classroom where a kid was sitting there with a belt buckle mark in the middle of his forehead, and the teacher hadn't noticed."

Today, typical of school systems around the country, only 60 full-time psychologists are responsible for 115,000 students enrolled in the San Diego Unified School District. "Last week I dealt with four kids who talked about suicide," said Worthington. "A few days ago, one girl actually slashed her wrist in class. Yet school psychologists still don't have a place to work in the schools and aren't respected by the school administration. I've worked in the back of a boys' bathroom, in broom closets, on auditorium stages. As in most of the country, we're almost prohibited from doing real counseling because we're buried in paperwork. The district is making us into piece workers: 'How many tests did you give today?'

"One girl told me that whenever she came to see me, she felt that she was bothering me because I was always testing and had so much paperwork to do. Sometimes I even felt guilty for taking the time to talk to her."

Later, this girl committed suicide on the way to school.

"Suicide is just aggression turned inward. These highly intelligent kids are cutting themselves with razor blades to ease the aggression they feel. I've had kindergartners run out in traffic and try to kill themselves. Very few of these kids are actually mentally ill. Suicide isn't built into them. They're reacting to something in their family; the kids are losing their families and their families are losing them."

What about all the school counselors out there? Surely they're helping kids deal with their psychological stresses? Not necessarily. Around the country, school counselors are going the way of school librarians and school nurses (considered expensive frills by too many school boards), or they focus increasingly on academic guidance rather than on the emotional lives of children. In elementary schools, where they're needed most, counselors are almost nonexistent.

A few decent-hearted organizations have insisted that schools attend more to the emotional needs of children. The Kiwanis Club, for example, raises tens of thousands of dollars each year for a few pioneering counseling centers in elementary schools. In Coronado, California, the local Kiwanis Club pays the part-time salary of the one counselor working in Coronado's three elementary schools.

"Think what these kids could accomplish if their emotional health was dealt with in school a couple hours a day," said Dennis Buckovetz, president of the Coronado Kiwanis Club. "Seems to me that mental health has something to do with academic achievement."

How are the Kiwanians raising money to hire the school psychologist?

"Individual donations," said Buckovetz. "And we sell hot dogs."

Does attention to the emotional well-being of children now depend on how many hot dogs the Kiwanians can sell?

As fine as this effort is, the absence of a far wider public effort suggests a disturbing lack of public understanding of the forces shaping childhood today. Yet if a group as traditional as the Kiwanis Club can so clearly see the need to weave a new web, perhaps the rest of the country is not far behind.

12

The Nature of Childhood

●

The natural world is the larger sacred community to which we all belong. We bear the universe in our being even as the universe bears us in its being.

— Thomas Berry, *The Dream of the Earth*

The natural world is the ultimate web, and essential to the emotional health of children.

Just as children need positive adult contact and a sense of connection to the wider human community, they also need positive independence and solitude (as opposed to ongoing isolation) and a sense of wonder. In the past, nature has offered this to children, or at least to most of them. But the children and parents I spoke with described a radically changing relationship between children and nature.

During my visit to Swarthmore, my friend Ralph Keyes and I went for a walk through the surrounding neighborhoods. To get home, we passed through a wooded area and crossed a little creek, stepping across large flat stones. It was spring, and the trees in the damp Pennsylvania countryside were still budding. As we crossed the creek, I looked north along the wavering line of water and dead leaves, into the gray trees. For an instant, as still happens in that part of my mind which still exists in childhood, I imagined Mohicans crouching. These fantasies still jump up sometimes, and I am both embarrassed and pleased at their presence. Tadpoles in the shallows scattered, making arrows in the water. I asked Ralph if his son, David, ever came down to these woods, and he said: "No, never. He's just not interested. He's interested in baseball and organized sports. I don't know if any of his friends come down here either."

I thought about this, on the way home, wondering how much our adult relationship with nature has to do with the fantasies we bring to it as children. As a child, I brought cowboys and Indians and Davy Crockett and war to the woods. They were prepackaged fantasies, and often violent, but most of them did attach human beings to nature, and served as doorways into unpackaged mysteries. Sometimes, at age eight or nine or ten, I would be in the woods alone with my BB gun, intent on shooting something (but succeeding only once), and I would end up sitting beneath a tree or next to the creek, listening, touching my finger to my tongue and wetting my nostrils so that I might be able to smell better, listening, breathing, watching for the small critters to reemerge, the frogs' eyes to pop up once again above the sheen of water. How many children of the fifties and earlier eventually became environmentalists, or otherwise deeply concerned with the fate of nature, in this way? Walking silently with Ralph, I wondered how the current generation of children will relate to nature in the future. What fantasies will they bring to it, what doorways in it will open for them?

Today's relationship between children and nature is a puzzling one.

On the one hand, children's sophistication about global environmental issues is very high — and intensely felt. On the other hand, they have much less physical and unstructured contact with nature. In the early eighties, an advertisement began to appear in national magazines which showed a little boy silhouetted in front of a cabin window, tapping at a computer terminal. Beyond the glass, trees could be seen, and a sailboat moved lazily across a pond. Could it be that, in the era of the bogeyman and Lyme disease, computers are viewed as more important to a child's life than access to nature? In southern California, Girl Scouts can attend a "High Tech–Computer Whiz" camp that has $50,000 worth of terminals and software. With the steady erosion of farmland and woods and streams and fields adjacent to housing, the increasing programming of children's time, and the evolving fantasies and obsessions of our national culture, nature — for children and adults — is becoming something to wear, to watch, to consume. We sport IRRESISTIBLE SEA OTTER T-shirts and view nature "mood videos" in which electronic images of streams flow to relax and distract us while the forests are cut, the sea despoiled, and hilltops decapitated to make room for more malls.[1]

A few years ago I interviewed Robert Stebbins at the Museum of Vertebrate Zoology at the University of California–Berkeley. He is an old man now and something of a legend. For more than twenty years Stebbins's book *A Field Guide to Western Reptiles and Amphibians,* which he illustrated as well as wrote, has remained the undisputed bible of herpetology, inspiring countless youngsters to chase snakes.

"We've got to teach children and young people that we're related to every living thing, even the AIDS virus," he told me. "Maybe that's an unfortunate example. We're not sure viruses *are* alive."

For a decade, Stebbins and his students drove to the California desert to record animal tracks in areas frequented by all-terrain vehicles (ATVs). Over the years, Stebbins discovered that 90 percent of invertebrate animal life — insects, spiders, and other arthropods — had been destroyed in ATV-scarred desert areas. When I spoke with him, Stebbins dropped scores of slides into an old viewer. "Look," he said. "Ten years of before-and-after photos." The pictures showed grooves and slashes, tracks that will remain for centuries; desert crust ripped up by rubber tread, great clouds of dirt rising high into the atmosphere; a gunshot desert tortoise, with a single tire track cracking its back; aerial photographs taken near Blythe, California, of ancient and mysterious Indian intaglios, carved images so large that they can only be perceived from the air. Across the flanks and back and head of a deer-shaped intaglio: claw marks left by ATVs.

Looking at Stebbins's slides, I wondered whether this destructiveness was simply the inevitable product of growing population, or whether our culture is producing a succession of generations with increasing disregard for their environment. This destruction amounts to a kind of species self-hatred, like lemmings throwing themselves over a cliff and calling it fun — the environmental equivalent of slam dancing. (In Missouri, river riding is a popular pastime: gunning big-wheeled all-terrain trucks down the middle of rural streams.) "If only these people knew what they were doing," said Stebbins. What upsets him most is not the destruction that has already occurred, but the devastation yet to come, and the waning sense of awe toward nature — or so it seems — that he senses in each successive generation.

Part of Stebbins is still a boy ranging through the Santa Monica Mountains, calling in the owls. For him, the world is still magical. "One time I was out watching the ATVs. I saw these two little boys trudging up a dune. I went running after them. I wanted to ask them why they weren't riding machines — maybe they were looking for something else out there. They said their trail bikes were broken. I asked them if they knew what was out there in the desert, if they'd seen any lizards. 'Yeah,' one of them said, 'But lizards just run away.' These kids were bored, uninterested. *If only they knew.*"

Stebbins's words returned to me when I read newspaper accounts of the boys who went "wilding" in New York's Central Park, raping and nearly killing a young woman. They exhibited behavior similar to that of some off-road vehicle users — the disrespect for life, the ignorance of consequences. But then, most of the current movie heroes are like that: machine-men who roll over whatever confronts them, running tracks right up life's spine.

Parents speak often, and sometimes defensively, of this strange divorce between children and the outdoors. One woman said: "It's all this *watching*. We've become a more sedentary society as a whole. VCRs, videos — all these machines that kids sit and watch. When I was a kid growing up in Detroit, we were always outdoors. The kids who were indoors were the odd ones. We didn't have any wide open spaces, but we were outdoors on the streets, in the vacant lots, playing baseball, hopscotch. We were out there playing even after we got older." Willie Thigpen, a physician, added: "Something else was different: our *parents* were outdoors. I'm not saying they were active like yuppies today, as far as joining health clubs and things of that sort, but they were out of the house, out on the porch, talking to neighbors. As far as physical fitness goes, this is the sorriest generation in the history of the United States. Their parents may be out jogging with their earphones on, but these kids aren't outside."

Another mother spoke movingly of a nagging, repeated dream: "Sometimes I dream that I am one of my own children, and I think to myself, What am I going to do today? In my dream, I go out to the back yard to play, but I've covered every square inch of the back yard before, and I cover it again in this dream. When the dream ends, I wake up feeling dissatisfied, as if I have played in my dream, but I haven't really played. It's a feeling of never being able to get beyond the back yard." This woman and her husband were planning to leave the constraints of San Diego, with its overcrowding, its overpriced houses with postage-stamp yards and dwindling access to nature, and were headed for Eagle, Colorado, where "kids can play in the fields and in the trees like kids used to, and where people actually feel safe enough to let their children out to play for hours — you know, normal, everyday behavior. Not like in my repeating dream."

I would have suspected, during my interviews in Kansas, that children there would still be playing in the woods and along the streams. But the middle-class parents of Overland Park viewed such activities as a vanishing part of childhood. Laura Beth Clark said: "No, they're not too interested. Even when they go skiing in Colorado down a beautiful mountain on a perfect, quiet day, they've got their headphones on. They can't enjoy just hearing nature and being out there alone. They can't make their own entertainment. They have to bring something with them."

She added: "Of course, we discourage them from going out in the woods alone. But we're trying as a family to encourage our kids to love nature. We take them camping, we try to get them to go on bike rides and walks. We even pitch the tent in the basement in the winter when it's too cold to pack or go outside."

Kathy Tuel said: "The only time the kids associate with nature is when it's a science project. They had an assignment in seventh grade — every morning at a certain time they had to go away from the house, somewhere they could be alone with nature and write things down. And that's the only time that they really would venture off on their own to do something like that — because it was an assignment."

I asked Kathy's husband, Mike, who on other topics had often disagreed with the group, how his kids related to nature.

"They don't. Very little. Very little."

"Don't say that," said Kathy. "They love to fish and boat and all that."

"Yeah, but they don't go out alone or in groups of kids," said Mike. "We used to live by a lake and we'd spend a lot of time out there fishing, but it was because the lake was there, it was something to do. If we lived by an amusement park they'd go do that because it would be handy."

One of the mothers, Bev Hughes, was perplexed. "I don't really know what you mean. I think that my girls enjoy a full moon, a pretty sunset, and flowers. They enjoy the trees when they turn. That sort of thing. I don't know what else you mean."

I clarified the question: What I meant was being *engaged* with nature — free, with time to connect with it, time to bring fantasies to nature.

"Let me address that," said Jack Hughes, who was raised in a farming community. "What you're talking about is something that's totally different today. Where I grew up you were outdoors. No matter which direction you went, you were outdoors — it was a plowed field or woods or streams. You couldn't walk a quarter of a mile without getting into something like that. We're not like that here. Overland Park is a metropolitan area now. The kids don't see that type of thing around here as much. They see houses being built. They see progress. What about these kids who grow up in New York? They've never even seen woods. They haven't lost anything because they never had it in the first place. What you're talking about is the transition that you made and I've made and most of us that grew up surrounded by nature made, and now it's not there."

The group was quiet for a moment. I was incredulous at this description of the use of the surrounding countryside in Overland Park. Yes, much of the farm land and woods were being graded and built on, and yet one could see woods from the windows of the house in which we were sitting. It was still there. Something other than simply a lack of access was keeping their children away from nature.

Kathy told this story: "When our kids were in third or fourth grade we had a little field behind us. The kids were complaining about being bored. And I said, 'Okay, you guys are bored? I want you to go out to that field and spend two hours. Find something to do there. Just trust me, just one time try it and you might enjoy yourselves.' They begrudgingly went out to the field. And they didn't come back in two hours — they came back much later. And I asked them why. And they said: 'It was so much fun! We never dreamed we could have so much fun!' They climbed trees, they watched things, they chased each other, they played games like we used to do when we were young. So the next day I said, 'Hey, you guys are bored, go to the field.' And they answered, 'No, we're already done that once.' They weren't willing to let themselves do it again."

From Streams to Screens

Perhaps too much can be read into these statements. Many children of the fifties, and earlier, chose not to have any contact with the natural world — they preferred their rooms, their basements, their friends' houses, their yards, their urban museums and back alleys (though back alleys and vacant urban lots could be considered a form of the natural world), and many of them grew up to discover nature as adults. (Some of the envionmentalists who have written the angriest and most persuasive essays against the destruction of nature grew up in the most urban of neighborhoods.) And yet, one senses among parents and children that something has changed in kids' relationship to nature.

One of the fathers in Overland Park said: "Our kids and the neighbor kids rush into the house and they head straight for the video games. It's almost like the house with the most kids in it is the house with the best Nintendo cartridges." Another mother added, "We can't get some of our kids' friends to come to our house because we only have kids to play with."

All these screens in children's lives can reverse the very polarity of childhood reality. One fourth-grader told me, "I like to play indoors better 'cause that's where all the electrical outlets are."

When I asked sixteen or so gifted students, third- to sixth-graders, in a class at Dewey Elementary in San Diego — children who spoke at length of their relationship with computers — how many would rather be outside with nature instead of working on their computers, twelve raised their hands. Kyre said, "With the computer I just have to sit there and I just press buttons and move the joystick around, but when you're outside you don't just sit there and move your hands 'cause you're actually outside and you're doing something." Another girl, pragmatically, said it all depended on the weather. "It's kind of a toss-up. But a computer will always be there as opposed to the good weather."

Paul, the future programmer with thick glasses, talked of his sense of isolation outside. "Me and my sister live on this street where there are not very many kids, there's no one really to play with if you want to go outside and play baseball or something. With the computer you can do things by yourself, and you don't need someone else to play with you."

And Ben, grinning, added, "For me it's a draw because no matter what I'm doing, whether it's spending time in nature or spending time on my computer, I'm going to run into bugs!"

Some experts on child's play contend that the movement from streams to screens is part of an ongoing evolution of play. Brian Sutton-Smith, a professor of both education and folklore at the University of Pennsylvania, is one of the leading experts on play. In an essay for the Please Touch Museum, he writes: "American children's freewheeling play once took place in rural fields and city streets, using equipment largely of their own making. Today, play is increasingly confined to back yards, basements, playrooms and bedrooms, and derives much of its content from video games, television dramas and Saturday morning cartoons."

The industrial revolution of the eighteenth and nineteenth centuries slowly removed economic and social life from home. Whereas children and adults had once spent their days and nights together, parents began to travel beyond the home to work. "Children were often left to run wild in streets or hills and to carry on the play that had been part of the earlier communal festivals," writes Sutton-Smith. "In the 20th century, this control over play has been increased still further, first by playgrounds and gymnasiums, and more recently through organized activities (swimming, tennis, dancing, sports), consumer entertainment (movies and shows) and, finally, through that most controlling of all instruments, television. . . . The shift in play has been steady: a taming of most violence; mechanization of toys, increasingly electronic in character; symbolization in games of language, information and strategy, which have largely replaced rough physical play; decreasing differentiation between play of boys and girls; increasing remoteness from direct experience through fantasy; and, most significantly, isolation."[2]

Some of this recent change in play is welcomed by many parents.

As I watch my older son enter grade school, I remember the fist fights, the dog-piles, the mud balls packed with gravel, much of the cruelty of a fifties boyhood in Raytown, Missouri. Certainly physical combat is still the dominant rite of passage in some neighborhoods, particularly inner-city communities, where violence escalates as economic and social conditions deteriorate. Yet many parents remarked that physical combat among children has been replaced by other forms of competition: organized sports and the battle of material goods — Jordache versus Lee, Reeboks versus Keds, Apple versus IBM. Still, if the forces shaping child's play today decrease children's free access to nature, those forces ought to be challenged.

Nature offers children a world separate from that of parents; it gives children a sense of their place in time. Unlike television, nature does not steal time from parents and children; it augments and enriches that time. For those children for whom family life is destructive, exposure to nature can offer healing. Nature nurtures creativity in children, in part by demanding visualization, the full use of the senses, from them.

Although children are spending less time physically in natural surroundings, they also seem to worry more about the disappearance of nature — in a global sense — than my generation did. At Kenwood Elementary in Miami, most of the fourth-graders in one class said they would rather play in their houses or on the streets. I asked them if they thought kids would play in the woods or the fields in the future. One boy, who had earlier said his ambition was to be an astronaut, offered, "Maybe, but not if the city keeps on making these new ventures, making new buildings and tearing down all the wilderness."

Among the other answers:

"I'm pretty worried, 'cause if all the nature goes, there's just going to be buildings and there won't be fresh air and people will probably get a lot more sick without the fresh air, all the smoke is going to go in the air and all the pollution is going to go in the water, and probably the earth will get more destroyed."

"There might be nature, but there'll be so many buildings that they might have really thick parks, they might put woods there and put animals there that are beginning to be extinct — not like zoos, but really big forests for animals. And people can go there and hunt deer."

"In the future if they tear down all of the woods and stuff there may be another planet where they have all wilderness and they take the animals, like in a rocket or something, they take them to that planet. Like Noah's ark."

I shifted the subject. These kids were going to be in charge of the environment in the future. What did they think could be done?

"Tell people to take off the smokestacks of the factories so the air wouldn't be polluted, and invent a stove that would have no fire, and a boat that would fly up in the air so the water wouldn't be polluted, I would tell everybody to plant more trees and get more seeds for the vegetables for rabbits."

"If I was in charge, in one part you would have city and the other part, most of it would be forest and you couldn't pollute it and if you do, you would get punished. You could live in the forest too but you wouldn't be allowed to pollute."

"Some business people just care about their business and they don't really know anything about nature and they just want to build and other people can't really do anything because the other people are more in charge 'cause they're higher. And the people who care about nature can't really do anything even if they want to."

"Since people who want to make money maybe they could not make buildings but they could make money by planting nature, like planting trees."

"If people pull down nature, if they pull down all the trees to put up buildings, how they going to make their living if they can't use the trees to build their furniture?"

These comments, it seemed to me, expressed some surprisingly sophisticated environmental concepts.

As a boy, I was intimate with the fields and the woods behind my house, and protective of them. Yet, unlike these children, I had no sense of any ecological degradation beyond my small natural universe. Children today may be less intimately involved with nature than many of us were, but they exhibit far more global environmental awareness. The electronic world that disrupts intimacy with nature has also been used to communicate to these children nature's distress. I wondered, however, about the intellectualized quality of this awareness of nature.

An intimate connection to the natural world can give children a sense of freedom and imagination and wonder; that intimate connection is endangered. And yet . . .

The Gift

One of my journey's last midwestern stops was at Southwood Elementary School in Raytown, Missouri, near Kansas City. This was my elementary school. The same swings (or so it seemed) still creaked above the hot asphalt, the hallways still shone with the same linoleum tile, the same pint-sized wooden chairs, carved and deeply initialed with black and blue and red ink, sat waiting in the crooked rows.

As the teachers herded the children in from several classrooms, second through fifth grade, I unpacked my tape recorder and glanced at the ridge of blue-green elms moving slowly in the spring breeze. How often had I dreamed of those trees. . . .

I turned to the children packed into the room and felt suddenly that they might have been friends from my own childhood. There were fewer slogans on the T-shirts than I remembered seeing in other schools. The girls in this class, many of them, wore cotton print dresses. Perhaps this sense of continuity had to do with the geography of Raytown, which still exists on the edge of farm land and woods. Developers seem to have lost interest in it and moved west, on to Johnson County and Overland Park. Whatever the reason, this school and these children seemed suspended in time.

I began by telling them that I had gone to this school, that I had lived on Ralston Street, and that there had been a big woods behind my house. The woods were all gone now, replaced by a housing tract — in which some of these children might now live.

I told them I wanted to know how kids felt about nature. I asked, How many kids there spent a lot of time in the woods and fields? Almost all of them raised their hands. I was astonished. This was the opposite of the response in every other classroom I had visited around the country.

"Well, me and Brett, he sits right there, we have like an old swamp in our back yard and lots of fields," one boy said. "I have two horses and a goat and some chickens in my back yard, and a big tree house and a creek that runs through the woods, and we always follow it to a fork."

"Let me ask you a specific question," I said. "When you go out into the woods and the fields, what are the fantasies — the images — in your mind? What do you think about, who do you pretend to be?"

The answers came quickly.

Many of them were connected to science.

"I'm some famous mad scientist out looking for some frogs or something to stick in a new chemical to make the world explode or something."

"I feel like I'm a scientist and I'm looking for cures for diseases. And like I'm finding some secret passages."

Several children mentioned "National Geographic Explorer," the television program, which feeds the fantasy life of children.

"What I imagine whenever I go in the woods and go look for stuff is I'm one of the world's great explorers and I'm exploring something else. I'm trying to look for something."

"I pretend I'm one of those National Geographic Explorers and I catch all these animals. One time I took a frog home and my mom got pretty mad at that 'cause she doesn't like frogs."

Some imagined the cosmos, and other mysteries.

"Whenever I'm out in the woods I like to think about things like 'Star Trek' and space and how it can go on and on forever and things like the Loch Ness monster and Bigfoot and if they really are true."

I asked if anybody pretended to be a cowboy or an Indian in the woods. Only one boy said he did. "Me and my friends pretend we're hunters and get our BB guns out. We go shootin' frogs. I think of it like Vietnam or something." Boys in the back of the room whispered, "Yeah!"

But surprisingly few of the kids connected nature with violence.

The fantasies these children take into the woods are more indirect than mine were. Rather than being associated with the cowboys, Indians, and frontiersmen of my boyhood, their fantasies were more likely to involve technology, space, and — particularly for the girls in the class — family issues.

"I just pretend I'm my grandpa. I have a little pair of overalls down at my grandfather's. I put those on and I do the exact same work as he does and it makes me feel like I'm a farmer."

"Well, when I'm in the woods, I play like it's just a home. I just go back to the woods and like with all the trees gathered together, and some of the trees split, it sort of looks like a home."

One remarkable girl, a fifth-grader, was wearing a plain print dress and an intensely serious expression. She later told me she liked to write poetry, and that she wanted to be a poet when she grew up. She said, "When I'm in the woods, I feel like I'm in my mother's shoes."

Nature, for children, seems to work on at least two levels.

For some children it serves as a blank slate on which they may draw the fantasies supplied by our culture. On this slate children replay the conflicts of their environment and incorporate modern society's symbols in their experience of nature. Given a chance, children will bring this

outside world to the woods and fields and creeks, where they can examine it in peace. (Today's symbols, with the exception of Vietnam fantasies, at first seemed gentler, more gender-neutral, and less racist than
the ones my generation took into the woods, or at least that is what
Raytown youngsters suggested. But as I thought more about this aspect,
I realized that many of my childhood fantasies in the woods were, indeed, gentle ones, and so perhaps were the nature fantasies of others my
age — though we did not share them then.)

At a deeper level, nature gives children itself, for its own sake, not as
a reflection of our culture. In addition to the sense of freedom and fantasy, access to nature also gives children a sense of privacy, of being
separate from the adult world, in a place older than the adult world.

"I feel like I'm free and I can do what I want and it's my land."

"I feel like I just want to go get a whole bunch of wood and build my
own house as big as I want it and then I'd have all this land to myself,
and I could just kind of move out of my own home, and just visit my
mom, and I'd get my own job, and I'd feel more grown up."

"Whenever I'm out in the woods, it feels like that's where I should
go, like it's your home, and you can do anything you want to because
there's not hardly anyone bothering you. You have the woods to yourself."

"I feel like I'm getting away from my brothers and sisters and I'm just
away from the house."

"It's so peaceful out there and the air smells so good and it doesn't
smell like that polluted city air. I mean, it's polluted but not as much as
the city air."

The little poet said: "For me it's completely different there. It's more
peaceful and it's like you're free when you go out there, it's your own
time. It's better to me than watching TV because there's nothing really
you can learn from TV. But when you go back in the woods, it's like if
your brain's empty, you got everything back there. Sometimes I go there
when I'm mad and then just with the peacefulness I'm better. I can walk
back and be happy and my mom doesn't even know why."

I wondered, How did their parents feel about their going to the woods?

Several of the kids said their parents didn't want them going to the
woods because of fear of strangers.

"They don't feel real safe if I'm going real deep in that woods. I just
can't go too far."

"My parents are always worrying about me. I don't know why. And
like I'll just go and usually I don't tell 'em where I'm going so that makes
'em mad so usually I go without them knowing 'cause I just want to go

freely. Like I'll sit behind the tree or something, or lay in the field with all the rabbits."

"My parents worry about me a little bit when I go out to the woods, and sometimes I have to take my brother and sister, but I let 'em play where they want and I just go to my own area."

One boy said his father didn't worry about him in the woods, " 'cause when he was little, he used to get a whole bunch of his friends, they'd go real deep in the woods, they'd find these vines. They'd start swinging on the vines like Tarzan and stuff and he showed me how to do it and the vine busted when he was on it and he fell, and he was laughing and everything. It was pretty funny."

Finally, I asked if any of them had had a favorite woods or favorite field replaced by a housing development.

"Behind my house we have a field. There's a track and trail where you ride your bike. It used to have jumps that you can jump on your bike. We rode back there all the time, and there was a family of foxes that lived back there and we'd see them, and one time last year on the way home on the school bus we saw 'em. We hid stuff back there when we played hide and seek. We had tree houses and we had an underground place and we had this big vine that we swung on, went back and forth, it was fun, and they just tore that all down. . . ."

"We had a field," said another boy. "They were going to tear it down, so we had this meeting, and we sat in this real tall grass where nobody could see us and we all discussed what we were going to do. We said we wouldn't let 'em. We moved our hideout to right on the edge of the field where they started to build and we started just sittin' there and sayin' to them that this was ours but they just said, 'Sorry kids, we already planned this out to make houses here so you're going to have to find someplace else.' That made us really mad."

The face of the girl who wrote poetry seemed to flush as she spoke urgently: "I had a place. There was a big waterfall and a creek on one side. I'd dug a big hole and sometimes I'd take a tent back there or a blanket and just lay down in the hole and just look up at the trees and the sky and sometimes I'd fall asleep back in there. I just felt free, it was like my place and I could do what I wanted and nobody could stop me.

"I used to go down almost every day and then they just cut the woods down. It was like they cut down part of me because every time I went back there I'd find this stuff and bring it home and show my brother because he was too small to go back there. I was waiting just till he was old enough to take him back there to show him because I had been wanting to take somebody back there for a long time. I ran back there when they were starting to tear it down, to get my blanket from in this hole. I ran back there to get it and they'd already thrown it in the dump. And they wouldn't give it back or anything. I had my special little place and then they just cut it down before my brother was old enough to go and I stayed in my room for a week and wouldn't talk to anybody."

She stopped, eyes glaring, shining, wet.

I asked her where she went to get those special feelings now.

Her voice turned flat, secretive.

"I go back in another woods."

The image remained with me long afterward: the little poet lying on her old blanket in the woods, staring at the trees above as they swayed in the wind, wondering — pulling together the strands of creativity, watching her dreams take form in the branches above.

Now a little girl, overweight, with thick glasses, spoke in a dreamy, story-telling voice. Perhaps she was only caught up in the moment, perhaps not. "I had a special creek and there was a goose that always came there and would drink the water," she said. "And so the goose he kept on biting at my toes, and finally I just told him that he should start biting on the leaves. So I stuck leaves in his mouth, and they finally tore it down. And the goose was killed."

How did she know that?

"'Cause I watched 'em tear it up and one of the machines killed him."

We do not fully understand how much we wound children by our destruction of nature.

The preservation of nature should be among the essential goals of the new web, not only for the protection of the least tern, but also for the mental health and the creativity of children. And this stewardship should be focused especially on the woods and fields at the end of the block.

It touched me deeply that these children still felt the way I had about the woods, that this part of childhood was not lost for them, and that for others, perhaps, it was only misplaced.

Listening to them, I remembered how, from third to sixth grade, I had pulled out hundreds of survey stakes — wooden stakes with bright orange flags attached to them. I knew what they were for. The year we moved out of that neighborhood, the woods were torn down and a new housing development went up.

I asked the children if any of them had ever pulled out a survey stake. More than twenty of them raised their hands. Enthusiastically. And I laughed.

I told the kids it was almost time to leave and began to ask another question, but one red-haired girl, who had not yet talked, began to wave her hand frantically.

"Behind Ralston Street!" she exclaimed. "There's still some woods back there!"

No, they were all torn down. I was sure of it.

"But some of it *is* still there, and there's a park back there."

The boy next to her joined in excitedly: "They have a creek back there, it's a big field that we like to go out and play in. The other night we went out and played war out there. There's also ponds down there and some kid this winter, he tried to go ice skating, and he fell through. He was okay."

The red-haired girl traced a map in the air with her finger. "There's hedges and then Ralston's right over here and then a creek right here and then the field's right in here. There's a big house hidden away. It's *your* woods!"

I had other appointments after the class period. But I found myself driving toward Ralston. I was sure that the kids and I were talking about different places. Still, I drove back to my old neighborhood and looked for the woods. Maybe part of being a parent is finding and reliving your own childhood, through your children, and then letting it go.

The kids were right. There was a little park. But where most of my woods had been there were now houses. A handmade sign read CAP GARVIN PARK. I got out of my rental car and walked the length of the park. A dog was barking somewhere. Some glass and a 7-Eleven Big Gulp carton and a beer can lay in the grass. It was just a long field, located at the extreme end of where the woods had been. A few trees remained near the end of the field.

As I passed under one tree, I remembered walking in the snow there once with my father, who was now dead. He had his old army coat on and was holding an air pistol, and we were looking for rabbits, and I saw the trail of ungraceful tracks across the snow through the trees. Over to the left, a trickle of water ran where the creek used to be. The old creek had become a brook. I remembered falling through the ice of the creek, and standing in water up to my waist pawing at the snow-covered bank as my collie looked down.

This part of the field was covered with dandelions.

A few old trees were still there. Up in the branches were the remnants of a tree house built a long time before: just four boards, one of them marked with black soot and rusted nails. There had been a small tree house down in this section of the woods, not as big as the triple decker that my friends and I had built farther up where all the trees were now gone.

I came to the end of the park. It was marked off with barbed wire. Across the wire was the old farmhouse, hidden in the trees and brush.

There had been an old horse down near the swamp, deep in the woods below, and I would go down and stand on a fence to mount it, and ride it wherever it chose to go.

From the fence on, the woods were dark, thick. Maybe the swamp was still there down below where the dam had been broken out, where at dusk I had once seen, in one of those blinding flashes, a great heron lift on the air, lift up above the old silo that stared with vacant windows out across the swamp — watched the heron lift up into the air and then fade away in the distance. The dog was gone, too, but maybe that swamp and those woods and that silo still existed. Maybe that part of childhood still existed. But this was the end of the park. If I had still been a kid, I would have crossed the barbed wire and gone down there. But now I was an adult.

It was good to know that the best part of my childhood was safe. I turned and walked back to the car and as I passed the little sign, I thought, Here's to Cap Garvin, whoever you are.

PART III

Weaving a New Web

●

If we don't find a way to prevent the painful abandonment, abuse
and exploitation of children, we will spend the rest of our lives
building mental hospitals and prisons.

—Karl Menninger

Modern technology has been created by the efforts of people
using stores of abundance in increasingly complex patterns of
interdependence. Each time we use such a typical product of the
system as (say) a jetliner, we are trusting a vast army of unseen
collaborators in our journey — all those who designed, built, sold,
service, fly, guard, and guide the plane. One slip in the huge
operation, and it ends in disaster. . . . Any breakdown in this web
of social links makes us vulnerable, no matter what our individual force of will or play of ingenuity. The self-reliant test pilot,
strapped in his seat in the travel section of a jetliner next to the
dimmest bureaucrat, will die along with him if the maintenance
people have not done their work properly.

—Garry Wills, *Reagan's America*

Weaving

●

Can we reverse the unraveling of the web? Can we weave a new one?

Given what I have heard from parents and from children, I believe that we can. Many of them understand, probably better than most policymakers, the need for change — not only the need for particular programs, but a new public consciousness about childhood and family life, a new sense, personally and politically, of what is important and what is not.

The first indications of what may be — of what must soon be — a ground swell of concern began in the late eighties.

In September 1987, in the first national survey of its kind, a Harris poll asked Americans if problems facing today's children are more severe than when they were growing up. Three out of four American adults agreed. The Harris survey found that less than half of the public believes that most American children are basically happy, or get a good education, or live in a safe neighborhood. Among blacks, 84 percent believed that children's problems have grown worse.

"It is plain that the American people are ripe and ready for leadership to emerge that will call upon them for some sacrifice to make it possible for government and the private sector to take action at last on behalf of children," said Harris, announcing the results of the poll. "A majority of adults, between 73 percent and 86 percent, said they would be willing to have their taxes increased for programs to trace missing children, for drug-prevention programs, for public schools, for day care, and for parks and recreation programs. Bluntly speaking, I doubt that this result in the poll could have emerged five or six years ago. But the times are changing and perhaps more rapidly than might be imagined. . . . When you get numbers as high as these of American people who think such problems are on the increase, then, I say, watch out." [1]

The long rise in the divorce rate seems, at least for now, to be leveling off. Among many working women and working men, there is a dawning sense of the price of excessive careerism. We need to begin devising answers to the problems created by these dislocations, and to offer one another the gift of hope. "We had a series of shocks that came so fast we didn't have time to adapt," sociologist Andrew Cherlin of Johns Hopkins University has said. "They're not finished yet, but they have slowed to the point where we can begin to figure out how to deal with it all. There is, for example, a shift in sentiment away from divorce — a feeling that it treats women and children very poorly." Thomas Espenshade of the Urban Institute put it this way: "We may have reached a clearing in the woods where we can stop and look around a bit, assess the changes, and see what needs to be done."

Now comes the weaving of a new web.

We can begin with this truth: no one raises a child alone. Parents who assume that this is possible find themselves entrapped by loneliness and fatigue, and their children are all the more vulnerable to influences beyond their families. But parents who view the raising of children as part of a larger process, within a larger web, may be liberated — not *from* responsibility, but *by* responsibility.

Paradoxically, the more control we have over childhood's environment, the freer our children can become. The more time we spend with them, and the more free time and dream time they can experience; the more nurturing and gentler the environment outside our homes, the less we need to program our children's hours. The more care we take with the growth of cities, the more exposure our children may have to nature. The more we attend to our own values, the less concerned we need to be with the direct teaching of values to our children.

Many of the parents I spoke with reinforce these truths within their families. And yet, within the parent groups (and within myself) I often sensed a timidity, a vague confusion, a failure of nerve. Americans on both sides of the fundamental divide articulate a fear of action: a sense that, by supporting new family constellations, they may in fact move further from what they have known, or believe they have known.

How do we move beyond this paralysis? In using the term *family liberation* I have consciously chosen two words that, in the historical context of the past few decades, may seem contradictory. Also, each of these words carries its own cultural baggage. Many people on the cultural Right have, in the recent past, felt repelled by the word *liberation* because of its association with feminism and other movements. Similarly, some people on the cultural Left have felt uneasy with the word *family* because of previously narrow definitions of what a family is. But a new marriage of family, defined in the broadest possible way, and liberation, defined by what supports us rather than by what divides us, is what we need to break out of the paralysis created by the fundamental cultural divide.

I do not presume to suggest that what is to come will actually be called a family liberation movement. Recently I have heard the term "parents' movement." It is essential that parents begin to organize politically and personally, but they should be cautious about consciously or unconsciously excluding nonparents — singles, seniors, childless couples — from this coming movement. Some of us are parents; all of us belong to a family. As the following chapters will show, the success of a pro-child movement will depend not on its exclusiveness, but on its inclusiveness. All of us, conservative or liberal, parents and nonparents, can find common ground by pursuing personal and public policies that give families more time together. We may not always use that time wisely, but at least we will have more choice, more ability to focus on our children (or our elderly parents), to relax, recoup, regroup. More than money, love demands time. Parents also need more time with other parents, and more parental involvement in the institutions that serve our children. In pursuing better family life for everyone, a family liberation movement's specific goal should be to offer children and adults what they most miss: more positive contact with each other.

To weave the new web, we must reimagine our institutions and our cities. More immediately, we need a synthesis of traditional and contemporary values, a more realistic approach to family life. Weaving the web will demand uncommon personal and political contact among parents, a degree of exposure to one another that we have not experienced in recent years.

And the weaving will also demand quiet, unrelenting heroism.

13

Hope in
Hell's Romper Room

●

Coming into north Philly I could see trash and blight everywhere. A
few of the blocks were attractive, with little row houses painted in
bright colors; other blocks were burned out, boarded up. The school
was a three-story brick building, scarred and gouged. Parts of the school
were boarded up, peeling in great blue strips, and some of the school
grounds were fenced in with a high chain-link fence topped with
rolls of razor wire. The school's sign read JAMES G. BLAINE PUBLIC
SCHOOL. The M was missing, and beneath the name graffiti announced, ACE POLO KID, ACE.

Madeline Cartwright is the principal of this little school under siege.
Despite its disrepair, Blaine is a clean, scrubbed island — a safe zone.

Cartwright came here in 1979. She was forty at the time, and a former
teachers' union organizer. She grew up in Pittsburgh's poor Hill District,
and she was determined to make a difference in north Philadelphia, one
of America's most drug-ridden, devastated inner-city neighborhoods.

In this neighborhood, like so many other pockets of America, children
grow up in a violent poverty beyond what we have previously defined
as poverty. If a new web can begin to take hold here, it can be woven
anywhere.

"All they have is us, you know, that they can really depend on. We
come every day so they can depend on us. I don't miss a day for anything. I don't miss a day," Cartwright said. We were sitting at a folding
table in the school kitchen/cafeteria, next to a rumbling washing machine. Cartwright is a tall, forceful woman with a do-it-now philosophy.
She talked awhile, hands flat on the table, about growing up in the
projects in Pittsburgh. "We didn't just have poor people there. The rent

was arranged according to how much people made, so there were many, many role models. My mother always worked. My sisters, when they were old enough to get a job, they had a job. Some went to college. Everybody went to church."

Sometimes, Cartwright said, she remembers Fanny Q.

"When I was a girl, my clothes weren't always as clean as they should be. It's difficult for children to wash. You can't wash your dress every day. That's crazy! *You* couldn't wash your shirt everyday. You couldn't! But I did the best I could, and I kept the outer ones pretty good. There was this little girl who lived next door. Her name was Fanny Q. Can you imagine someone's name was Fanny Q? Fanny didn't have a mother. Her father wasn't as brave as my father, you know what I mean? She had a lot of disadvantages, many more than I had. By the time I got to be seventeen, Fanny Q was still behind the eight ball. And she'd remark about how nice my clothes were. And I'd say: 'Fanny Q, this skirt cost me forty-nine cents. And you smoke cigarettes. If you didn't smoke those cigarettes, you could take forty-nine cents and buy you one yard of material — that's all I got here, one yard of material.' And I said, 'I'll make you a skirt.' So Fanny Q listened and talked, but she never did bring me the one yard of material for forty-nine cents. She never had the kind of molding that it took to be successful.

"She was six feet tall, Fanny Q was, and twelve years old. One day, in class, the principal said to her" — Cartwright's voice boomed — " 'Fanny! You haven't been to school in two weeks! How come you haven't been to school!' Fanny Q said, 'Mr. Anderson, I don't have no shoes.' 'You don't have no shoes? It's because your feet are so big! You can borrow mine!' And the whole place just laughed, the kids were falling out of their chairs. And I looked at that man and I didn't laugh, and I looked at Fanny Q and she just cried and cried. And I wondered how that man could have said that to her. There's no way I'd treat a child like that.

"That principal inspired me. I said to myself that the Fanny Qs in *my* school are going to get help, not ridicule. I'm tellin' you, there's things you can do!

"What have these people got if they don't have us? One lady came to school and told me somebody stole her front door." She laughed disgustedly. "Took the door off the lady's *house*! A man sees this house, it's not in bad shape, just needs a door. So he takes this lady's front door and puts it on his vacant house. You go out and somebody steal your toilet while you're gone. I'm serious! They took one woman's television. While she was sitting there watching, a man walked right in, ripped it off. There was nothing she could do. The cops don't protect her. If I were to call the cops, they would come right now because the kids are in the school. See, they'd be afraid the newspapers would be here. But let school be over at four o'clock, and I get a call from a house across the street and a woman say, 'There's somebody beating me up,' and the cops ain't coming. There's no help for these folks."

Many of the people in the neighborhood, the ones not making out on the drug trade, live in some of the abandoned, burned-out houses surrounding the school.

"Our parents move up the street, down the street, across the street. Take a mother, she has one child. Welfare gives her a hundred and thirty dollars every two weeks, so she's making two-sixty maximum, from the welfare. Can she pay rent, two hundred and fifty, three hundred dollars? With that? So they just move and move. They live in these abandoned houses, no running water, with an electric wire that came from next door to their house. The kids take a two-liter soda container and go borrow water. That's how our children live. Many of our children don't have addresses. They don't have anything.

"The preachers and doctors and all the rest of the black middle class that once set examples for children, those people are all gone. I don't have enough working families to use as role models. So my role models are my welfare families who take care of their children, who keep a clean house, who keep the children dressed up, who send the kids to school. Now I'm seeing *these* role models go right down the crack drain."

A few days before my visit, a mother had walked into the principal's office at Blaine Elementary School and sat down and waited. The woman, her hair in frizzed-out tufts and her eyes bloodshot and bleary, wanted to know what to do with her child. She had no money to bury her daughter, who had died suddenly from a bad heart and lousy health care. She sat in the principal's office waiting.

"She didn't have enough money to bury her child. She had no money, she had nothing except a dead kid." So Cartwright made phone calls, helped the woman fill out papers, and disposed of the body of one of her brighter students.

"Another morning, a mother and four of her children were sitting at my desk, waiting for me. The mother says, 'What do I do now, where should I go?' Her daughter had died the day before. This girl, her brother shot her; he's on drugs. Fifteen years old. Double-barrel shotgun, he pulled both barrels. They were fighting with each other. I'd met this little girl in the third grade. Very hostile child, but she had an inner good. After a while you can tell who's hard-core crazy, and who's just surfacy crazy, and she was just surfacy. The mother asked me if I would go with her to the undertaker to see the child, because she said she was not so sure what the body would look like because he shot her in the face. And she wanted to make a decision as to whether she should have an open or closed casket, and she wanted me to help her make that decision. So we went.

"The little girl didn't look like herself, but she was not grotesque. And the casket was elaborate. How the mother could afford that, I don't know, unless it was drug money."

Cartwright looked out the window at the kids spreading out on the asphalt. It was recess time.

"I had asked this mother if her girl could come spend the summer with me, because I could see that there was nothing good in this kid's life. Nothing at all. The mother said no, so I dropped it."

The washer behind us had entered another cycle.

Not long after she arrived, Cartwright bought a washer and dryer for the school. She moved them into the kitchen/cafeteria, and each morning she and her staff personally wash many of the children's clothing. A Philadelphia chemical company supplies her with free soap powder.

This may be, she said, the only way many of the children in her school will know what it's like to have clean clothes. Her own son, Tyrone, a first-grader, attends the school, and she washes his coat right along with theirs. "Always. I never wash his coat at home. I wash it right here so they can see that Tyrone missed recess too because his coat was still in the dryer.

"This is one of the things you can do to bring about a change. My kids look *good*."

A few pupils, the offspring of dope dealers, come to school wearing gold chains and $200 bomber jackets and designer jeans. Cartwright washes their clothes along with all the other kids' ragged clothing.

"Just 'cause they have fancy clothes doesn't mean their parents know how to wash 'em!

"I've seen youngsters good in the first grades, and then all of a sudden they're *gone*. Won't do anything. I say, 'I'm going to call your mother.' 'Call my mother for what? She's on crack, what can she do?'

"So when the mother is cracked out, this child becomes the head of the household, feeding younger children. 'How you gonna tell me what to do when I had to find food for my brothers and sisters yesterday?' The mothers sell the food stamps to buy drugs.

"This one boy, not a day over fourteen, I washed him every day. He was from one of the ill-kempt families. Every day I washed him because they all slept together, they wet each other. He come to school smelling. Then one day, here was this child, standing there dressed up in a little suit. He was clean. He reaches in his pocket to buy a bar of candy — we had a candy sale that day — he takes out a wad of money and peels off a bill to buy a bar of candy for him and his sister. I said, 'Are you dealing drugs?' He said, 'I'm not telling you.' He just smiled and left.

"Out on the streets, kids ten, twelve, fifteen sell drugs. The drug pushers don't use adults as runners, they use children. They're carrying double-barrel shotguns; they keep the gun in the house so that if anything goes wrong with a drug deal, they have protection from the drug supplier. Two weeks ago, this kid was killed, drug pusher put a gun to his head and shot him — thirteen years old. They use these kids because there's no bail to get them out. The mother can get 'em out. So I don't allow any money in this building. We sell homework books for a dollar twenty-five, and we sell pretzels twice a week for twenty-five cents, and that's it. If they bring money, they have no business with that money and I'll take it. I don't give it back. If a youngster's dealing drugs, he can't do it in this building."

She led me down a bright hallway to one of the classrooms, where the walls were freshly painted yellow. On the teacher's desk there was a ceramic elephant with a JESSE JACKSON button fastened to it with a rubber band.

I asked the fourth-graders my usual first question: Was childhood better or worse today than when their parents were kids? At first the answers were surprising.

"I think it's better. Well, the girls had to wear skirts to school, and underalls, and we can wear pants."

"My grandma told me when she was back in those times, they only pay fifty cents where she worked. Fifty cents a day."

What kind of work did she do?

"Clay potting. She was back when Dr. Martin Luther King was living."

"I think it was better in those days than these days because there wasn't so many drugs," a girl wearing corn-row braids said. She was a pretty, delicate-looking girl with big eyes and a tiny voice with a fierceness in it. "It wasn't so trashy in the neighborhoods like now. They didn't have to worry about their children coming home late or nothing because back in those days, when the children just went straight home, it wasn't a lot of parties or anything and right now, they worry about their children getting kidnaped or hooked onto cocaine or something like that, or child abuse or something. My grandma said when she was a child my age they didn't have drugs like they do now and some kids they just get on drugs and they die from it."

"In my life, I see that if you get hooked on drugs, too bad," said a girl wearing a clean white pullover. "You could faint or die. Somebody in my family used to do drugs and they were glad they got off of it because the feeling they had every time they came home, they were throwing up and stuff."

A little boy said: "I have three uncles that's on drugs. One of them is on pot, the other one has a drinking problem, other one will try anything. My mother and my grandmother they're trying to quit. I keep telling my uncles to stop 'cause it will mess up their brains, and they won't be able to think right. I don't think they listen to me."

"On my block they got cocaine capsules all around the ground and the dirt," said the girl with the corn rows.

I had to bend over close to hear her.

"My friend, she was nine, picked up one of the capsules. She put it on her tongue and she swallowed it and then she went in the house and got some water, then came out and she started spitting out white and red blood and then she died."

"In front of you?"

"She just fell out on the street."

She looked down at the desk and didn't look up.

The kids told how they walk to school each day, their shoes crunching empty crack capsules; how they must pass the crack houses and the groups of young men selling dope on the corners. They told how they watched a favorite store where they bought candy go up in flames after, as one kid put it, "some men argued, and they had a bag of cocaine and they were pulling on it, and then one man took out this pouch of gasoline, and then he took a lighter and lit it." Another child told how one of the men had gone crazy one night, and "he raped his girl, her baby . . . the baby died, 'cause it fell on the back of his head. In glass."

"You saw this happen?"

"Yes."

They see it all happen. They're growing up in the real living room war.

One boy said, "My cousin Anthony sells drugs." Anthony, he said, was ten years old. "He delivers 'em for his dad. To adults. He steals stuff from people, like coats. He sells the coats to people to get the money and take it to his dead. He stole three watches from me. He stole my bike because he was delivering drugs once. He took my bike to a drug house."

Another boy offered, "There's this boy named Tyson that live down the street from my grandma, he shot hisself in the stomach."

Cartwright spoke up: "Tyson was selling drugs. When the supplier came for the money, he didn't have it, so rather than taking a chance that the supplier would shoot him, he shot himself. Tyson went to this school. He was fifteen or sixteen. He was a quiet youngster, always dressed very well."

All but three kids in the class said someone in their family was doing drugs.

What did they think about adults in general? I asked.

One of the girls said: "Even if they do it, I don't care if they do it or not, I've got respect for 'em. I know that they have a problem. I see the boys today, they throw rocks at them. They don't got no respect. I just say, they still people, they human beings, they have a problem and they need some help."

I was shaken by the stories these kids told. And I was amazed at what was still alive, deep in their eyes, still shining. Childhood.

On the way back to the principal's office, I mentioned this to Cartwright. She nodded, but said nothing for a few moments. Little kids were trailing her down the hall like baby chicks. Then she told me how a few months earlier some of her students, on the way to school, had looked up and seen a man standing on a front porch holding his wife's severed head in his hand, holding it up to show them like a trophy. The man had killed his wife in an argument over who would take care of the kids.

"But they're still children," said Cartwright. "Still children."

By fifth or sixth grade, the childhood starts to leave their eyes, and something else moves in.

Madeline Cartwright faces the fear in this neighborhood squarely, faces it down. Early on, she determined that the school was the heart of the neighborhood and as long as the heart beat cleanly, then the body around it had a chance — but that the heart could not beat without the body.

On the night after she arrived in north Philly, someone broke into the school and stole televisions, record players, basketballs.

"Next morning, I went right down to the street corner and told these young men: 'Somebody broke in last night and here's a list of what was stolen, and I'm the new principal, and I got a new Cadillac sitting right there in front of the school. See it? The payment on that Cadillac is two hundred and seventy-five dollars a month. I can't pay my car bill if I lose this job. How am I gonna look, first day on the job, if I got to call the superintendent and tell him somebody broke in? Whatever's in that building, if you want to use it, you let me know.'

"All that stuff was back on the front counter the next day. And they have not ever broken into this building and taken out anything since."

She pointed to the basketball court on the school grounds, at the young men out there *thump, thump, thumping* the ball.

"When I order basketballs for the school, I throw them a couple. They borrow stuff, record players, microphones, and they bring them back. I say to them and I say to my students, 'You may never own property anywhere else, but you own this school. *This is yours.*' "

She answers the office phone herself every morning.

"I read that a principal in Glassboro, New Jersey, improved attendance fifteen percent because he answered the phone. So I started answering the phone. I say, 'Good morning, this is the Blaine School, this is Madeline Cartwright.' They hang right up. Two, three minutes later, phone rings again. 'Good morning, this is Blaine School and still Madeline Cartwright.' Hang right up. Next time the phone rang, I said, 'Good morning, this is Mrs. Cartwright. If you're going to take off today you have to talk to me, you either talk to me or you come to school, simple as that.'

"This school is the *only* thing these kids can depend on. I tell the teachers, 'As old as I am, you haven't had any disease I haven't had, so you come to school, no matter what.' Snap! Teacher broke her leg, wanted six weeks off. No way I'm going to have that! So I said to her, 'I'll come and get you and I'll put you in a wheelchair and I'll roll you to class.' I says, 'You can write halfway up the blackboard. Guys come back from Vietnam who don't have any legs and they work every day. Some as teachers. You've got just *one* broken leg and you want to stay home?'

"When I rolled that lady down that hall in a wheelchair, the word went through the school the new principal's *crazy*. Best thing I ever did."

After this, attendance of teachers and students shot up.

The most important thing Cartwright did when she came to the school was round up people from the neighborhood and browbeat parents into getting involved in the school. At her first parents' meeting, the *Philadelphia Inquirer* reported, "the parents were spellbound and the teachers were dumbfounded by the size of the crowd, the first sign that things were changing."

"I told them this was my first school, and I came from the same cir-

cumstances they came from and that the sky is the limit. You can go as
far as you want and that I was there to help them take their kids as far
as they could take them. I said, 'Nobody apologizes for me being rag-
gedy when I was a little kid, so I don't apologize for my Cadillac.' I told
them I had to have the job to keep up the payments on the Cadillac, and
I could only keep the job as long as *they* helped me keep it.

"When I came in, this place was black as soot. I told the parents:
'This place is dirty! How can your kids go to school in a place like this?'
One of the parents said, 'You must think you're in the suburbs.' She
expected her neighborhood to be dirty. I said to her: 'The dirt in the
suburbs is the same dirt that's in north Philadelphia — if you don't *move*
it. And the same detergents work here.'

"I told the parents: 'We're going to clean this building this summer.
Raise your hands if I can depend on you. Keep your hands up! Somebody get their names!' So the first of July, eighteen parents showed up
here in their jeans and sneakers and rubber gloves. And we started to
clean this building, and we cleaned it, cleaned it good. I made these
parents know that you don't accept anything less than that which is
right because you live in north Philadelphia.

"The problem with parents in this type area is they feel threatened.
And also many of us as educators don't realize the real worth of parents.
We went through a period in the late sixties and seventies where the
federal program demanded parent participation. We put them on the
payroll. We had the problem of having to have input from parents who
really were not capable of giving quality input, so we started pushing
them back. But with the right parents involved you have a better school,
because teachers know the eye of the community is on them.

"Today, my auditorium is overflowing with parents. I make the children bring them. I say: 'You *must* bring your mother. Your mother has
to know what is going on here.' I give the students a doughnut or a
pretzel the next day if their mother came. Now, pretzels cost me nine
and a half cents. Very cheap.

"I'm telling you there's things you can do. I tell the children: 'All the
things that look like big problems to you are not big problems to adults.
You can't even *think* of a problem that I can't solve. So if you're having
a problem, come to me and I'll solve it for you.'

"Then I tell the parents at all the school meetings: 'If you are having
problems, you come to me. I can direct you to a place to solve these
problems. If you've moved and you don't know how to get your electricity going or your telephone on, come to me.' And they do. They
come. Parents come in and they feel at home, that's the first thing. We
have a parents' scholar program where we pay them to come. We give

them two hundred fifty dollars, and they come one time a week for ten weeks, and they volunteer in the classroom.

"My children are less abused because the parents around here know if they send that child to school dirty, that's neglect. I'm going to clean that child up. And I'm going to ask that mother, 'Why is this child dirty?' I'm not going to let it go. I'm going to speak right to it. They know that these kids tell me everything. And when these children tell me they've been hurt, I talk to the parents. I call them in. I don't go sneaking to call the child-abuse hotline, afraid to use my name. I call the parent and say, 'This child looks to me to be abused, so I'm going to call the child-abuse hotline, and when they come, you'll know I sent them.'

"And if a child isn't coming to school, I'll go into a home and bring kids out. I will! I'm scared to go by myself so I take a lady friend. One time we went down and we knocked on this door, and here stood this man, and he's talking to this little fourteen-year-old girl at the door. I said, 'Where's your mother?' She said, 'I don't know.' So I said to the man: 'Who are *you*? What are *you* saying to a fourteen-year-old girl?' So he said, 'Miss, I'm just trying to help.' And I said, 'What are you trying to help *do*?' He kind of got quiet, and I came into the house. I didn't find the mother. I found another girl, sixteen, and another man. And two little kids.

"This place was cruddy. I mean beyond anything I could ever imagine for little children to live in. The kitchen was a hot plate sitting on a drain board. I saw no refrigerator, there was no running water and no electricity, there were dirty dishes, food caked in piles, the bathroom had a bedspread wrapped around the bottom of the toilet. And the toilet was full to the brim with human waste. To the *brim*. And a little girl had one foot on one side of the toilet, and one foot on the other and she squatted over this toilet while she used it, and it was seeping over the sides.

"So I said to the man, 'You're gonna help.' He said, 'Well, I can't, I can't.' I said: 'You got a snake at your house? A plumber's snake? Can you go get it?' He said, 'You can't get no snake in there.' I said: 'Yes, you can. I'll get it started and *you'll* finish it.' I took a plastic container, maybe Ready-Whip or something, and we got buckets from the school, and we dug this mess out of this toilet and took it to a vacant lot. While we were in that apartment, we scrubbed the floors, took all the dirty clothes out, all the sheets off the beds, brought them back to the school, washed them up. And we left food for dinner, from our school lunch.

"The mother came home to a clean house and clean children. This lady had gotten so far behind the eight ball, she didn't even know where to go to get out."

Cartwright looked out at the playground again and at the trash-filled lots beyond it. "Sometimes, I wonder what happened to Fanny Q," she said suddenly. "Her sister, I know, was finally locked up. But I don't know whatever happened to Fanny Q."

Maybe there are a lot of Madeline Cartwrights out there, spinning the strand of dreams. They need encouragement.

The week I visited Blaine I also spoke with the officers of Philadelphia's parent-teacher organization. It had occurred to me that schools might adopt what could be called a Do It Now program, something like the Just Say No campaign. School districts could come up with a laundry list of things that could be done, *right now,* that would not cost a lot of money — the kind of things that Madeline Cartwright had mentioned, using student and parent volunteers. The philosophy might be: we can't wait for a great national philosophical transformation or a political messiah. Time moves too quickly in the children's time zone; we've got to do what we can now. Here's a list of suggestions — select what you believe is appropriate for your school, or your community, and do what you can with the tools you have available *now.*

I asked Philadelphia's parent-teacher officers, Would that kind of Do It Now approach work in Philadelphia's schools?

The response was silence. A long silence.

"Well, yeah, I think it could work. . . ."

And then they started talking about bureaucracy — "But you'd run into this problem, and then you'd run into that problem. . . ."

Cartwright's response, when I described this scene, was "I tell my staff: 'Don't tell me what I can't do. I can do something if I want to. It can happen.' It's like people say to me, 'You cannot wash this child's clothes.' I said: 'I have a problem, and I have a solution. I am going to take off this child's clothes, put 'em in the washing machine, and give him some clothes to put on. I can do that.'"

She described her dream of "infiltrating the neighborhood with role models." She wants the state of Pennsylvania to set up what she calls "mentor houses" — move salvageable families, mothers and children, into vacant houses in better neighborhoods, and appoint, even pay, families "with the right kind of values" to watch out for them. "I'd like to be a mentor," she said.

"There are vacant houses on my street. It's a good street I live on. I could bring some of these troubled families into my neighborhood, and then agree to watch out after them. I could cosign with the mothers to get those food stamps, and we could go shop with the food stamps, and when they get their money for their children, I could help them budget their money, so they could pay for the electricity and the gas, and keep those kids clean so they'd be proud of themselves. These mentors would have to be people who are not afraid to get their hands dirty. And why not pay these mentoring families, say, several thousand dollars a year?

"I have a little girl in mind right this minute. I think about her all the time. I guess I'd have a stroke or something if anything happened to her. She's a very pretty girl. And I say that because that's a disadvantage in this area. The pretty ones are preyed upon first.

"I've talked to a lot of people about this idea. I talked to a lady who keeps old people, and she began to tell me this zoning business you have to have, the fire regulations you have to have, in this house, but I'll work all that out."

She escorted me out across the playground.

The kids ran up, dozens of them reaching up and grabbing her and hugging her, and I could see the basketball players across the asphalt. They turned and watched, and one of them rolled the ball slowly in his hands. Cartwright said she knew a couple of them who snatched purses. She walked me out to the car. She wanted to make sure I got there safely.

I drove out of north Philly, past vast lots where the trash and garbage was knee deep, where every square foot of every flat surface was covered with graffiti, past beautiful old buildings with windows and doors covered with plywood or steel plates, past men urinating in the gutters; then into a more populated zone, past a corner store called People's Pharmacy (oddly, the name was written across the front wall in sixties psychedelic lettering and decorated with huge paintings of pills and capsules), past two men going through the trunk of a car, past a twenty-four-hour auto repair shop lit like a prison and surrounded by razor wire, past signs crusted over with rust. The faces of the fourth-graders seemed to rise, now, into the windshield, with the childhood still in their eyes. And then turning down Broad Street, I saw Philadelphia's City Hall with the statue of William Penn on top, silhouetted against the late afternoon sun. And I wondered, Can one person accomplish much, for long, alone? Yet this is the way the new web begins — not with grand political schemes, but with strong individuals spinning out their strands.

Maybe Madeline Cartwright's dreams are naive; maybe not. But they make a kind of mathematical sense: one safe and clean school, one set of clean clothes, one clean toilet, one safe house — and then another safe school — and another — and another.

"I'm tellin' you, there's things you can do!"

14

Reweaving the Family

●

During recent years, some Americans have viewed childhood's future as a purely private issue. Many of us have searched for personal exemption: if only we read the right how-to-parent books, if only we enroll our children in the right preschools, and on and on — then, we feel, our children will be safe. But even if we succeed for a while at sheltering our families, sooner or later our children will encounter those who have grown up without a web. At the same time others of us have viewed childhood's future as a collection of public policy issues: if only the government would increase the education budget, or declare war on poverty or war on drugs, then what threatens children — particularly poor children — will recede into the shadows. Certainly a vast public effort, much of it by government, is needed. But the truth is that we need both private and public change. In pursuing this change, no one class should be targeted exclusively. Each family needs to reevaluate its own private values — and recognize how those values shape part of the whole of childhood's future.

Many of the families I met are doing that.

Not far from Madeline Cartwright's little school in north Philadelphia, in upper-middle-class Swarthmore, the Fitzsimonses were cleaning up the breakfast table.

The kitchen was still filled with kids — all sorts of neighborhood kids, plus Tom and Beth's own, Devin, Biz, and Justin. Now Beth sat down at the table and asked Justin to call his grandmother and tell her about his pierced ear. "This has taught us a lesson: be careful what you promise," said Beth, turning to me. "If we had said he would get a Jaguar for getting on the honor roll, we'd be in *big* trouble now." She set her coffee cup down. "The ear-piercing only cost eight dollars. I guess the honor roll's worth it." She grinned. "But now we've got to break it to his grandmother. Gently."

A stranger meeting this family for the first time might incorrectly stereotype the Fitzsimonses as politically liberal and parentally permissive. Politically liberal they are; permissive they are not. Both worked for the civil rights movement, both came of age during a time of widening personal freedoms, both are feminists. But today they work hard to find a balance, for their children, between personal freedom and license.

For example, Tom and Beth do not allow their kids to spend time in the house without adult supervision. They believe that teenagers need after-school sitters as much as small children do. Beth admits that it helps, of course, to be able to afford after-school sitters, and that not everyone has that ability. Even so, this is one way they have consciously synthesized traditional family values with new economic demands.

Beth worked part-time until her youngest child, Devin, was three, and then went back to work full-time as an executive head-hunter. "Two parents *can* work and not neglect the kids," said Beth. "But it's a constant juggling act. We've had good luck so far. Good in-home child care has really been the hinge that everything else is attached to. Having a sitter in our house after school for the kids rather than sending them to an after-school program or day care works out to be more cost-effective, because there are three of them. Most importantly, we feel more in control."

"Three up, one down," said Tom. "We've had four child-care people. Three of them have been great, and one of them was — *hmm* . . .

"We pay well, you understand," said Tom. "We pay six dollars an hour, about four hours a day. Our friends and relatives have always thought we paid too much. If they're sick, we pay 'em. And we pay them for two weeks' annual vacation, even though they're part-time. We do this because we have to rely on them. If our baby sitter doesn't show up, we're really in trouble. So when we advertise, we get tons of responses. We discount the people who write in and tell us how clean they'll keep the house and how well they cook, but never mention children. One woman wrote that she liked children and didn't beat them much. . . ."

Out of the stack of letters, and later phone calls, Beth narrows the field to two people and arranges for personal interviews. "During the interview, the kids usually meet them for a couple of minutes, and sometimes we leave the room."

That day the Fitzsimonses had a new sitter, who was in *charge*. She ironed and cleaned (though these tasks were not part of her job description), and had laid down a new rule in the Fitzsimons house: when the kids and their friends were home, girls and boys could not go upstairs — only boys and boys or girls and girls together.

"She's the boss on that one," said Beth. "Not a bad rule at all."

Biz admitted that, all things considered, she's glad she has had a sitter, even as a twelve-year-old. "Most of them are nice. And you know, they really worry about you. They pay attention to you."

In addition to avoiding any latchkey hours, Tom and Beth ban television during the week — unless they make the program selection for the kids. "So the kids read," said Beth. "They think." The Fitzsimons children aren't allowed to go to R-rated movies; they can't go to any movie, in fact, until one of their parents has seen it, or read a review of it, or knows someone who has seen it whose opinion they trust. "If the kids say they're going to a friend's house, we call to make sure the parents are going to be home," said Tom. "I remember calling one of our kids' friend's house and the kid answered and he put the phone down and yelled, 'Dad, it's Mr. Fitzsimons on the phone, checking to see if you're a responsible parent!' "

Were Tom and Beth ever accused of being overprotective? "Sure, by relatives, friends," said Beth. "And by our kids, all the time."

Justin interjected: "My parents aren't going to let me go out until I'm elderly. They won't let us go out much after five o'clock, or even hang out at the mall!" He seemed a little perturbed at this, but also — proud.

Did Justin get any flak from friends about his parents' strictness?

"Not really. It's like, okay. Sometimes."

"When is it, like, okay?" asked his mother.

"I don't know, but if it ever happens, I'll tell you." He grinned sheepishly and fingered his new earring.

Although the strict rules governing their children's environment suggest Tom and Beth's conservatism, the earring represents their liberality. Within certain limits ("No Mohawks, no dog collars . . .") they encourage their children to express their individuality. For the most part, how the kids dress isn't that big a deal. Better to be a "scummie," as Biz, who dresses quite creatively, put it, than a "trendie" who "won't wear anything until half the United States is wearing it."

"If the kids can argue a rule in a lawyerly way, they can convince us to change it," said Tom.

Justin nodded. "That's true *some* of the time."

"We decided a long time ago that we would rather have half the neighborhood in our house than have our kids hanging out in environments we couldn't control," said Tom. "We didn't realize we were going to become Penn Station. But it's worked out anyway."

Some of the neighborhood kids started to show up as we talked — scummies bursting through the living room and into the kitchen, toting bags of Oreos and Devil Dogs. One of the boys wore braces and a long black coat festooned with what he called a "rash" of little silver studs in the shape of human skulls.

Sitting there in the kitchen, I thought of Madeline Cartwright and her dream of creating mentoring houses for the children of north Philly. The Fitzsimonses, without naming it such, have created a mentoring house for some of the kids of Swarthmore. Their house might well be the most popular teenage hangout in the neighborhood, even though — or perhaps because — some adult is always around, listening.

And here came the kid with the Mohawk.

"What happened to you?" somebody asked.

"Chemotherapy," he said.

Beth looked at him with an arched eyebrow, smiling slightly. "The reason Justin has never come home with a Mohawk," she said, "is that he knows that there is a special and secret punishment that we have been saving for an infraction like that."

One of the neighbor kids joked, "My parents tried that line, but they forgot what the secret punishment was."

"We don't forget," said Tom.

Toward Common Ground

I admired Tom and Beth's mix of traditional and modern values, their openness to their children's unique characters, their insistence on personal responsibility. And I thought of the yearning for equilibrium that so many parents described.

"Parenting styles may have become more lax after the sixties," said one father in Boston. "But I know among my friends who are parents, there's a desire to find some kind of — balance — to find a way to have more parental involvement, to be more supportive — neither authoritarian nor permissive. My parents went to most of our functions, whether it was a piano recital or that type of thing. But I don't remember holding any kind of intimate conversation with my mother or father. Having grown up in the Depression, they were committed to meeting all their kids' physical needs. They made sure that we were clothed well, fed well.

But there was really no effort made to find what was going on inside our minds." He suggested that "we should be proud, as fathers, that we tend to be more open with our children. We should hang on to that."

One good way to begin the bridging of the fundamental divide is for parents to admit the frequent discrepancies between what we say about gender roles and what we do. This subject was often among the first to surface among the parents I interviewed; they attacked the subject with relish and subtle relief.

"It's been bewildering and confusing to me," said Steve, in the Overland Park group. "I don't want to teach my kids the old, rigid structure, but there *are* differences in gender roles that kids need to be aware of."

"I think gender roles are God-given," said one of the more traditional mothers.

"What's that supposed to mean?" said someone else.

"I think there *are* natural differences in gender roles," said Kathy, another mother in the group, "but people in the past *worked* at it to make the boys wear blue and the girls wear pink." Kathy believed that sorting out gender roles — what is God-given and what is merchandised — would be much easier for her children's generation than for her own. "Our kids are exposed to female doctors and male doctors. They can go to the store or school and see that the boys are wearing pink and the girls are wearing blue. All of this seems very natural to them, God-given."

Her husband, Mike, added: "I don't know if I'm a feminist or not. Who needs labels? But I made a conscious choice from day one with my children to take an active role in rearing and maintenance. When I say 'maintenance' I mean things you've *got* to do — changing diapers, feeding them. I did it because I like it. I want to do it, I want to take an active role. If the kids are going to get screwed up I'm going to screw them up myself."

Even with their commitment to gender equality, many parents express confusion about the gap between their spoken family politics and the wiring of their hearts. This internal wiring, along with the new gender roles, sends spasms of conflicting messages to mothers and fathers — especially to mothers, who feel pulled in a dozen directions.

Among working parents, for example, women still do far more housework than men. Clearly, this is unfair. Yet some surveys have suggested that most women are not particularly comfortable with handing child care over to their husbands — though they do want husbands to do more chores around the house. Internal wiring set decades ago sometimes translates into subconscious agendas and unexpected territoriality.

All of us harbor contradictory values. Our confusion reflects a society that, as study after study suggests, believes firmly in traditional family values — and feels surprisingly negative toward day care — but also believes that women should not return to their traditional roles.

The way out of that dichotomy is toward a new kind of traditionalism.

In the late eighties, the cultural mood began to shift away from the excesses of the countercultural revolution of the sixties and seventies, as well as from the supply-side ethics of the early and mid-eighties. Although the emerging cultural mood still prizes personal freedom, it has also begun to make peace with traditional family and religious values. This is not to say that nascent neotraditional values are without severe internal contradictions, or that feminists and fundamentalists are about to embrace. But parents of divergent philosophies are beginning to find personal and political common ground.

Only a few years ago, parents would have been much more divided in their definition of gender roles than were the parents with whom I spoke; liberal parents would likely have been far more ideological in their defense of identical working-parenting roles for men and women; more conservative parents would have been more dogmatic in their defense of traditional, Bible-based roles. But whereas the public debate remains paralyzed by the split between leaders carrying either the nostalgic traditionalist or the high-tech modernist banner, many of the followers — the parents — have already moved to a higher level of sophistication. Some cultural leaders understand this shift. Betty Friedan (whose *Feminine Mystique*, a seminal work of the women's liberation movement, described the family as a "comfortable concentration camp") now writes that "equality and the personhood of women never meant the destruction of the family, repudiation of marriage and motherhood, or implacable sexual war against men." That myth, she suggests, was fomented by young radicals "without firm roots in family or career, who gave vent to their rage in a rhetoric of sexual politics based on a serious ideological mistake." Friedan has called for a revival of the American family, and she says the time has come to "affirm the differences between men and women. New feminist thinking is required if American women are to continue advancing in a man's world, as they must, to earn their way, and yet not become like men."[1]

This new family consciousness must go beyond the sometimes distracting discussion of gender roles. It requires liberation from the exclusiveness of the Left or the Right, from preconceived gender and family roles of either brand. The neotraditional family is being formed from the yearning, pushing, groping, often fumbling effort to get beyond current labels to find a better life.

Shortly after writing an article about changes in family forms I received a letter from Katharine Lewis, an unmarried woman without children. She had thought long and hard about the meaning of family. She suggested that people's attachment to traditional ideas about family may be part of the reason the family is in trouble. She sees too many of her contemporaries desperately trading their families' welfare for the sitcom symbols of family life — nice houses and expensive cars, appliances, designer jeans. "The money required to finance all those expectations," she wrote, "sets up a conflict of values, and puts enormous pressure on any marriage."

> I think about my mother, who died several years ago. An intelligent woman, she was not able to go to college. Once my brother and I were beyond toddler-hood, she felt she had nothing to do, had no role, had no value or self-worth.
>
> She poured herself into gardening and reading, but never felt she had any options outside the domestic role society sanctioned for her. Increasingly frustrated, she became an angry and bitter woman. I have often thought she made herself ill . . . rather than go on feeling so useless. She passed on to me a panoply of ugly feelings about domestic life, about families, about the value of being a woman.
>
> Perhaps because of this experience I believe very much in the essential value of families as secure ports in personal storms, places of nurturing, warmth, and gentle humor. But unlike the traditionalists, I also believe that a humane society does not dictate roles, does not value life by a paragon of marketed expectations.

This letter made me think harder about one aspect of what it means to be a liberated or neotraditionalist family. Such a family would be liberated from certain guilts: the sense of shame that it does not, for whatever reason, conform to some material form prescribed by tradition or television or commercial marketers.

Beyond the Labels of Family Politics

"I don't think conservative and liberal family values are mutually exclusive," said Beth Fitzsimons. "This has been a feminist family for years. Feminism hasn't hastened the demise of *this* family. I should say here that some of how my kids have turned out — and I think they're doing pretty well — comes from sheer luck. We're challenged more by Justin than we are with the other two, because he's the oldest. But when push comes to shove, he makes very good judgments. Some of that is luck, but some of it is because we're always in their lives."

Tom added: "A new level of family health is going to have to develop quickly or this society is going to go to hell. In the sixties and seventies, people had the ability to do whatever the mind could conceive, but if you don't know where the lines are, you don't know whether or not you want to go across them. I think that we're coming to the end of the period where there were no lines. And I think that those lines are starting to be penciled in, almost accidentally.

"They're being penciled in by AIDS. And they're being penciled in by economic constraints. There's got to be a point some time within the next ten years where we stop spending two hundred and seventy billion dollars a year more than we collect in taxes, because the economy isn't going to stand it. Economically, it's going to be increasingly difficult for families to split up. With so many families in the United States dependent on both parents working, how can we *afford* to run around? I'm talking about the mothers and fathers who work so that they can live in a house, have a basic car, and eat well —"

Now Beth spoke, rapidly. "What Tom is talking about goes way beyond who's going to wash the dishes. The kinds of constrictions he's talking about are all happening at the same moment that people's tolerance is about at its end. We've been indulging in the wrong kind of tolerance for too many years. Tom's very philosophical, but I'm very concrete. I'm getting real sick of being screamed at by lunatics on the street in Philadelphia every day. There's one guy on the corner at Seventeenth and Sansome. I avoid that corner because some day I'm going to bash him. He's just some poor guy who should be hospitalized. He screams foul, disgusting things at women when they walk by.

"This poor soul is a tiny bit of concrete reality to what Tom's talking about. He's been allowed to live on a vent and practically freeze to death every winter because somebody says it's his *right*. Well, I refuse to think of that as any kind of freedom. There's a whole bunch of people who avoid that corner because they don't want to listen to the offensive things he shouts at them, so that's now *his* corner. Instead of making it his right to get decent mental health care, we've made it his right to live on a vent. That's the kind of society and the kind of definition of freedom that we're giving our kids. But I don't think we're going to keep going in that direction. I refuse to continue to be tolerant of that kind of suffering and the message that it sends to my children. And I refuse to be tolerant of the kind of social tolerance that lets so many kids disappear through the cracks. So in that way, I'm getting pretty traditional, or conservative, or liberal, or whatever you want to call it."

So it was with many of the families with whom I spoke. Growing in number, these families are attempting to pencil in the lines, trying to get beyond the stereotypes. These are people who understand that family values cannot be confined to the home. To survive, these values must extend outward, as strong filaments of the new web.

Indeed, two years after I spoke with Tom and Beth in their kitchen, I was to learn that their lives and their children's lives, since then, had not remained quite so idyllic. Tom and Beth discovered that, no matter how much thought and time they invested in their own family, eventually they were compelled to reach out to other parents for solace and for help.

15

The Weaving of
New Parent Networks

●

What is most striking about parents today is how isolated many of them are from family, and from each other, and how hungry they are for new ways of making contact with other parents. "I'm on my own," one said, "*on my own*. That's just the way it is!"

Invariably, after my interview sessions with parents, several would mention how extraordinary it was for them to be able to hear other parents describe emotions that they themselves felt. This was particularly, painfully true of single parents. At Dewey Elementary School's child-care program in San Diego, single parents described how they spoke with one another only briefly in the morning and evening when they dropped their kids off or picked them up. A few had never sat down and talked with any other parents in the program. "It's nice to know that there are other people like this, that I'm not the only one that's out there," said one mother, sitting at a school table for this rare meeting with other single parents. "It's nice to know there are other people out there going through it." These parents had no time, they said, to take advantage of any psychological services or networking programs.

One of the mothers said: "There are parenting classes that I'd love to attend, but it's a question of priorities. Is it more important to cook my son's dinner or see that the laundry is done? Any number of things."

I asked these single parents if any of them ever picked up the phone and called a friend for parenting advice. "I call my mom," said one woman. Another mother said: "I don't have any other friends who are single parents, or even parents right now. But I can call my sisters. They adore my daughter. And my boyfriend will help out when I run out of patience and I can't handle it. But I don't know any other single parents. They're too busy, I'm too busy."

Joanne Hill, director of the Dewey child-care center, described one imaginative woman who had a child in the school, who has started bartering with other parents. "She's learned how to network through her business experience. She used to be a hairdresser, so she might do Delane's hair. And Delane makes beautiful birthday cakes, which is what she barters. Or they trade baby-sitting time." Such trading of skills and time can go a long way toward easing the burden. "This parent has created her own extended family. We have offered group sessions to try to discuss bartering, to assess individual needs and what could be traded, but then trying to get these parents organized is next to impossible. They simply don't come to the meetings. They don't have time."

This isolation translates into a lack of political power. "Recently we had to put a freeze on our enrollment here," said Hill. "So typically, I'll get a single parent on the phone who is desperate for child care and tell her, 'Look, the governor vetoed the bills that would help us and if you want to do something, write the governor.' But the parent will say, 'I don't have time to write the governor! I've got to find child care!' "

Isolation among parents helps create isolated kids — or more specifically, kids isolated from the adult world, more vulnerable to their peers.

Why are parents, whether single or married, so isolated? The demands of work are a major reason: parents are spending more hours in the work place or on longer commutes, or both parents are working. Most neighborhoods are empty during the day. The networks that once connected parents within their communities — coffee klatches, churches, neighborhood schools — are gone or transformed.

And, in a curious way, America has become anti-parent.

Threatened by international competition, the nation's economic engine demands increasing devotion from its workers; the engine monitors its own production, but fails to monitor the stress on its parts. As the bolts and widgets are pushed, their metal fatigue grows, unseen.

The central problems are not so much that the work places and institutions of the economic machine invade parental privacy, but that the institutions and work places operate as if family pressures do not exist. As a logical consequence, too many parents act as if other parents do not exist. In the work place, parents seldom discuss parenting among themselves or with their bosses because parenthood is too often considered a career hindrance. Who wishes to admit such an antiproductive handicap?

Avoidance of parents by parents extends to the neighborhood.

"I'm *afraid* of other parents, afraid for my child to play at other children's houses," said one mother. "You never know what kind of weirdos are raising your child's friends."

Another mother said: "I think Western society mistrusts parents in general. I think about my own feelings of trust. I wonder, To what extent do parents want to do the best for their children? I'm not sure. There are the parents I don't know, and the ones that I do know. I assume that the parents I know want to do the best for their children; I'm not so sure about the parents I do not know. I assume that they're the ones who don't care as much. But maybe this is just a societal prejudice I've picked up, a prejudice that comes from a lot of sources, including Freud."

The machine and the people have lost the sense of positive linkage between children and the future. As a consequence, many parents feel defensive about bearing children — particularly if they have more than one or two.

The topic of this defensiveness came up when I visited with a group of home-schooling parents. Some had chosen home schooling for religious reasons; others had chosen it because they felt the need for more control over their family lives. Most of them had made extraordinary financial sacrifices to keep one parent at home. We met in a cramped two-bedroom apartment where two of the parents lived with their three small boys.

One of the mothers, Sandy Meeks, a religious, soft-spoken, and extremely committed mother, said: "I'd like a little bit more respect from parents. When I chose to stay home with my first child, other parents, including my old workmates, couldn't understand that. They thought I must be bored to death. When I had my second child I was relieved because people quit asking me, 'Well, what do you do with your time?' I would explain that I had two children and they would respond, 'Oh, you're busy, aren't you?' But by the time we had our third child, people started making negative comments, such as 'This *is* the last one, isn't it? My *goodness,* you have a lot of children. My *gosh,* you have your hands full!' "

Her husband, Brock, added, "They would say" — he imitated a beer-belly voice — 'When you gonna *stop,* you baby machines!' and all this bull."

Sandy continued: "I find a lot of satisfaction in home schooling. It alleviates that awkward feeling you have that, as a parent, you're not doing something important. 'We home-school' is a good thing to say to strangers because it shifts the emphasis away from feeling defensive. It makes me feel like I just moved my piece across the board."

These home schoolers had created an elaborate system of peer support with monthly parents' meetings and social events. They admitted that the system was inbred, isolated from mainstream society. But such a specialized system was, they said, better than no psychological support system at all, which is what most parents experience.

Attack of the Parenting Experts

Instead of support, we get advice — a booming how-to-parent industry. Books on one-minute parenting, videotapes, audiotapes, Better Baby Institutes, *pregnophones*. Parents are overwhelmed by the avalanche of advice pouring down on them. Sure, we want to do the right thing. But which right thing? As social historian Barbara Whitehead pointed out, "It's almost as if parenting is now considered bad for kids."

One goal of a family liberation movement would be to respectfully rethink parental submission to experts — particularly in the context of parent and family isolation. Based on the history of the how-to-parent industry, we have plenty of reason for resistance and skepticism.

Since 1914, the U.S. Children's Bureau has produced a booklet entitled *Infant Care*. In its first edition, parents were advised that the child's biological impulses were bad, repeating the Victorian expert advice warning that rocking horses, swings, even teeter-totters might encourage masturbation — which was blamed, in the nineteenth century, for everything from baldness and epilepsy to insanity. Some experts suggested that parents pin the offending child's sleeves to the bed sheet or place the child's arms in stiff cardboard sleeves. Infants who cried to be held or sucked their thumbs would likely become self-indulgent. During the twenties, writes historian John Sommerville, John B. Watson, the American behavioral psychologist, "applied Ivan Pavlov's conditioning techniques to children." Sommerville describes how Watson "recalled a two-hour car ride in which one child had received no less than thirty-two kisses from mother, nurse, and grandmother. It nauseated Watson. He feared that this kind of conditioning led to sentimentality, dependency, and an invalid complex." Never hug and kiss children, Watson advised; never let them sit in your lap.

By the fifties, the pendulum had swung to the other extreme. In the era of Dr. Benjamin Spock, the experts assumed that the child's desires were natural. Affection and play were important. "Parents read that their children should be allowed to dress, talk, play, and 'have the same allowance and privileges as the other average children in the neighborhood.' In short, they should not be made to feel different." [1] Since the fifties, Spock himself had moderated some of his ideas; each new edition of his *Baby and Child Care* has encouraged more parental guidance — and less peer influence.

In the nineties the pendulum swings in shorter, quicker arcs, from the guests who appear with Donahue or Oprah to Pat Robertson. Some of the how-to-parent advice is excellent, but the sheer volume of it leaves many parents feeling inadequate. A Boston father remarked: "You see these fads come and go and you don't know which experts to trust, or which *era* of experts to trust. What bothers me the most is this feeling that everything, including our children, has got to be perfect. Our parents thought that life was hard — they were raised with that idea, and anything good that came along was gravy. Baby boomers were raised just the opposite. We thought life was supposed to be great all the time and we're surprised when it isn't. Hard times and personal difficulties are nothing to be ashamed of. There's no reason to feel guilt; life is not perfect. But because I was wired to think that life was perfect, I assume that *I* should be perfect. And my kids *must* be perfect." [2]

In an age that values information over wisdom, many parents or prospective parents rush their infants or even their unborn children into educational settings, including, for example, the Prenatal University in Fremont, California, and the Better Baby Institute in Philadelphia. [3]

Much of the overstimulation of babies and the concern with childhood perfection is a direct outgrowth of the dearth of family time. Parents find themselves cramming child rearing into smaller, more compact periods of time. In that context, maximizing experience by turning to experts makes ironic sense.

Richard Farson, director of the Western Behavioral Sciences Institute in La Jolla, California, and a leading advocate of children's rights in the seventies, believes that the how-to-parent industry could actually increase child abuse by parents. "As you increase the loneliness and frustration of parents, as you increase the fear of parents of the community, their job gets harder and harder, and *community* — which is the real preventer of child abuse — becomes more and more difficult to create," said Farson. "We're the only culture in history to leave child rearing only to the parents. No matter how helpful the parenting books might be, they send a metamessage that parents don't know what they're doing.

"The thing that most people don't understand about child rearing," according to Farson, "is that what you do *deliberately* as a parent doesn't matter as much as who you are, and kids have a way of finding that out."

What we need isn't training; it's education. There is, as Farson pointed out, a difference. "Training is essentially an attempt to get everyone to use the same skills. But parenting is reinvented continually. First, parents need to understand the history of parenting, and how the advice has changed over the years. Second, parents need each other — to be able to talk straight, rather than looking to so-called experts or only to themselves. That is what community is all about."

I do not mean to diminish the value of expert help from psychologists, school counselors, teachers, or other helpers; such advice and expert help is often essential. But other parents are still the best experts for parents.

In Overland Park, I asked parents this question: How did they feel when they went into bookstore and saw a big rack of how-to-parent books?

"Walk right by them. Don't even look," said Mike.

"I don't rely on books as much as I rely on my buddies," said Kathy. "I call 'em up — my friends. You know: 'My children take off their diapers! They paint each other! They tear the mattress apart! Is this normal?' And it helps to find out how my friends cope with these daily problems. Trouble is, the friends aren't as available for most parents as books are."

Parents as Experts

Wonderful things can begin to happen when parents do get together. I learned this firsthand in my interview sessions. At the beginning of a session parents would usually squirm and hesitate, but ten minutes into the session they would be relating their experiences — often with amazement that other parents experienced problems like theirs.

Here is one example of the kind of nascent wisdom that parents, given a chance, can share with one another. At a seminar session at the University of San Diego, I asked fifty or so primary and elementary school teachers, most of them parents, to share what they do to conserve time — what time tricks their families use to get more family time. The time tricks they described combined the traditional with the inventive, and they are worth sharing.

Time Tricks in the Car

"When my kids were tiny, I used our time in the car to talk or teach, and I'd sing the colors of the stop lights to them. In the car, one's attention is almost guaranteed — at least we don't have a car phone! Over the years, the car has continued to be a place where important topics are questioned, analyzed, and discussed.

"We've graduated to teen sex, marital infidelity, and living together before marriage. Teaching them colors by watching stop lights sure was easier on a mother's blood pressure. But I treasure the time we have in the car. I often hear what is most important to them there."

Culinary Time Tricks

One teacher said her family schedules a dinner out once a week "specifically to talk and listen."

Another suggested: "Lower one standard so a higher-priority item is saved. Example: a high priority — sitting down to dinner as a family. Standard lowered — dinner may be a basic salad and a frozen pizza via the microwave."

Time Tricks with Chores

Several teachers said their families considered chore time as talking time for the family — particularly grocery shopping.

Don't do a lot of housework until it gets overwhelming and then it's done as a family! Live by the rule 'Don't sweat the small stuff!' "

Ritual Time Tricks

Sundays (remember Sundays?) are still official family relaxation days for some families. "We walk around the lake or go out to brunch, without stress or pressure." "We go to church."

Some families regularly turn off the television. Or, as a family, they watch the same television show regularly, and then talk about the show. As an alternative to television, board games and cards are popular rituals.

The evening before trash collection day is good family time, suggested one mother. "My younger son and I would go around the neighborhood with a wheelbarrow — which was also found in the trash — and collect treasures other people had discarded."

A kindergarten teacher reported that the parent of one of her pupils keeps her child out of school one day each month to visit the museums in Balboa Park on free admission day.

"When my daughter was young, I would invite her to 'spend the night' with me playing games, watching TV, or talking just as overnight friends would do."

"Dr. Spock may not agree, but as a family with children ages three and six, we take a shower together in the morning."

Outdoor Time Tricks

"We took the boys camping in a van with a seat built so they were close to us and we could talk. We were all trapped together."

"Camping and the beach when we were poor." Later this woman's family bought a small boat, and the kids went fishing, water skiing, and boating — sometimes under protest. "But today, they talk about how wonderful it was." Her family also put a pool in the back yard — "letting our home be a neighborhood fun center — and we bought a mountain cabin for family togetherness. It's very noisy now, as the four have multiplied to fourteen." These activities, she pointed out, "were subsidized by a working mother."

Time-shifting Tricks

"Shower at night. Get up before the kids to satisfy the need for alone time. Appreciate the *now* — simple things."

"I get up at four-thirty A.M., an hour and a half before my husband and daughters. Don't get me wrong, I don't like getting up at four-thirty, but it does resolve the Me-versus-Us conflict."

One woman suggested staggered bedtimes, so each child could receive focused attention. Another teacher said her retired husband, Tom, "is the mom at our house." She described her eight-year-old son, who is enrolled in a home-study program, as a second-grade dropout. The reason was primarily time. Her son spends three hours a day doing schoolwork with his father. Then they, and sometimes the other siblings, are free for field trips.

"They go to the library," she reported. "They go fishing, visit boat yards, cook, sail, drive to the mountains. Dishes don't get done and the laundry is still running at twelve A.M. because Tom and the troops don't like *that* group activity. Since my husband grew up in foster homes, he is raising his kids the way he thinks the Beaver lived. The Beaver never had it so good."

Even the strongest families need other parents. When I called Beth Fitzsimons a couple years after meeting her and Tom, she told me how, after two of her children had entered high school, she and her husband discovered that they were not prepared for the roller coaster of their children's adolescence. "It's been a hard adjustment," she said with a strain in her voice, a touch of self-doubt I had not heard before. "I used to think some of these troubles would only happen to somebody else's kid. No more. The number-one thing that has helped get us get through this period was turning to other parents.

"One night we attended a meeting about alcohol and drugs at the high school conducted by two fine teachers. They showed a film, and then about thirty parents sat around for a long time talking, sharing their experiences. We were all amazed to find out how much we had in common. This session took place near the end of the school year, and the teachers announced that it had been so successful that they would sponsor more meetings in the fall. But the parents said, 'No! We can't wait that long!' So several parents took names, and we're now conducting more meetings on our own.

"Tom and I are also turning to some neighbors of ours who have children older than ours. They've been through all of this and they have helped us deal with it. Maybe it's just us, or maybe not, but I get the sense that parents are beginning to catch on that parents themselves are often the experts, the ones with experience."

Perhaps, she said, parents are moving away from this conspiracy of silence.

"One of the hardest things we've had to learn, and we've learned it from other parents, is about 'good parents' and 'bad parents.' If you judge your parenting only by your child's behavior, you'll make yourself crazy. Sometimes, no matter how good a parent you've been, your kid is going to do something wrong, and your kid — not just you — has to accept some responsibility for that. You can't do it alone, and no matter how hard you try, you can't assume all the responsibility.

"I remember one particularly clear moment at one of these parent meetings. One of the mothers said she had told her teenage daughter that if any of her daughter's friends came to her house drunk, she would call the police. Some of the other parents were aghast at this, but I wasn't. I'd be furious if she let my kid go back out on the street drunk.

"I remember how, when the kids were small, the neighbors would get together to socialize around the pool. If one of the kids fell in, some parent would be there in a flash to pull the kid out. I remember how that was and I wonder why we lose that when the kids get older. As a community of parents, we have to figure out a way to continue to be there for each other's kids, even when — especially when — they reach adolescence. We can't do it alone."

Toward New Parenting Networks

Many parents who understand their need for other parents are creating imaginative new connections. Creating time and a place for groups to meet — sanctifying them within established institutions or within the work place — could go a long way toward decreasing parent isolation.

New Single-Parent Support Networks

The need to decrease parent isolation is especially crucial for single parents. The first objective for single parents should be to take a close look at the advice and the lack of support they have been getting from government.

Under the Reagan administration, numerous social agencies tried to reduce the likelihood that a single-parent household would include other adults, particularly unmarried partners. In the mid-eighties, Reagan administration officials even discussed reducing the level of allotments for households in which a *grandparent* joined the single-parent family.

This thinking is shockingly myopic. Studies by Stanford University researchers, for example, indicate that the presence of any other adult in the household brings adolescent control levels in single-parent families closer to those found in two-parent families. This finding suggests that there are functional equivalents of two-parent families — that nontraditional groupings can do the job of parenting, and that the raising of adolescents is not a task that can easily be borne by a lone parent. Single mothers who choose television's "Kate and Allie" model, in which two single parents join forces and share the burden, report that housing costs decrease (and the comfort and size of the house usually increases), baby-sitting headaches lessen, and emotional support increases.[4]

Government should be encouraging such extended families rather than viewing them as deviant. A few private organizations, such as Roommates for Today's Family in southern California, match single parents. Schools, for example, could offer formal or informal help to single parents under financial duress (since such stress can affect a child's grades as much or more than a learning disability) by helping them find support networks or supportive living situations.

Extended support networks could also be offered by churches, government, private organizations, and employers. Such networks could take a variety of forms. A program called Project Self-Sufficiency, for example, sponsored by the city government of Huntington Beach, California, offers a self-esteem workshop to help single parents and other low-income parents make the transition from public assistance to employment and economic self-sufficiency. The basic theory of this program, which grew out of a drug- and alcohol-abuse prevention agency, is that the best way to prevent child abuse and substance abuse is to promote a positive self-image among single parents and their children.[5]

Some single parents have already established more informal models for the rest of us. One woman in Los Angeles, a veteran of the women's movement and a friend of mine, suggested that new parent networks are a logical extension of feminism and the self-help movement that followed the women's movement — all those twelve-step programs for compulsive drinking, gambling, overeating. "You find the same emphasis on the group, the consciousness-raising group — leaderless, nonhierarchical, structured so that everybody has time to participate. These groups are basically nonjudgmental, though there are a set of norms and values attached," she said. "People make fun of the self-help movement, but you don't solve problems by making fun of people. One woman in the group I attend [for overeaters] also belongs to Alanon, a self-help group for families of addicts; she joined because her child is a cocaine addict. She needed this group of other parents who were facing the same problem with their children because her family of origin just didn't know how to cope; if anything, their advice made the problem worse."

The parent network movement may hearken to the feminist movement in this sense: the personal will eventually become political.

My friend, a single mother for eighteen years, continued: "I'm a child of my times — I'm connected with both these movements. In the sixties I connected with other single parents through an alternative public school which we helped start. We could just as easily have linked through church or synagogue, but we didn't go. Rather, we did politics together and what survived the politics was friendship and connection. We were all single parents. We formed an informal extended family. With the exception of Dr. Spock, I've never read a how-to-parent book in my life; I have my friends. It's revealing, I think, that most of us who made these kinds of connections can truthfully say today that our kids are okay. The parents who didn't make those connections tend to be the ones with kids with severe problems. Those of us who connected with each other shared resources; it's the people without human resources who are so terribly lost, in part because human resources often lead to other resources.

"The group was nonhierarchical, but I did consider some of the people in my group to be expert parents, because I saw them parenting. However, you don't turn to the same parent every time. Some parents are good at some kinds of advice; others are good at other kinds of advice. I was an expert on schools, so other mothers turned to me for advice on that. And I knew about how to collect child-support payments. Word spread. Other parents were experts on finding a baby sitter or pediatricians. This was not a group that met formally. It was simply a group of women, and some men, too, who talked frequently on the telephone. I didn't know *networking* was a word eighteen years ago. In a sense, networking is a spurious term. It simply means connecting with people."

As I spoke to my friend on the phone, her call-waiting line beeped. The caller was a single parent she had met seventeen years ago, a member of the informal parenting group.

"You see, this doesn't end," said my friend when she returned to the line. "Our children are in their twenties and we still turn to each other for parenting advice. Right after the San Francisco earthquake, several of us reached out to each other because our kids were in the Bay Area. We figured out how to get through to our children — by car phone!"

She added one more thought.

"Sometimes I realize that I was lucky to be a single parent. My mother and grandmother were as helpful as they could be but they were out of touch. So in being alone I was forced to turn to other parents, and that made all the difference."

Innovative Networks for All Parents

In my travels around the country, I was impressed with the sheer variety of the new networks beginning to emerge for parents. So far these networks, like isolated solar systems, remain unconnected to each other. But a parenting-center movement is building. The number of parenting centers grew from fifty member organizations in 1983 to two thousand in fifty states by the end of the decade, according to the Family Resource Coalition, a national organization that coordinates the efforts of parenting centers.

Parents from all economic and social groups are involved in these centers, often located in libraries, schools, Y's, churches, synagogues, hospitals and community health centers, Junior League chapters, child-care programs, and union halls.

At the Community Y in Lansdowne, Pennsylvania, reading and cooking classes are offered to children and adults; there are classes for pregnant women, retired adults, and for children as young as eighteen months old. The Y sponsors teen dances and camps for kids, a thrift shop, and a booming child-care facility. Most interesting is the Buddy System, a program for children from single-parent homes who are matched with volunteers who can spend time with the child.[6]

The Early Childhood Resource and Information Center in Manhattan, under the auspices of the New York Public Library, is one of the nation's pioneering parenting centers. It offers both parents and professionals a ten-thousand-volume library, and about twenty-four thousand adults and children come to the center yearly for early education and parenting skills taught by staff educators and such experts as Benjamin Spock and Kenneth B. Clark.

Some of these centers connect parents to each other, through parent support groups — a far more important function than connecting parents with experts. In New York, the Parents League, established primarily to help parents through the hurdles of private school enrollment, conducts workshops for parents. Parents who attend these workshops, particularly at-home mothers, often ask how they can meet other parents. One Parents League officer, Pat Girardi, explained: "It's clearly difficult for parents to make contact. One of the ways is through courses. I don't think my own mother ever thought of taking a course on parenting, or going to a parenting center. But a lot of parents who enroll their children in parent-child courses do it for themselves as much as for their children. They want to be with someone with whom they can talk."

Another officer, Myra Lipman, added: "Our emphasis is on encouraging parents to trust their own gut reaction. But some parents resist that message. They're still looking for a 'solution,' not a range of solutions." Over time, with exposure to other parents, these parents often grow to appreciate the diversity of solutions to child-rearing problems. "Our success with the parent workshops suggests that we're replacing the park bench where mothers used to spend time with one another," Lipman said. "I remember how I used to sit in the park for hours trading notes with other mothers. Of course, there were mothers in the park then, and there are many fewer now. Our most successful workshops concern allowances and birthday parties — those are the kinds of subjects that parents would chat with each other about on the park bench, the nitty-gritty details of being a parent."

The Parents League officers expressed delight with some of the other imaginative ways parents are making contact in New York. One restaurant, for example, encourages mothers and their children who have just moved to the city to drop in on Wednesdays at noon to meet each other.

The restaurant offers a meeting room as well as publishes a newsletter for parents. Parents also meet each other through a growing number of playground committees in New York which oversee neighborhood playgrounds, report vandalism, and organize play groups.

"A mother in one of our toddler workshops," said Girardi, "signed up with a play group in her building, with other moms with children the same age. The group meets in the nighttime because all the parents are working parents. It was put together by the *doorman* in her building." She laughed with pleasure. "Each parent had asked him if he knew of other parents with young children, and he got everyone together."

The Electronic Back Fence

Among the most intriguing new forms of parent contact is something I came to think of as the electronic back fence. On several computer bulletin boards around the country parents log on, via modem, and participate in ongoing forums. Often late at night, after work and family duties have ended, these time-shifting parents use their computers to seek the kind of parenting advice they can't seem to get from parents they encounter during the day.

One particularly active bulletin board is part of the international computer network USENET, which connects universities, research labs, and high-tech companies. Just as parents once compared notes in the park or talked about their kids over the back fence, these parents discuss everything from disposable diapers to corporal punishment by way of computers. One USENET forum is dedicated to parenting. Scrolling through the messages, one gets the feeling that a lot of these people are using work time to discuss their kids with other parents. Parents from Oregon, California, New Jersey, Arizona; from Denver, Boulder, Boston, New York, Toronto; from universities; from Citicorp, Hewlett-Packard, and AT&T — all chatter away, sometimes using their names, sometimes communicating anonymously.

The buzzing variety of discussion suggests how well some of these new parent networks can function, and how much parents have to say once they sit down with one another — even if they live on opposite ends of the continent.

For example, a father logged on and asked for advice from other parents on traveling on airplanes with a baby. "Two things bother me about flying with a baby," he had tapped out on his computer. The message could be seen for the next several days by thousands of other USENET parents. "First, the baby doesn't get a seat. Second, there is no way to restrain the baby with a seat belt."

A day later he was advised by a parent who lives a thousand miles away: "The airline (or the FAA) does not allow you to use car seats. So, you are left holding the baby. (You are told never to do this in a car.)"

Another parent posted this response: "I've seen car seats that claim to be FAA approved for use on an airplane. If this is true, and you're willing to pay for the extra seat, you need not hold the baby." And another father, a week or so later: "On BOAC in Britain we were given a loose seatbelt which attached to the parent's seatbelt, to belt the kid in with. It wasn't that secure, but it was better than nothing and at least they didn't make the pretense that holding the kid in the lap was safe."

Several parents shared their concerns about disposable diapers: "Does anybody have any comments on various store brands?" One mother complained about the poor quality of one brand's sticky tabs. Other parents discussed discipline: "Those of you who warned [one mother] to firm up or pay later are doing her a disservice. I was told many times by people that I needed to be more firm with my daughter. I am sure that children are as varied in personalities as we are in opinions."

One mother described what she called "baby rodeo," the sport of getting her two kids dressed. And the subject "Purple Hearts," or "Injured in the line of duty" drew a string of war stories, including this one: "My son, the 1.75-year-old astronaut, likes going into our room, crawling in our bed and trying to wake us up. (You know, opening our eyelids, putting his fingers in our ears, honking our noses, etc.) He decided to try something new one day and bit my wife's nose. All hell broke loose."

The electronic back fence isn't an ideal form of parent networking, but it does suggest how eager many parents are to share their experiences. Such electronic contact is especially helpful if it leads to face-to-face encounters — and eventually, to parent organizing.

The Return of the PTA

What about the PTA and other parent-teacher organizations? How might they help create a new web of parent connections?

Norman Thomas, president of the Georgia PTA and a rising star in the national organization, is a black male in a largely female and white organization. I met Thomas at a California PTA convention in Anaheim. We were sitting in an empty room down a hallway from an exhibit area, where candy companies were setting out bowls of free chocolates to lure delegates to their booths. He told me: "The so-called yuppies have developed a great deal of sophistication in making a living, but as a result of that emphasis they also experience a vacuum in their lives.

For example: a couple waits until they're in their late thirties to have a child, and though they feel competent in the work place, they may feel less than competent as parents. Where do they turn? The PTA is a natural."

Or almost natural.

Unfortunately, with the trimming of school budgets, many parent-teacher organizations have become so consumed with fund raising for their schools that the most important work — helping parents, children, and teachers communicate about the daily issues of living — is given short shrift. However, if PTAs can rediscover their original purpose — the networking of parents and teachers to build personal and political power on behalf of children — they may yet be among the most important strands reconnecting parents to each other.

One obstruction is the skewed nature of the membership.

For ninety years, the organization has fought successfully for children and public schools, but the membership has remained almost entirely middle-class, white, and female. Today, Hispanics and blacks constitute the majority of urban grade school populations. Urban white flight has emptied many of America's major cities of traditional PTA leaders. In fact, in Boston, Philadelphia, and New York the PTA has disappeared completely — replaced by private parent-teacher organizations, PTOs, which tend to be more focused on individual schools rather than on citywide, statewide, or nationwide issues involving parenting and children.

"The PTA needs to reoccupy the cities," Thomas said.

Thomas is chairman of the national PTA's Big City Project. Its goal·figure out how to recruit blacks, Hispanics, and other groups that have traditionally shied away from PTA membership. In Atlanta, Thomas targeted black leaders for PTA recruitment to fill the vacuum left by whites. He moved PTA meetings from school cafeterias to the housing projects. "That was their turf. It was elemental: go to where the people are." In Atlanta, he increased PTA membership from ten thousand members to thirty thousand within three years.

Race isn't the PTA's only challenge. So are the new time and logistical problems faced by families.

"In Georgia, all of our key officers work at full-time jobs," said Thomas. "We've switched almost entirely to night meetings, and we spread out the responsibility more." Many PTAs now offer child care during the meetings.

Some state PTA organizations are also beginning to enroll parents at the day-care level — a development that could improve the quality of day care by adding an additional watchdog organization, but more important, would connect day-care parents with the public schools.

But the chief goal of PTAs should be to connect parents with each other — directly.

Some parent-school associations are beginning to address the issue of parental isolation by encouraging parents to meet in groups, matching their children's grade level, to talk about issues common to children at that age and their parents. Movement in this direction needs to be quickened.

In a conversation with one PTA president, a woman intensely committed to her children's elementary school, I asked if the PTA had ever organized meetings where parents could gather and discuss parenting.

"Oh, yes," she said, "we have experts come in and speak to us."

But what about parents simply talking among themselves about parenting?

She paused, surprised.

"No, we've never done that. *I* could sure use some of that. Sometimes I feel like I'm the last parent on earth."

The Search for Heroes

Improvement in the lives of families with children is not going to occur until parents organize themselves. We cannot expect government or the corporate world to reach out to us until we reach out to each other.

Given the American concept of family as a kind of frontier fortress, this reaching out will not come easily.

Indeed, I find myself recoiling slightly from the concept of parent groups. Perhaps my response comes from learned feelings that parenting is a private, almost secretive endeavor. More likely it comes simply from the fact that I am not, by nature, a joiner. However, I realize how much I have gained personally, as a parent, from these many interview sessions with parent groups. Like the parents I interviewed, I came away feeling uplifted and less isolated as a parent. And I realize that, if childhood's future is to be reshaped, such personal connections must eventually reach into the political arena.

This movement is already gathering quiet, largely unheralded strength.

Anita Shreve, in her book *Remaking Motherhood*, advocates a "second stage of consciousness-raising" which would aim to follow up the early gains of feminist support groups. She proposes that more working parents form groups to share advice and then become active in encouraging schools, businesses, and government to accommodate the needs of working parents better. Such groups could press for mandatory parental-leave laws, on-site day care, and a flexible work structure that would make good part-time jobs and job sharing more widely available. "Working parents, if you think about it, could be the biggest special-interest group in the entire country," Shreve says, "and their voting power is absolutely enormous." [7]

The examples I have described are striking in their similarity to the tools of other liberation movements, particularly the feminist movement — networks, support groups, the building of self-esteem in a community of peers.

The movement also has roots on the Right, in home schooling (which actually spans the political spectrum) and in the parenting self-help movement, which goes largely unreported, among fundamentalist Christians. The trick will be to transcend political and religious dogma and stereotypes.

The common denominator among all of these new parent networks is that parents, if they give themselves the opportunity, can offer marvelous support to one another. The support is often more flexible and appropriate than that pressed on them by experts and by the lonely shelves of parenting books. Experts are useful, but only in the context of community. The building of self-esteem among single parents or an electronic discussion about disposable diapers may seem, as political events, less than revolutionary. But something larger is being born — the creation of a new community of parents. The coalescing of that movement will be among the most important social and political forces of the nineties.

The parents' movement should include, on its agenda, four important goals: first, although it will be rooted in self-help techniques, it should reach beyond the personal to the political; second, it should bridge the fundamental divide; third, it should enlist the help of nonparents and senior citizens, rather than viewing them as enemies; and fourth, it should not be confined to the middle class. In fact, some of the most powerful parent networks are beginning to form in low-income neighborhoods — primarily to fight drugs — and could serve as models for the rest of the nation.

In conversations with children, I became increasingly convinced of the need for new parent connections, the necessity that parents reach beyond the boundaries of the family itself. One reason is that children need flesh-and-blood heroes — quiet heroes committed to American renewal.

Each year the *World Almanac and Book of Facts* conducts what it calls its "Heroes of Young America" survey. In 1989 the top ten winners, in order, were Eddie Murphy, Michael Jordan, Bill Cosby, Oprah Winfrey, Patrick Swayze, Arnold Schwarzenegger, Oliver North, Mike Tyson, Jesse Jackson, and Larry Bird. With the exceptions of Jackson, North, and Ronald Reagan, there hasn't been an important political figure on the *World Almanac* list in years.

Children model themselves after the most powerful people in their environment. Change the models, and you change the behavior.

Mike Barnicle, a columnist with the *Boston Globe,* described how drug dealers in an inner-city neighborhood had staged a recreational event for children: "Friday afternoon, a 13-year-old and a 15-year-old . . . distributed leaflets around [a] project offering a free bus ride this morning to Riverside Amusement Park. The leaflets stated there would be free prizes, free lunch and a raffle with the winner getting a choice of a microwave oven, VCR, bicycle or 13″ TV set." In the absence of a real support system, drug dealers offer their own web of support, albeit a sick and destructive one. Meanwhile, in Los Angeles some suburban kids wear beepers in imitation of inner-city crack dealers. A sheriff's deputy specializing in gang activity told the *Los Angeles Times* that "the only time they'd get beeped is when their mothers wanted them home for dinner."[8]

When I asked kids to name their heroes, the question was often met with silence. After the initial puzzlement, the students' answers revealed a hunger that went deeper than the *World Almanac* survey would suggest. "Ivan Boesky, he's my hero," joked one kid cynically. "Serve two years, get out, pay the government a hundred million dollars, and still get rich." One girl asked, "What's a hero?" Another kid answered: "A hero is somebody who's in the public eye, who's taken control of his destiny and done things they like and have been really powerful with what they did. I really like watching someone like Jack Nicholson just 'cause he's so passionate about what he does." One boy said his heroes were sports figures. "But I'm kind of embarrassed about that. Athletes aren't the best people."

Nobody had mentioned any politicians, I noted.

"Pardon me?" someone said, and the class laughed.

Again and again, young people defined a hero as someone who took control of his own life, who shaped his own destiny, who grabbed what he wanted — which usually included money and media attention — and moved on. But ideals? Get outta here. Ideals were for religious nuts. There was one exception to this subtraction of idealism from the definition of heroism: Martin Luther King, Jr. In Alexandria, an upper-middle-class black kid who said he was politically conservative told me: "My heroes are Dr. King and Malcolm X. It's not really their ideas that I like, but the fact that they did something. My problem with the black community is that they wait too long for the government to help us. King and Malcolm X didn't sit around and wait. They went out and did something."

It's a mystery why King's name didn't show up on the list of young Americans' heroes in 1989 — especially considering that six of the ten most-admired Americans on the current *World Almanac* list are black. Part of the reason is that ideals don't mean much these days. Another is that such a hero demands hope, and a lot of kids live in circumstances without much hope at all.

I asked students in a class in drug-devastated north Philadelphia to name their heroes. No hands went up.

Jesse Jackson had made a campaign stop in the neighborhood on the previous day. I mentioned his name. "He doesn't make me feel like I could run for president," said a tough-looking sixth-grader. "I have my own influence, and my own opinions, and I don't think I want to run for president." A few of the students named, halfheartedly, some of their heroes:

"Oprah Winfrey." "The army." "My conscience."

"Your conscience?" I asked.

"Because my conscience, it tells me what to do."

"Where do you get a conscience?"

"From your mind."

"Who puts it there?"

"I do."

Then one girl with thick glasses and a fierce look in her eyes spoke up. "The reason why I don't have a hero is 'cause nobody has done what I want to do. I want to take this world. I want to change it all around. Stop and destroy everything like guns, cannons, and all this junk and just make the world like it was before. When God first created earth where it was free, peaceful, nobody tried to fight anybody, nobody tried to hurt anybody." She paused. "But I do want to be like somebody in real life."

"Who's that?" I asked.

"Donald Trump."

"Why's that?"

"Because I plan on going into business when I get older. I just want to work my way up in a high company and I want to build my own. Manufacturing, management. I just might take over the world."

Well, Donald Trump's a better hero than no hero at all — though it would be good if heroism in the nineties came to reflect more than the art of the deal. Maybe the times are about to change. Irony, fashionable boredom, and cultural hopelessness are boring after a while.

Even so, as I asked this question around the country, only a handful of kids named any person in their families and no one named a person in their neighborhood or community as their hero. That could change with the formation of new parent networks — particularly those that grapple with neighborhood violence and drugs. The real importance of the so-called war on drugs is not that it will stop illegal drugs — it will not — but that, at the local level, it sends a clear message to children that their parents are still connected to the world, that a world still exists outside the electronic bubble, and that personal connections and networks among parents must eventually become political.

In a living room in far-less-than-affluent southeast San Diego, I sat for a while with eight extraordinarily ordinary people. Magdalena Osuna, a soft-spoken grandmother, spoke of how she wasn't going to stand by and watch her neighborhood be taken over by crack dealers. Her hands fluttered up and grabbed an imaginary broom.

"When I'm outside sweeping, I take license plates," she said. One hand moved to another. "I write the license plate numbers down in the palm of my hand, and I write what kind of car the drug dealer is driving. And my neighbor is a photographer, and she hides in the bushes and takes pictures. My daughter, she's in the house yelling at me, 'Mama! They're going to kill us, I tell you! You're not Columbo!'"

Magdalena Osuna's hand fell back to her lap and the fingers bent and the hands turned into little rocks, tough and hard.

"I'm not afraid anymore. No more."

Not since she hooked up with the San Diego Organizing Project (SDOP), a network of church-affiliated community organizations established a decade ago — but now beginning to show real muscle. The people in this room represented about ten thousand families associated with churches throughout San Diego.

Most of the active members are middle-class and low-income parents. Indeed, many of the neighborhood anti-drug parent networks are emerging first in lower-income neighborhoods, where the drug problem is most visible. But this movement is likely to spread as the residents of upper-middle-class neighborhoods begin to realize the power they can muster in shaping their children's environment (and their own), just as they have realized that neighborhood action, through block watches, can lower local crime rates.

In 1987, SDOP decided to ask people in the neighborhoods what was troubling them. What they discovered (long before George Gallup did) was that drugs were the number-one issue. So the people of SDOP — the housewives and janitors and schoolteachers and secretaries and carpenters — decided to educate themselves about drugs. Methodically, they fanned out and interviewed beat cops, narcotics agents, government officials, judges, drug-treatment program administrators, representatives from the city manager's office.

What did they learn? That even though drug-related crime consumed 70 percent of the city's police resources and 80 percent of court resources, no one in city or county government was offering a broad strategy against drugs. The city manager's office had fifteen departments, dedicated to traffic, economic development, utilities, and so forth, but no one city official was assigned to coordinate anti-drug efforts. They asked, Why was there no special unit in the district attorney's office to handle street dealing? Why were at least 50 percent of all cases plea-bargained? Why street dealers being given citations instead of serving jail time? Why, when the city had more than 160,000 abusers, did it only have publicly funded treatment space for 40 juveniles and 120 adults? And why did the school system's effective, police-based anti-drug education program reach only 72 of 181 public and private elementary schools?

At one by now nearly legendary meeting with Mayor Maureen O'Connor, SDOP turned out a thousand people who packed a Catholic church and listened politely to what O'Connor said she had accomplished in the war on drugs, and then, in midspeech, asked her to sit down. Then the people told the mayor what they wanted accomplished. As one woman there put it, "Your honor, words are not enough."

After that meeting, SDOP has — along with similar organizations in Oakland, California, and other cities — intensified pressure on government officials and pushed local officials to make a number of changes. Indeed, no force is as powerful as sustained, organized pressure on bureaucrats and politicians — who have yet to realize fully that not since the Vietnam War has any issue had so much rage attached to it. One bitter SDOP leader said: "I have two children that are involved in drugs, and there was a time that I couldn't say that publicly. I was ashamed and it hurt me, but if I don't do something, then who will?"

"We're trying to look beyond just the programs, and beyond drugs," said Fern James, a former systems analyst for the federal government. "We're looking at the whole social fabric. The churches used to hold things together in the community." What happened to the churches?

"The people in the churches went and hid behind their walls. The churches need to take responsibility again."

Some of us may live in impotent times, but not these people.

They speak of creating a widening web of churches and community groups to confront drug dealers and absentee landlords who allow their buildings to become crack houses. They speak of creating a new kind of relationship with the police. They speak of holding the bureaucrats' feet to the fire. They speak with one voice, a wave of rage rising up, pushing, gaining strength and power as it rolls forward.

And most of all, they speak about their children.

"The main thing is to know you're not alone anymore," said Dorothy Kwiat, a single mother who works as a word processor. She told how she helped organize the meeting with the mayor, and how she insisted that her two teenagers attend the event, which they did, grudgingly. And she told how, when her kids walked into the church and saw what she had helped accomplish, she looked in their eyes and saw for the first time "that I was a hero to them."

She added softly: "Do you understand how important that is? *We must become our children's heroes again.*"

16

Toward Fourth-Wave
Child Care

●

As new parent networks form, they must begin to create ways for children to spend less of their lives in institutional care and more time with their families, and they must reshape the way in which children are cared for by people other than their families. Both goals are interdependent.

There have always been alternatives to day care, though these have usually received short shrift from the media. In the late sixties, for example, Barbara and Ralph Whitehead (she is now a social historian, he a professor of journalism at the University of Massachusetts–Amherst) had their first child.

"I was a student, and Ralph was working as a reporter at the *Chicago Sun-Times,* and we were poor and predictably liberal," Barbara remembered. "But as we tried out day care — these were the very early days of organized day care — we became more and more conservative on that topic. So in 1969 we bought, with two other couples, a three-flat house with a playroom in the basement. Each family had two young children. This was not a commune. We were very middle-class. Each family lived separately in their own apartment. The extent of our adult communal living was that we had breakfast every Sunday.

"What we shared was child care. Each of us were committed to staying home with all the children for one day each week, and our school work and jobs were flexible enough that we could juggle our days."

"The kids came to know each other almost as if they were brothers and sisters," said Ralph. "For the parents staying home for their day, apart from a little diaper changing and dispute mediation and meal making, it wasn't too demanding. This was child care, not early childhood developmental education. No flash cards or karate."

Barbara added: "Today all of the kids are in college. Two are fathers. For us, that period was financially difficult, but these kids have the happiest memories of that time. They look upon it as their golden age.

"If the goal was to balance work with child rearing, we certainly succeeded. We got time with the kids and we got our work done; what we didn't get is time with each other."

But that goes with the territory, I noted.

Barbara laughed. "Of course!"

Ralph said: "What the kids got, too, was a community! Not only other children, but other adults. A community of adults."

Looking back, Barbara ponders the self-consciousness of this arrangement. When she was a girl, she said, such contact with grownups occurred naturally, through church and neighborhood. "Ralph and I had to create an environment where there was good contact for our children with grownups."

Today the Whiteheads live in suburban Amherst. "Our other children are grown, but we have a ten-year-old son now. I often think about how he has more privileges and money, because we're more affluent now. What he doesn't have is that stable community of children and adults."

One hears of few such creative child-care alternatives today. Perhaps they go largely unreported, or perhaps these alternatives are rare, given the growth of the child-care industry and the isolation among most parents today, caught up in the accelerating pressures of the economy and careerism.

During my interviews, it became clear that few parents or children are satisfied with the current realities of child care in America.

Yale University is among the few large institutions that has actually attempted to find out what parents think about child care. The university offers a variety of child-care benefits, including seven day-care centers and a university child-care coordinator. Yet until 1987, little was known about how parents used child care at Yale. University administrators did not know, for example, the number of young children employees had, how many employees used child care, or what kind of child care parents preferred.

So, in 1986, Yale began to survey its employees. As an article in *American Demographics* magazine points out: "The survey results make one point clear: any employer-sponsored child care should take into account the wide ranging needs of employees. . . . Because of these variations,

employers may find it difficult to emphasize one type of child care benefit to the exclusion of others."

Among the findings:

• "Most parents are happiest when a relative, baby-sitter, or housekeeper provides care in the child's home. . . . Parents whose children
are cared for at home are frequently dissatisfied with its cost, but they
are rarely happy with anything else. They are particularly pleased with
the location of the care. . . ."
• "Upper-income parents are more likely to use day care centers and less
likely to use family homes. Parents with household incomes of less than
$20,000 a year are much more likely to put their children in family
homes; rarely do they use day care centers for infants and toddlers.
They are also more likely to leave children with friends or relatives than
are higher-income employees. Yet lower-income parents are only slightly
less likely to use the more expensive choice — in-home care by nannies
or full-time baby-sitters — than are upper-income parents."[1]

The problem is finding good in-home care.

One Option: The Nanny Brigade

Here comes the nanny brigade, just in time.

"A nanny is not a baby sitter," according to Deborah Davis, an associate professor of education at California State University–Los Angeles. "A nanny [or if it's a he, a "manny"] is a trained professional who
comes to your home and takes care of your kids and knows what she is
doing."

By Davis's count, based on a nanny network of individuals, private
training schools and recruitment companies, and a handful of community college programs, only five hundred nannies were graduated from
some kind of child-care training program in the United States. In 1987,
these programs were deluged with 250,000 applications from parents
seeking in-home child care.

"This is a brand-new industry in the United States. The old-timers
have been in the business three years," Davis said at the International
Nanny Conference held at Scripps College in southern California in 1987,
the first time that U.S. nannies have banded together to form what Great
Britain has had since the forties — an official organization and national
training standards.

Among the first issues on the agenda (along with the name *nanny*, which some nannies consider frumpy and want to dump) is price. Can Americans afford nannies?

The going rate for a trained nanny, depending on the region, is $200 to $250 a week, often including room and board, use of a car, and health insurance. Who can afford that? Highly paid professionals, mainly. Many nannies are employed by physicians who place them on the office payroll.

One nanny I spoke with suggested a share-a-nanny system — two families dividing the cost of one nanny. (It occurred to me that a small network of parents could, indeed, share the costs of part-time in-home care.)

She was soft-spoken, almost timid, but when I pressed the issue of cost, she flared with anger: "Look, some of these parents are going to have to get their priorities straight. They'll spend thirty thousand dollars for a Mercedes but won't spend ten thousand a year on quality child care!"

But the average family (with a Chevy) earns only $28,000 a year. So Davis has another intriguing suggestion: company nannies. "A lot of companies are thinking about offering child care, but they're locked into this idea of on-site child-care facilities. What companies ought to do is put their money directly into care givers, pay substantial salaries and benefits to a cadre of nannies and use them flexibly," she said. Company car, company nanny.

Some of these nannies, Davis suggested, could be employed exclusively for individual families; others could be used as "pinch sitters," stepping in to take care of an employee's children when they're home sick. Davis believes such an approach would also attract more and better nannies. "You'd have a lot of girls saying, 'I wouldn't mind working for Xerox.'"

Do we really want the company in our homes watching our children? A number of complications spring to mind, including liability and privacy issues. Nonetheless, powerful forces are moving companies and parents in that direction. Current sources of in-home child care are dwindling. The new immigration law, which includes employer penalties, is already discouraging couples from hiring undocumented immigrants. Because of the demographic aging of the nation, fewer teenagers are around for baby-sitting.

At the same time, employers are facing the effects of the baby bust, a smaller supply of young workers to fill entry-level jobs. So companies are going to be forced to pay more attention to valued, trained employees — and to deal with what *Fortune* magazine bemoans as the "vexing" loss of productivity due to parents' worrying about who's minding their kids. "Working parents," according to a recent *Fortune* cover story, "seem to be trying to assuage their guilt by cutting corners on the job." [2]

"There is no pain quite like not knowing if your child is in good hands," said Davis. "This is going to be the mental health issue of the nineties."

Consequently, child care is likely to become the fringe benefit of the decade, and nannies could play a part in that.

I spoke for a few minutes with Janet Shannon, president of the Nanny Company of Austin, Texas. I told her I was writing a book on childhood. She gave a wry smile. "Are you for it or against it?"

She explained why she had started her nanny business.

"I looked at the demographics. By 1990, the consensus was that in this country we will be spending ten to twenty billion dollars on child care or child-related services."

"The other thing that is very subtle: a lot of mothers don't want to be usurped. They don't want the child to love the nanny best. This is a legitimate fear. I have seen very aggressive, assertive nannies who are a real put-off to mothers. Some women — maybe fifteen percent — call in later and say they just can't take it."

Half of her nannies work part-time, at least fifteen to twenty hours a week. "I have a client right now with two small children who needs help with the 'arsenic hours,' between three to seven P.M." Part-time nannies, Shannon said, "are going to represent a burgeoning portion of the nanny business."

The new market for nannies is primarily on the East and West coasts, but most of the recruitment for nannies occurs in Mormon Utah and the Midwest. "Los Angeles is one of the worst places to recruit," said Deborah Davis. "The girls there aren't interested. Short attention span, different expectations."

I sat for a while in a lunch room at the college with a group of nannies from St. Louis. They called themselves "Happy Nannies Now."

"We're happy now," one of them said. She was thirty-three, attractive and articulate. Divorced nine years before, she had no children of her own. "When you first get into this, you're naive, and you can end up with a bad family."

Another said: "You know within three hours, three days, that something is wrong. Motherly instincts, gut feelings. The husband and the wife are shouting at each other, 'Go ——— yourself' — you know. You stay, and you do it for the child because you love the child, but no matter how much you pretend, that child is not your child. You have to learn when to get out."

The oldest nanny, in her fifties, said: "I have six children of my own. I'm a registered nurse. I had nurse burnout. I was sick of taking care of sick people. But I loved children and I thought, Parenting is what I'm good at. Why not do it and be paid for it?

"I told my nanny family, 'Please stop me if I start giving you too much advice or start mothering you.' But they said they needed mothering, they needed someone who wasn't in the family but could care for them."

Being a nanny is like being married, explained the youngest nanny at the table. She was twenty-three. "Except you're married to a family, and when your job is done in a few years, you move on to another family.

"You know," she said, "when I'm sixty, all these children of all these families will be grown, but they'll still call me on the phone and visit me and wonder how I'm doing. How many older people these days have that in their lives?"

The Second Option: Reshaping Day Care

Outside of rare cooperative arrangements among parents (arrangements that may form more easily as parent networks grow), few families will be able to afford in-home child care. Consequently, the day-care industry — both family day care and organized day-care centers — will continue to grow. What shape it will eventually take is still an open question.

The idea that day care is evolving toward some yet-to-be-defined form came up often in interviews with parents and child-care providers. So far, the child-care debate has focused mainly on the brick-and-stone issues of day-care availability, on hard numbers and utilitarian concerns. Day care in America is still seen as something of a panacea rather than part of a larger web of support. Yet people are making their own way, slowly.

Eric Nelson, director of the Child Education Center of the Cal Tech–Jet Propulsion Laboratory Community in Irvine, California, among the handful of day-care providers who can truly be called pioneers, breaks the recent history of day care into three periods: first wave, second wave, and third wave.

Whereas family day care — provided by the woman from down the street who cares for several children in their home — has always existed, the first significant wave of organized day care did not arise in the United

States until the early seventies, when a few companies, including the Boston shoe manufacturer Stride Rite, and one union, the Amalgamated Clothing and Textile Workers Union in Chicago, opened on-site day-care centers.

"These projects would get started because of an enthusiastic executive, who would either find out it cost more than they planned, or their economics would change," said Nelson. Also, after the last year of the baby boom, 1964, the demand for day care tapered off for a time. By the late seventies, however, the second wave began as women began to move into the work force. The new generation of top management was somewhat more understanding than managers at the outset of the decade had been. Nonetheless, on-site day care in the work place was slow to bloom.

"By 1980, a lot of us thought that employer-related child care was really taking off. Wrong. In May 1980, in San Jose, I attended a conference called 'Child Care: An Idea Whose Time Has Come.' I'll never forget that." He laughed. "In 1981 the economy went into a tailspin. The second wave just went *smack* on the shore."

During the third wave, which began a few years later, the growth of chain day cares took off. By 1987, Kinder-Care Learning Centers, started by a shopping mall developer, was included in *Business Week*'s annual ranking of the top one thousand American public corporations based on their market value.[3] By the late eighties, Kinder-Care operated nearly 1,200 centers in forty states and Canada, with a capacity for over 115,000 children — far ahead of its closest competitor, the 520-site La Petite Academy of Kansas City. The company zeroed in on growing suburbs, especially in the Sunbelt. As this third wave of child care progresses, the chief issues are quantity and quality — especially quality.

Only about 20 percent of child-care programs in the United States are of adequate quality, Nelson estimated. "If you've worked intimately with the finances of child care as I have, you understand quickly that as soon as you decide to make a profit you're in conflict between the children and the investors."

One hindrance to quality is pay. Child-care workers earn less on average than janitors, house cleaners, and garbage collectors, according to a study by the Child Welfare League of America. (The median annual salary for garbage collectors is $14,872; the median salary for day-care teachers without college degrees is $10,800.)[4] Not coincidentally, most of these workers are women. Day-care workers, more than government, are the chief subsidizers of child care.

A more difficult hindrance than pay to achieving quality child care is defining *quality*. For example, some day-care centers and preschools offer intensive early education, which is often defined as quality day care. But Lillian Katz, professor of early childhood education at the University of Illinois, stresses the importance of play and unstructured learning for pre-kindergarten youngsters. From her point of view, the growing trend toward enrolling toddlers in competitive learning-intensive preschools — rather than in relaxed, play-oriented schools — is harmful and should be avoided. The emphasis, she says, should be on the encouragement of imagination. American preschool teachers, according to Katz, tend to structure their classes too much, telling young children exactly what to draw or how to complete projects.[5] Another quality marker is the staff-to-children ratio, but state governments cannot agree on an appropriate figure. South Carolina, for example, licenses centers that have at least one adult for every eight babies, whereas Maryland insists on a ratio of one care giver for every three infants.[6]

Results — good or bad — always depend on the specific children and the home from which they come. There is no one answer and no one question. And that, for parents, is the most unsettling aspect of the debate about day care. The truth is, we do not know the final effects of day care.

"We will not know the ultimate effects of infant day care until these infants have grown up and become parents. We have a whole generation that we should be watching," contends psychologist Edward F. Zigler, director of the Bush Center in Child Development and Social Policy at Yale, who calls the search for quality child care a "cosmic crapshoot." Zigler, who helped originate the Head Start program in the sixties and was the first director of the federal Office of Child Development, believes that America is developing a two-tier system of child care, with affluent people being able to afford relatively decent care and the rest having to accept "mediocre or even dangerous care for their children" — often, for just those children who "are already vulnerable, or at risk, because they come from single-parent homes or from families with little money, a lot of deprivation and poor health care. And they are being placed at even greater risk by being put into very inadequate child care settings." The nation — and its children — cannot afford the long-term effects of such a system.[7]

In March 1990 the House of Representatives finally passed a bill to expand day-care programs and provide more money to programs that already exist. The bill, put forward by the House Democratic leadership, was hotly debated over issues involving pay for child care and whether federal funds should subsidize day care provided by church groups (another battleground defined by the fundamental divide). The bill would bolster the Head Start program, provide bloc grants to states to expand day-care programs, and give vouchers to parents to pay for child care of their choice, including that provided by religious institutions. At this writing, differences remain to be settled between the House measure and an earlier bill passed by the Senate in June 1989, differences centering on how increased federal child-care assistance would be administered. If the Senate version dominates, the White House has threatened to veto the bill. Nonetheless, more government support for day care does seem to be on the way.

In the coming decade, the day-care debate will likely move on to other questions: How much day-care subsidy is enough? How do we test the quality of day care, and its effects on infants and children? How do we decrease the need for day care?

And how do we create a new, whole-family approach to day care as part of a wider, more complex system of family support?

Toward Fourth-Wave Child Care and New Family Centers

In the fourth wave in the approach to child care in this country, day care will begin to be viewed as part of a larger family and community web as *quality* comes to mean what is good for the family rather than what is good solely for the child or what is good for the employer. Instead of the efficient warehousing of children (one parent called some of the more utilitarian settings "day-care dumpsters"), the fourth wave will be concerned with family liberation.

A look at other countries places our patchwork child-care system in perspective. In 1988, a global review of child-care arrangements presented in the *World Monitor* found that many countries take a more sophisticated approach. In the best systems, day care is seen not as a panacea but as part of a much larger child-rearing network.

In France, for example, public nurseries are supplemented by licensed, in-home "mothers' assistants." These helpers can be called on by women returning to their jobs after sixteen weeks' maternity leave, during which they receive 84 percent of their regular pay. Such services are funded by local government, by parents contributing on a sliding scale according to income, and by a national family allowance.

In Sweden, families are assisted by a parental leave policy that provides twelve months' leave, with the state providing 90 percent of lost income; the leave may be shared by mothers and fathers — nine months for the mother and three months for the father. (The Social Democratic government plans to extend the leave to eighteen months in 1991.) In addition, mothers may take an additional six-month leave at 70 percent pay. After-school programs for seven- to twelve-year-olds function during vacations. Sick leave for parents who work is supported by insurance, which reimburses them when they stay at home to tend a sick child. Some children in day care and preschool are placed in "sibling groups," mixing ages as they naturally occur in families. Funding comes from local taxes, parents' fees, and state subsidies financed by employer payroll taxes. Municipalities are responsible for building and operating child-care institutions and programs. Also, tax deductions of $4,000 for each child under six and $2,000 for those aged seven to twelve are supplemented by credits for the poorest families.[8]

As I listened to children and parents describe their feelings about child care, it seemed to me that some of their negative feelings emanated from their sense of being detached from one another by economics and institutions. In-home child-care providers were perceived by both parents and children as a more personal, though sometimes intrusive, solution. Yet few of us can afford extensive in-home care. Assuming that neighborhood homes and institutional care are going to be a growing reality, what should they be like? What emerged from the interviews suggests that day care as we know it should be replaced by family centers that do everything possible to serve the family's need for interaction.

When I spoke to a group of thirty or so day-care workers from a variety of facilities who were gathered in a community college classroom, several mentioned that day care should offer more to parents — it should offer a sense of community. "That's absolutely something we could be doing more of," said Karen Shelby. "In the morning, when the parents come, some of them will be late to work because they're standing and touching base. Or you get two or three moms that are all pregnant and they stand there and talk. We have parent orientation every year, and the parents discuss common problems — biting, whatever."

One of the women in the class, Kim Pham, a Vietnamese immigrant, offered her perspective on this issue. "I came in 1975 and now I have three children. My parents end up watching the kids. We grow up to be a very close family, not like over here from what I'm seeing. A lot of grandparents here don't even really care about their own grandchildren. They don't care even about their own daughter or own son. I wasn't going to go to work, but my mom said you go ahead and work because we need that second income. So she's watching them and she doesn't complain. But the guilt is on me, because I'm having the child and she has to be taking care of my child instead of me. So what happened was, about a month ago I went in to quit my job as a computer programmer, and the boss said no. He told me he had to give me another raise. I didn't quit, but I will in January."

Why?

"To open a day-care center" — one, she said, that would replicate the village life that she had left behind: "So relatives, friends, uncles, aunts come and help."

Some cooperative day cares now require parental involvement — one morning a month when a parent serves as a teacher's aide.

Indeed, one theme that I heard repeated often by working parents was that, just as day care has become a new neighborhood for children (while the streets in front of their own houses are often empty of children), day care can also offer a focal point for parent contact and parenting advice. One woman, a college professor, said: "I came here from England. My family is three thousand miles away. Day care really did give us a sort of extended family. When we were trying to make a decision as to whether to enter our daughter into public school this year, it was the day-care teachers to whom I turned for advice, and they gave this advice to me in a way that was very loving and yet dispassionate."

Other parents, particularly those in cooperative day cares — in which parents must share time caring for the kids — said their primary contact with other parents was through the day care. "But it takes effort to make contact with the other parents," said one. "There needs to be a mechanism at the day care that encourages parents to stay a few moments and visit with other parents. Sometimes I think we should have our own time-out room to de-accelerate from work, drink a cup of tea, talk with other parents before we rush our kids home to dinner and the bathtub."

Despite my misgivings about the lack of permanence in child-care relationships ("It's still a business," said one day-care provider), it seems to me that the whole-family day-care approach may well have been the more important missing ingredient in third-wave child care. The problems with day care do not arise primarily from geography. Where a child spends his or her time makes less difference than how, and with whom.

Indirectly, the feelings of parents, children, and providers suggest this vision: the transformation of child-care centers into family centers where children would spend time while their parents were at work, but which would include parents and other family members as much as possible in daily operations, events, and teaching. Family centers could be structured in such a way that services to children would be part of a larger whole: the centers could offer classes for parents, meeting places for parent groups, and social activities for families.

The centers could be sponsored by public schools and private businesses. Such family centers might also offer day-care services for elderly family members and involve them, too, in the nurturing and loving of the newest generation. In these centers, the presence of parents and grandparents would improve the adult-to-child ratio and decrease parent and child isolation. Day-care operators could shape and market their centers as extensions of the family rather than replacements.

The coming of such centers could, indeed, fill part of the unhappy hole left by the disappearance of the old neighborhood structure, and they would become small hubs in the new web.

A "Family Ties" Proposal

I'd like to propose a new law that will release an army of day-care inspectors, help prevent child abuse, and almost immediately improve day care, elder care, and the schools. Call it the Family Ties Bill.

Consider the McMartin child-abuse trial. It has become clear that the courts are the worst place to police day care. For example, state licensing inspectors are responsible for day-care safety, but day-care facilities are inspected only once every three years. Who, then, are the best day-care watchdogs? Parents, obviously. Some states, including California, require day-care centers to allow parents to drop in without advance notice, and without discrimination or retaliation by the day-care center.

"Some of the parents who do drop in at their day cares report mistreatment of children," according to Amanda Gomez, an inspector with the San Diego County Department of Social Services. But Gomez estimated that fewer than 1 percent of parents take advantage of this right. Even though state law requires parents to be informed of their visitation rights, parents aren't fully aware of them or of how important they are. Also, some day-care facilities subtly discourage parents from visiting. Considering the shortage of quality day care, many parents don't want to risk offending providers. But the most important reason more parents don't police their children's day cares is because they can't get time off work.

Here are the chief elements in my Family Ties Bill:

• Employers would be required to give every parent two to four hours a month to visit their child at day care, or if the parent has hired a baby sitter or nanny, at home. The parent could split this time up into either several short visits or one long one. Preferably, the visits to day-care or elder-care settings would be unannounced visits.

- In order not to discriminate against nonparents, all employees would have the right to use two to four hours a month to visit their parents in elder care, or to do volunteer work in elder-care, child-care, or school settings.
- Employers would have the right to request proof of the visit and to ask for up to one week's notice. Ideally, Family Ties time would be considered paid time off. Companies with fifteen or fewer employees might be exempted from the requirement. No employee would be required to volunteer.

Precedents for my Family Ties proposal already exist: many companies, in their employee contracts, allow workers mental health days, paid days off for anniversaries and birthdays, and paid and unpaid pregnancy leave. Also, employers are required by law to allow workers to take time off for jury duty.

The cost of the Family Ties Bill? In the long run, very little. In fact, the Family Ties legislation would actually save companies money by increasing the work-place productivity of parents, which has been linked in some studies with employee anxiety about child or elder care. Those companies that offer more family-time provisions experience improved employee retention and recruitment. In addition, enacting this proposal could help save taxpayers millions of dollars in court costs by decreasing the number of litigated child-abuse cases, by slowing the growth of child protection agencies, and by decreasing the immeasurable long-term human expense.

I asked readers of my column in the *San Diego Union* to comment on the idea.

Perhaps predictably, reaction from politicians was dry, suggesting that no matter how much chest-beating they may do about the fate of children, most policymakers are reluctant to envision anything beyond the status quo.

But as we say in the business, the letters and phone calls poured in. Nearly all of them were from enthusiastic parents. The response indicated that both parents and nonparents are ready to support change in the work place to benefit families. One mother, Kathy Cross, wrote: "It would be delightful to be able to do a couple of volunteer hours a month in [my daughter's] class. . . . Her daddy would also love to do it." And Kathryn A. Bearss wrote: "I did have one day care that was leaving my

18-month-old son unsupervised — exactly for how long I don't know. Luckily, I found out within six weeks of placement. I found out because I showed up earlier than scheduled."

Ed Weingartner, a member of the board of education in the Santee, California, school district, sent this response:

> In 1986, when I was board president, I tried to identify major employers in the San Diego area where the parents of our students might be employed. Nearly 200 employers were identified. I then sent a letter proposing that they join the Santee district as partners in education by adopting policies to encourage employee participation in their children's education. Among the ideas set forth was paid time off (four hours per month) which employees could use to visit schools, volunteer time in the classroom, attend PTA meetings, etc.
>
> The response was underwhelming. Less than a handful of employers even bothered to respond to our letter. Those who did respond were not interested in such a policy. Some took the time to boast about their existing ties to the local schools, others sent a form letter. My own employer didn't respond at all.

Interestingly, not one employer wrote, either to argue with my Family Ties proposal or to support it. Until Southland called.

Now and then a company does something remarkable for its employees and for the community around it. The huge Southland Corporation, noted for owning or franchising every 7-Eleven convenience store in the universe, is one of those companies.

In recent months, Southland had been negotiating with Japanese interests for a buyout of the company, but that's not what three Southland executives wanted to talk about when we met for breakfast a few mornings ago. They wanted to talk about Family Ties.

"We read your column about making business give time off to parents, and frankly, it irritated us," said Gary Anderson, Southland's San Diego division manager. "If you think government can mandate the private sector to do this kind of thing and expect it to be successful, you're wrong."

However, Southland has announced its own corporate program, based on my Family Ties proposal. On March 12, 1990, Southland sent a letter to its two hundred corporate office employees within the San Diego division announcing what Paul Schmitt, Southland's regional human resource manager, now calls a Family Ties program.

"We wanted to have this thing in place before we made it public," said Don Cowan, publicity manager for Southland. (Cowan's wife, incidentally, operates a family day care in her home in Dallas.) "The program we're adopting is almost identical to the one you proposed."

With two exceptions. First: no government involvement. Second: the program will be what Schmitt calls a "shared cost" plan.

"Psychologically, employees have to have a stake in this," said Anderson. "If they don't share in the sacrifice, this idea won't take."

Under the Southland program, an employee will be able to take up to four hours a month off work to visit or volunteer in a day care, elder care, or school. (The arrangements are slightly different for salaried and hourly employees.) The employee would donate one or two work hours, for which he would not be paid, and the company would pay for one or two extra hours.

Fair enough. Cost sharing seemed to be an improvement on my proposal.

"My main interest is in improving education," said Anderson, who, by the way, has no children. "The stories I hear about the schools, and what that means for business, are frightening. We've got to get people more involved in the schools."

Over the next six months, if all went well, Southland planned to make the Family Ties option part of its permanent corporate benefits package.

"The next step will be to spread this idea through all of Southland's other regional division offices," said Cowan. "The idea could then be extended to Southland's approximately four thousand company-run 7-Elevens, and recommended to about three thousand franchisees and the fifty-two hundred stores operated by independent licensees, mainly overseas."

Potentially, the adoption of this idea could follow the same course as Southland's pioneering crime prevention program, which began in the San Diego region during the seventies and then spread nationally. "News of the Family Ties idea is already spreading within Southland nationally," said Schmitt. "It's possible that some of the divisions could set up test programs of their own, or adopt it outright even before we do. We haven't heard of any other companies doing anything like this."

Of course, success depends mostly on how employees respond to the idea. So far, signs are good.

"When we announced the program last month, we expected a 'ho-hum' response from the employees," said Anderson. "But they were excited. They said, 'This is great!' "

How could the company encourage high employee involvement? One way would be through a continuing education program to convince employees — who may have good reason for suspicion — that the company really does value good parents and community volunteers. Another way to guarantee success would be to sponsor, with company time and space, parent support groups. Southland executives were discussing these approaches, too.

I still suspect that government must eventually encourage business, perhaps through tax incentives, to allow more parenting and volunteer time. If nothing else, the threat of government action tends to concentrate the corporate mind. But Anderson is right: if the private sector can make family-time provisions work without government involvement, the programs will be better ones.

The long-term benefit of the Family Ties approach would go beyond preventing child abuse. Most child abuse does not happen in day care, but in the home. The best child-care and elder-care centers and the best schools are all empowered by family participation that, in turn, can improve the environment for the child at home.

Theoretically, the Family Ties approach could be something that conservatives and liberals could agree on, a bridge across the fundamental divide.

And a step toward a new kind of day care.

17

The Family-Friendly
Work Place

●

I heard this refrain from many parents: *What we really need is a job and a half.* As Judith Owen, a Swarthmore professor and mother, put it, "For my husband and me, it's not that two careers are too much, but two careers as they're presently shaped are too much." What does she want? Not two careers of 52.2 hours a week (the average workweek of professionals in America) but "two thirty-seven-and-a-half-hour weeks, or two thirty-hour weeks. That would be fine — if companies and government would establish some adequate support systems for parents."

She continued: "It seems to me that the whole society must shift its expectations away from the notion that the more you work, the more valuable a contributor you are. I've begun to see the beginnings of such a change, at least within the colleges, which are frequently at the leading edge of social change. For example, when I tell my department administrators that I must leave because I must get my son to soccer practice at three-thirty, they say, 'Oh, sure. We'll see you tomorrow,' and there isn't any hesitation. Maybe we'll see that attitude spreading in the corporate environment soon."

That new disposition won't spread without intense pressure from parents. How do we create a family-friendly work place — how do we *demand* a family-friendly work place?

In June 1989, a Louis Harris poll reported that job satisfaction among office workers was lower than in 1978 — a year when job enthusiasm was already in the pits. Disgruntlement on the job is especially strong among parents, who are torn between the worlds of work and home. At work, we feel we should be home more. At home, we feel we should be at work. Nowhere is the right place to be. This sense of conflict, sometimes called "transitional stress," is particularly characteristic of women. But men feel this sense of disconnection more intensely than commonly thought. "We tend to think working moms have a monopoly on guilt, but it's not true," says James Levine of the Bank Street College of Education in New York in *The 1990s Father: Balancing Work and Family Concerns.* "They're feeling that they're repeating the same pattern of their own fathers, not being around enough." Fran Rodgers of Work/Family Directions reported that many men are beginning to seek a balance between work and family — "they don't want to work overtime, they don't want to relocate, and they don't want their performance measured in terms of hours put in on the job. The intensity of feelings is greater for women; but they're there for both." An AT&T study found that among people with children under age eighteen, 73 percent of men and 77 percent of women deal with family issues while at work. Also, 25 percent of men and 48 percent of women spend "unproductive time at work because of child care issues." Indeed, dissatisfaction with child-care arrangements may be the most reliable predictor of employee absenteeism and unproductive work time.[1]

Yet despite much sound and fury in the media regarding the need for family-friendly work places, the nation's businesses are not moving swiftly toward new options. "Modern, paternalistic corporations," as one writer calls them, are offering medical, dental, and psychiatric health plans, matching-stock investment programs, meal subsidies, free haircuts, and even in-house gyms and health bars — everything *but* help with child care.[2] Although the percentage of employers offering some type of child-care assistance is increasing, by 1989 only three to four thousand out of six million U.S. employers provided such assistance to their employees.

Several factors hold back change, including the fact that today's typical top executives are still, after all these years, white (98.6 percent), male (97.7 percent), and married, and according to one study the typical executive's "wife, like his mother, does not work outside the home."[3] Our work institutions are encumbered with tired agendas.

Parents share some responsibility, however. Why don't they fight harder for family-friendly work places?

Several reasons: they're tired; their interest in creating pro-child work places lasts only as long as their children are small; they're isolated from other parents. And parents are often secretly ambivalent about either corporations or government being more involved in the daily care of their children. Also, the fundamental political divide in family values paralyzes the debate.

As parents, we can unlock the paralysis.

To do that we must face our ambivalence and ask two central questions. First, do we desire a system in which the company becomes the provider of day care and, in rare cases, even the provider of elementary schooling for our children, or do we wish to be helped by the company in ways that widen our options as parents outside the company? The second question is, Will we allow ourselves to be tracked, shunted to the rear of the work place for being parents?

The Integration of Children into the Work Place

The first option is the integration of children into the work place through company day-care facilities or other innovative approaches.

Some parents speak almost longingly of a future when the company will truly become an extended family, helping them even in caring for children; others are not so sure that this ideal is a worthy one. Wanting company day care and working for it are, it seems, two different things.

Oddly, no strong grassroots push from employees for on-site day care has arisen, though many studies show that Americans think companies should offer it. The reason for this inconsistency may be what *California Business* calls an "information barrier," the invisible wall between parents and employers. What employee wants to admit that his or her child-care problems are costing the employer money? Who wants to admit he's late, absent, distracted because he is a parent? To do so is to admit to what is, in too many employers' minds, a disability. The lack of a movement for company child care is symptomatic of parent isolation.

Another reason companies are slow to develop on-site company day cares is frustration with government regulation, usually designed for commercial child-care facilities.[4]

Jeanne Martin, an employee of a small computer technology company in Berkeley, California, told this story of trying to create an on-site day care at her small privately held firm: "This was the owner's idea because she brings her child to work with her every day. Her boy is three now. He's come every day since he was seven days old. He has a separate room off the owner's office with a crib and special carpeting and a rocking chair. He was nursed on-site. He's a child with eighty-five adults who love him, carry him around, talk to him. We have a party every Friday and it's readily accepted that the children are brought to the parties. If the children are nearby, at other day cares, the employees will leave a few minutes early and go get the child and bring him back for everybody to see. We know who the children are, how they're growing up. Some of our employees use child-care centers and occasionally these places close down, or things go on that the parents aren't happy with so they have to find new situations. At least one person gave us her resignation because she had a four-year-old and a new baby and her *au pair* left after three months.

"Over half of our employees are women, and we're over fifty-percent minority — mainly Thai and Laotian. Many of these women are having children. So when we bought a new building we thought including a child-care center would be a natural. We talked to our insurance agents and they said, 'No problem.' They didn't see much additional risk. The parents were all going to be on-site — we weren't taking children from the neighborhood at large, we were taking children only from our own employees. Even nursing mothers could come down and feed their children.

"Then we started contacting the state agencies and finding out that we needed so many square feet inside, per child, and so many square feet outside, per child, and a separate kitchen, and that we couldn't use the same kitchen for the preparation of the children's food that we used for employees. And there had to be so many caretakers, per child, and *they* needed so many supervisors per caretaker, and there had to be so many medical people, if not in residence then at least on call and within a certain radius. Even if we could have afforded to put in an extra kitchen, we still physically couldn't deal with the outside requirements for the sidewalk structure. A lot of the safety rules and regulations assume that the parent is completely absent. But our parents were there. Any parent working there could have walked in at any time to see their child.

"We gave up. The state won this battle and it's something that we clearly would have done."

Inappropriate government regulation is only part of the reason companies are slow to adopt on-site care, however. Something else is at work among parents: the often unexpressed unease with the idea of their company's having so much power — not only over their lives, but potentially their children's lives.

Barbara Reisman, director of the Child Care Action Committee, alluded to this resistance: "I used to work for a union years ago that was helping the workers of General Electric Company. The workers said, 'They have me for eight hours a day — I don't want them to have my kids, too.' We've got to bridge that trust gap. Workers should have some control over what goes on in that child-care program."

I asked Reisman if there had been too much emphasis by children's advocates on companies' supplying day care. "There's been way too much," she said. "Companies have to do a lot more, but I don't think they can carry the whole burden. They certainly can't build a coordinated system of child-care delivery throughout the community." That effort, she said, must come from government. "We don't ask companies to build hospitals, train doctors, and provide on-site surgical centers for their employees. We say companies should provide health insurance, but there are thirty-seven million workers in this country who get no health insurance. The notion that all these companies are going to run out and build child-care centers is ill-founded." Moreover, as technology and traffic patterns encourage more companies to decentralize in satellite offices and by allotting tasks to at-home workers, centralized company day care may become less attractive to both employers and employees, who may prefer other methods of child-care support.[5]

When company day care is adopted, it will likely be created not by individual companies but by private, shadow governments — interlaced corporate governments, government agencies with no elected representatives, public-private partnership, consortiums, community associations — none directly accountable to the public. The new relationship between companies, government, parents, and children is in its infancy. But while conventional government falters in its approach to family issues, these shadow governments are beginning to provide day care.

In Miami, I visited one possible future.

I pulled up to the empty guard station. A disembodied voice gurgled forth. "Come on through," it said. An iron gate slid open. Up ahead stood one of those gleaming glass monuments now so common in suburbia — this one the headquarters of Bankers Insurance Group. It seemed an unlikely site for one of the nation's most provocative experiments in public education. Out in front, someone pulled up in a car with her new baby and a dozen women gathered around, admiring the infant. Next to the building was a preschool playground with a padded play area, swings, a slide, and a jungle gym.

What is most extraordinary about Bankers Insurance, however, is not its on-site day care but its on-site public school.

Not far from the headquarters, just across a long grass field, was a small two-room schoolhouse — the nation's first corporate-based, publicly supported satellite learning center. At the time of my visit the Dade County school district was considering establishing other similar public/corporate-sponsored satellite schools. The Dade County school district would pay the teachers at these schools; participating companies would be asked to pay for construction, maintenance, custodial work, utilities, and security. Parents provide the transportation, so busing isn't a cost factor. The up-front savings: $219,000 for every new classroom built by a company instead of government.

This idea could spread.

After two years in operation, the Bankers satellite school, established in 1987, planned to extend its curriculum from kindergarten only to second grade. And eleven other Dade County companies had expressed interest in providing company-based public schools. Inquiries about the concept have come from as far away as Japan.

"Bankers made the decision to do this based primarily on our excellent experience in day care," said Phil Sharkey, Bankers' no-nonsense senior vice president for human resources. "Not only is this an excellent recruitment tool, but a phenomenal retention tool." According to Sharkey, the company's annual rate of employee turnover is 17.6 percent, but among those parents who enroll their children in the company day care or the satellite learning center, the turnover rate is only 4.2 percent. Absenteeism has been reduced by nearly 30 percent, and "tardiness is nonexistent because they have to get their children to school punctually," said Sharkey. "We figured three hundred and twenty-five thousand dollars [the cost of building the school] amortized over fifteen or twenty years is a pretty cheap price to pay if we can keep the retention rate as high as it is."

He smiled and pressed his fingers together.

"This school is money in the bank for us."

At the satellite school, housed in a temporary building (the company planned to build a fancier permanent structure), Roberta Keiser said: "I'm the teacher and the administrator here. I make decisions on the spot. No faculty politics. I don't have the daily contact or perhaps the daily heartache."

In a company conference room, several parents described their experience with the satellite school. The parents were enthusiastic about the ability to spend break time and lunch time with their children and volunteer in the classroom.

"My children just beam when I'm there," said Trish Otero, a document control supervisor. "When I'm not in the classroom, Mrs. Keiser will sometimes pick up the phone and say, 'Your daughter just amazed me.' Where else can you get that kind of contact?"

Julia Leon talked about her husband's anxiety about their kids before they entered the company school. "My husband works fourteen-, sixteen-hour days. Most of the time he gets home when the kids are already in bed — sometimes it will be a week before he will see them. He's a manager for a chemical company. Before the kids were in the satellite school, when they were in a private nursery, he was constantly asking, 'Who is the kid's teacher today?' and I would have to give him a daily report of what the kids had for lunch. God forbid it was cold lunch. He would ask: 'How tall is the fence in the school? Can they jump over it? Is the gate locked?' " But her husband worries less now that the kids are in the school.

"My husband is a little bit different," said Trish. "He'll call me maybe once a day: 'Have you seen the kids?' 'Well, honey, I've had a very busy day, I've had a lot of meetings.' He goes, 'Trish, come on, you've got this great benefit, take advantage of it every day.'

"But there is such a thing as overkill. The kids say: 'What are you doing here again? I'm going to see you tonight.' "

Manola Gutierrez said the small satellite school offered her child a smoother transition from preschool to kindergarten. "We're not just letting a five-year-old loose in some huge school. Most of the kids in our kindergarten were in day care here, and they know each other. This way, they enlarge their universe in smaller steps. My mother and my mother-in-law love this company — they know it's the closest thing they can get to my staying home with the kids."

All the parents agreed that the program had dramatically increased their loyalty to the company. One woman said she had turned down a job offered by another company that would have increased her yearly salary by $10,000.

Couldn't $10,000 buy her child the best private school?

She shook her head. "It's not the same. I can't be with my kids at the private school, at least not as frequently. Child care was driving me crazy. I was driving to two nurseries. I had to be at both nurseries before six, and I figured that one of these days I was going to kill myself on that road. The nurseries were charging five dollars per kid for each fifteen minutes of overtime. Plus, if you showed up late, they'd look at you like you were a child abuser. For me it wasn't just the inconvenience but the peace of mind. With all the crazy stories in the newspaper about what's happening in the day-care centers, child abuse and all that, you have no peace of mind if you can't check on your kids often."

"Until I came here, my kids viewed work as something that was taking Mommy away from them," said Manola. "They didn't know what work was, they didn't know what an office was. To them it was this black box, this big secret, this monster. They couldn't understand why I was gone eight or ten hours a day. One day my child said, 'Just kill that ugly monster and stay home, Mommy.' Those were her exact words."

Now that she drives her kids to work — and to school — she said, "They understand my work, and that I'm safe, and that I'm going to pick them up."

Had they mentioned the monster since?

"No," she said. "The monster's dead."

I came away from Bankers Insurance impressed with the company's efforts to be family-friendly, and yet vaguely uncomfortable.

This particular company is surely benevolent toward parents and children. But not all companies are so straightforward in their priorities.

Economists David Bloom and Todd Steen have suggested that one way to increase the supply of workers as the baby bust creates more demand "is to raise labor-force participation rates. Men's rates have been declining steadily and should continue to decline through 2000. In contrast, more women are willing to go to work. . . . Better child care could bring substantial numbers of workers into the labor force." They cite a Census Bureau report suggesting that fully 26 percent of non-working mothers with preschoolers say they would look for work if reasonably priced child care were available. And, write Bloom and Steen, "better child care would also allow many women to work more hours, further magnifying their impact on labor-supply growth."

The good news is employers will be more likely to offer on-site child care; the bad news is that even fewer parents will be at home with their kids — and mothers and fathers will probably be working even longer hours.[6] Particularly in non-unionized regions of the country, some companies may come to view on-site day care as a way of squeezing more hours from their employees.

The strands of the new web, particularly where the company and government are involved, should be woven with caution. Yes, we need company help with child care. But we need to scrutinize such help through the lens of family liberation, not merely that of convenience. If a company offers on-site day care and then expects us to work longer hours, who is liberated? The parent? The child?

Company day care is an important piece in the puzzle, but too few companies are talking about the host of other approaches that, when combined with good day care (corporate or otherwise), increase family time: flex-time and flexible scheduling; part-time work with benefits; job sharing; family leave; career breaks; telecommuting; a four-day workweek; and several hours a month available for visiting day cares or elder cares or volunteering in schools. These goals may seem out of reach today, but as the baby-bust generation creates a labor-seller's market, families should be asking for more.

Toward a New Work Consciousness

A new work consciousness is needed — a new sense of balance between work and family, a public understanding that an essential employee benefit is more family time even for families without children.

This is not to degrade the psychological worth of careers to men and women. Some parents are better parents when employed; some are better parents without a career; but an increasing number of parents need a mix. Consequently, an important goal is work-place choice — allowing parents a degree of flexibility so that they can determine for themselves what mix of work and at-home time is best for their families. Today that choice is too narrow, but many parents already have more choices than they realize.

Amy Stillman, president of the support group Mothers at Home More, described what might be called the parent preparation gap. Parents, she said, seldom talk to one another about how the work place could be changed, or what their roles should be in that change. "Parents do not prepare themselves for the future," she said. One of the reasons is that many women think that families and work are mutually exclusive, separate realms. Not surprisingly, that is also how their employers view work and family. So when women become pregnant, employers think, Well, that's it for them! Never see them again! They're gone! Because of this, women are reluctant to talk at work about family needs. They keep this part of their lives to themselves. They consider family needs to be personal."

Talking about family issues and needs at work is a taboo — an invitation for discrimination.

"One of the reasons for parent/employee isolation is human nature," said Stillman. "Whatever choices we make we try to justify. The at-home mothers clip out the newspaper articles regarding studies that describe how great it is for them to be at home. And all the working parents clip the articles that say day care is good for children. Each side tends to be defensive about the choice they have made, and when you are defensive it's hard to converse with someone who has made a different choice."

No option is perfect, she added. "It is important to talk about your decisions, so that other parents who are making choices will know how to make good ones. I'm encouraged, though, that more parents are beginning to discuss these choices openly."

Mothers First, an organization based in Washington, D.C., advocates at-home parenting, but one of its goals is to encourage parents, in twice-monthly meetings, to communicate about home/work decisions — how best, for instance, to deal with income loss if the decision is made to stay home. Mothers First is currently establishing chapters around the country which will serve as support groups.

"Clearly, the companies are not as flexible as they should be," said Stillman. "Simultaneously, parents are not as aggressive in trying to arrange flexible work options as they could be."

To begin with, parents could think through what it is they really want. "A great many parents, nearing the birth of their first child, start considering how they will balance work and family, and their first inclination is to think in all-or-nothing terms," Stillman said. "They take their maternity leave and go back to work and they miss their baby. If that doesn't work out, they go home, and shift into the Nothing Mode — a sense of giving up identity in favor of the baby. Their sense of self-esteem gradually falls. That doesn't have to happen. If parents want to maintain part-time or at-home work, they need to think this option through early. They need to ask themselves, How many hours a week will it take to do a part-time job? While you're still working full-time, begin to keep a diary: 'Do I need to do all the tasks personally? Could I share some of them? Could I do some of them at home?' It's important to first ask those questions, to analyze your work that way, and *then* go to your employer with a proposal. So often, parents go to their employers and say, 'I'm not sure how much I want to work — what do you think?' But the burden is equally shared. It's in the employer's best interest to keep the employees, and it's in the employee's best interest to maintain his or her work and income. So if you go to your employer once and the employer says, 'No, that's not going to work,' regroup and go back! Keep proposing options!"

Such pressure, applied often enough by enough parents, will lift the consciousness of employers and other parents.

The more parents arrange and take alternative work/family options and succeed in the work place and at home, the easier it will be for employers to make such options available to more parents, and the easier it will be for future parents to demand and expect these options. The aging of the population will make some options — the career break, for example — more palatable for parents and for employees, Stillman pointed out. "I'm planning to work until I'm eighty, whereas the earlier generation thought of stopping at sixty. But the work environment has become more technological, and the tasks are less physically demanding, so people work longer into their lives. Taking five or ten years out of your meteoric rise will not be that crucial."

Part of the new work consciousness, too, is this question: With or without company day care, should we be working this hard?

In the iconoclastic and thought-provoking newsletter *New Options*, Sam Keen, a long-time contributing editor of *Psychology Today*, contends that the traditional Left and Right have made a tacit agreement not to discuss how parents' dedication to the company is shaping their kids, and how to raise a compassionate generation. "In many ways this society has said, 'Look, we're too busy for our children,' " says Keen. "But what the kids get, the metamessage, is that they're not important — not important enough for our parents to spend time with them. And that's not going to create a compassionate people."

Frank Rubenfeld, co-founder of Psychotherapists for Social Responsibility, is a first-time father at the age of fifty-one. "I think men's spending time with kids just has to deepen their appreciation of life," he told *New Options*. "If men have day-to-day contact with an infant, I think it has to affect their view of the vulnerability of life, the preciousness of life. It would elicit and enhance their feelings about wanting to nurture and serve. And I think it would affect the kids' own view of the self and men and the value of nurturing." To make this experience more likely to occur, Rubenfeld supports generous parental leave policies for both women and men. "This is a very tender area for many, many families. You're touching on families' deeply held beliefs, and there are some families that want to be more traditional. And that's their privilege. But for those that want to try this other way, I think they should have that opportunity. Just the fact that [paid parental leave for men and women] would become an issue in public policy might intensify the change in public consciousness — by making the general public aware that more and more men are wanting to spend more time with their children." [7]

Changing corporate attitudes, despite favorable demographics, will not be easy. Parents themselves, and their favored elected representatives and unions, must force the issue. Typical American employers treat child rearing as an idiosyncratic act bordering on the irresponsible. With the growing internationalization of capital and labor, some large employers privately believe that they have little economic reason to make a commitment to the education and well-being of American children. Why should they, when they can move their factories offshore and automate? The answer to that dismal shortsightedness is international social competition. In much of Europe, government and private companies pay family allowances, subsidize child care, encourage alternative work schedules, allow parental absence for children's illnesses, and offer long job breaks. In most European countries, child rearing is seen as a service to the wider community, not simply a private act of procreation. This European attitude toward children may seem superfluous to American corporate leaders now, but as the sixteen-member European Community begins to flex its economic muscle, the payoff for European companies, because of pro-family policies, will be a work force far more technologically capable and personally secure than our own. That outcome is ensured, unless a family liberation movement quickly reforms the American work place.

The Need for Family Leave

Among the essential elements of a truly family-friendly work place is adequate family leave.

For the first three to four months of life, an infant should be in the care of its parents, according to Dr. T. Berry Brazelton, associate professor of pediatrics at Harvard Medical School. "Parents that know they are going to have to give up their baby too soon to another caregiver go through an automatic kind of grieving," he says. They suffer denial — denial that it matters, denial that the baby will suffer or that they will suffer. They project onto other people the responsibility for their baby, and they feel detachment, "not because they don't care, but because it hurts so much to care." Mothers are often forced by economic necessity to return to work prematurely, before they have recovered fully from childbirth. Parents and siblings have little time to adapt as a new member reshapes the family unit. Yet, according to a survey by the labor organization Nine to Five and the National Association of Working Women, most working women — three in five — are employed by companies with no form of maternity leave.[8] This is true despite the fact that 85 percent of working women will become pregnant at some time during their careers.

Edward Zigler of the Bush Center in Child Development and Social Policy at Yale points out that the lack of support for a working family at the time of birth can create stress for fathers as well. Child psychology experts recognize the importance of fathers in the development of their infants, that the early attachment between father and child is crucial to their future relationship. Yet, typically, the father is not allowed any significant time off work to deal with inevitable loss of sleep, to help with child care, to give the mother needed emotional support. "Caught in a series of escalating stresses, he is severely hampered in his ability to fill the multiple roles that society is beginning to expect of him," writes Zigler.[9]

In recent years Connecticut, Minnesota, and Oregon have passed legislation providing some parental leave to either parent. In addition, twenty-five states had legislation pending in 1988 on parental or maternity leave.[10] No state has yet mandated paid maternity leave, however. By contrast, guaranteed, paid infant-care leave exists in every industrialized nation other than the United States and South Africa.

In Japan, for example, women are entitled to six weeks' maternity leave both before and after childbirth, at 60 percent salary. In West Germany, parents can receive six weeks' paid maternity leave before childbirth and eight weeks' paid leave afterward, with an optional partially paid four-month leave.[11] As was mentioned in the last chapter, Swedish parental leave policy provides twelve months' leave, possibly to be extended to eighteen months in 1991, with the state providing 90 percent of lost income. Mothers may take an additional six-month leave at 70 percent pay.

In the United States, pressure is building for family leave, but so is the resolve of opposition. In 1990 Congress passed the Family and Medical Leave Act, which would have provided twelve weeks annually of job-protected unpaid leave for any employee for the birth, adoption, or serious illness of a child or dependent parent. The bill did not apply to companies with fewer than fifty employees. Its chief supporter, Republican Representative Marge Toukema of New Jersey, described the bill as "so minimal it's almost an embarrassment to present it." Lawrence Perlman, president and chief executive officer of Control Data, described it as a "moderate and appropriate response to dramatic changes in the American work force." Two years prior to passage of the bill, candidate George Bush said, "We need to assure that women don't have to worry about getting their jobs back after having a child." However, President Bush vetoed the act, which fell fifty-four votes short of an override. At the state and national level, we must strengthen our resolve.

Arguments against such proposals are often made on the basis of national productivity. The U.S. Chamber of Commerce, for instance, claims that the Family and Medical Leave Act would cost $16.2 billion a year in lost productivity. But how much productivity and creativity are we losing now — and how much will parents and companies lose in future decades if we accept, without question, a society in which parents work longer and harder and children spend more and more time in institutions?[12] The Chamber of Commerce offers no accounting of that loss.

It also neglects to mention that most of the costs of parental leave are borne by the parents themselves, who lose weeks or months of salary while newborn or sick children are boosting family expenses.

William Even, assistant professor of economics at Miami University in Oxford, Ohio, believes that, if companies are forced to offer maternity leave, they will begin to discriminate against women when they discover how expensive a maternity leave policy is. "They may try to offset these costs by not hiring women, or lowering salary or benefits," says Dr. Even.[13] This criticism is answered by including men in paternal leave policies — and by pointing out that, as the baby-bust generation enters the work force, experienced workers are too valuable to lose through discrimination.

Moreover, corporate America could clearly benefit.

A study by the U.S. Chamber of Commerce itself confirms the view that parental leave can make companies more productive. A survey of companies offering parental leave found that more than 60 percent cited "recruitment and retention" of good employees as the main reason for the program. J. Douglas Phillips, senior director of corporate planning at Merck and Company, one of the nation's largest pharmaceutical firms, says that his company's child-care leave policy has resulted in savings. Phillips estimates the cost of losing an employee at $50,000. But by permitting a worker to take a six-month child-care leave (cost: $38,000), the company achieves a net improvement of $12,000.[14]

In *Personnel Journal*, Catalyst, a research organization that helps corporations foster the careers of women, reports that the interim costs to Southern New England Telephone of maintaining health-care benefits for those on leave was a minuscule one-quarter of 1 percent of the company's total health insurance costs. Catalyst asserted that the cost of not supplying parental leave is best measured against that of employee turnover, and one estimate indicates that turnover for any position can cost companies approximately 93 percent of a first-year salary — the cost of recruitment and training, plus the cost of lost productivity during the time it takes a new employee to become accustomed to the job.

Many companies surveyed by Catalyst did not know the true costs — and savings — of parental leave because they do not keep any statistics on the subject. Others, aware of the economic advantages, have developed good family leave policies, among them Campbell Soup, American Express, Aetna Life, and Johnson and Johnson, which provides up to one year of unpaid family leave with full benefits and a promise of reemployment for anyone who has to care for a child, a spouse, or a parent.

One major consideration, according to Catalyst, is the development of plans to handle the work flow in the absence of regular employees. In New York, Time, Incorporated uses an in-house supplementary replacement system to fill in for employees on any type of leave and employees for the jobs they fill.[15]

The debate about family leave should eventually revolve less around whether family leave should exist than how long the leave should be, and other negotiable details. A panel of experts at the Bush Center recommends an optional six-month protected leave for either mother or father at the time of birth or adoption which would include continuation of medical and other benefits, with a 75 percent salary replacement up to a reasonable maximum for three months. The panel suggested that this salary be paid through an insurance fund to which employers and employees would contribute. This fund could be administered by the federal government or by the states.

Another approach would be a career-break plan. In England, for example, under the provisions of a new Return to Work plan, women who have worked two years for Lombard North Central, a London finance house, can apply for an extended leave to care for babies or toddlers. Lombard's plan is, according to *Christian Science Monitor* writer Marilyn Gardner, one of a small but growing number of career-break programs British companies are devising to help working parents and to stem the loss of trained employees. A typical leave lasts five years; some companies, such as Lombard, offer a possible two-year extension. Most firms require participants to complete two weeks' paid work each year to maintain contacts and update skills. Mothers on leave are not strictly employees during their absence, explained one Lombard administrator: "They're more like members of a club." They receive no salary or benefits, but are kept informed of activities and changes within the firm. If the company does not have a suitable opening available when a worker is ready to return, the employee is kept on the plan until an opening occurs.[16]

To working parents in the United States, a leave of several years to care for small children seems a distant dream — yet imagine the sense of security such a policy would offer parents, and the corresponding security of a company that would enjoy the support of a reserve force of trained individuals. With the coming labor shortages among highly skilled workers, such a policy would be more practical than utopian. At-home parents on a planned career break might be called on by their companies to do part-time or occasional work. Besides the emotional (and technological) connection with the company, the parent would have a source of occasional supplementary income. Of course, legal and contractual safeguards would be needed to protect career-break workers doing occasional work at home or in the office from economic exploitation or unsafe working conditions.

Toward a Smorgasbord of Family Time Options

Is company day care, then, an idea whose time has passed? Possibly. Certainly a broader, mix-and-match approach will likely become a more popular option than company day care. Levi Strauss, for example, whose at-home employees resisted company day care, now offers up to five months' disability and child-care leave for both men and women after the birth or adoption of a child, plus flex-time and job sharing.

A family-friendly work place might arrange for a discount with established private child-care facilities, or make voucher payments toward whatever child-care arrangement the parent chose. A company might also provide temporary emergency care for those days when an employee's regular arrangements fail, or join networks that identify and recruit good day-care help and pass that information on to employees. A family-friendly company might financially sponsor existing day-care facilities used by employees. In Texas, the Corporate Child Development Fund matches centers that need money with altruistic companies willing to fund them.

Jacquie Swaback, child-care coordinator for Sacramento, recommends that more companies adopt a "cafeteria" approach to benefits so that an employee can choose among child-care reimbursement, more vacation days, and health insurance. A two-paycheck family doesn't need two health-care plans, so if one spouse has health care, the other spouse can choose a child-care benefit. The company, then, gets a tax write-off for offering either a voucher for child care or on-site day care. Interestingly, by eliminating redundancy in benefits, society's expenditure on child care becomes more a matter of shifting resources, from health insurance companies to child care, than a major new outlay.

This approach can also be part of a potential new relationship among government, business, and labor. For example, Sacramento has negotiated union contracts that include cafeteria benefits and the provision of child-care assistance.

A handful of large companies are defining what it means to be a family-friendly work place. Merck and Company, one of the nation's largest pharmaceutical firms, offers job-protected parental leaves for both fathers and mothers for up to eighteen months. Merck also allows flexible working hours and several on-site or nearby child-care centers. Other leading companies, including American Telephone and Telegraph, Corning Glass Works, Levi Strauss and Company, and Steelcase, have shown similar leadership and creativity. Among unions, the Service Employees International Union and the Communications Workers of America have emphasized the importance of family support benefits in contract negotiations.[17]

Katherine Tanelian, with the elaborate title of "world wide personnel communications manager" at Hewlett-Packard, described how her company, noted for its humane personnel policies, defines a family-friendly company: "This isn't just one problem — day care — it's seventeen. We offer a flexible time-off program which combines traditional sick leave and vacation time. Now employees receive fifteen flexible days off to use at their discretion — in addition to eleven paid holidays. We treat people like adults. We don't ask for doctors' notes. We realized that we had a lot of honest working parents who would call in and say, 'I have to take a vacation day because my son is ill,' while others would simply say, 'I need sick leave.' It's now accepted in the company culture that people will call in and say they need a flex-day — flexible working hours for that day — because their child is ill. You can even take this time in hourly increments. In addition to that, we have flexible working hours. You can come to work anytime from six to eight-thirty and work your eight hours. We trust you to do that, we don't have time clocks. There are a few exceptions. If you're in a particular environment — say, an assembly line — your hours are not as flexible. You have to make an agreement with your group. If you're going to take several days off, you need to give some notice."

As part of its benefits package, Hewlett-Packard also makes it relatively easy for a new parent to take a leave of several months. Combining all the available increments of paid and unpaid time, a new mother can usually take up to three months off. Plus, using the company's job guarantee stipulation, a mother could take an additional four months — though she may not be returning to the same job.

Hewlett-Packard has also introduced a new part-time policy. A new mother may, after having a child, decide that she doesn't want to come back full-time. At that point, she and her supervisors determine if her existing job can be done part-time or if another part-time job is available. "We have some jobs that lend themselves well to that," said Tanelian. "For instance, in telemarketing, people spend almost all their time on the phone communicating with customers. We've discovered that telemarketing is often done *better* in less than eight hours — because of burnout." Other jobs appropriate for job sharing include those of receptionist, software developer, and technical writer. So far, less than 5 percent of Hewlett-Packard's employees are part-time workers, but Tanelian reported increasing interest in part-time work.

"Sometimes time is not the problem, finances are. So instead of an on-site center, we offer pre-tax accounts for dependent care [for the old or young]. You can estimate how much you spend for child care or parent care and set it aside for an account that is not taxed. That helps offset the burden.

"Another reason we don't offer on-site day care is equity. We offer the same basic package to all employees, so building a child-care center would not benefit the people who do not have kids. Cost-wise we could afford to do it, but it doesn't feel very equitable."

Yet Hewlett-Packard and the few other companies that offer such options remain outstanding exceptions among corporations. Too often the attitude of employers is epitomized in the statement of one boss, a recently divorced man with no children, who told me: "I resent all these parents asking for special treatment. Every time one of them wants time off, one of the other employees, without kids, has to take up the slack." The fact that these employees are shaping America's future employees escapes him. Although small entrepreneurial companies might be excused for such an attitude, large corporations should not be.

A crucial element in any family-friendly package is for companies to follow Johnson and Johnson's lead and adopt training programs to sensitize supervisors to the need for balancing work and family.

What we will see, then, in coming years will be three kinds of companies: those that offer little or nothing to families; those that offer company day care in an increasingly controlled work environment; and those that offer a range of choices, flexibility, and time — with or without on-site day care.

Beyond the Mommy Track

If we are to create a truly family-friendly work place, one final question is extremely important: Will we allow ourselves, as parents, to be passed by for work-place advancement because we have supposedly special needs? The suggestion that such work-place discrimination — creating a so-called Mommy Track — would be good for parents and good for business was made by Felice N. Schwartz, author of a now-famous article published in the *Harvard Business Review* in 1989, "Management Women and the New Facts of Life," in which she argued that corporations should recognize two different groups of women managers: those who make their careers their chief priority and those who need a flexible schedule to put children first.

Schwartz declares that women in management cost corporations more than men do. Her article argues that employers would do best by identifying whether a woman is "career primary," which means she can be worked long hours, promoted, relocated, and generally treated like a man; or "career and family"—oriented, meaning she is valuable to the company for her willingness to accept lower pay and little advancement in return for a flexible schedule to accommodate family needs. Schwartz offers little evidence for her claims. The article cites only two studies, both by companies Schwartz does not name in order to preserve confidentiality.[18]

One study, by a multinational corporation, found that the rate of turnover among the best women managers was two and a half times greater than among male managers of similar abilities. (Could this be because there are fewer women managers than men, and they are therefore more competitively sought after by companies?) The other, by a "large producer of consumer goods," found that half the women who took maternity leave returned to the job later than they promised or not at all. (Could this be because most companies offer obscenely short maternity leaves?)

Some corporate spokespersons jumped to support Schwartz's statements. In a letter to the *Harvard Business Review*, Richard Lewis, chairman of Corporate Annual Reports, called the article "a historical point in the discussion of women in business."

But feminists attacked the notion of the Mommy Track as enormously damaging to the women's movement. Fran Rodgers of Work/ Family Directions estimated that more than 80 percent of women who take maternity leave do return to the job. "What's so disturbing about Felice Schwartz's article," she said, "is that it is devoted to fitting women into the existing culture instead of finding ways to change that culture. And this idea of dividing women into two groups, but completely ignoring the diversity among men, is just horrifying."

Those of us dedicated to a family liberation movement should view any attempt by business to create a Mommy Track as dangerous to children. For example, the economic welfare and career advancement of single mothers would worsen under such a plan, further deepening the feminization of poverty. Moreover, by singling out women to be tracked, such companies would be actively discouraging ambitious women from expecting any company arrangements for family time. Political cartoonist David Horsey summed up the approach succinctly in a cartoon for the *Seattle Post-Intelligencer*. In the cartoon, a woman in a business suit pauses before an office entrance. Next to the doorway are two drinking fountains — a clean, new fountain with a sign above it reading CAREER WOMEN ONLY, and a small, shabby fountain; its sign reads BREEDERS ONLY.

The Mommy Track proposal makes strategic sense to corporations resisting family pressure: divide and conquer by dividing women among themselves, women from men, and parents from other employees. (Notice that the very name "Mommy Track" uses the diminutive form of *mother*; notice too that the proponents do not prescribe a Daddy Track or a Parent Track.)

With the certainty that new work arrangements will have to be made for parents, is there an alternative to the demeaning Mommy Track?

Yes. Call it the Family Track — by which I mean provisions for all employees who belong to families, including families without children. A major goal of a Family Track approach would, of course, be the welfare of children, but children and parenting would be viewed in a larger context. Family-friendly work places will not become a reality, at least not in any fair form, as long as women and men, parents and nonparents are seen in competition for special needs. We need a different approach. First, parents should be seen not as having special needs but needs central to the welfare of society, essential to any company concerned with the care and feeding of its future workers.

Second, this approach should complement other family needs for time, for help with their parents' care, and for a better balance between work and other human requirements. In other words, mothers should not be patronized within a company. The essence of family liberation is connection, not exclusion from or opposition to or even competition with other social groups.

A generation ago it would not have occurred to new fathers to take time off for the birth of a child, an increasingly common practice today. But nearly three-fourths of fathers in a study of AT&T employees said they had to deal with family issues while at work. Almost half of du Pont's male workers reported difficulties making child-care arrangements. A national study in 1989 by Opinion Research Corporation of Princeton, New Jersey, found that male managers under forty are the group in the work force least satisfied with the amount of time their jobs leave for family life. According to the U.S. Census Bureau, while Mom is at work, no one — grandparents, baby sitters, and day-care providers included — looks after more preschool-aged children than do fathers.[19]

According to a survey by Du Pont in 1988, 33 percent of the company's male employees said they would like to work part-time and be with their families more. Du Pont, Corning, Merck, and many other big companies already have "family interest" policies — carefully worded to be nonsexist — that would allow men to take a greater part in child rearing. Very few men have signed up, however, probably because they're not encouraged to.[20] The Mommy Track, if implemented, will only make the situation worse. How will a man be able to claim his family needs him if his wife's whole career has been restructured so *she* can be available?

If business can be flexible about the shape of women's careers, it can be equally flexible about men's. Why shouldn't there be many career patterns, based on interests besides parenthood? According to Arlie Hochschild and Anne Machung, authors of *The Second Shift: Working Parents and the Revolution at Home,* many people are starting to feel they ought to be able to pursue outside commitments other than family. Some would like to go back to school, maybe for a work-related degree, but maybe not. Others are committed to volunteer projects such as working with the homeless, or to a pursuit like making scenery for a local theater — something that calls on talents that don't emerge on the job. Hochschild and Machung say that allowing time for such commitments makes good business sense: "Companies would cut down on absenteeism, low productivity and depression if they'd allow employees to live balanced lives."[21]

Imagine a family liberation movement in the work place which aimed to benefit all of this larger context, including men and nonparents with family needs. Suddenly the idea of a demeaning Mommy Track fades; instead of creating a company minority ghetto of underpaid, under-appreciated women, a Family Track approach would appeal to a coalition of groups — perhaps more than half of all workers. Such a political alliance would not only make family-friendly work places more possible politically, but more pleasant places for everyone to work. And that principle — viewing improvements for children as improvements for everyone — is crucial to the weaving of the new web.

Families need a lot more than day care. They need a work environment that redefines the best way to achieve productivity — an environment that encourages family time and discourages the current headlong rush into national workaholism. Ultimately, they need to refashion personal attitudes about the value of work. In the words of one Wichita parent, "Maybe we need to start questioning how many things we need, and whether it's really worth it to work this hard and be away from our children so much."

18

Heading Home

●

Some parents are balancing work and family life by heading home —
in a new way.

During the fifties and sixties and even into the seventies, most women
stayed home with their children. But then came the feminist movement
and an economy transforming from industrial to service jobs, which
brought women overdue economic power. Sometime in the seventies,
staying home went out of fashion.[1]

For many parents, and some children, Mom's going to work was an
overdue liberation. Indeed, some parents found they were better at parenting when they worked. "I spent the first two years of my oldest son's
life with him, and I regret it," said a financial officer at Bankers Insurance Group in Miami. "I got anxious and irritable. I was spending a lot
of time with my son, but it wasn't productive time. I just had to go back
to work or go nuts. Does that make me a bad parent? I'm a better one
now, that's for sure." And one woman, a college professor, recalled: "As
a little girl I wished that my mother would go to work. She was a very
bright woman, and I grew angry watching her fall further and further
behind intellectually. Her role was to be a good housewife, a good cook,
mend fences with the neighbors, make sure that the community as a
whole held together — and she was very good at this. But after a while,
I couldn't talk to her anymore about politics or anything intellectual.
And I resolved as I grew up that staying home with the kids would not
be enough for me." She paused. "On the other hand, I can remember
coming home from school and being glad that she was there, because I
used to spill out my heart and soul to her and she would listen. That's
the selfish little girl in me speaking, wanting all of my mom.

"Even if I wanted to, it wouldn't be that simple to stay home. When I was a little girl, the neighborhoods were overflowing with children. Today the street on which I live is absolutely empty. When I was a little girl, a network of mothers at home helped each other. You know where I turn to get that kind of help? To the day-care teachers. But still, I'm very ambivalent about this."

Because of this same ambivalence, which can tip in either direction, many women — and a few men — have taken a look at the quality of their lives and their children's lives and have headed home. For them, going home is one way to begin to reweave the web. It's not the only way, but it's one way.

Dreams in Collision

There is nothing easy about the decision, nothing clear about the price or the payoff of heading home.

The economics of the decision reveals two American dreams in conflict: one, the dream of hearth and home, the yearning to spend more time with children and family; the other dream of upward mobility, home ownership, improving one's station in life, saving for college, being fully insured, having material goods beyond day-to-day necessities.

At Bankers Insurance Group, a stylish and professionally dressed woman described how she regretted "leaving [her] children with strangers at six weeks old when they couldn't defend themselves," and yet she felt she had no choice. "There's no way I could stay home and have everything we needed. There's certain things in life you want to give your kids. You just don't want to pass with what you can have. It's hard to explain. You always want the better house, the better car, you want to take the kids for a vacation. You want your kids to have better than what you had. So I decided to go out and work, and about the only thing I regret in my life is not staying home with my kids for the first two years."

Still, some families seem to do just fine despite the hardship of cutting back to one salary.

Lucinda Dyer, West Coast publicist for Christian-oriented publishers, told of the sacrifice she sees fundamentalist families making. "We took a survey in our fellowship and eighty percent of our members have been to college, thirty percent to graduate school. This discounts the popular impression of religiously conservative folk as uneducated, simple people who don't know what they're missing. They feel the same pressures to be seen as successful, yet they choose to stay home with their kids and make what some people currently view as very un-American sacrifices."

One at-home mother spoke with anger about the people who believe keeping one parent home is economically impossible. Dena, who considers herself a feminist, said: "I guess we stay-at-homes are just ignorant, barefoot in the kitchen. We don't know how hard it is to have to go out to work. And we just can't appreciate how much some people have to sacrifice for their new drapes, their brand new car, the new carpet. They say to me: 'Well, you're just fortunate that your husband can support a family of five. Aren't you lucky?' Well, shit, I'm not lucky. I have garage-sale furniture; it's no better than it was in college. I had a cousin call me the second week in January, in tears, absolutely hysterical. This is someone who works for Xerox and has a high-paying position, saying, 'Oh, I just know when I bring that baby into day care that I won't be able to talk with her again until she's twenty-four.' She's mortgaged to the hilt. She and her husband believe they have no choice at this point. They'd lose money selling the house, but who put them in that position? Why did they choose to go that way?

"Don't get me wrong. I think the women's movement is correct. My grandmother is seventy-six. When her husband died, she took his job and did the same work for one-half the pay so that she could maintain the family. But I think that feminists really missed the boat by not demanding respect for all we do, for providing emotional support for husbands, children; for bringing healthy, capable people into this world."

Parents often mentioned their unease with how they would be perceived by parents who worked outside the home — or, in fact, how they would be perceived by their own children. One mother said: "I often say to my husband, 'What kid likes their mother?' I wonder about when my kids grow up, what they'll think of me. If I stay home, are they going to look at me as somebody who helped them the most? Or are they going to make fun of me, like I make fun of my mother and mother-in-law?"

Despite the isolation, the economic sacrifice, and the colliding dreams, most of the at-home parents I spoke with said they had no regrets. In fact, some parents who have gotten a taste of staying at home after being temporarily laid off, or because they decided to stay at home for their baby's first six months, find it difficult to return to outside work. A woman in Seattle told this story: "Until about a year ago, I was a working parent. Then my husband's company got on its feet, so I decided to stop for a year and be with my children. It's nice to know that dinner will be ready and the laundry will be done. Just the little, basic nice things about life. Now I have to return to work, and I told my son, Jeff [a thirteen-year-old], and he said, 'I understand, Mom. You always liked working.' Later he wrote a note to his aunt, and the first line just said, 'Thank you for the five dollars for my birthday.' And then the rest of this letter was how he felt about my going back to work."

How did he feel?

"Scared. And to tell you the truth, so am I. For this last year, Jeff has been coming home and talking to me a lot about how he feels. He's a real open kid. I've always made sure that everybody in the family talked a lot. He has a real good relationship with me and he does with his dad too, but when I quit work he began to come home every day to talk to me. Before that, I don't think he was getting enough contact with me or any other supportive adults. He knows that, and he says, 'Which adults can I trust?' And I see people all the time who are crabby and unreasonable and that includes teachers, and I think, They're stretched so thin. . . .

"I ran my own business — we're talking a lot of hours. I do production work. My husband is a builder, and everybody knows builders work pretty long days. My kids aren't neglected, I want you to know. It's easy for that to happen and I've seen other parents who care a lot who do end up neglecting their kid. And they have no intention of doing it. I have to confess that when I was working, I was kind of like, 'Don't talk to me now.' But there's been a great difference at home since I've been off this year. I love being there to bring the kids home from school, being there for them and looking after them. It's been such a treat. And, you know, I love to work and I have to confess that I gain the greatest sense of personal growth from working, but it's so frustrating . . . that these little children are with you for such a short period of your life. I don't know what I'm going to do!"

For many mothers, staying home is not a rejection of feminism but an expansion of it — or a recognition of an uncomfortable and unjust economic reality: the spouse with the smaller salary, usually the mother, is almost invariably the one who quits work to stay home. Ironically, when women do stay home, their action encourages employers to rationalize the Mommy Track — companies' relegation of mothers to a diminished status. Census data indicate that few married men stay home with their kids, despite the impression created by a flurry of magazine articles about househusbands and at least one movie, *Mr. Mom,* in the seventies and eighties.

An essential goal of family liberation must be equal pay for equal work, regardless of gender. Equalizing male and female income would encourage more men to stay home with their children, and child care would no longer be a gender issue.

We should also support policies that allow families to keep a parent — mother or father — at home. Government will probably be subsidizing more and better day care, but families that choose to keep one parent at home should also be encouraged. An editorial writer for the *Colorado Springs Gazette* offers this intriguing proposal: "Raise the personal exemption from $2,000 per child to $6,000," which would allow either the father or the mother to stay at home on a part- or full-time basis. Such a tax break would also help single parents make ends meet.

What else would encourage more men to stay home? William R. Beer, who has done one of the few studies on househusbands, writes, "It is still a threat to many women to have a man take over aspects of household work, and especially of child care, that traditionally have been performed by women." Legally, married women are not required to support their husbands.

> In fact, if a man does not work for money, if he stays home and devotes all of his efforts to household work, he can be sued for divorce on the grounds of nonsupport. . . . In two thirds of the states, a wife is not required to support a husband even when he cannot support himself.
> Sweden has one of the longest-standing and most comprehensive programs to encourage male participation in family life, including househusbanding. In addition to comprehensive day care and parental insurance, Sweden offers child care training classes for boys in secondary schools, voluntary parenting classes for fathers of newborn babies, and a law that gives both parents the right to reduce their working day from eight to six hours.[2]

When American fathers do stay home, they often continue to do part-time work. In Swarthmore, Ralph Keyes, who is a writer and the father of two sons, described what being a part-time househusband was like: "When you're home with your kid there's a real rhythm to the day. You develop a kind of psychic — *psychic* is too strong a word — but you and your child develop an awareness of each other that you don't develop in any other way. As a result of our time home together, I'm very in tune with Scott, even though he's in day care now. I have an intuitive understanding of Scott in a way that I didn't with David, our older boy. When he was a toddler, I was working my butt off on a book. He would stand at the bottom of the stairs pleading with me to quit working and come down and play with him. Sometimes I did, more often I didn't. Either I didn't have time for him or when I was with him I was always distracted. When the book was finally done, I was down in the living room just lying with David watching a ball game and Muriel [Ralph's wife] had tears in her eyes. She said, 'That's the first time in years that I've seen you lying with your son like that.'

"I feel pretty good about my relationship with David now. So I don't think there's any lasting fallout from that period, when I wasn't giving him any attention. But it was painful at the time. Now occasionally David will make a comment like, 'When are you going to write another book?' And I mentioned that to Muriel and she said: 'He doesn't want you to write another book. He wants you to have written another book.'

"But when Scott came, I made this deliberate decision to gear down on my work and give my family the better part of my attention. I'm glad that I have the flexibility to spend time that most two-career couples don't have. But I've ignored my career development significantly. And I'm a guy that likes to work. But I'm glad we have two kids and I'm glad we have this family. I wish we had more money, and I wish we had more flexibility, but I think we just have to accept there's certain things in life that are very difficult. This happens to be one of them."

Pioneering At-Home Working Parents

Particularly for women, the new work/family pressures demand a new kind of at-home parenting.

In an opinion piece in the *Wall Street Journal*, Carole Gould writes:

> Although many people warned me of the difficulties of motherhood, no one mentioned the one I find most onerous: There are no tangible signs of success in the task of raising a child. No promotions, no raises, not even interim performance reviews. Nothing along the way to tell you that you are moving in the right direction. Women of my generation may feel this lack of feedback and recognition especially hard. We were schooled in the competitive '70s, when success was easily and quantifiably measured in a steady procession of the alphabet tests: SATs, LSATs, GREs, MCATs. My generation was taught from a very early age to be goal-oriented, to set a pattern of work and accomplish it. In motherhood I found there are no such clear guideposts, no measuring how well I do my job.[3]

Is it possible to be a successful at-home parent and still maintain a professional identity?

Christina Donovan thinks so. The "new at-home mother" has arrived, she said, and has more in common with her working-mother contemporaries than with the at-home mothers of a generation ago. Donovan is co-publisher of the *Woman's Workshop Quarterly,* a national newsletter produced from her home in Coronado, California. She defines an at-home mother as a woman who does all or almost all her own child care. She said the media, pandering to stereotypes, fail to recognize the new at-home parent, and that there are many more at-home mothers than popularly believed, if one counts women working part-time at home.

One widely quoted figure is that half of all mothers with children under one are working outside the home. In fact, this figure is cooked. First, the Labor Department's Bureau of Labor Statistics report (the most frequently quoted source on this matter) includes mothers with children up to twenty-three months old in its count of working mothers — though this item is often reported in the media as children under a year old. Second, the bureau reports "women in the workforce," not women working outside the home. By the bureau's definition, a woman in the work force can work fifteen hours or more a week as an unpaid worker in a family-operated enterprise, or as little as one hour a week as a paid civilian worker. In other words, a woman at home on a farm, taking care of the kids and keeping the books, is considered a member of the work force.[4]

What's more interesting than the fried figures is the changing role of the at-home parent. But Donovan is determined to change the public's perceptions. The new at-home mother, said Donovan,

- Wants an independent and productive life of her own and expects to or will have to reenter the work force at some point.
- Wants to maintain her professional contacts and continue her education part-time while at home.
- Often earns money, either by working from home or by working around her children's schedules, through part-time or flex-time employment.

"Generations ago, even one generation ago, getting married and staying home to raise a family was a relatively secure lifestyle for a woman (it was certainly considered more secure than being a working woman). This is why today's at-home mothers should not be lumped with the previous generation of at-home mothers, most of whom didn't have to face these challenges in large numbers," said Donovan. She advises those at-home mothers who haven't previously established careers to start building one by working part-time from home or in carefully chosen volunteer work — which can lead to full-time employment when the kids are grown. (The same advice could apply to at-home fathers, but Donovan focuses her attention on mothers.)

Donovan's newsletter (which she publishes with her partner, Deborah Dawson, who lives a few blocks away from her) does not argue for or against staying home. But the pages fairly bristle with exuberant advice for those who do, with such headlines as THE ROAD TO A SUCCESS-FUL CRAFT BUSINESS; LEGAL CONSIDERATIONS FOR AT-HOME MOTHERS; WALKING OUR WAY TO SUCCESS; and FROM KITCHEN TO GREENHOUSE: SPROUTING FOR THE WHOLESALER.

Curious about some of the authors, I called them.

After her husband died eleven years ago, Gerry MacCartee of Coronado, with two small children at home, started the Coronado Touring Company, which conducts historically oriented walking tours of the island. She and her partner, Nancy Cobb, also with children at home, earn about $700 a month each. They work a couple of hours a day and share baby-sitting. Their goal is to transform the part-time work into full-time careers, with, according to MacCartee, one proviso: "Now that my children are getting more independent, I would still rather be at home when they get out of school. Owning our own business, we can control our own time. We're not at the mercy of another employer."

Another at-home mother discovered that her years at home have redirected her life in unexpected ways. Now in her forties, with two young children, one in kindergarten, Michelle Dodge of rural Worthington, Massachusetts, quit her job as a bank branch manager.

"We planned it all," she said. "Before our income was cut in half, we paid off one car and sold the other one. But suddenly we realized that a lot of the extra activities that schools used to provide — music lessons, art lessons, gym — had been cut. So I started the business to pay for the extras." The business was raising sprouts (of the vegetable persuasion) in her kitchen and selling them to restaurants. She sells enough sprouts to earn approximately what she did as a bank manager — after subtracting all the hidden expenses of working, that is: professional clothes, commuting costs, day care.

The only problem was that the sprouts began to consume her life. "We couldn't even go away for the weekend because we needed a sprout-sitter." So now she works part-time for a local health center, operating a play group for children — and for their parents. That job began as a volunteer position.

Did she have any inclination to go back to being a branch manager?

"Nope. At the bank, I worked with machines and computers. Now I work with people. This has changed the direction of my life."

Paul and Sarah Edwards, nationally recognized working-from-home gurus, operate an electronic forum on the subject of at-home work on the computer information service CompuServe. They described what they called "open-collar workers" who work from home, contending that 75 percent of at-home workers choose to work at home not because of what they will avoid, but for what they will gain — feeling more in control of their lives, saving money, and spending more time with their families.

When I posted several questions about at-home working parents, one particularly interesting response was sent to my electronic mailbox by Judith Wunderlich, who operates a typesetting firm, the Wunderlich Graphics Agency, from home in Schaumburg, Illinois:

> Here's my two cents about working from my home with children: I quit the corporate ladder-climbing rat race after the birth of my first child, who is now 3½, but I hadn't yet formulated exactly what type of business venture I would start, as I had several options. So I took it relatively easy for two years, doing free-lance typesetting work for about 12 hours a week. I used day care while I was freelancing, but it was usually a disaster, and sitters moved away on me without notice. The birth of my second child in 1987 led me to realize that I didn't want to play the possibly dangerous day care game with another child. I realized I had to get busy and get a business going that would bring in sufficient income and keep me mentally occupied enough so I wouldn't turn into a Sesame Street mush head. I decided to start a home-based typesetting business and shopped around for used equipment. Luck was on my side, and I was able to get a system from a previous employer for a song!
>
> However, soon after embarking on this venture, I realized that caring for two small children and trying to conduct business and making pick ups and deliveries was harder than I realized. Then my husband, who would make someone a wonderful housewife and is a great father, volunteered to change to the night shift, thereby allowing him to be with his kids all day and allowing me to run the business.
>
> The situation has worked out fantastic, but is not without pitfalls. For instance, my parents think I'm a terrible person to impose on my poor overworked husband by letting him take care of the kids all day (plus he ends up doing a lot of housework) and then working a full-time job at night. They can't accept this semi–role reversal. However, they think nothing of a woman working a full-time job, then coming home and having full responsibility for the kids and the house.
>
> Here's some more reflections:
>
> #1. My husband now can't imagine not being with his kids during the day. We've grown much closer as a family, and we do things, both simple and exceptional, that we probably wouldn't have the time to do on just the weekends.

#2. We've found that because both Mom and Dad are at home most of the day, the kids try to take advantage and demand almost constant attention. We've had to firmly let them know that though we love playing with them, we're not here for their constant amusement. We've found that our 3½-year-old would actually rather play with other kids her age, but almost all our neighbors with children are employed outside the home and the kids are in day care (it's like a ghost town around here during the day!), so we take her to the local YMCA or park district for different classes or activities so she'll have kids to play with. This also gives Mom and, especially, Dad a little breather.

#3. I'm not sure what other people call our situation. My business is grossing over $4,000 per month now, but I only work part-time hours. Yet I think my husband actually spends more day hours with the kids, but he can't be called a househusband because he works full-time at night. I guess we have a unique, but immensely workable, situation. And I don't have to worry any more about baby-sitters or day care.

Another at-home pioneer, Kris Kyes, an editor and writer for medical trade publications in Los Angeles and New York City, works from her home office eight thousand feet up in the pine forest twelve miles outside of Santa Fe, New Mexico. "The company I was working for in Los Angeles relocated to New Jersey," she said. "I refused to go, and they said I could edit from home." So she and her husband asked themselves, Why not edit from the mountains of New Mexico? Today, through her phone, computer, and fax machine, she edits three medical quarterlies; in addition, she taps into CompuServe's MEDLINE medical data base for research. "I love it, my publishers love it, my children love it, and the phone company does, too," she said. "The most rewarding sensation is interviewing big shots in medicine who presume I'm sitting in my elegant office, but I'm wearing an old bathrobe."

Like Wunderlich, Kris Kyes has succeeded financially. "Overall I'm only making two-thirds of what I did full-time. But instead of sixty hours a week, I'm working twenty hours, a lot of it at night when the kids are asleep," says Kyes. By working at home, she saves money on baby-sitting, commuting, and power suits, so her real income is 34 percent higher than it was in Los Angeles. However, working from home does have its drawbacks. "I haven't learned yet how to separate my work life from my personal life," says Kyes. "I sometimes find myself editing manuscripts in the bathtub."

Some labor organizations see the at-home trend as a way for businesses to avoid paying for benefits or providing decent working conditions. Nonetheless, Kyes says at-home work life is worth it, particularly for her kids. "We own several acres in the pine forest where the kids can be explorers instead of being prisoners in their own house like they were in L.A."

As attractive as this route may seem, it would be wildly inaccurate to assume that a majority of families who wish to keep a parent home can do it. Keeping one parent at home — even one who works part-time — still demands one good salary and usually involves a steep drop in overall family income. When both parents work, living standards seem to climb automatically, eating up much of the second paycheck. Yet few parents I interviewed mentioned being able to afford extravagances when giving their reasons for sending both parents into the work force. They mentioned house payments and health insurance, the often unrealistic but emotionally compelling fear of poverty and homelessness, and saving for a child's college education.

Still, heading home is a real possibility for those parents who can master the new home-office technology, and more important, are capable of shifting the center of their lives from the office park to the neighborhood. The at-home movement will also encourage the growth of parent networks outside the corporate work place. If enough people can manage to do this, the neighborhoods might once again come alive for workers and for their children.

19

The Global Child

●

Some of the newest strands of the web are being woven by immigration and changing racial patterns. Today's children constitute America's first truly multicultural, multiracial generation, a fact that is expanding and reshaping the experience of childhood. Some parents view this aspect of their children's childhood with a mixture of denial, dismay, and fear. Other parents, however, view this change with delight — as do an even higher proportion of children and teenagers. The multicultural influences on children add to the puzzlement of today's childhood, but also to the possibilities. The new racial mix is bringing new frictions to childhood, more generational fragmentation, but also new possibilities, including a fresh reworking of traditional family values.

America has always been a nation of immigrants, of course, but until the sixties, the nation's immigration laws were intentionally shaped to encourage European immigration and to radically restrict immigration by Asians, Hispanics, and Africans — people of color. In 1964 immigration law was reformed, attitudes about race began to change, and so, slowly, did the complexion of childhood. In less than a century, current levels of legal and illegal immigration and a continuation of present birthrates will create a U.S. population in which whites will no longer be the majority. By the year 2010, Hispanics will become the nation's largest ethnic minority. By 2077, non-Hispanic whites will constitute the largest minority in the nation.[1]

Immigrants are already becoming America's fountain of youth. That's the startling theme of a study conducted in 1986 by the trend analysis program of the American Council of Life Insurance. "We hope the companies will move fast. That's why we're alerting the industry," said Niels

Christiansen, the council's director of social research services. The bottom line, he added, is that "people who have more children are likely to buy more life insurance." In the future, the report concludes, such issues as retirement income and nursing home care will have an interracial as well as an intergenerational aspect:

> We must ask not only if younger Americans will feel a responsibility toward caring for the growing elderly population, but will younger Americans — who will be increasingly non-white — feel responsibility toward the growing elderly population of which a majority will be non-Hispanic white?[2]

The answer to that question will depend on how well the current generation of parents understands, and adapts, to the new ethnic and racial realities of childhood. So far, the kids are way ahead of us.

The New Language of Childhood

The nerve centers of the emerging multicultural childhood are the schools. Unfortunately, the United States has made little progress in desegregating its public schools since the early seventies. Hispanic students in particular are becoming increasingly isolated. Many minority students are being shortchanged in their education by teachers who fail to recognize their cultural differences and relegate them without sufficient cause to lower sections of their classes. In classrooms serving minority children "one finds a near absence" of academic content. "Instead, there is often a heavy-handed concentration on the development of the lowest level of basic skills," says Lily Wong Fillmore, a professor of education at the University of California–Berkeley.[3]

Still, irresistibly, the tide is toward new cultural and linguistic awareness in the schools. A little more than one in three public school students is now a minority student. In America's thirty largest cities and in some entire states, notably California and Texas, the very term *minority* needs redefinition since in each state the so-called minority makes up a majority of the school-age population. In California, one out of four students comes from a home where English is not the primary language.[4]

While the debate continues over bilingual education, the probability is that the new multicultural childhood is in the country's long-term economic interest.[5]

The drastic decline in language course enrollments during the sixties and seventies is over. During the eighties, New York State's language enrollment nearly tripled. In Texas, enrollments in French and Spanish more than doubled in the same period. "We're experiencing a phenomenal language boom in Oregon," said Sally Malueg, who heads the department of foreign languages at Oregon State University. "It's student-led. Students are demanding languages at a lot faster pace than we can supply them." Traditionally, liberal arts students were the ones who took languages. Today students in business, science, and engineering dominate the language courses.[6]

Because of the neglect of language study in past years the supply of language teachers isn't keeping up with student demand. One Oregon school district went to China to recruit a teacher for its new Chinese program. "If we're going to compete with Japan, we've either got to make better goods or be better salesmen, and if we're going to be better salesmen in a global market, we've got to know the languages of the customers," said Dr. J. David Edwards, executive director of the Joint National Committee for Languages in Washington, D.C. (Edwards, incidentally, speaks only English.)[7]

Smart parents see all this as an opportunity.

In San Diego, parents line up to get their children into Longfellow Elementary's language-immersion magnet school.

On the day I visited, two Longfellow fifth-graders, both African American, were sitting at a small round table. One kid's name was Chezar Hines. "Not like no ketchup," he said. The other kid's name was Dona Hill. Offered Dona, "Don't ask me for my middle name, 'cause I got three middle names: Jerome Damien Cornelius!"

Every weekday morning the two boys are bused from a predominantly black section of San Diego to a predominantly white neighborhood, where they take part in Longfellow's Spanish language immersion program.

At Longfellow, the grim classic portrait of George Washington hangs next to a Mexican flag. The wall of one classroom is covered with a mural of Aztecs worshiping the sun, and the textbooks are in Spanish. From kindergarten to sixth grade, all the students who come to this school are taught in Spanish. The program is not bilingual. The students come from English-speaking families, but English is never spoken in the classroom. From day one it's '*Abren los libros.*'

"Makes me pretty happy," Chezar told me in English. (I am monolingual.) "It's really great to know two languages. When I went to Tijuana one time they called me a bad name and I knew it."

Dona was excited. "When we grow up we're gonna buy a boat and sail away to other countries and see what other people are doin' —"

"Or be like that guy Mr. Bentley on 'The Jeffersons,' " Chezar cut in. "He's a translator for the U.N. He gets paid a lot and that's why he can live in that rich building."

"We could start a school in T.J., like for poor Mexican kids."

"Yeah, we could!"

Dona and Chezar weren't alone in their enthusiasm. There was a sense of excitement and pride at the school. Thirteen American cities have some kind of partial- or total-immersion language program. Approximately thirty U.S. public grade schools offer either partial or total language-immersion programs. The attractions go beyond traditional academics. Children in immersion programs score significantly higher in measures of creativity and in acceptance of people who are culturally different. San Diego's Spanish program is the largest publicly financed total-immersion program in the United States. The program involves five schools, and the results are remarkable.

By the time the students reach fifth or sixth grade they can speak, read, and write in two languages, usually with no accent. Surprisingly, tests show that children in immersion programs do just as well — or better — in basic school subjects as do students in regular programs. These results hold true whether the children are tested in English or in the second language, and regardless of socioeconomic background.

"Most of our students enter school before they've learned to read in English," said Maria Potter, a resource teacher who oversees the Longfellow classes. "Children taught to read in Spanish first are able to transfer the skills to English. It's a fascinating process. Essentially, your brain learns the decoding process necessary for reading only once in a lifetime."

Language-immersion students do experience a delay of several months in learning to read compared with children in regular programs, primarily because learning to read usually depends on having an oral vocabulary already in place. Also, Spanish students at Longfellow tend to lag slightly behind in learning to read in English. So a few hours each week some students, those who entered the school after the second grade, are taught in English.

But that gap soon disappears. By the beginning of the fourth grade, language-immersion students usually read in English at the same level as children in regular schools. Moreover, they consistently score a whole grade level higher than the district average on mathematics proficiency tests.

"We don't know why the kids are so much better at math," said Potter.

No studies have been done, but one hypothesis is that teachers using the immersion method must first teach the vocabulary before teaching the concepts. In English-speaking classrooms, the teachers often assume that kids already know the vocabulary.

Fifth-grader Dona had a different explanation: "Me and Chezar are in the sixth grade for math 'cause we're so *awesome.*"

Another fifth-grader, Lara Summerville, who takes great pride in her Spanish fluency, said: "Sometimes I can't think of English words, especially ones that describe feelings. Those are easier to think of in Spanish." [8]

Language programs like Longfellow's are gaining status with upscale parents. On the day I visited, Pam Carleton was working as a parent volunteer. "Friends either think it's terrific that you've got your kid in this program, or that you're nuts," she said, and laughed. "When I was a girl growing up in Delano, California, there was a feeling that it was beneath us to take Spanish. How foolish. But today that's changing. More and more, parents want their kids to know Spanish. The way the demographics of this region are changing, kids who grow up bilingual are going to have a lot better shot at jobs. That's what it comes down to. *Jobs.*"

A Prophecy of Conflict

Socially, most kids seem to be adjusting better to the new multicultural childhood than adults or, for the most part, institutions.

Other winds are blowing, including the cultural literacy movement advocating the teaching of Western values in schools. Reestablishing these shared values will be an important aspect in the reweaving of the web. Still, the nation's economic and social future increasingly depends on cultural and linguistic understanding of Pacific Rim and Latin American countries and on deeper understanding of our African American heritage. To forgo the teaching of multicultural literacy is to help create a climate of cultural conflict.

Economic pressure is creating cultural and political stress that runs like a silent fault line beneath the surprisingly smooth surface of the multicultural childhood. Adults spread this resentment and fear, often in the name of children.

In Watts, for example, a black high school teacher, Ezola Foster, and her white associate, Leslie Dutton, are leading the resistance of some blacks to the infusion of Hispanic immigrants. Foster campaigns against the Latinization of Watts on radio talk shows and in her organization's newsletter, which has a circulation of twenty thousand and features such headlines as TERRORISTS AND ILLEGALS HOME FREE IN THE U.S. and SOVIET ALIENS ON WELFARE.

Foster, an unsuccessful Republican candidate for the California Assembly, also writes commentaries for large-subscription newspapers, arguing that, as she stated in one piece, "black Americans are facing the very real possibility of a complete reversal of civil-rights gains . . . due to U.S. policy on illegal immigration across the Mexican border." She predicts a "bitter confrontation between Hispanics and blacks" and says that "Watts is no longer a black community, it is an illegal-alien community." Watts has become more Hispanic because of immigration, a comparatively high Hispanic birthrate, a steep decline in the black birthrate, and an exodus of black middle-class families to the suburbs. As Foster sees it, when violent racial conflict comes, if it comes, it won't be white against brown, but black against brown.

But the school officials I talked with dismissed Foster's point of view.

At Bell High School, now 90 percent Hispanic, principal Mary Ann Sesma, an expansive and impassioned defender of cultural diversity, called Foster a "professional, excellent teacher." But Sesma became visibly angered when I mentioned Foster's charge that Bell was a finalist for a prized technology grant from IBM because, as Foster put it, "corporations value cheap Latino labor over blacks."

Sesma asked, "You want to know why we're in the running for that grant?" She pointed at an award on her desk inscribed, FIRST PLACE, FOR PHYSICS-TEACH-TO-LEARN, CALIFORNIA SCHOOL ASSOCIATION. "That's why we're in the running. Because we earned it." She added: "Every human in this world bleeds red. As educators, we only look at the color of the blood."

At Jordan High School, surrounded by a steel fence thick enough to stop a tank, I stopped to talk with two teachers: Bob Norris, who is African American and has taught in Watts since 1958, and Matt Scanlon, a white rookie teacher "from middle-class America." They told me that the neighborhood suffers because of gang warfare, but that the fighting is as much black against black and Hispanic against Hispanic as it is between the races. Surprisingly, both men mentioned the enriching (Norris called it "mellowing") influence that Hispanic and African American students have had on each other. "To be racially or ethnically isolated," said Norris, "is to be shackled by your own experience."

At Jordan and at Bell, Hispanic American students join African American students in ceremonies for Martin Luther King, Jr., and African Americans participate in Mexican dances during Cinco de Mayo.

Out in front of Jordan High, principal Odaris Jordan, a black woman, spoke of the "common cause" between Hispanics and blacks. We had been talking about Ezola Foster. She paused to tease a disheveled kid wearing an earring and a baseball cap. "Take that hat off," she commanded, and then laughed. "And pull those pants up before you lose 'em." Her voice lowered. She chose her words carefully.

"Yes, someday blacks and Hispanics will turn against each other — if we keep believing they will."

Toward Multicultural Family Values

Despite the potential for spreading racial violence, kids are often the quiet resisters of multicultural hatred. American children, though they may be ignorant about geography, are already learning multicultural literacy — from each other. What kids today express is a liberality about racial issues, especially dating, unacceptable in America a single generation ago. But this liberality is often mated with immigrant children's otherwise conservative attitudes about family values. The combination makes for quite a hybrid.

I spoke with a class of juniors at Franklin High School in Seattle. The class included immigrant and first-generation Chinese, Japanese, Filipino, Vietnamese, African American, and European American students. When I asked them what they had learned from each other, one particularly popular girl of Filipino, Hispanic, and Samoan extraction said: "We learn the difference between foods — Japanese food, Chinese food. The way they dress, their gods, what they believe in religion-wise."

Another girl, a blond, apparently middle-class eleventh-grader: "Everybody here celebrated Chinese New Year. You give out lucky candy so they'll have a prosperous year. We learned about the Chinese dragon dance. It's not like, 'Oh, wow, that's weird!' It's like, 'Oh, that's *nice.*' And it's just accepted."

The popular Filipino-Hispanic-Samoan-American girl added: "If you go to a school with a lot of different cultures you understand the way certain people think — say, how black people perceive Asians. If you just go to school with basically one color, when you go out in the real world you probably won't know how to talk to somebody else or know how to approach them, or you might insult them accidentally."

She grinned suddenly and added, "For several months this year I'd only go out with black guys because Chinese guys can't dance!" The class good-naturedly booed her.

In part, the new racial and ethnic tolerance is due to the sheer variety of racial and ethnic backgrounds in public schools today, which no longer reflects the black/white dichotomy. Because of integration and immigration, and because so many schools now celebrate linguistic and cultural differences, mainstream American children — perhaps a majority — no longer see people ethnically unlike themselves as particularly odd. Everybody's odd. Everybody's an outsider. Everybody's global.

Our baby-boom generation may well be the last generation to whom interracial dating and marriage are generally taboo. "We are probably going to have a browning of America over time," said Lawrence H. Fuchs, director of the Select Commission on Immigration and Refugee Policy from 1979 to 1981. "It will take six or seven generations, but ultimately, I believe, a majority of the population will be nonwhite. That is likely to occur because of immigration and increasing rates of inter-marriage between darker-skinned people and whites. But concepts of color and race will probably change, and it's possible that questions about color won't even be asked in the Census a hundred and fifty years from now."

Certainly among the kids I interviewed, racial differences were of little importance when it came to romance. At Franklin, multicultural variety can make it a chore to restrict one's romantic interests only to members of the same race. "It's the parents who don't like it," said Franklin teacher Richard Nagely. "The parents still have a lot of control over their kids on this, but the kids basically don't see any problem."

One would be mistaken, however, to believe that the new demographics automatically mean a liberalization of values regarding gender and family. In fact, immigrants and their children often bring conservative family values with them, and at least for the first two or three generations after these families arrive in America, their values remain resilient. Indeed, new immigrants may, for a time, help spur stronger family trends among the general population. The American Council of Life Insurance report points out that Asian immigrants show a strong sense of responsibility toward providing for the needs not only of their children and their elderly parents but also of their other relatives. Asians in particular, according to the report, are attracted to life insurance products that provide savings for college educations and which protect parents and relatives as well as immediate families.

I got a taste of these more conservative family values when I visited William Cullen Bryant High School in Queens, which boasts the largest Greek population of any public high school in New York City. The students there speak twenty-five languages — including Greek, Italian, Korean, Farsi, and Spanish.

Laraine Pacheco, Bryant's principal, is a first-generation descendent of a Polish mother and a Russian father. Pacheco believes immigrants have been getting a bad rap — what with all the debate about illegal aliens and amnesty and English-only referendums, many Americans have turned fearful and angry about anyone perceived as foreign. The assumption is that immigrants only take. But these kids, Pacheco demurred, and their teachers are proof that immigrants give — always have, always will. And the giving isn't easy.

Rose DePinto, a Bryant teacher, described a Vietnamese teenager named Tran, who came to America alone. "I still don't know how he got here. He was seventeen when he arrived. He works all night long — we're all convinced he doesn't sleep. Yet after six months he got his own apartment, and he's an excellent student — he won a United Federation of Teachers scholarship."

Change is afoot. The attachment to native languages has increased in recent years, not only for Hispanics but for other immigrant groups as well. Gerald Jabocowski, a math teacher, told how he made phone calls to the parents of thirty-eight students to explain a new math curriculum, and not one parent spoke English. "Most of my students in advanced placement college-level calculus don't really speak English well, so we speak in calculus." He laughed. "We just point and grunt and groan and we do pretty well."

Pretty well, indeed. An extraordinary number of Bryant students have been national winners in the Westinghouse Science Talent Search.

Once upon a time, immigrants sliced away their emotional ties to their native lands. But not now — not with cheaper transoceanic communication and nine-hour flights from New York to Athens.

"Of course, political refugees are here to stay and thankful for it. One of our children, from Romania, was in prison for four months," said Pacheco. "But the parents of many of these kids really believe they're going home someday. These very traditional, conservative families come here, and there is so much more divorce, so many more problems and complexities for kids. In some ways, America is a harder country to come to than thirty or forty years ago. The parents are deathly afraid of what America can do to their families. If anything, this family orientation has become more pronounced over the years — and this is rubbing off, I think, on nonimmigrant kids. It's a gift to us."

A gift. In this strange new culture, where so many parents consider bearing babies a higher form of shopping, immigrant kids are often smothered with love and family traditions.

The students I spoke with at Bryant were, like most teenagers, ambivalent about their parents' conservatism — straining to get away from it, yet holding to it tightly.

"My mom wanted to come to the prom with me, I mean seriously!" said one girl, and the class laughed with appreciation. "Our parents believe that once you meet someone, you should just marry him. Not only that, but they have to be older than you, and well established. And if they're not from Greece —"

"If they're not from the same island!"

"— don't even bring him in the house!"

These kids understand that they're enriching each other, and the rest of us, culturally, possibly because most schools now encourage cross-cultural awareness. The students described, with excitement, what they had learned from each other. They mentioned Greek food — dol-mathes — and Colombian soccer and a Caribbean dance called me-rengue. A Colombian girl said, with awe, "My boyfriend taught me that in the Greek Orthodox religion, if the priest is holding a closed Bible in his hands, he's blessing you, and if the book is open, he's teaching you."

I asked them, What were they and their families contributing to the United States? A young woman answered simply, "Us."

I came away from my interviews with immigrant kids feeling admiration for the hard workers — particularly those who had saved so much money — and a sense of hope. But I should also confess a concern that I may have romanticized what I learned from them. After hearing so much pain expressed by other classes with fewer immigrants, I may have grasped the hope in this room too tightly. And yet the multicultural childhood offers so much raw material with which to work.

If we resist our fear of the foreign bogeyman and, instead, nurture the inherent strengths of the new global children, this particular expansion of childhood experience will enrich our culture. As the general experience of childhood grows more electronic, scattered, and commercialized, the multicultural experience injects fresh blood and older values into childhood's future in America.

20

Bringing the
Generations Together

●

Now to weave the strands of the generations.

Children spoke often of their yearning for contact with grandparents, or with any people older than their own parents. During my visit to Shawnee Mission North High School, in Kansas, a class of juniors latched on to the subject and would not let go.

"My grandmother and grandfather on my mom's side live across the street from me," said one young woman, smiling brightly. "So I see them every day and sometimes it's really cool because she makes cookies and pies every morning. And she gives me the recipes. But sometimes she's like a pain in the butt. She calls up and says, 'Oh, put that dog inside,' or 'Let the dog out,' or 'What are the birds doing flying around the house?' " The class laughed. "I don't know what she can hear. You can turn the radio on really low — 'What are you doing over there jamming that radio?' She'll call up on the phone and sometimes it is a real pain but I guess — I mean, I love her and everything — she's great but still sometimes she can be a pain."

She grinned in a way that said "and worth the pain."

A second girl, with a brooding look, said: "My grandma, I can tell her things and she won't tell them to my parents. I don't know, she's like a friend — she's not like a grandma. She won't go and tell my parents things that I don't want her to."

Some spoke of distance: "I rarely, rarely, rarely see my grandparents because they live in Iowa. A lot of people don't like old people because they're like, slow. My grandma is full of energy and she's a lot of fun to be with. But I can't really talk to my grandparents because I don't know them that well."

"My grandparents live like twelve hours away and the others live sixteen hours away, so I don't get to see them. But when I do, my grandparents are the greatest things in the world. Because they never nag at you and they always see the good things in you." She grinned. "And they tell you bad things your parents did."

Some of them spoke of the role that their grandparents played in their lives after their parents' divorce. "When nobody else was around my grandparents were there — so they were like my second parents. Until I was nine I always called my grandmother Grandma Mommy and my mother Mommy Grandma, and I always confused them. So I'm still really, really close to her."

Even when kids spoke of their grandparents with anger or bitterness, I sensed in their words and voices that their lives were given more meaning and depth because of the contact across the generations — when that contact was possible.

Some parents spoke of trying to mend ties with grandparents, strained or severed by the mobility of society. One Kansas woman said, "We spent twelve years in Mississippi after we graduated from college and I think our family missed a lot by not being around their grandparents, aunts and uncles and cousins. And now that we have moved back to Wichita, we're trying to rekindle those relationships. We're trying to make up lost time, trying really hard to track down the memories, and trying to be together more and fill each other in on what we have missed. It is a very hard thing to do. Maybe it's impossible."

So many children do not have contact with grandparents; socially, demographically, and politically, the generations seem in danger of drifting apart. And yet, tentative new connections are also being made.

The Expanding Role of Grandparents

Just as the nature of childhood, politically and socially, is changing, so too is the relationship between the old and the young. New pressures are being brought to bear on both, creating what amounts to a generational realignment. And this evolving relationship is ultimately a hopeful one.

Surprisingly, little is known about the modern role of grandparenting. A fascinating study by Andrew J. Cherlin and Frank F. Furstenberg, Jr., charts this change. As Cherlin and Furstenberg point out, popular television series such as "The Waltons" conjured up a nostalgic picture of large, extended families with strong, loving grandparents, but in reality it was a rarity for children fifty to a hundred years ago to grow up with a close relationship with a grandparent. Proportionately, many more grandparents, particularly grandmothers, are around today than just a few decades ago. For the first time in history, most adults live long enough to get to know most of their grandchildren. Only one in four children born in 1900 had four grandparents alive when they were born, and only one in fifty still had four grandparents alive by the time he or she was fifteen. In comparison, in 1976, nine out of ten fifteen-year-olds had two or more grandparents still alive. Grandparents today spend more years of their lives being grandparents.

Not only do they live longer, but grandparents also have more leisure time. Long retirements were a relative rarity until just before World War II. The expected retirement was ten years in 1970, seven years in 1940, and only four years in 1900. Today, the average man can expect to spend fifteen years of his adult life out of the labor force, most of it in retirement.

Though grandparents do tend to live farther from their grandkids today, they also have more money to spend on them, they're less likely to be still raising their own children, and they enjoy new ways of communicating with their grandchildren. As late as the end of World War II, only half the homes in the United States had a telephone.

The popular conception is that, as the economy has shifted from the farm to the factory and office, grandparents have become less important to the family; they're no longer needed as mentors and teachers. Yet if one holds today's realities up to the light and turns them slightly, one can see other possibilities in the relationship between young and old. A family in the thirties may have had to band together because of the threat of starvation; the enemy was identifiable, tangible. A family's enemies today are more elusive. Unemployment of a parent can pose enormous hardships for a family, but today *over*employment — and lack of time for children — can be just as destructive to family life. Grandparents (and other retired people) may be more useful to their young families today than in past decades because they have — and can share — our era's most valuable commodity: time.

A number of social scientists have described the grandparental role as empty, ambiguous, roleless. Yet Cherlin and Furstenberg report that "there has been an increasing emphasis during this century on bonds of sentiment: love, affection, and companionship." The researchers asked grandparents whether grandparenthood had changed since they were grandchildren. "Their grandparents, we were told, were respected, admired figures who often assisted other family members. But again and again, our informants talked about the emotional distance between themselves and their grandparents. . . . Grandma may have helped out, and she certainly was respected, even loved; but she often was an emotionally distant figure."

The emerging relationship between the generations awaits a new definition. Grandparenting may, in fact, be returning to the more functional role that was widespread several generations ago.[1]

In some families, grandmothers are vital to the early upbringing of children. The growing affluence of the elderly has enabled more grandparents to help their children (who, as a group, have dropped in affluence) buy homes. The very instability of the American family — the high divorce rate, the number of teenage pregnancies, the growing legion of single mothers — has given many grandparents more to do.

Witness the increasing number of quiet heroes who come before the nation's probate courts. Often it is a grandparent — or an aunt, uncle, or older sibling — who assumes guardianship for a neglected and endangered child. Grandparents who take in children have always existed. What's new is the influence of drugs, the sheer number of abandoned and abused kids, and stiffer requirements by health care insurers and schools. Another reason for the increase in guardianships (fourfold in San Diego between 1985 and 1990) is that probate court often is more effective in protecting an abused child than are the bureaucratic, overloaded child protective services. These new guardians face extraordinary financial and psychological stresses. Some grandparents in their forties and fifties are caring not only for their grandchildren but for their own parents as well. Ten years ago few support groups for grandparent guardians existed; now they're springing up all over the country. Government and the private sector must shift from their sole focus on the nuclear family to helping the extended family. As an activist for grandparent guardians told me, "The guardianship movement isn't a division of the family but a coming together again."

Old and Young: How They Could Join Forces

Frightened by the changes they see among younger Americans, an increasing proportion of seniors are withdrawing into "adults only" housing developments. As the nation ages and housing patterns continue to fragment according to age, will the young and the old have less and less contact with one another?

Possibly. Certainly the political stage is set for such a division.

Just as all politics is local, most politics in late twentieth-century America is also generational. Children's issues are not simply children's issues but *intergenerational* issues. The "attack of the granny-bashers," the "next civil war," "kids versus canes" — these are the ways some observers have described the conflict between the old and the young. As the granny-bashers see it, the old, by moving behind the walls of their adults-only communities, by refusing to support school bonds or spending on children's health, are turning their backs on their own children and grandchildren.

Though the elderly are growing in number, wealth, and political power, 20 percent fewer eighteen-year-olds entered the work force in 1988 than only a decade before. A decreasing proportion of productive workers will be supporting an increasing number of older people. As a result, Medicare may well face a funding crisis; by the time the baby-boom generation retires, Social Security and Medicare could be biting as much as 40 percent out of the paychecks of working Americans.

Phillip Longman, author of *Born to Pay: The New Politics of Aging in America,* has pointed out that the growth of the older population will cause the funding of public pension and health-care benefits for the elderly to become ever more difficult, but that rising poverty among children and the crisis in education threaten to swell the ranks of dependent Americans still more. Today's poor, undereducated children will become tomorrow's marginally employed workers. Instead of paying taxes to support elderly baby boomers, they will more likely collect public assistance themselves. Society's resources, rather than going to help the elderly, will be committed to pay for police, jails, private security guards — for protection against a growing underclass.[2]

Rather than a generational war, however, the stage may just as easily be set for a new relationship in which the old accept a call to arms on behalf of the very young. Such a call will demand a new kind of leadership from the political lobbies of both the young and the old.

Interestingly, the confrontational approach that has been employed in the past by the Americans for Generational Equity (AGE) lobby hasn't worked. AGE changed its focus in 1987, according to J. J. Wuerthner, executive director. "A year ago, *Fortune* magazine called us a kids' lobby, but now we're an organization looking at all generations. In the very early stages, we employed a direct-mail firm and there were some rather intemperate things said about the elderly." The ploy, he admitted, flopped financially and alienated seniors, whose support is essential for any additional assistance for the young. In addition to growing proportionally, the sixty-five to seventy-four age group has the highest rate of participation in congressional elections. So in any political confrontation between young and old, the old win, hands down. Moreover, most people understand intuitively that in any conflict between the old and young, everyone eventually loses because everyone gets old someday.

The real challenge will be to show the generations how interdependent they are — to convince older and younger Americans that it is in their interest to pay for education, quality child care, and other youth services. "We've found that what happens to one generation has an almost immediate effect, or a long-term effect, on other generations," said Wuerthner. "So we've broadened out." He suggests that if you can't beat 'em, enlist 'em. That approach might be especially effective among the so-called young-old, the growing proportion of Americans too young to die, too affluent to wither, too interested in life to withdraw, who could help mend the gap. In some cities the young-old and the elderly are becoming champions of the young — out of self-interest.[3]

The need to find generational unity is urgent. Many of the problems people are having with small children they're also having with their parents. The "sandwich generation" of Americans find themselves caring for aged parents and their own growing or grown children at the same time. Advances in medicine have lengthened adult life spans and saved children with disabilities who in an earlier time would have died. Yet because more wives are working and more parents are single, the number of relatives available to take care of the infirm elderly or children is decreasing.

American society thus faces this threat: a generation of the very young and a generation of the very old without an adequate system of care. For the individual family, this is a formula for guilt and stress: imagine the constant feeling of being torn between your responsibilities toward your spouse and children and toward your elderly parent. There are 6.6 million older people who need long-term care, and 80 percent of that care is provided by family members. In many single-parent families, one person, usually a woman, must take care of both her children and her aging parents. "The family is the workhorse care giver in our society, and all too often an exhausted workhorse," said Leah Friedman, coordinator of the Gerontology Education and Training Center at San Jose State University. "For a long time, we thought the family was dead as a care giver. Now we realize it's alive and what a burden it faces."[4]

Who will pay for the rising social and medical costs of an aging society? The nation has several options: increasing the working population by producing more babies; inviting more immigrant workers to the United States; or ensuring that the children now in school gain the best education and the best emotional support possible so that they will be extraordinarily productive adults, able to compete in the world marketplace and to carry the financial burden of an aging society.

Another, not often mentioned option is that aging Americans might work longer and retire later, thus paying more taxes and becoming more supportive of both themselves and the young. The growing physical health of older Americans should not only make this fourth option possible, but to many of them desirable. Among those aged sixty-five to sixty-nine, fully 40 percent of Japanese men are working, compared with only 25 percent of American men.

Changes in retirement and Social Security laws might encourage older Americans to stay in the work force longer on a part- or full-time basis. The earnings test under Social Security tax on the incomes of many Americans who choose to work past the age of formal retirement discourages seniors from working. U.S. corporations have failed to tailor jobs to fit older workers — including the creation of flexible or part-time positions (a structuring of jobs that would also help parents).

J. J. Wuerthner pointed out that an enormous cadre — fifty thousand technically oriented people — retires each year from science, business, and academe. Yet more than two thousand high schools are going without a qualified math teacher. Senior power should be tapped directly for the schools. Imagine what older, experienced Americans might contribute to currently understaffed and underfinanced public schools, day-care centers, and preschools. Day-care providers are fast recognizing the special advantages of hiring mature workers. Rather than taking punitive measures toward seniors — for example, bleeding their Social Security benefits — society must develop a more positive approach: the encouragement of seniors as a national resource, valued both for themselves and for the skills they can offer to younger families and children.

We need to devise ways to share rather than duplicate resources. In addition to legislation to help with long-term nursing home costs, we need family centers where the elderly can congregate and where children can receive care. These centers could share the costs of the same buildings and in some cases the same personnel. Parents could drop off both the elderly grandparent and the child. These centers would provide grandparent figures to those children with no grandparents or grandparents who live far away, and older people would receive the nurturing of the young. Company benefits should encourage the use of family centers. Such centers would offer children one more way to obtain what they need most: positive contact with adults.

A number of other imaginative intergenerational approaches could be taken. In Sacramento, for example, Riverview Plaza, a frail-elderly housing project, will match "foster grandparents" with children in a child-care program called "Grandpa and Grandma's Place." Nutritional meals prepared for elderly residents will also be offered as take-out meals to parents of children in the child-care facility.

In Branford, Connecticut, an intergenerational program combines a day-care center and a hospice; each day, two dozen children, including three- and four-year-olds, are in daily contact with terminally ill patients. Familiarity with the patients has enabled some children to cope better with the death of their own grandparents or parents.[5]

Closing the Generational Divide

Driving through the aging Seattle neighborhood of Ballard, I passed a billboard for a local hospital that announced, BALLARD'S HAVING BABIES!

The billboard signals quite a turnaround. During the seventies and early eighties, this neighborhood lost many of its children. It's a postcard community, Norman Rockwell with a twist. There's the Rocket Comics store down the street from the China Theater, whose marquee is in Chinese pictographs. The past is very close to the surface here, and so is the future.

The older people have watched the neighborhood change from a largely white, middle-class neighborhood to 32.9 percent minority — Asian, native American, black. Young people are starting to come in, fixing up the little brick houses, and the children are coming back.

Many of the older people in Ballard fear the newcomers and their families. And yet, the oldest and the youngest members of society have always shared an affinity for each other, and that understanding is fully visible in the library at Whittier Elementary School, where seniors from the neighborhood sit in the little light oak grade school chairs next to third- and fourth- and fifth-graders. Hands as gnarled as bark and hands as smooth as unripened peaches or darkened plums turn the pages of books together; voices murmur and heads nod in agreement.

In 1978, the city of Seattle decided to use some of its extra school buildings — the "temporary" structures set up on playgrounds during

the height of the baby boom — as senior citizen centers. One such senior center was established at Whittier, where every afternoon the sep-
tuagenarians and octogenarians would walk the thirty feet from the center to the school, then down a hallway to the cafeteria for a hot lunch.
The old people and the kids seldom interacted; they might as well have
moved in parallel universes. For ten years this went on. During all that
time, no one tried to create a formal relationship between the old and
the young. Not until the summer of 1987 did Monica Roberts, the school
librarian, watching seniors moving like ghosts down the hall, think to
herself: What a waste. We could *use* those people.

As a result, the Whittier Senior Reading Partners program, possibly
the first of its kind and financed with private money, was begun. Now
the seniors arrive at the school library in the morning and sit with children — many of them homeless or abused children from emergency
shelters. These children have the lowest reading scores in the school.
"They're desperate for some kind of adult contact," said Roberts. "At
first we weren't sure how the kids would respond to the seniors, but
now we have kids — good readers — on a waiting list to get a senior
reading partner. It's the contact they're after. That's what they're missing
most of all: ironically, that's what the seniors, too, are missing. I look at
these elderly folks and the kids sitting at the same tables, holding the
same books. I see these kids' reading abilities and attendance improving
dramatically. I think, this is what our future could be; we should get
more of these folks out of mothballs."

I spoke for a few minutes with a boy named David and his reading
partner, Paul Eaton ("I'm always eatin'!" he said). Eaton had sold insurance for thirty-five years and taught school for thirty-four years. David,
a shy boy who said he is "nine, going on ten," added, "I think these
people should get a reward or something 'cause they help people read."
He said that Eaton had helped him "with a *lot* of words. . . . I learned
good words."

"Like this word," said Eaton, pointing to a page in the open book
before him.

"*Trouble*," said David.

"And like this word."

"*Curtains*."

I asked David if he had learned anything in addition to reading from
his reading partner. "Magic," he said. "I learned some magic. I learned
how to do this one pencil trick!"

"Levitation," said Eaton. "Now there's a word."

Grace Stanfield, eighty-three, who makes two bus transfers to get to the center, said, "We were kind of afraid of these little kids, but soon we got a rapport with them." I asked her what she had been afraid of. "That we wouldn't do as well as we think we should. But then we got to thinking, Well, gosh, this is their future."

One woman said: "There is nothing frightening about children. They're so open to you. Sometimes in the hall a child will stop and say, 'You're from Reading with a Friend, aren't you?' And I'll say yes. And they'll say, 'Well, when can I go?' And this might be a child who has no problem at all with reading. One of the big reasons the children want to be here with us is they get one-on-one attention. I became interested because my great-grandson is eighteen and cannot read a book. They just passed him through each time. He can't read any letters that I write to him."

Roberts, the school librarian, spoke passionately about the possibilities beyond Whittier. "If somebody worked at this, they could get an army of old people volunteering in the schools. An *army!*"

Loye Carrington, a reading specialist at Whittier, explained that it was not always easy to bridge the generational and cultural gap. "For example, we have difficulty getting some older people to use the word *black* instead of *Negro*, or worse. But often the toughest thing is to convince older people that they're worth something. There's this boy named Jerome, a black youngster. His senior reading partner, Margaret, didn't have a lot of self-confidence. One day she just quit. I had to tell Jerome that she wasn't going to come anymore. I had to make up a story for Jerome about doctors and her health, and I hated doing this. But I asked her to talk to Jerome just one more time. Margaret looked down at him, and then looked away, and finally said, 'Well, maybe I can change my doctor's appointment.' And Jerome started to cry. And Margaret started to cry. And she's been here ever since. She just didn't think that she was needed or wanted."

After my meeting with the seniors, I walked over to the SPICE (School Programs Involving City Elderly) center in the temporary building next to Whittier's original brick building.

Several couples were ballroom dancing, including two older women who were dancing together. A few people were playing cards. An old gas stove stood in the middle of the room, hot and sizzling.

Sitting at one of the card tables, Ken Camper, the director of the Seattle-wide SPICE program, described the gulf between young and old, which is exacerbated by the media. "The young often think older people are worthless, and the old tend to think of schools as rough, out-of-control places where spoiled, disrespectful kids set their own agenda," he said. "The only solution to overcoming those superimposed images is to get people together." When SPICE began, the senior centers were placed only at elementary schools. Then the program moved into two junior high schools and a school for seriously handicapped children. "People said: 'Oh, they'll never come to that. It will be too depressing. The wheelchairs, and the handicapped kids, and it will remind the old people of their own disabilities, and they won't want to come.' Today that's our biggest site. The handicapped students serve the lunches to seniors each day. We've had seniors volunteer to take kids to regular therapy appointments. The seniors have raised money to help the school buy special equipment. And they see those kids overcoming much worse handicaps than what they're suffering."

Extending the program into high school was the last frontier.

"There were misgivings on both sides. One principal was adamant that it would not work. She thought the kids would be too rough. She thought the kids would be unsympathetic. She kept raising concerns about physical danger. She thought the seniors would get trampled in the halls."

Four years later, the high school program is a success.

High school students in wood shop have built cupboards for the center and repaired lawn mowers for seniors.

"We had a series of drama classes where SPICE seniors put on dramatic productions with the kids. They did a lot of role playing and role reversals, and we videotaped this into a special production."

"These kids are going to live longer than any other generation has before," said Camper. "They're going to need to know about aging."

Bumper's Buddies

In the unlikely city of Miami, something like a battalion has organized around the mutual needs of the old and the young.

During the past decade, anyone looking for evidence of economic conflict between the old and the young could find an ample supply in Florida — a state that demographers say foreshadows how society will be in an aging America.

In the late seventies and early eighties Florida seniors, represented by powerful political lobbies, voted to cut school spending and nearly gutted some youth services, including Head Start. Back then, a policeman's wife captured the mood perfectly when she told a reporter, "The problem with the O.P.'s [Miami slang for 'old people'] is not how to take care of them; it's how to keep them from killing the rest of us."

But that was then and this is now.

In March 1988, Dade County voters passed the largest school-bond issue in the history of the United States — nearly a billion dollars. In the close election, the bond was supported by 72 percent of the senior vote. "The condo congregation — the seniors — they were the ones who turned the tide," according to Freeman Wyche, former Dade County PTA president. The bond issue was crucial because Dade County, the fourth-largest school district in the nation, is overflowing with a new generation of immigrants and children. Ironically, the groups that one might have expected to be more supportive of school spending voted against the referendum. "We were amazed," said Wyche. "The seniors came through."

How and why did this happen?

In part, the shift may reflect a change in attitude among the old toward the young. More specifically, proponents of the school bond organized an effective person-to-person, young-to-old sales campaign that employed a guerrilla tactic: PTA and school officials infiltrated the senior condos with kids. "The PTA and other groups went to the retirement condos and sold the bond issue directly," said Wyche. "One of our appeals was that if you don't pay now, you pay later — if you fail to educate our citizens, they'll be illiterate, they'll be on welfare, they'll be stealing, they'll be breaking into your homes. But if you educate them, they can become productive citizens, and that's going to lower your taxes later."

"We took kids into the condos and the convals [convalescent homes]," explained Ramona Frischman, Dade County's coordinator of senior volunteers in the schools. "We brought music groups in. We thought, Well, the seniors will enjoy the music, and they'll see that the children are adorable; we'll get in and make our pitch. And it worked." [6]

The foundation for the Miami campaign was laid several years ago when the Dade County school district created six aggressive senior volunteer programs — which now enlist the help of twenty-five hundred senior citizens. These volunteers help children learn basic skills.

"When kids and seniors get together," said Frischman, "both groups realize that they don't get a lot of respect. We've sent high school kids out to interview seniors, and when the kids talked later about those interviews, they said: 'The seniors feel they don't get a lot of respect because of age. We teenagers feel the same way.' The seniors were saying their big problem is inadequate transportation; well, there's also inadequate transportation for teenagers, who don't all have cars. Both groups suffer from discrimination in the work place.

"The Gray Panthers are sponsoring a student essay contest: the students must assume that they're county commissioners and there's a pot of money and it's to be spent to either build a senior center or a youth center. We hope that they'll say they'll build a 'multicenter' that everybody can use — old and young!"

Bit by bit, politically, socially, Frischman's program is weaving the young and the old together.

At Miami's Westview Elementary School, I met Wesley Wilson.

Out in a grassy square between the school's temporary buildings, Wilson fussed with a row of plants as little kids trailed after him. "I think they ought to take talent from everybody," Wilson said in a raspy voice. "In other words, if you retire, you take your expertise and use it with kids. My background is horticulture."

Wilson had started a garden club with the students, mainly inner-city black kids, who usually have little contact with gardening.

I asked the kids, who had begun to dig in the dirt around a row of plants, what they were learning from Wilson.

"Plants. He teaches us how to plant 'em and all that."

Did they all know about plants before he came?

Scattered noes came from the group.

"Like a cactus. I had a cactus," said one boy. "I watered it like I didn't know what! The thing died on me. I took good care of it, but it just died. And then when I came here, I found out that a cactus needs very little water."

I asked how many of them now had a garden at home. All the hands were raised. "Corn trees, and I got apples trees, and avocado trees and —"

Another boy, carrying a deck of baseball cards, said firmly: "If Mr. Wilson doesn't get some kind of award for his horticultural knowledge I think there's something wrong. He deserves some sort of honor."

Shortly after my visit, Wilson was given a statewide award for his volunteer work with children.

At the other end of the yard, Richard Dillman, in his late fifties, was working with another group of kids. Dillman, along with Wilson, is one of the sixty-two senior mentors in the county. A retired veterinarian, he works with potential dropouts. His specialty: pet therapy. Dillman's fourteen kids — most of whom also live in the inner city — spend part of each week at the Miami Agricultural School, where they care for several dogs, rabbits, pigs, and a steer, Bumper.

"We use pet therapy to keep these kids interested in school, keep their minds open," explained Dillman. "These are high-risk kids, but their attendance this year went from fifty-six percent to ninety-seven percent.

Most people think of pet therapy as a device used in nursing homes, convalescent homes. But we're realizing that pet therapy can be effective for children with learning disabilities, and it's a natural link between old and young. We use pet therapy to work with children, and then the same animals will be used, with the kids' help, to address the needs of senior citizens in the nursing homes. So with the animals as a link, we're creating a new relationship between the child and elderly person. When they work with animals, the kids and the seniors relax; they feel like human beings."

"Bumper a *special* steer," said a fifth-grader as the group gathered around. "He play with you, he bump you!"

What was special about him? I asked. "He was hand-raised." "He fun!" "He'll play with you." "Take his food away and he bump you!"

But how did they feel about hamburgers?

"Fine!" "No, not from Bumper!" Another boy offered, "If it was his father, I would eat him!"

I asked them what they had learned from the pets. "That they have feelings. Like Bumper, he loves to be pet. Animals like the way you scratch their ears and stuff like that." Didn't they know that before? "No! Well, I already knew they could get mad and all." A girl said authoritatively, "In order to do the training you got to get it, like, when it's first born."

One boy said: "When I first went out there, I thought that Bumper was a rabbit. I didn't know he was a steer." Another boy said, "I thought it was like a *horse*."

A girl explained: "This girl had found a baby possum, and we gave it a home. Dr. Dillman handled the baby here, like feed him from a bottle, because his momma was gone, and he was small."

"Yeah." "And it grew up." "He cute! His momma left, and then we found him, so we had took him in."

How did they feel about his momma leaving him?

"Bad!"

"He probably fell off while she was running."

"They was scared."

The children told about how they take some of these animals into nursing homes, where the door between the young and the old is opened.

"The old people tell stories about when they was young," said a fifth-grader, with a quiet of awe. "What they used to do in them days, pets they used to know. We go there and then we sit down at a table and we talk to our grandparent and then we eat." An adopted grandparent? "Yes — well, it's in between. We adopt each other. My grandparent tol' me the story that he was eighteen and was in the army and stuff, in French. They used to ride in the boat and then they had to rush and they fight." Whom did he fight? "He ain't tol' me. But he tol' me that they rode on a boat and they had fightin' in the middle of the night and they had to rush. . . ."

What kinds of things did they tell their adopted grandparents about themselves, about their own lives?

"I tell 'em what grade I'm in, like what school I go to, like what I'd like to be when I grow up, what kind of problems I'm having at school."

Did anybody tell the grandparent about problems at home?

"Only with my room."

What was the problem with his room?

"I gotta clean it up."

Another boy said: "We're going to take the pets and let our grandparents touch 'em and hold 'em. They're gonna have a pet at their feet. A pet again, like what kind of pet they used to have."

Another boy, wide-eyed, added, "But it's like, if we take 'em in there, and some of them people might be scared and have a heart attack."

How many had pets of their own?

"Me, me . . ."

"I got three birds, six dogs, and five chickens, and three cats."

"I got a bird."

No steers?

The kids laughed. Several were wearing BUMPER'S BUDDIES T-shirts that Dr. Dillman had had made for them.

How did these animals, and the old people, make them feel about themselves?

"Proud!" one boy said. A chorus joined in: "Yeah, proud!"

Tested this year, these kids have shown remarkable improvement in their attitude toward older people, in their conduct, in their school attendance, and in their grades, which went from a C-plus to a B-plus average.

To publicize the program, Dillman and "Bumper's buddies" plan to take the steer downtown to meet the school board members. "It's going to be interesting," said Ramona Frischman drily. "We already know what the headline is going to be: A LITTLE BULL IN POLITICS. But the real story here is that when seniors and kids join forces, remarkable things can happen."

21

Creating the
Family-Friendly City

●

We can reduce the isolation of children and their parents by reimagining the city.

A friend of mine, who is twenty-four, was talking about what it had
been like to grow up in the city, and how different it was now for her
sister. "In the long summers, I lived in the neighborhood park," she said
a bit wistfully. "There were classes in tumbling and a gym and a rec
room, and in the summer there were little day camps, and movies for a
quarter. You felt wanted by somebody, you felt wanted by the city."

Today her sister, who is fourteen, never goes to the park, which has
been taken over by adults, mostly single yuppies taking private classes
in tennis and ceramics and self-defense. The neighborhood kids play in
the street, or hang out at shopping malls. My friend's sister spends a lot
of time sitting alone in darkened movie theaters.

But many parents are beginning to look around at how the urban
environment treats children, and they don't like what they see.

To paraphrase Winston Churchill, we shape our buildings, and thereafter they shape us. To the planners and builders of cities, children are
nearly invisible. In Sir Banister Fletcher's classic textbook, *A History of
Architecture*, 1,621 pages long, the index lists only one reference to children: "Children's Hospital, Beijing, In-patient department, 1960."[1] "I'm
afraid to tell you," said Michael Parrish, director of the urban studies
and planning program at the University of California–San Diego, "that
our courses don't deal with children."

Current municipal tendencies regarding children have decreased the
livability of cities not just for children but for all of us. In the seventies
and early eighties in Dallas, Houston, and Denver, between 70 and 90

percent of all newly constructed apartments were strictly for adults. Nationwide, at least 10 percent of condominiums are age-restricted. Some cities, eager to tap the expendable income of single yuppies and the senior citizen tax base (and to avoid providing expensive municipal services for children), allow developers to build higher-density complexes in exchange for the no-children restrictions. In many major cities, nuclear families have been moving out. Seattle, for instance, lost 36 percent of its children between 1970 and 1980. Much of this flight, of course, is due to busing, congestion, and crime, but some of it is directly related to the wider message being sent to families with children.

"A lot of people in Seattle thought the family exodus was just fine," said Art Skolnick, a former city official. "I remember arguing with an economist who said children didn't belong in the city anyway; they were the cause of crime, taxes, a drain on the public coffers. Childless yuppies, on the other hand, are a good source of taxes, they're affluent, they party a lot, they keep money in circulation, and they demand fewer services. What they want, mainly, are flashy restaurants." When Skolnick ran for a seat on the King County Council he proposed that King County create a children's commission to confront such issues as housing discrimination against families with children. "My opponent said, 'King County already spends millions of dollars on children — look how much we spend on juvenile courts!' "

Skolnick added, "My daughter, who is sixteen, says: 'Put yourself in my shoes. Look at the library hours cut back, schools down, parks down. . . . It looks like you people don't care about us.' " Another Seattle city councilman put the concern this way: "The city must have a living memory. You cannot import your whole population each generation. If public policy does not affirm the importance of families, then the city very possibly does not have a future."[2]

Children have specific ideas of what they like and dislike about cities, said Robert Aldrich, the former chairman of the department of pediatrics at the University of Washington Medical School. "In Japan, children have a word, *harappa*, that means 'loss of grass, trees, and flowers where we used to make our games and play.' " The word applies to America's urban areas, where a proliferation of high-rise developments and the disappearance of open space are pushing out family life. Families are often clustered in the areas with the fewest amenities for children. "There is something about living in those areas of a city that is not good for children," Aldrich contended. "They don't develop their learning capabilities. But I figure that if we can build a city to produce functionally retarded children, we can unbuild it and build it differently."

Imagine a city where children are the priority. Aldrich and the children of Seattle did just that.

KidsPlace

In the mid-eighties, a Seattle civic group started what has since been named the KidsPlace project, the first organized effort by a major American city to make the urban environment pro-child — to create, in effect, citywide habilitation. Aldrich (who, in the early sixties, started the National Institute for Child Health and Human Development) and the other participants began by taking groups of elementary school kids on field trips around the city. The kids were asked to draw pictures and write stories and poems about what they saw and then, at the end of each trip, meet for a few minutes with the then mayor of Seattle, Charles Royer.

The youngsters described the obvious. They didn't like the downtown waterfront, said Aldrich, "because there wasn't any place to touch the water." And new buildings with blank walls at street level "scared the kids."

Surprisingly, the project was accepted with enthusiasm by developers and architects convinced by Aldrich and his civic group that a pro-child urban design could increase retail profits in commercial districts. Among the eventual improvements: the waterfront architects, more likely to listen to kids than sociologists anyway, laughed and went back to the drawing board to design new places for wading and touching the water. The city determined that, on future buildings, street-level blank walls would be discouraged.

Most large buildings offer no open places where kids and adults can congregate, but developers of several new Seattle buildings are now considering whole floors devoted to children, short-term day-care centers, and shopping areas aimed at kids.

Teenagers were invited to sit on some of the city's planning committees, and an urban design "good idea" competition awarded the young winner with the post of Mayor for a day. "A number of projects involve teenagers in actually doing things for the city that need to be done, for which they'll receive recognition," said Aldrich. "American cities aren't very good at that. Generally we tell our teenagers to get lost: we don't employ them or ask their opinion."

KidsPlace also created a campaign to encourage retail stores to exhibit KIDSPLACE window decals. These stores advertise themselves as places where kids and parents are welcome. (For businesses, this could be a profitable endeavor.) Volunteers from each business area educate clerks that if children and parents are treated with respect, they spend more and shoplifting drops off. Aldrich, who travels internationally promoting these ideas, said that one of the things that has surprised him in his journeys "is that if you go into a store in Italy, the salesperson will spend five minutes playing with the kids before they get around to what they can do for you. This is true in Japan, China — they really star their children. Americans, some of them, treat kids just marvelously, but I think it would be a worthy goal to encourage clerks, people in stores and restaurants, to be much more considerate of people with small children. We've all been in a grocery store when a parent grabs and slaps a kid. That can often be prevented. If a clerk takes notice of the kid, bends over, shakes hands, it changes the whole ambiance, changes the behavior of the kid. But too often young families get the message that they aren't wanted."

Aldrich's KidsPlace concepts acknowledge a powerful motive: profit. Welcome families spend more money. And if a city treats its children well, they'll treat the city well later on — commercially and socially.

The answers gathered by KidsPlace surveys are instructive in suggesting ways to reverse anti-child urban damage, and for suggesting how urban life could someday be for all of us, whether or not we have kids. For example, here are some of the answers garnered by a KidsPlace survey conducted in San Diego (by an Aldrich-guided replica of the Seattle program) given to thousands of children in the public school system. Notice that the children make little differentiation between social ills and urban design — a sophistication more urban planners should exhibit.

> I would try to find the street people a home so they won't be making downtown look dirty and bad. And I would add more ramps for the handicapped and more bathrooms.

> Stop building so many buildings & houses before we are ugly like Los Angeles. . . . Too many bums . . .

> I would give the kids more chances to learn the jobs of the grown-ups and let the kids replace their parents or other people for a day.

> . . . an information booth for kids.

> I would have one day a year that kids can be in charge of court & police system — to see how justice really works. I would also have a kids day where everything for one day is half price for people under 18.

First I would build a place where kids could go on weekends. There would be a movie theater and a dance place and an indoor aquarium with different kinds of fish, a wishing well and finally day care so we could bring our little brothers and sisters.

I would ask for money to create a center just for children. A place that would be centered not only on their futures, but also on their present.

Organize a teen-center where kids could do things they really liked. There would be a free shuttlebus.

More places for kids, a bus and trolley only for kids, make a big family fun center and a skating rink.

I would ask for a special shopping mall for kids. The mall would be called *"The powerful shopping mall for kids only."*

. . . more crosswalks so that kids can cross the street by themselves.

Make a bike trail so kids will not get hit by a car or by one of the trolleys. Now that's my statement.

The results of a more extensive survey in Sacramento were also revealing. Imagine living in the Sacramento community that children imagine:

If kids planned Sacramento, we'd have more bus service and bike lanes. . . . Kids would build wide, shaded sidewalks away from busy traffic, where they could walk, ride a bike, or sit on a bench. These sidewalks would go from neighborhood to neighborhood (so kids could visit their friends), go to shopping areas (so kids could run errands), go to transportation centers (so kids could lock their bikes and get on a bus or light rail train), and go to places of employment (because kids want to work).

Our libraries would have computers, because kids realize that they will be learning from computers as well as from books. Schools, parks, and libraries would be places where kids could have paid or volunteer jobs, helping younger children, building, cleaning, repairing, gardening, or running errands. Kids would also like to learn practical things there, like how to deal with emergencies and how to prepare meals.

Now, our young people often meet their friends at the movies or the shopping centers. However, they would like Sacramento to have more community swimming pools and places to dance where they could also get food. In addition to continuing to emphasize sports, students would also provide more places where they could participate in music, art, dance, and theater.

Kids would design our commercial areas to include benches and drinking fountains for very short people. They would include child care centers and supervised play areas in shopping centers, so kids wouldn't have to always go shopping with their parents (after a while, it gets boring to just see knees). They'd have businesses put posters in their windows, indicating that it would be O.K. for young people to go into the business and to ask for help. And kids would plan Sacramento so that there were more safe, non-alcoholic places where teen-agers could meet old and new friends.

In terms of residential planning, kids would build houses in which their bedrooms were big enough to include desks. They would plan our neighborhoods so that kids could safely get to places without a car, and so that they could see and safely play with other kids near these streets and sidewalks.

For younger children, students would provide child care, but would also include flex-time in businesses, so that a parent could sometimes be home when the kids were home. For older elementary school kids, they felt it was O.K. for them to be home alone, but would also plan programs for them at the school, park, and library.

A second Sacramento survey queried parents also, whose chief concerns included bicycle education programs, well-lighted stops, bike racks near bus and light rail stops and stores, and mechanisms such as pedestrian light switches to be used by bicyclists to get across the street safely.

One revealing difference between parents and children: kids are much more interested in creating jobs for children and teenagers. Kids should be encouraged by business people, program directors, and parents, the Sacramento report concluded, to take on nonacademic responsibilities. Among the report's suggestions:

- "Clean-up days," when kids would help pick up trash, water, weed plants, paint, and help build things, could be established.
- Junior high and high school students could assist in taking care of younger kids before and after school and during vacations, helping them with sports, art, drama, crafts, music, and so on.
- Business and industry should be encouraged to maintain part-time entry-level jobs through which young people could be successfully integrated into the paid work force.[3]

In Search of Mister Rogers' Neighborhood

Robert Aldrich's KidsPlace approach is a wonderful technique to use for retrofitting cities with family-friendly thinking. But what if this approach were used preventively, before developments are built?

Driving up through the outer reaches of San Diego County one can look out along the rolling hills now being sliced off, beheaded really, as the earth movers rend and tear the muscle from the land to make way for houses. Whenever I drive up the freeway, looking out at all the new developments, I wonder what they're going to be like in twenty or thirty years. I wonder what kind of culture we're creating. Will the children who grow up in these places have any sense of commitment to them? Or will these developments someday become vast, soulless slums? What's been forgotten is that it is our culture that is being shaped, not just housing. People need homes; there is no question of that. But in recent years, Americans have been spending more and more for less and less. Houses should be built cheaper, say developers; let's cut corners, shave lawns, slash red tape. The developers — and their co-conspirators, the politicians — insist we want instant colonies that look like a kind of stucco algae, faceless and grim (despite recently applied pastel cosmetics); amenity-filled private enclaves surrounded by walls and divorced from their surroundings, locked into place by strict covenants.

I asked an editor for the *San Diego Union*'s Homes section about the press releases that come to the paper from developers. What developers themselves consider the important amenities of their new communities are views of the eighteenth fairway (that is, open space managed by someone else), security systems, trash compactors, ceramic tile entries, miniaturized fireplaces, cathedral ceilings, wet bars, and three-car garages.

Were front porches or sidewalks ever listed as desirable amenities? I asked.

"No," the editor said. "Those things are never mentioned."

Why not? Why are so few developers building neighborhoods safe for children and other living things?

Developers continue to maintain that, because of economics, we have no choice. But surely a front porch and a wide sidewalk are no more expensive than a wet bar and a three-car garage.

The new neighborhoods that we shape eventually shape our children. What if all new developments required a children's environmental impact report?

This suggestion is more than half serious.

Most developers would resist the idea, but not all. Some would recognize the market for healthy environments for children and families.

A wealth of ideas is waiting to be tapped by smart developers.

In Seattle, architect and planner Art Skolnick proposes this idea: just as some schools have been designated magnet schools, why not create magnet neighborhoods for families? These neighborhoods would include affordable housing, recreation facilities for kids, and "walk-to" schools and libraries geared toward group participation. Such neighborhoods would not necessarily be patterned only on the "Leave It to Beaver" model. Surprisingly, the Sacramento KidsPlace study showed a preference among sixth-graders for apartment living. (One theory about why children expressed that preference: they may view apartment complexes as having more of a built-in sense of community than the empty streets of many suburban neighborhoods.)

As an increasing proportion of middle-income U.S. families with children purchase condominiums and townhouses, will these developments be pro-child? In *Housing as If People Mattered,* Clare Cooper Marcus and Wendy Sarkissian observe that many condominiums were designed for adult play but contain no play areas at all for children. They point out that designating some corner with a sandbox or a flat, green park area (often underused) as a play area is not enough.

Children need private spaces for themselves where they can build tree houses, forts, clubhouses in woods and fields away from public view. They need to be able to wander over to a friend's house without a formal invitation to play. To gain a sense of independence, they need to be able to travel safely farther and farther from home. Wild or leftover spaces, more attractive and useful to children than any play sculpture or swing, should be left undeveloped and incorporated into new neighborhoods. Some housing developments in Denmark include "play woods" adjoining traditionally equipped play spaces; in Holland, landscape planners often plant urban woods ahead of construction so that the woods are ready for use by the time families move in.[4]

What if parents were also questioned in preparing a children's environmental report? When asked, parents offer an array of suggestions, some banal, some fresh and creative, about how pro-family communities could be designed and the services they could offer.

The Sacramento study asked parents, all of whom were members of homeowners associations, to list the housing services they would most want. The answers suggest profitable marketing items to developers as well as possibilities for community associations and other neighborhood groups in existing communities:

• Security features
• On-site manager who can give assistance to children
• Recreation center for children and adults
• On-site children's playground (supervised)
• Pay-as-used on-site day-care center

• Pay-as-used dining room for prepared evening meals
• Pay-as-used baby-sitting service to care for sick children

The flexible "pay-as-used" approach could relieve a great deal of stress on families pushed by so many inflexible schedules — those of day cares, schools, and work places.

What This Country Needs Is a Few Good Developers

A handful of visionary developers and urban planners are reimagining the way cities and neighborhoods could be for families. The newest idea in development is an old idea — the nineteenth-century town. "In a small but rapidly growing number of American towns," writes Philip Langdon in the *Atlantic Monthly,* "designers and developers are rejecting the dominant modern methods of creating new residential areas. They are coming to view the community-development practices of the past few decades as a terrible blunder and returning to the town-planning traditions of the early 20th century and before. A new traditionalism is on the rise. . . ."[5]

An outstanding example is a new development called Seaside, in the Florida Panhandle. Built on an old-fashioned grid plan with shopping within walking distance, Seaside is strictly down-home: no picture windows, sliding glass doors, or aluminum siding. Instead, cupolas and towers rise from some of the roofs, creating a skyline reminiscent of long-ago rural towns, though these houses include many of the best interior design features of modern homes. But what is most striking about the board-and-batten houses is their deep front porches.

These are homes with human faces.

At Seaside, neighbors sit on porch swings, waving to each other across the narrow, straight streets, watching their children play out front in the dusk. The houses are open, visible, outward-looking across shared, defensible space; they provide their own natural security.

I asked Robert S. Davis, the developer of Seaside, what he considered the essential design elements of a pro-child community environment. He responded with a detailed letter:

> Seaside seems to work particularly well for children, and I think this is primarily because the streets are designed as outdoor living rooms. Automobile traffic is a secondary function of the street; the primary function is human habitation. This includes strolling, hanging out, and, especially, children's play.

The streets work because they have the right scale and texture. They are lined by trees and by picket fences and by houses with front porches. People sit on those porches and watch other people using the streets; the porches are close enough to the street for conversations between strollers and porch sitters to be quite comfortable. In addition to comfortable streets, there are also footpaths between lots and running alongside people's backyards. These footpaths are used much more by children than by adults.

It would be nice if every community, even after it is built up, could leave at least one construction site for children to explore. This certainly seems to be a source of endless fascination for most children. Almost any community could and should leave a section of woods in a completely natural state. Children like woods much better than manicured lawns or gardens.

I think that the critical issue in community-building is one of scale. A town, or a quarter or a city, should have limits and these limits are quite closely related to the distance that an adult with a child in tow would be willing to walk to get from one side of town to another. Eighty to ninety acres seems to be about the right size. Even in large cities, districts or neighborhoods effectively work as small towns with a commercial core surrounded by residences all within walking distance of the core.

While well designed settlements should have boundaries, they should most definitely not have walls. One of the truly absurd aspects of modern life is the degree to which being a parent means being a chauffeur. Not only do parents spend an inordinate amount of time driving their kids to all sorts of activities which, in a real town, would be within walking or bicycling distance, but also parents often find themselves driving their children to visit another child who lives 100 yards away as the crow flies.

I am firmly of the belief that activity on the street and eyes on the street will form a sense of neighborhood which provides a greater degree of safety than the walled compound.

Playgrounds should also be small and accessible. They should be located near adult activity centers. Seaside does not yet have a school, but when it does it will be within easy walking distance for any child in the community. It is far better, in my opinion, to have a larger number of small neighborhood schools for basic instruction. Specialized subjects can be housed in larger, more centralized facilities which students could attend once or twice a week or, better yet, could be taught by roving teachers. I think that bureaucrats, far more than true educators, are impressed by economies of scale and advantages of centralization.

Seaside's nineteenth-century American vision could be a twenty-first-century vision — if other developers and politicians are paying attention.

A few years ago I visited another alternative development, Village Homes in Davis, California, a pioneering, solar-powered planned community. Rather than manicured plots of grass, Village Homes was overgrown with decorative vegetable gardens. Rather than a communal jacuzzi, it had a day-care center. Rather than a surrounding wall, Village Homes was encircled by almond trees. Children harvested the almonds and sold them in a tiny "farmer's market" in the village square. Cars were tucked out of sight, behind the houses; homes had front porches and patios facing inward toward walking paths. Village Homes suffered none of the lawsuits common to planned communities. It boasted the lowest crime rate in Davis and a long waiting list of people who wanted to live there.

This family-friendly development has drawn visitors from all over the world — including François Mitterrand, the president of France (whose helicopter landed on the green one day), who wanted to duplicate its innovative design in his own country.

Walking through the pathways one afternoon, Michael Corbett, the community's designer, told me that a few U.S. developers had stopped by over the years. "But nothing comes of it," he said. "Not one developer in the United States has tried to duplicate Village Homes. Not one."

If the president of France has visited Village Homes, why don't politicians from our own cities? Why don't they visit Seaside?

Maybe we need some help imagining what we can barely remember. We need visionary political leadership that will educate people that they do have options. If developers really believe they're giving us what we want, why don't they offer us a real choice?

So far, Seaside has gained more serious attention than Village Homes. Philip Langdon calls Seaside "the most celebrated new American town of the decade" and suggests that, in America's search for home, "town-planning traditions that have been ignored for half a century are serving as a generally trustworthy guide."

Surely there's a market for neotraditional, family-friendly housing.

Looking at the photographs of Seaside, I was struck by the familiarity of the houses. The development looked much like the rare older neighborhoods for which young families compete feverishly and pay extraordinary prices in many cities of the Sunbelt. Families with children are drawn to the traditional, functional design of the neighborhood: the front porches on the houses, the feeling of community, the wide sidewalks perfect for tricycles, the narrow streets and slow traffic, the fact that one can walk to the pharmacy and the parks. Surely smart developers could create approximations of this kind of pro-child, pro-adult neighborhood and, in due course, make a profit.

Developers might profit in other ways. If people were to look out across the stretches of new housing and see real towns rising up — inviting, friendly, familiar places — they might feel differently about their opposition to new development. And if sociologists and psychologists who study the nature of community are correct, a return to early twentieth-century community design could eventually create a less expensive society with less need for security systems, SWAT teams, psychiatrists, and electronic diversions.

A City of Family Centers

Part of the reason for the loss of families in cities is the deconcentration of American life, the outward movement of people toward what I have described in another book as America II — clusters and nodes of development which are not really urban, not really suburban.

As society deconcentrates into such nodes and clusters beyond traditional cities and towns, we need to recognize this movement and plan pro-child, pro-family hubs within it. Many now lack centers — hearts, connective points. How can children or parents feel at home in places without identifiable meeting places? The nature and quality of this kind of development (which in rural areas is known as "buckshot" urbanization) leave both parents and children with a fragmented sense of place.

Ultimately we need to rethink this evolving urban form, reconsider how to reorganize it around community. To create a pro-child and pro-family environment within this new reality, we need to reshape our thinking about the physical places where children and parents make contact. The new web has no one center, but it should have many if it is to hold.

Some advanced thinking on this subject is going on in the unlikely city of Phoenix. Like the Blob of science fiction, urban Arizona consumes everything in its path. To their credit, community leaders in Phoenix are determined to reinvent the American city, to move away from the twentieth-century mold (which it now exemplifies) of endless sprawl, possibly toward a post-freeway, twenty-first-century city. In 1987 the city council adopted a general plan to guide growth in Phoenix until the year 2000. The plan formalizes the urban village approach, with a goal of creating smaller "towns" inside the big city, guiding future development into them, and making them into true communities.

In theory, urban villages

• Allow families to live and work close to home, which should cut down on commuting time and increase family time.

• Contain one or more higher-density cores (sometimes a shopping mall, preferably a "festival" mall, with housing and office space), with the density decreasing to single-family homes at the edges of the village. This would give each urban village a sense of identity and place, and a focus for family centers.

• Are buffered from each other by greenbelts, parks, or agricultural or mountain preserves between the villages.

The urban village plan aims to give sections of the city a sense of identity and community. Downtown Phoenix would become the Super Urban Village, the first among equals. But a lot more emphasis will be placed on all those new "downtowns" out there, the urban villages. The plan virtually throws out the old ways of zoning and accepts urban villages as the guideposts of future development.

Phoenix is already making progress in developing the natural buffer zones between its urban villages. Some of the planned villages have been designed so that mountain preserves and other natural buffers separate them from existing villages. The region could eventually be freed from overdependence on freeways. Though provisions for mass transit aren't spelled out in the new plan, city planner Rick Counts believes that a light rail system could link all the urban villages with the downtown core and Sky Harbor Airport. Counts admitted there's not much of a constituency for light rail now, but "someday traffic problems are going to force people to choose between light rail and building even more freeways — which are noisy, disruptive of neighborhoods, demand a huge right of way, and aren't very fun." Much of the urban village vision for Phoenix is, Counts acknowledged, "pie in the sky, years away," but the design of truly pro-child and pro-family cities will demand such visionary thinking.

In the meantime, more practical goals can be met; existing urban facilities can be transformed into family hubs.

We need to think of malls, for instance, as powerful environments. Like our residential neighborhoods, malls shape our children; therefore, we need to reshape malls.

Malls as Family Hubs

Malls are, in fact, the new downtowns, the new playgrounds for teens and, increasingly, for younger children. If we accept this reality, how can they be made to be pro-child?

"I'm always terribly ambivalent in malls," said one father. "I do and

I don't like taking my kid there. We have a whole ritual: I take David first to see if the parrot will talk, then go browse in books, then a children's clothing store that has some playground equipment and he plays, and then we look at the toys I'm not going to buy for him. There's always tension, because of all these goodies available. Malls are ambivalent places. On the one hand, they're self-contained villages, contained for families, and on the other hand, they're amusement parks, and they don't seem quite real and *I* don't feel quite real when I'm in the mall."

Temple University professor Martin Millison studied the kids of mall culture in his doctoral thesis. "I think they do grow up faster," he says about children who frequent shopping centers. "They become more worldly." [6]

Commercial interests certainly understand the potential of having children in the malls. The vice president of Trend Facts in Detroit, Dana Blackwell, who conducts market research sessions with children around the country, has been impressed by the extraordinary amount of time children say they spend in malls. Malls are where other kids are, and kids go also to see what's new and to spend money. Since the proportion of Americans under thirteen is expected to increase dramatically in years to come (as that of teenagers plummets), the children's market is going to explode. That explosion may well mean an entirely different kind of mall.

How can malls be made more humane places for kids — how can they be made into family hubs?

Applying some of Robert Aldrich's KidsPlace principles would be a good place to start. But the use of such public-minded ideas in private spaces will undoubtedly meet resistance. Sanford Goodkin, a nationally known urban consultant, said most mall designers are "elitists in love with two things: affluence and the status quo. They're inoculated against joy and unpredictability and fun, unless it's on the damn golf course." Until recently, the assumption has been that shoppers want malls to be sterile and predictable. (Enforced sterility is still all too common: some malls have banned Salvation Army bell ringers because they distract shoppers.)

But now three trends are converging: the "overmalling" of many cities, which means that new malls must come up with gimmicks that make them different; the emergence of a new breed of shoppers, raised on unpredictability, who want it when they're shopping; and the rise of a new generation of kids, who consider malls their natural habitat.

Already, one can see evidence of what could be called mall redevelopment — little things like newly planted trees down the center of an old mall, and benches placed there for people-watching.

The newer malls are becoming cities unto themselves. In Houston and Dallas, the giant Galleria malls contain their own hotels and underground tunnels. Goodkin is helping design a mall in Denver that will be part campus, with student housing, possibly as an official arm of the University of Colorado. "Malls are becoming theme parks without the rides," said Goodkin. Along with James Rouse, who designed the giant "festival malls" in Baltimore and Boston, Goodkin envisions a shift toward nonretail mall tenants: doctor's offices, aerobic dance studios, television and radio stations, even residential housing.

The next logical step, then, is to take children seriously in this redesigning.

Among the features of a pro-child mall: play areas, children's museums and teen centers, school extensions, public day-care centers or family centers, and drop-in counseling centers for kids and parents. The latter could include on-site counselors (in private rooms) for immediate crises and referrals, nurses, parenting classes, abuse information. A few developers think that malls are not complete without a part- or full-time day-care center, said Goodkin, "but others feel they're a pain in the butt, more theoretical than practical. My feeling is every development should have one, and if they're managed and merchandized as well as other stores, they would be widely used."

What about parenting centers, and family information and counseling?

"I like the idea," said Goodkin. "Ironically, in one sense the mall is an escape mechanism — that's why they're evolving toward the theme park — but it makes sense to create places where those kids and parents who need help wouldn't feel they were going to some institution for the abnormal. Place these kinds of services in the mall, and you've placed them in a very positive, nonthreatening context. School systems should get involved with this, working with the mall developer."

As malls take on more of the role of the "downtown," more public control will be required of how mall space is designated and how much freedom of expression is allowed. That is not an attractive idea to some mall developers, but the visionary ones may eventually see the commercial wisdom of allowing a little mall glasnost inside their walls, along with the kids.

The Last Safe Place: Libraries as Family Hubs

In addition to malls and schools, public libraries could become more active as family hubs.

There has always been something churchly about libraries — the humming quiet, the sense of wonder. I like to think of the public library as the last safe place. So do a lot of parents, including the parents of thousands of latchkey kids dropped off at libraries each day. Indeed, the idea of government's lending something out for free and trusting people to return it is a radical idea. The library may well be one of the few places where the strands of trust still exist. Programs for illiterate adults are far more effective in libraries than in schools, where these adults were often humiliated as children. Said one librarian: "Libraries and bus stations really are the only place people can go and be with other people and not be approached, at least most of the time. We encourage people to socialize at the library, especially young people. It's a good alternative to the 7-Eleven or the mall." Libraries could help provide some of the glue necessary to hold together a rapidly decentralizing society.

"Traditionally, people went to check out a book. Now they go to sit down and read, to attend a lecture, use a copy machine, or use a computer terminal," said California state librarian Gary Strong. "They're expressing a new set of wants and needs."

A California State Library study issued in 1986 showed that users were as likely to say they were helped by a library in emotional ways as they were in getting information: 93 percent said it helped them to get motivated, feel good about themselves, calm down, or feel hopeful; 89 percent said the library helped them in reaching goals, finding out what to do, and how to do it; and 72 percent expressed happiness and pleasure when they visited the public library. Strong concluded that the study "confirms something that librarians have always known. Libraries are more than just places where books and information are stored and disseminated."

Los Angeles County's head librarian, Linda Crismond, believes that the future of libraries, particularly in the Sunbelt, will be shaped by the endless suburbs of population sprawl. California, she points out, is leading a "nationwide trend where our cities are coalescing into collections of urban villages — office, industrial, retail, and housing focal points amidst low-density cityscapes. If the library is not in these urban villages, we may find ourselves on the outside looking in." She recommends that libraries develop more partnerships with social agencies to improve shelters and child-care services and to provide job information.[7]

Gary Strong proposed a particularly appealing vision of the library of the future which incorporates technology and the human touch. He believes future libraries should offer the kind of atmosphere and services of the old town halls. They could include community centers, meeting rooms for community and parent groups, education and media areas, and concert facilities. Libraries could offer banks of videotaped or audiotaped samples of local work — high school band performances, local theater productions. In addition, people would be able to use their home computers to tap into library data bases, downloading anything from Shakespeare to local bus routes. Rather than simple book depositories, libraries could become quality-of-life centers, the physical and electronic hubs of communities. "We've fallen away from human dialogue," said Strong. "Conversation has moved, literally, to the barroom, to the Happy Hour. We need to step back and take a look at what we've lost — the old town meetings, the discussion groups, the sharing of ideas. Everywhere you look, you see gyms and recreational centers to keep our bodies fit. I think we need mental fitness centers — to regenerate the mind." The central focus of such mental fitness centers should be the family.

Despite dismal funding for libraries nationwide, many libraries are becoming de facto family centers. Sydney Stanley, a San Diego librarian, said: "As librarians, we desperately need people who can welcome children and make them feel at home and help them with reading. It's very difficult to introduce kids to the books appropriate for their age because they're so overexposed to visual images. Unless they're given tremendous support at home, these children are just lost. I see a growing inability to function in the library. I've seen kids and adults come in my library who can't read the instructions on the photocopy machine. Children's services in the library have been financially cut back, but our volunteer program, Friends of the Library, has taken up some of the slack. With two hundred and fifty volunteers in the city system, we save several thousand dollars a month in labor that we would otherwise have to pay for. But only a token number of volunteers work with children; most of what they do is clerical. It takes qualified people to work with children, and that costs money."

Though some public library systems have become increasingly restrictive about latchkey kids, some libraries (with money) have moved in the opposite direction. For example, Greenville County Library in South Carolina has created a latchkey program that serves nearly fifteen hundred children. Carolyn Cody-Fuller, the library's director of youth services and coordinator of the program, sent strands of her library's web out to eight neighborhood centers to identify children to be included in the program. Initially, some of the children were suspicious, hostile, and reluctant to get involved. "Some of the children believed that we were coming to see them because they were poor and disadvantaged and we pitied them," she says. "We took time to tell them that was not our purpose. We had come as friends interested in their welfare. The library set up bookcases in the neighborhood centers, each containing about a hundred thirty books, which covered such topics as first aid, dental care, preparing easy meals, general safety, pet care, baby-sitting. Staff members visited each center and presented an 'Introduction to the Latchkey Program,' in which the library staff required the children to make a list of emergency telephone numbers for their parents' work place, the sheriff's department, a neighbor, and the fire department. The most popular program — how to prepare meals — showed children how to make snacks without using the stove because the stove is a potential danger to children." [8]

How much more humane this approach is than handing latchkey kids brochures or videotapes.

Linda Crismond writes in *Library Journal* that public libraries should eventually be recognized as part of the educational structure, that library hours should be changed and lengthened. Customers will check out their own books, pay their own fines, and update their information files — presumably leaving librarians freer to work with kids. "Join me in a brief look forward to the inside of a 15,000-square-foot community library in one of our Sunbelt cities in the year 2000," she writes. "The first thing that catches our eye is the number of people present. There are people all over the place, adults and children . . . computers or terminals are all over the place, linked with other library collections near and remote." There are small group spaces, and small study spaces created from modular office equipment. "If we listen at the door, we will overhear the Thursday Afternoon Investment Club. . . . Another group is practicing their French for their upcoming trip to Paris. . . . A third group is rehearsing a play and preparing to stage it in the library's 150-seat meeting room. . . . As we turn to leave, we realize that we have just been in a true learning environment, a true community center. We are aware that here, in this one small building, we could access the whole of human knowledge, and that no one would question us as to why, or what, we were doing or wanted. It is such a fine feeling. The public library, the People's University, the community center!" [9] It is a place where children and their families can find a sense of place, of identity, of belonging.

Beyond malls and libraries, other family hubs can be identified and expanded — existing community centers, YMCAs, churches, and most schools. What is most important is that families, parent networks, and government recognize the crucial psychological importance of these hubs in our increasingly deconcentrated, lonely cities. These family hubs are the focal points to which the strands of the new web can be attached. In establishing these hubs, we might begin to redefine the kind of institutions most needed in the family-friendly city.

Part of the reason for the institutionalization of childhood is that so many of the supportive institutions we used to rely on have faded: for example, the extended families or churches that once took up more of the slack of troubled families. At a meeting of social workers at the Kansas Children's Service League in Wichita, one woman elaborated, "When I was a girl growing up in a small town in Kansas in the forties, a thirteen- or fourteen-year-old rural girl could go to the city and get a room at a Lutheran home and look for a job and she'd be protected." This protection, she said, was neutral — not in a moral sense, since the young women were taught and expected to adhere to religious values, but in the sense that the institution "didn't assume you were a runaway, didn't treat you like a criminal." She said she believed that one of the reasons the amount of reported child abuse and the number of runaways and throwaways has increased is the community's decreased ability to absorb stray children naturally.

This point seemed to me to be subtle but crucial: we need more institutions for children and youths which are neutral in their judgment of children and of families, institutions that would provide for many young men and women a bridge into the adult world, as the YWCA, the Conservation Corps, and others did in the past.

Childhood and family problems have risen as the number of neutral or nurturing, facilitating institutions (extended families, caring neighborhoods, the Boy Scouts and Girl Scouts, and so on) has decreased. These facilitating institutions have been replaced by commercial, curative, sometimes punitive, purely protective institutions — the juvenile justice system, child protection agencies, residential treatment centers. But by their nature, such institutions usually come into play after a child's emotional problems have already become severe. By contrast, facilitating institutions often help prevent problems from becoming so serious.

As individuals, we can support the remaining facilitating institutions, even if we do not particularly subscribe to their entire doctrine. For example, one father said: "I'm in church not because I'm religious. I'm known as a nonpracticing atheist, but I'm active in the church partly for the fellowship but also because of the important role that churches have in socializing our youth." Indeed, those churches that are growing and thriving are those that recognize the socialization of youth as a major role. Churches might also more actively sponsor parent support groups and parent networks. A key for the success of church programs for children and parents is that churches perceive themselves not as insular islands serving only their memberships but as family and neighborhood centers.

In short, the difference between a child-abuse agency or residential home on the one hand and a facilitating church, school, or neighborhood on the other is the difference between the safety net and the larger web — the difference between reaction and prevention.

Here is an example of the kind of facilitating institution that might, if it were a reality, help bridge the fundamental divide.

The lack of a supportive network for children who get pregnant means that abortion is used as a form of birth control. (Whether or not one supports the freedom to seek an abortion, few Americans see abortion as a preferable form of birth control.) One-third of all abortions performed annually in the United States are for teenage girls.

In the seventies, after the Supreme Court legalized abortion, homes for unwed mothers fell out of fashion. Nationwide, more than half of the homes closed. Religious Right leader Jerry Falwell has admitted that conservative religious groups have done little themselves to offer more avenues for adoption. However, a small but growing number of sectarian maternity homes are popping up around the country, such as King's Ranch in the Alabama countryside, which is supported mainly by religious organizations. In the sixties, only half of existing maternity homes were operated by religious groups. Today the figure is close to two-thirds.[10]

One possiblity is that sectarian organizations might begin to move into this arena — perhaps feminist groups. The religious Right may have a more acute interest in providing alternatives to abortion, but organizations on the other side of the divide could pursue their own aims in this way as well. What better way, for example, to break the chain of child and spouse abuse, to offer young women adequate prenatal care, psychological help, career counseling — a doorway into a better world — than during these precious and vulnerable nine months? Such facilitating institutions could even be established as joint ventures by groups on both sides of the fundamental divide to offer prevention and healing to parents and children in the family-friendly city.

Marketing Family-Friendly Cities

Some cities will soon begin to recognize the economic advantages of becoming family-friendly.

A few years ago, states and cities would do just about anything to attract high-tech businesses. The ads in business journals went something like this: "Hi, I'm Governor Bob Rebob of the great state of (*enter name here*). We're pro-business! We've cut our sales tax and abolished our corporate taxes; in fact, we'll pay *you* to set up business here. We'll throw in a free industrial park. So leave that dreary old tax-burdened state you're in, and come on down!"

Such lures worked fine for a while. Businesses hopped around the country like cats in a fish market; but as time went by, most competitive states and cities, including some of those dreary old northeastern states, were offering the same deal.

So what special new premium should states and cities offer now?

How about child care, and family centers, and family magnet neighborhoods, and schools, and libraries and malls that serve as community hubs, and employers who offer generous family-leave policies?

Cities could begin to market themselves as pro-child and pro-family.

Think about it, says Jacquie Swaback, Sacramento's child-care coordinator. An entrepreneur at heart, she once operated her own economic development consulting firm. She buzzes, blurts, fizzes with ideas. Swaback wants to make Sacramento among the first major cities to attract business by marketing pro-child policies.

Where there's demand, there's opportunity. A family-friendly city could gain a competitive edge by promising potential new employers easier employee recruitment, less turnover, and higher productivity because workers wouldn't be worrying about their kids all the time. "Child care will either support or sabotage economic development," Swaback said. In Sacramento, which has more child-care centers than most cities, the waiting list for infant day care, private or public, is over a year long. One step in creating a marketable family-friendly city is to create more child care. To accomplish this, Swaback's first principle might be called constructive avarice. San Francisco charges hefty developer fees to pay for day care in downtown office buildings, but Sacramento employs a jawboning technique. "We have purposefully not charged fees," she said. "We may in the future, but not right now." She instead convinces developers, in her no-nonsense way, that they can make money with child care. She does this through an intensive blitz when the developer applies for a building permit.

As a result of her efforts, in two years ten out of Sacramento's twenty-five major developers have built or planned child-care facilities in new developments. "As a developer, who are you going to lease your building to?" she asked. "Companies with employees needing child care, that's who." Besides, it's a lot cheaper to put the facilities in from the beginning than to retrofit buildings in a few years. The same logic can, given a forceful presentation (and the subtle threat of later regulation), be effective even with residential developers. "Smart developers realize that if two-paycheck families are the only folks who can afford to buy houses, two-paycheck families are going to be a lot more interested in buying a house in a development with day care and other family services."

Once all these facilities are in place, how are they paid for? Partly, said Swaback, through creating a new system of benefits among family-friendly companies and family-friendly government employers. She launched an intensive campaign to persuade Sacramento employers to take advantage of two Internal Revenue Service provisions that were passed a few years ago but are only now emerging from IRS regulatory confusion. Under the first provision, IRS 129, the so-called income reduction plan (which is used by Hewlett-Packard), employee pre-tax dollars are placed in a fund to reimburse child-care costs — thus saving tax dollars for both the employer and the employee. The second provision, IRS 125, the cafeteria benefit plan, allows employees to pick from a smorgasbord of benefits.

Persuading cities, and the employers within those cities, to market themselves as family-friendly will become less difficult as the shift to a service economy becomes more complete — and as more parents work outside the home, whether they want to or not.

Swaback's techniques have so far been directed mainly at increasing available day care, but they could also be used to create family-friendly housing developments, family centers, parks, family hubs in libraries and malls, and play areas, as well as to preserve natural areas.

If Swaback's energetic approach pays off, and if other cities and states catch the fever, perhaps we'll be seeing new ads in the journals soon:

"Hi, I'm Governor Bob Rebob of the great state of (*enter name here*). We're pro-business because we're pro-family!"

By rethinking how our cities treat children, we rethink how we all want to live. A family-friendly city is a liberating place to live because of its increased efficiency, and because of the physical web of support it offers which reduces stress and provides more time for us to be full human beings rather than breathless servants of the freeway and the work place. Part of the hidden agenda of KidsPlace innovator Robert Aldrich is, he says, "to get people to look at the future — which is much more easily done if you ask them to look at their environment through the eyes of the children. I think we're going to see a kind of rolling change." Indeed, we have a chance to build real, caring communities that everyone will want to live in.

22

Schools and the
Reweaving of Time

●

No other crisis — a flood, a health epidemic, a garbage strike or
even snow removal — would be as calmly accepted without full-
scale emergency intervention.

> — Carnegie Foundation for the Advancement of Teaching,
> *An Imperiled Generation: Saving Urban Schools*

During the past few years, most of the talk about the future of public
schools has dealt with academic achievement, and apparently with
good reason. This is the educational system, remember, that turns out
kids who think that Peter Ustinov was the leader of the Russian Revolution and that King Alfred conquered the Dames. In one study, youngsters aged eight to eleven were able to name more brands of alcoholic
beverages than former presidents. However, the most exciting discussion about future schools won't be about content and curriculum but
about form.

Some visionary educators are coming to believe that the most important school reform has less to do with curriculum than with community — with strengthening the invisible web that connects the school
and its children to parents and other adults in the surrounding community. Public schools could become the most important of community
hubs for families, complete with large counseling centers, day-care facilities, and in-house and outreach parenting programs. Schools could increasingly serve as part of the child's extended family.

We have already embarked on the path toward this future. Schools
have taken on the role of the shaper of psyches, the smoother of ethnic

and racial differences, and the enforcer of laws. As with day care, parents are ambivalent about this developing role for schools. The role goes unacknowledged, and is insufficiently supported by most communities.

Indeed, even as many parents directly or indirectly ask schools to take over more family responsibilities, parents often resent them for doing so. In return, parents are often resented by teachers and school administrators who feel overburdened by these growing responsibilities. The reason for this double-sided resentment is that, with few exceptions, schools and parents have yet to develop a partnership with a winning strategy.

One goal of family liberation, then, will be to reshape schools so that they reduce the isolation of students, teachers, and parents. Schools should augment the family rather than replace it. The difference is subtle but crucial, given the justifiable fear many parents express about being replaced by institutions. Families need help, but they need to be supported, not replaced. The question should not be how schools can replace parents, but how schools can liberate families — and how families can liberate schools.

To understand the new role of the school (or rather, the reversion to a much older role), one needs to understand how far schools have drifted from the ideal of the community hub.

First, the physical plants of many public schools have decayed to the point of child endangerment. In *An Imperiled Generation,* published in 1988, the Carnegie Foundation for the Advancement of Teaching eloquently reported:

> Cities have spacious convention centers, new hotels, and banks that look like great cathedrals. But what about the schools? If urban America, regardless of its gleaming high rises and impressive skylines, is a place where education is neglected, then the glittering signs of "progress" remain a shameful facade. . . .
>
> One high school in Cleveland is near a once bustling intersection of commerce, but so many surrounding buildings have been razed that now the vacant land makes the school look like a forgotten outpost in an underdeveloped country. A sprawling playground is rendered useless by a carpet of glass. Inside, lavatories for students have no light bulbs, the stalls have no doors and there is no toilet paper in the dispensers. There is an atmosphere of hopelessness among the students, mirroring the outside world. . . .
>
> We visited urban schools where peeling paint, cracked plaster, torn window shades, and broken furniture are so common no one even seems to notice. In New York, for example, we saw schools that were filthy

because the budget allowed for sweeping the floors only once every other day. And at one school, two drinking fountains were in working order for its 2,000 students. . . .[1]

In school after school, tutoring sessions are held in converted restrooms and guidance counselors work in gym shower rooms. In New York, some custodians earn more than principals, and only 171 truant officers chase 200,000 truants.[2]

Second, the new and grudging recognition of the school as extended family comes in the wake of several waves of educational reform which have produced less than stunning results. One push for reform, beginning in 1983, produced a longer school year, longer instructional days, tougher graduation requirements, higher standards for teachers, and a renewed academic focus. The "back to basics" emphasis of the early eighties on math and reading gave way to a focus on curriculum content, a revision of what students learn about English, science, history, and social studies — substance and ideas rather than learning skills. The open-ended curriculum was replaced with a coherent grouping of shared knowledge. The content reform movement arose suddenly, dramatically, with the publication of the best-selling books *The Closing of the American Mind* by Allan Bloom and *Cultural Literacy* by E. D. Hirsch. This reform effort met with some surprising resistance. Albert Shanker, president of the American Federation of Teachers, blamed some of the resistance on what he called the nascent anti-intellectualism among many education administrators. At a speech to 150 high school principals in 1987, Shanker asked how many had heard of Hirsch's *Cultural Literacy*. Only three hands were raised.[3]

The academic results of these waves of reform are mixed. Most educators agree that, after half a decade of educational reform, the average public school in America provides a better learning environment today than before, with more academic subjects taught and more time spent teaching in class. As a higher-quality curriculum is introduced, SAT scores are generally rising. By the late eighties, almost every American high school graduate could handle simple arithmetic, but testing data suggested that virtually no progress had been made on the more complicated mental tasks increasingly sought by employers. Only half the nation's seventeen-year-olds, for example, could solve mathematics problems at the junior high level; fewer than one in fifteen could cope with problems at the high school level that required several steps or involved algebra or geometry.[4]

The larger uncertainty is how the effects of educational reform should be measured. Unlike virtually every other industrialized nation, the United States lacks a commonly accepted instrument for assessing academic performance.[5]

Contrary to popular belief, SAT scores began to rise in the mid-seventies, well before the school reform movements of the eighties, according to a Congressional Budget Office study, which also suggested that cultural and demographic factors such as family size and levels of drug and alcohol abuse may have more to do with the learning process than efforts to reform the curriculum.[6]

Moreover, we do not know how much improvement shown by testing is due to cheating by teachers and schools. In 1987, all fifty states reported above-average scores on standardized achievement tests, and 82 percent of 3,503 school districts surveyed reported above-average scores for elementary students, which makes one wonder where all the average students have gone. In April 1987, sixteen California schools cheated on the California Assessment Program test given to sixth-graders; state officials identified the sixteen schools by checking test booklets with a computerized scanning device for dramatically high numbers of erasures. They then looked at the booklets to see how many of the items with erasures were answered correctly. (Presumably, the students were coaxed by the teachers.)[7]

For individual schools, much is at stake. Test scores have become the most common gauge used by parents and real estate agents to judge a school, and funding is based largely on enrollment.

Madeline Cartwright told me about the testing in her school: "When I came here, test scores were the most important issue to principals in Philadelphia. Principals worked toward getting the scores as high as they could. No matter how, you got them high. When I came to this school, I saw that these test scores were higher in this building than they were in the rich areas of Philadelphia. Our scores were higher than theirs! So I called the teachers together, and I said: 'Look at this. How can you tell me that our first-graders are above the eightieth percentile?' I says, 'Make sense to you? This is crazy, this is not right.' For some of these teachers, the test becomes a follow-up to the lesson they just taught!"

The kids, she said, would look to the teachers for subtle guidance in the form of smiles and frowns.

"So I said to the teachers, we are going to test and we are going to follow the book right down the line. If the book says there's twenty minutes to a test, that's how long we're going to have. I assigned every teacher a watcher. They had to work in pairs. A teacher and a watcher." The result? "Our scores went straight down, from the ninetieth to the twentieth percentile. Here comes the local superintendent. She says to me, 'I want to speak to you about these test scores. . . .' "

Where does this overemphasis on testing lead? Sanford Dornbusch of Stanford University warned that "the only thing that keeps the ship afloat is the pressure of testing and standards, but the testing movement is a time bomb. We're headed for national testing. If we go too far with this, testing will drive the system. The teachers will teach only for the tests."

At least a quarter of all U.S. students attend schools untouched by academic reform — whether or not the reform works. Few inner-city students have reaped any real rewards. According to the Carnegie Foundation, at one Chicago high school only 10 percent of the entering tenth-graders were able to read effectively; in New Orleans, the average high school senior was reading at a level exceeded by 80 percent of the students in the country. Only 229 of the 1,918 students at one Los Angeles high school scored at grade level in reading. According to the citywide Educational Coalition in Boston, not only do 44 percent of Boston's high school students drop out before they reach twelfth grade, but over 40 percent of those who do reach twelfth grade are functionally illiterate.[8]

By the year 2000, the national dropout rate could reach 40 percent, according to *Trends in Learning,* a biweekly newsletter published by TRAC of Alexandria, Virginia. The current rate, 25 percent, has begun to rise for the first time in twenty-five years. At the same time, the job market has grown more educationally demanding. In the late sixties, a high school graduate was 30 percent more likely than a dropout to have a job. Today that figure is 60 percent. By 1990, three out of four new jobs will require more than high school training. In lost productivity, the economic costs of the escalating dropout rate are immeasurable. Most inmates in the nation's prisons were dropouts.[9]

Indeed, visiting schools and listening to teachers and students and parents, one comes away with the feeling that the reform movements of the eighties, obsessed with the basics and with content, may have walked right past the most important door to childhood's future. One key to this door is the amount of positive time children have with their parents, particularly in their early years. Another key is early childhood education, yet the United States remains the only major industrialized nation of the world that does not have a carefully articulated public policy for the early years of childhood.

Teachers speak almost with one voice: the most important issue is not the academic life of the student, but the emotional life of the child.

The Isolated Teacher

One way to understand the importance of the emotional life of the student is to understand the emotional life of the teacher. No group is more skeptical about reform than teachers, and with good reason: many of them have seen reform movements come and go in dizzying succession with little real effect on students, and with little positive influence on their own sense of isolation. At one vocational school, a savvy, seen-it-all principal (chewing Red Man tobacco) dismissed the famous *Nation at Risk* report of 1983 [10] in this way: "I retitled it in my own mind, 'Teach the Best and Shoot the Rest.' " In Philadelphia, another teacher remarked: "When I first started teaching, we emphasized the basics and then, later, 'do your own thing.' Now the pendulum has swung back the other way. We finally understood the new guidelines and the pendulum swung again. I feel we need a combination of both ways, both basic and innovative. Instead everything is political, and the pendulum keeps swinging to extremes."

At Van Asselt Early Childhood Center, a Seattle elementary school, an angry teacher spoke of increasing demands and decreasing resources: "They want us to teach values, they want us to teach a tougher curriculum, they want us to parent their children because they don't have time — and 'Oh, by the way, we're cutting your budget.' "

On the day I spoke with this woman, the school district had announced a $9 million cut in the budget. The teachers at Van Asselt had already resorted to using their own money to make up for shortages in classroom supplies — including paper. "We were ready to march on district headquarters," said Sheila Mae Bender, one particularly free-spirited Van Asselt teacher. A woman in her early forties, she wears her long hair pulled back tight. When I talked with her, she was wearing a long, flowered dress reminiscent of the sixties counter-culture. She grinned. "We had this little rhyme all ready to go: '*A mind is a terrible thing to waste — we want paste! Can you take the hint? We need newsprint!*' "

I wondered, How do teachers feel at ten o'clock at night, when they're brushing their teeth and thinking about the next day, about the pressure to innovate on the one hand and the pressure to work within a tight budget on the other?

"You don't think about it," said one teacher. "If I did, I'd be crazy."

A black teacher at Van Asselt whose daughter is in a private school said: "*I* think about it. I read the paper, I watch the news. It eats at me. I can't stand the way society is going, I can't stand to think about the future of my kids and the rest of the black kids out there, or the Samoan kids or whatever. It eats at me. I worry about what the future holds for them."

"It's crazy, that's what it is," said Robert Femiano, young, bearded, intense. "The feeling out there is, Teachers don't deserve money. I have twenty-five children in my class. Twenty out of that twenty-five are on the free lunch program. That means they're below poverty level. Twenty-two out of twenty-five are minority, four are special ed, five are nonpromotive, ten are bilingual, thirteen are at risk of dropping out." His voice was getting louder. "People want changes — I think they ought to be asking *me* where the changes need to be. But instead, you get people like William Bennett [then secretary of education] up there telling me what works. Let him step into a class of twenty-five children that all seem to be having troubles, who all have needs and demands that come before academics — we're talking the *real* basics."

One reason for teachers' sense of isolation is violence.

I sat with a group of teachers at East Harlem Performing Arts School in New York. This is a prestigious public school for teachers — a good place to be, a good place to teach — if you survive. The teachers were sitting in the principal's third-floor office. The walls were covered with gauzy posters of ballet dancers. The office door was covered with steel plating and spanned by a four-foot-long, three-inch-thick steel bolt that could be locked from either side of the door.

"They break into the school and they go immediately to the offices because that's where the expensive video equipment is," explained one teacher. She said the word *they* as if she were referring to some kind of subterranean creature. "The doors leading to each floor are chained and bolted. One time they got to the second floor and ripped cabinets off the walls in the art room. I just had five windows shot out in my dance room. At a school I used to work in, we'd triple-park on the street right in front of the school. We'd just leave notes on the cars for the police saying, 'Tow us away if you have to.' We'd run from the car into the school. Our car batteries were stolen constantly. You would have to go to the corner where the guys hang out and buy back your battery. We would mark our batteries — paint, say, a little star on them. That way you could say, 'I'll take the one with the star on it,' and you'd know you were getting your own back."

Of course, New York is always useful as an extreme example. But the problem of battered, fearful, and discouraged teachers is a growing national phenomenon. Students at many schools across the country now routinely pass through metal detectors to cut down on the number of guns and knives in the classroom.[11]

Bureaucracy can be just as isolating.

A few years ago, even if teachers in some New York schools had extra time to spend with their students, schools under custodial union contract were closed promptly when classes were over unless enormous fees were paid to custodians to keep the buildings open. If teachers wished to prepare for classes before eight in the morning, they were obliged to sit in their cars or in restaurants because custodians would not allow them to enter the building.[12]

The similarity of teacher isolation to the isolation of children and parents is striking — and related. Teacher isolation is part of the wider reality of the vanishing web. One Seattle teacher told me: "When I was going to school here at Franklin High, eighty percent of the staff lived within a mile of the school. It was a big advantage. I saw members of the staff all the time. I saw them at the supermarket, I saw them on the street. And all of that is gone. And the kids saw us too. We were their role models outside of school as well as in school." But few teachers now serve as role models to students. In overcrowded classrooms, teachers rarely get to know their students well. And few teachers live in Franklin High's neighborhood. "I think some of the attitude you see among teachers here is a lack of vested interest in the neighborhood."

"Most teachers operate in self-enclosed classrooms, behind closed doors," said Sanford Dornbusch of Stanford. "One teacher told me, 'I could drop dead, and the only way my principal would find out would be from the smell after a few days.' She was convinced that the students would never squeal." He added: "Here's a shocking reality: our studies show that teachers who report more criticisms from principals are happier with the evaluations of their principals than the teachers who report few negative evaluations. You know what the reason for that is? The teachers know somebody cares, somebody's watching."

Considering the isolation and frustration of many teachers, it's not surprising that so many young people don't want to become teachers themselves.

In 1987, only 7.3 percent of college freshmen expressed interest in teaching. The Rand Corporation estimates one million teachers will be needed between 1989 and 1993 to meet the demands of a mini–baby boom, but only 650,000 teachers will receive their credentials during that period. To cope with the shortage, some school districts are recruiting outside the United States. Georgia has solicited teachers from West Germany. Other districts simply lower standards.

According to Rand, outdated recruiting policies and unattractive assignments for novice teachers are why many schools are losing the brightest new educators. Half of all novice teachers quit within their first five years; 70 percent of teachers drop out within ten years.[13] This recruitment and retention crisis is especially devastating among minorities, even as the nation's public school population becomes more heavily minority. One PTA official told me, "We can make all the noise we want about making regulations to hire black and Hispanic teachers, but if there's no pool of minority teachers coming in, who do we hire?"

In an off-campus coffee shop in Alexandria, Pat Welsh of T. C. Williams High School discussed his own struggle to make sense of daily life at school. Trained as a lawyer and author of *Tales Out of School,* an exposé of high school life, Welsh is a tall, irreverent man. He is clearly respected by most of his students and his fellow teachers and resented by some administrators and teachers.

When he describes today's high schools, he takes no prisoners: "School is a colossal bore to most kids and teachers. As a teacher, you're isolated in the classroom and nobody comes in to help you improve. These administrators come in and take notes in the back of the room and observe you, but they're just going through the motions. Teachers work behind closed doors. They face these distracted, bored kids who are getting all their information from television. School gets out at two o'clock in the afternoon and the kids can do whatever they want. They can go home and get laid or do drugs or do nothing. What do the schools offer? Longer days and longer courses. But longer days and classes of what?

"Who's going to want to teach unless something changes? Nobody wants to say it, but some of these kids are driving everybody out of school. They're driving teachers out, they're driving good students out. You have these real sociopaths walking around — maybe fifty people out of twenty-three hundred — and the whole school revolves around keeping them in check. We spend a fortune sending letters home to parents about their absences. The postage that's involved in keeping these creeps in line! We just pass these kids through. This year we will graduate two or three hundred kids below sixth-grade level, maybe a hundred who are functionally illiterate, and a whole bunch of other ones that are pregnant. The process dehumanizes students *and* teachers.

"The best a teacher can do with these particular kids is control them. The teachers who are good with these students use sixth-, seventh-, or eighth-grade material with them. One teacher has a system: he'll show movies that are based on short stories, and he'll hand out quizzes with true or false questions. As these kids watch the movie, they answer the questions, and this teacher sits in the back of the class and laughs. He says, 'I watch their heads. During certain parts of the movie, all the heads go down — like robots — and they answer the question.'

Incredibly simple questions that a fifth-grader could do. And you're doing this for *eighteen-year-olds*. But it controls them.

"You hear these people constantly bitching about the public schools — while their kids go to private school. The bureaucrats and government reformers live in this dream world where they assume that everybody is middle-class and literate and should be reading the classics. They're missing the fact of all these high school kids who cannot read. Unless our approach changes, the good teachers aren't going to be there to bail us out in the future. They're not going to be teaching, and they're not going to be encouraging their own kids to be teachers."

If Welsh were secretary of education, I wondered, what would he do to improve his school?

"Smaller classes, so you can get to know kids. More team teaching so that you've got two or three teachers exchanging information on individual students and getting to know the parents. There's just a lot a teacher never gets a chance to know. And schools have to become smaller to do that. One thing we've started at our school is a teacher's advisory: ten to fifteen kids meet every day with one teacher to shoot the breeze about anything, so that there will be some adult that a kid can talk to, even if it's only for fifteen minutes. The kids like it and it helps them to hook on to the school somehow."

What about money?

"I don't think money is the main issue. You've got to deal with the teacher morale problem. Money is part of that, but you've got to be willing to boot more kids out.

"The most important reform would have to do with the parents. The kids who make it — every one of them — have one powerful parent in the home, usually the mother, who insists they study and keeps an eye on them and gets involved in the school, and never lets them drift, and is on their back all the time. Those kids, even though they may be very poor, do well. I'll tell you what makes a good school system. A good school system has a high concentration of kids with the right parents."

I also asked teachers at Van Asselt what they would do if, for a time, they could shape the future of schools.

"Ongoing teacher training," said Robert Femiano. "And you need to look at school boards — how well equipped are these people? In Seattle, you can't be on the school board if you're a teacher. That's absurd!"

He would guarantee smaller classes and enough materials to work with. And he would focus on the whole child — on the child's physical and mental health, on the child's sense of connection to the world. "Those are the real basics. Somebody who tells us to go back to basics is just dreaming. It's just wishful thinking. We don't need to go back to basics; we need to go forward to *fundamentals.*

"We need to be paying more attention in the schools to child development, and applying the current research. Look at the population we're serving. A lot of these children are coming to school hungry or emotionally deprived. Some come to school in the wintertime with no coats, no socks, no shoelaces, torn dresses, pants that smell. You go to the home to find out why, and there's garbage on the outside of the house, garbage in the middle of the living room, no furniture, no bed, parents on welfare. All of these things you have to deal with before you can even get to teaching. Who do you think winds up dealing with child abuse? Teachers do. Schools do. It's the school's responsibilty, because our laws say that if we have any suspicion, we must call the authorities. In a day's time you may have to deal with two or three cases of child abuse. And it doesn't matter whether you go to Bellevue or Holly Park, whether the family is rich or poor, the parents aren't home. In this society, everyone's caught up in this thing."

Sheila Mae Bender spoke now, softly, insistently, quickly: "One of the first things we learned when we all went to education school twenty years ago — to work with the whole child. I don't know how we got away from that. But we have. Once we start meeting the needs of the whole child again, we'll begin to see real academic improvement, but not until then. I think we can do this under the umbrella of the school. We can begin to do this not by taking away nursing time, but by adding more nursing time. We need to attach more social workers to the school who can go into the home and provide more services *directly* to children and families, taking care of bad teeth and nutrition and abuse. If we wait until people are in their twenties, it's too late. We've got to do this *now*, in the preschools and the elementary schools — and, in fact, before the child is born, with good prenatal care for mothers. We can't do it later. There's no way."

How Schools Will Reweave Time

One reason for the sense of isolation within schools — and the gap between the school and the surrounding community — is time.

In Swarthmore, the mother who was also a college professor said: "Whenever my schools ask for a parent volunteer, they never call and ask what my husband is doing. They always, *always* call and ask for me. There is a complete lack of understanding of working families in our school district. We are frequently asked to do things at the last minute. I was asked to host a school party on three days' notice. I said, 'Gee, I happen to be lecturing to sixteen college sophomores that particular day and it's really very difficult to cancel that.' This hit the teacher and the at-home mothers completely out of the blue. 'What a strange idea — you work.' "

You would have thought, she added, that schools would have devised methods of involving working parents more, recognizing that times have changed. "At the very least, they could recognize that I need more notice than at-home mothers in the past to get time off work, to plan."

Schools could indeed become more flexible in their scheduling. For example, schools could better meet the needs of working parents by offering teacher-parent conferences on Saturdays or during the evening.

To high school students, schools could offer work-study and weekend programs, five- and six-year diploma options, independent study, and early college entry programs. Some young people drop out of school not because they are failing but because they have so many other obligations to fulfill. The Carnegie Foundation considers flexible school calendars essential: "The school calendar and daily schedule, as now constituted, often do not mesh with student needs — particularly the need (at least the perceived need) to work." [14] What this amounts to is flex-time for children. Helping kids match work and school time is one reason to move toward school flex-time; a more important but seldom mentioned reason is to match the parents' schedule with the child's to give them more time together. Such an approach is the mirror image of the changes needed in the adult work place.

The Carnegie Foundation also proposes that the last two years of high school become a "transition school": "The purpose is not to provide less academic content, but to arrange learning in a more manageable format. . . . Class work could be stretched over five or six years. Students could scale down the number of courses they take, mixing work and study, possibly pursuing no courses for a semester without being considered a drop-out." The transition school, with attendant counseling and guidance, would also offer "networks of learning" that could be established outside the school, blending school with college study and with what students have learned outside the classroom — in the work place, for instance.

One way many schools are already reweaving time is by lengthening the school day. The lengthening of school time is a mixed blessing. The primary concern is that lengthening the time children spend in school furthers the institutionalization of childhood. However, doing so does offer many children a better environment than they would experience outside school. The quality of the extra school time is crucial.

Judging from the way schools now use time, the question of quality is highly speculative. Schools today suffer from a kind of time inflation. Kids go to school longer hours but seem to spend a diminishing amount of time with teachers.

At Hocker Grove Middle School I visited Ned Williams, my seventh-grade teacher. The year I was in his class had been his first year of teaching. I remembered him looking nearly as young as his students. When I visited him twenty-seven years later he still looked young for his age, but his eyes were wearied.

I asked him to compare teaching then and now. He glanced off to one side. "In some ways kids are much more difficult to handle today. I don't think we could get away with some of the ways of controlling kids today we used then. I don't mean we tortured you years ago, but . . ." He thought for a moment or two, looking out the window at the long lawn and the ridge of trees now grown in the spring.

"Mainly, it's an issue of time. We got to know the kids better back then. I had you in class three hours a day, in unified studies. Very few schools still have the old core curriculum or unified studies as we knew it then. I ended up with some of you kids four hours a day, over half the school day. Most of the teachers today don't even have kids two hours a day. And I think some of them think, Gosh, I can't stand some of them for *one* hour." He laughed. "Maybe they shouldn't be in teaching."

The current push for more time in school has far more to do with academic competition than with whole-child emotional support. However, some schools are attempting at least to ensure academic quality during the extra hours.

As Boston slowly backs away from busing, it heads for a radical restructuring of school time. Laval Wilson, the city's first black superintendent, opposes busing, in part because it uses up precious time.

Wilson's public relations representative told me: "We're not calling neighborhood schools 'neighborhood schools' anymore. We're calling them 'convenience schools.'" Seriously? Convenience schools as in convenience marts? "Seriously." The term *neighborhood school*, he explained, has become code for "segregation."

"I'm not against busing in principle," Wilson told me. "But now we're busing black kids from black communities to white communities where there are mainly black kids in the schools. So the original purpose is no longer there. We have an equitable distribution of supplies and buildings now — *all* our students are in bad buildings, some of the worst buildings in the nation." Rather than spending time on the bus, Wilson believes, students should spend more time in school. A lot more time.

Boston's Project Promise, a cooperative effort of the schools and the business community which currently targets students at risk of dropping out, has extended the number of school hours during the week by up to a third for these students. For participants in Project Promise, each school day is extended ninety minutes; three hours of classes are offered on Saturdays. In September 1988, sixth- to eighth-graders scoring below the fortieth percentile on the Metropolitan Reading Test began spending three days a week learning reading and writing and two days learning math.

Early testing of students in the handful of Project Promise pilot schools showed dramatic improvement in some subjects. Other time rearrangements are on the way.

A citizens' task force set up by Wilson recommended the elimination of grade levels (instead, students would be enrolled in small groups based on their competence in particular subjects) and the establishment of a full-time evening high school — a kind of 7-Eleven convenience school. "But the main thing we've learned is that the more time spent on a task," Wilson said, "the better students become at it."

"When Wilson first pushed Project Promise, the teacher's union went after him with a vengeance," said principal Mary Grassa O'Neill when I spoke with her at Timilty Middle School in Boston's rough Roxbury neighborhood. "After all, working longer hours goes against the whole idea of unionism — even if you're paid for it."

Nonetheless, Timilty School has prospered under Project Promise.

"By state law, we couldn't make students come in on Saturday, but ninety percent of our students show up then," said O'Neill. "We sold parents on this idea by telling them it was the chance of a lifetime — 'This is what expensive private schools do, but you're going to get it free!'"

To its credit, Timilty School is also redistributing its student body into smaller clusters that compete with each other academically. Part of the idea is to give kids more extended time with the same small group of students and to teams of teachers assigned to the clusters.

Schools are also resetting the school clock by establishing year-round school — another mixed blessing. Charles Ballinger, executive secretary of the National Association for Year-Round Education, explained the concept: As of 1989, there were 485 (elementary and junior high) year-round schools in the country; 386 of those were in California. "Westerners don't mind winter vacations. Easterners tend to hunker down," said Ballinger. Most of the year-round students go to school on a "forty-five/fifteen" schedule — forty-five school weekdays, then vacation for fifteen weekdays — which eliminates the long summer vacation. Some overcrowded districts, however, use a multitrack schedule, thus utilizing school facilities every day of the year, which Ballinger claimed will save billions of dollars across the nation by the end of the century. "A quarter of a trillion dollars of public buildings sit largely empty during the summer," he pointed out.

Remembering what so many kids had told me about the overstructured nature of their time, the lack of dream time, I expressed personal misgivings about year-round school. What happens to summertime creativity? I asked. Ballinger replied: "I really question whether there's more creativity in the summer than in the winter. Most museums of art, for example, have major collections available in the winter season rather than in the summer season."

But what about exposure to nature during the summer?

"What about the springtime?" he answered. "Do kids *now* get enough time off from school to experience nature in springtime, fall, and winter?"

Of what value is it, he asked, to have thousands of students in our cities and suburbs largely unoccupied, unemployed, and unsupervised for three months each year?

Don't students burn out? "No," said Ballinger. Academic achievement appears to stay at about the same level in year-round schools. "Vacation is always right around the corner."

He added, "When I talk with parent groups the first question they ask is, 'What about child care?' They're worried about those two-week stretches." But for working parents, he said, arranging two-week stints is usually easier than arranging three months of activities.

In Denver, a new kind of recreational system is being created, partly to match new school hours. The school district, city parks, and recreation department have signed contracts to work together to assign child care, both before school and after school, year-round — including the inter-session periods — from six-thirty in the morning to six-thirty in the evening.

"Some of the kids are there twelve hours," said Ballinger, "which is probably better than latchkey life, but not as good as having parents home. They call it surround care, or "one-stop care."

But the central question remains: will the movement toward more school hours — toward surround care — mean more warehousing of children, or more nurturing of the whole child? The answer will lie in whether the school becomes an isolated fortress or a true community hub.

Schools as Community Hubs

Without outside scrutiny, schools can be oppressive places. The rearrangement and lengthening of school time — like the day-care issue — should be approached with caution and appropriate ambivalence. Extended school time is undoubtedly a good idea for children with dysfunctional or absent families. But pressuring functional families in this direction suggests a troubling possibility. If children and parents need more time with each other, longer school days, weeks, and years may well send the wrong message to parents. Just as the old-fashioned nine-month school year was established to fit the agricultural economy's need for extra summer hands, a not-so-hidden agenda in the move toward more school hours is the work place's demand of longer hours from Mom and Dad — as well as from school-age workers.

The primary engine driving the current wave of school-time reform is the competitiveness myth, the notion that more school time (like more work time for adults) will necessarily prepare kids to compete in the new world market — whereas in Japan there is worry that the nonstop robotic approach to education is stunting that country's creativity.

How much of who we are, as creative adults, was formed long ago on a slow summer day, watching the trees move? The Japanese educational system may produce better workers, but Japanese automobile manufacturers have established several design centers in the United States — in part because they believe that America contains that spark of anarchic creativity missing in Japan. Yet American schools are steadily moving toward a regimented, year-round, dawn-till-dark educational system not unlike Japan's.

We need a more humane reason for the reweaving of school time than the assumed need to meet some international quota for personal productivity.

In recent years, there has been much discussion about the disappearance of shared knowledge, and how curriculum reform is needed to increase the sense of common historical and cultural roots among children. But the cure to diminishing shared knowledge lies also in the nature and design of institutions and urban life, including schools. The desire for shared knowledge presumes a need for it. But is there a need if our lives are vacant of community?[15]

Not competitiveness, not convenience, but *community* should be the principle reason for reweaving school time.

Certainly, when the community diminishes around it, the school can become a last refuge of comity and care. Setting aside for a moment some of the fashionable bitterness many of us feel, sometimes justifiably, about the nature of school when we were kids, we might remember school's hidden worth: the feeling that it was a kind of small town. If things were not so good at home, if the beer bottles collected like bowling pins beside the couch as the weekend wore on, then some of us surely looked forward to Monday morning.

Some teachers teach, I believe, because school was for them a safety zone, and they wish to pass the safety on to their own students. Sheila Mae Bender of Van Asselt told how she had grown up in an impoverished neighborhood in Yakima, Washington. "As a child, I looked around me and saw no hope anywhere, except at school," she said. "When I was in eighth grade, my parents wanted to take me out of school and put me to work in a factory. They did not have any concept of education. My mother was put out to work for fifty cents a day when she was in sixth grade during the Depression. There was a lot of pain in my family, but school was a place to have some happiness and a sense of success and to hope for something different. As I grew up and went to college, my father never said anything to me, never asked me what I was taking or what I was learning. When I made it through — I'm the first person out of both sides of my family to ever finish college — he finally said to me, 'I don't understand how you didn't end up like everybody else in the neighborhood.' He didn't comprehend that the reason could have been *school*. I saw that there was hope. That's why I became a teacher. I wanted others to have that hope and to be able to relieve some of their pain and help them change their world."

Given the number of weapons and the amount of danger seeping into some urban schools, it may be difficult to think of schools as places of refuge, but the danger is relative.

Fred Morley, principal of a grade school in Liberty City, a neighborhood in Miami, described how he had opened the school on Saturdays for basic schooling — one hour of uninterrupted reading, one hour of writing, one hour of math. "On the first Saturday we did this, we prepared for fifty kids and two hundred came. And those two hundred are still with us," he said. "The PTA prepares a snack for these children. We pay the teachers an hourly fee, but they would do it free. I figured that the kids would eventually quit coming on Saturday. Why come to school when you can stay home and watch cartoons on Saturday morning? But they kept coming because they want to learn. Even if they didn't learn anything academically, the fact that they are here is important. They're here, instead of being out on the street, where the pimps and the prostitutes and the dope pushers teach them something else."

We need, however, to look beyond the school as refuge to the school as a catalyst of community rebirth. If parents and other members of the outside community are present in the schools — if schools become community hubs, anchor points for the wider web — then a kind of community magic invariably begins to emerge. Schools can begin to give all of us, not only children, a way to make contact — child to teacher, parent to parent, parent to teacher, and most important, parent to child.

Psychiatrist James Comer, director of the Yale Child Study Center, is a leading thinker on the idea of the school as a community hub. According to Comer, children begin to drift toward influences outside the home at about eight or nine years old. Now that extended families, churches, healthy neighborhoods have been bulldozed, spindled, and mutilated, to whom do kids turn? Television. Their peers. The street.

Public schools step into the vacuum and provide what kids need most of all: positive adult contact and a sense of belonging. Comer was quick to point out that this kind of school isn't an entirely new idea. "Prior to the nineteen-forties teachers thought of themselves in a much broader fashion than they do today. They thought of themselves not only as people who taught facts, but as people who helped kids grow up."

That was particularly true in black schools, said Comer, who is black. Though he remains an unwavering supporter of the civil rights movement, he suggests that some aspects of urban life were better in the forties — when black communities instinctively and actively supported kids, from the living room to the street corner to the school.

The main problem with education, Comer believes, isn't the curriculum, but the environment of the school and how it fits into the surrounding network — whether schools become the focal points for building community.

In exceptional schools around the country, charismatic principals have reimposed a sense of pride and community — for example, north Philadelphia's Madeline Cartwright, or controversial Joe Clark, who attained nationwide fame at Eastside High School in Paterson, New Jersey, for carrying a bat and a bullhorn to fight drugs and crime. When charismatic principals leave, however, the schools usually return to their former torpor. Comer's technique is more likely to succeed over the long haul. Its essence: give more power to parents and teachers, and allow them to design their own school plan. The main goal: provide the kind of warmth and adult contact that many kids don't get at home.

In more than fifty schools around the country, Comer's parent-teacher teams have devised their own plans. Some have decided to keep students with the same teacher for two years; some have replaced window frames and painted walls to make the schools look, literally, more like home; some have decided to focus on math and reading; all have invested great energy in the schools. His schools are operated by teachers, by the principal, and most important by parents, who are brought into the very design of the learning process. At one Comer-influenced school in New Haven, Connecticut, parents work as class aides for minimum wage. At Katherine Brennan Elementary, also in New Haven, 92 percent of the parents visited the school more than ten times in 1987.

In New Haven, the first city to apply Comer's ideas, the dropout rate has plummeted from 42 to 15.5 percent in the eighties, and the number of kids going on to higher education rose from 45 to 73 percent. At Columbia Point Elementary in Landover, Maryland, student scores on the California Achievement Test shot from the fiftieth to the eighth percentile in the eighties, and student suspensions, once twenty to thirty a year, virtually disappeared. These results weren't gained by climbing on whatever curriculum bandwagon happened to be passing by at the time, but by building community. "The back-to-basics movement is based on the simplistic notion that kids are learning machines, that if you just teach more they will learn more," said Comer. "But that's not the way human beings function. Much of learning is unconscious and related to the surrounding environment." A true back-to-basics movement would recognize that community — particularly ongoing and positive relationships among adults and children — is the most basic missing element in education today.

"In an individualistic society such as ours we like to believe that we accomplish everything on our own," Comer added. "But we forget that the talented flourish because others create the climate for them to do so, and that we are motivated by an invisible web of kin, neighbors, teachers. Children internalize this support in their attitudes, values, and ways, and so do parents."

Parents to the Rescue:
One Way to Decrease School Isolation

If public schools have a future, parents are going to be in it, in ways yet to be imagined. Like it or not, the new economic realities of family life will mean longer school hours and schools' taking on some of the responsibilities previously assumed by the family. One way to keep schools from becoming oppressive warehouses for bored and overregimented children is extensive parental involvement within the schools. If kids can't spend more time at home, then parents (with the help of employers) should spend more time in the schools. Parental involvement can help decrease teacher, student, and parent isolation, and also help deinstitutionalize the school, make the school part of the community rather than a fortress within it.

Giving parents a choice of schools within public school systems is one important step in ensuring parental involvement. But the more public schools offer the kind of parental involvement often seen in many private schools, the better they will be able to compete. Some private schools, in fact, require parents to serve as classroom volunteers a certain number of hours a month. The Carnegie Foundation concludes that schools have an obligation to view parents as co-teachers and recommends that "parents spend at least one day each term with their child at school." A recent Stanford study revealed just how powerful a small investment of time can be. The study was designed to isolate factors other than socioeconomic standing which could improve a child's grades. The most surprising finding: if a child's parent made at least one visit to the school or a school function during the year, that child's grades were likely to improve. Why? The visit convinces the child that parents really do care about school, communication is improved between the teacher and the parent, and the parent is helped to understand how the school works.[16]

However, despite almost universal approval of the idea of parental involvement, relatively few teachers reach out to involve parents in the home or in the classroom. Schools of education offer little direct training in parental involvement techniques. A University of Minnesota report on improving teacher education listed what researchers identified as the thirty-seven most important teaching skills. Incredibly, learning how to work with parents was not among them. Some teachers resist parental involvement, citing experiences with pushy parents and contending that the implication that they need help from parents diminishes their professionalism.[17] But when teachers do involve parents in their children's education, parents usually view the teacher as *more* professional. Joyce L. Epstein has written: "For most parents, the home-school connection is made when teachers involve parents in learning activities at home. When teachers were leaders in parent involvement practices, parents reported that they knew more about their child's instructional program than they did in the past, had more ideas about how to help their children at home, and rated the teacher higher in interpersonal skills and overall teaching quality." Moreover, both principals and parents gave higher evaluation ratings to these teachers, and students gained more in reading achievement classes. The students had more positive attitudes toward school, saw the school and home as more similar, and had better homework habits when teachers involved parents in learning activities at home.

But the partnership role will not be adopted by teachers or school administrators until it is common in teacher training. "Currently, teachers receive little direct training in parent involvement practices," Epstein writes. "Many teachers are taught that being 'professional' means keeping all of the authority in the classroom for themselves. Few are taught that being professional means managing resources — including parents — to meet specific goals for students." Yet particularly when teachers are trained to be managers of parental involvement, they too begin to see themselves as more professional.

Epstein suggests that parental involvement programs could be among the added responsibilities or specializations of senior or lead teachers. Her data support "the unexpected conclusion that school and family partnerships can, in some important ways, increase teachers' autonomy, professional status, and respect in the community."[18]

Yet most parents are not involved with their children's schools. The Carnegie Foundation's *Imperiled Generation* report (to my mind among the most important analyses of what must be done to improve education) reveals "a startling 70 percent of teachers in urban schools say lack of parental support is a serious problem." At a New Orleans high school that required parents to pick up their children's report cards, 70 percent of the cards remained unclaimed two months after the marking period ended.

"The one line you hear from parents all the time is 'I can't, I work,'" an officer of the Shawnee Mission PTA told me. "That was going to be my logo. I CAN'T, I WORK. Draw a big circle around it with a line through it, just like the traffic signs: I CAN'T, I WORK. Well, I work too. I don't get paid for what I do. But that's not a good enough excuse. I can see what's happened to the high school children. I remember in grade school, their parents weren't involved then and they still aren't involved, and those kids are in trouble today."

Why aren't parents involved? Partly because their priorities are scrambled; partly because two-career and one-parent households suffer from new time and geographic constraints; and finally, many parents don't feel their voices count.

A Seattle teacher said: "It would be wonderful if you could have someone come and work on a regular basis, say, every Monday from one to three, but I just don't seem to be able to schedule anything like that. You start out the year thinking that you're going to have a lot of volunteers — and that's one thing our school district puts an emphasis on. But frankly I just haven't seen it. Busing may have something to do with it because we bus students from across town. That could be a hardship on a family, for a mother to drive all the way over here, maybe thirty-five or forty minutes in heavy traffic with two other little kids in the car, or to have to make baby-sitting arrangements for other children in the family, and then drive all the way back. But if the people within the neighborhood who don't necessarily have kids in the school could just feed into the school, just walk up here and volunteer regularly, that might create a different situation."

How do we make it more practical for adults to volunteer in the schools? First, parents need to be taught how to give teachers more support from home. For example, some schools now suggest that teachers assign parents homework — or more specifically, that some homework be assigned that the child and parent do together.

Second, schools need to recognize the new time constraints on parents and offer more evening and weekend appointment time for parent consultation and more neighborhood meetings in which teachers and administrators meet with parents in homes and churches. Some volunteer activities — reading and math tutoring, for example — might be conducted during the early evening hours.

New schools could be located in residential or commercial buildings close to where students live or parents work. Employers should be encouraged to allow their employees to visit their children's schools periodically. One approach is the Family Ties proposal described in Chapter 16, which would encourage or require employers to allow parents two to four hours a month to volunteer in schools or visit their children at day care.

George J. McKenna III, superintendent of the Inglewood Unified School District in Los Angeles, argues in a commentary in the *Los Angeles Times* that it is no accident that students progress at a much higher rate in school communities where parents are deeply involved in the operation of the schools, or that this involvement is conspicuously absent in schools designated to educate the children of the working class and the poor. This absence is not because of parents' indifference, but because overworked parents have no work-place vehicle for that involvement.

We have the practice of releasing employees to serve on jury duty, or as subpoenaed witnesses, with no penalty to their salaries. If we are prepared to support the criminal justice system through corporate cooperation, why not the educational justice system? Rather than tuition tax credits for private schools, we should establish corporate tax credits for employers who give their workers paid time to visit their children's schools. Since government is a primary employer, and supports many of these parents in other ways, local, state and federal agencies could begin to implement this plan while encouraging private industry to become involved.

To be sure, there will be some resistance to this idea, including the unfortunate position taken by some teacher and school administrator groups that parents on campus pose a threat to the educator's autonomy and would disrupt the educational program. This institutional resistance is another form of classism that keeps the parent, who pays our salaries, at arm's length.[19]

One possibility would be for states to adopt McKenna's tax credit plan; if too few companies participated voluntarily, they might then move to a mandated approach.

"No one sees the daily pain of these children, and the daily struggle of teachers, unless they're *here*," said Sheila Mae Bender. "I'll tell you what it's going to take to create better schools. It's going to take parents coming into the school. Their attitudes change very quickly once they're here. Everybody thinks they know exactly what we should be doing in the classroom, but somehow you never see those people in the classroom. My own relatives sit there at family gatherings and put teachers down. But nobody comes in and finds out what we're doing. We're asking you to come in, but not just to watch. Come in and put your hand to the plow and *help* us."

One aspect of volunteer involvement in schools which is often overlooked is the effect that it has on the volunteer — whether parent or nonparent.

At Van Asselt, a group of parent volunteers described how volunteering in the classroom had not only changed their view of public schools but changed their lives. "I barely graduated from high school," said Robert Hunter, a thirty-six-year-old former steelworker. "I had all these bad thoughts about school, didn't want to go near another one." A few years ago, Hunter was hurt in an industrial accident and placed on disability. Bored without work, he began to volunteer in an elementary school on a whim. "I was astounded, happy with work for the first time in my life."

Hunter has gone back to college to become a teacher.

"I've recruited three people to volunteer here, all women," he said.

"The fathers think it's wimpy. They say: 'What do you want to do something like that for? There's no money in it.' Basically, there's one reason why people are afraid to work with small children. They don't think they can handle it. But they can handle a lot more than they think they can."

"I was raised in a rural atmosphere, went to a small school," explained another volunteer, Don Mitchell, a retired master sergeant whose granddaughter attends Van Asselt. "I was surprised to find that school — or at least this school — hasn't really changed that much since I was a kid. I see the same dedication in the teachers. They try their best within the means given to them. What *has* changed are the external influences."

Several other volunteers agreed. One woman said she had started volunteering because she needed to decide between public and private education for her son, then in preschool.

"My fear of public schools came from friends and the media," she said. "I decided to find out for myself, to go into the school and get involved. I expected the fault to fall on classes that were too large, and curriculum that was too hard. Instead, the fault falls on parents who are not involved in their children's lives."

The most important role for an adult volunteer is surrogate parent. "More than anything else, I've been overwhelmed by the emotional needs of these children," this volunteer added. "One little girl I'm working with is unwilling to learn anything right now. She just wants me to hold her, to be — touched, to be hugged, and to lay her head on my lap. I find myself — more than teaching them — I find myself trying to love them. To love away the hurt." The woman began to cry. "It can't be done."

"Yes, it can," said Robert gently. "Some of the hurt can be loved away. And if you don't do it, who will?"

Other Ways to Decrease
Isolation Inside the Schools

Decreasing the Institutional Isolation of Teachers

Teachers need a stronger web of support, beginning with teaching colleges. One Rand Corporation recommendation: creation of "induction schools," fashioned after teaching hospitals, where senior teachers would be paid more and have more administrative clout in exchange for working at traditionally unpopular schools, where new teachers would be trained. Another option is ongoing teaching-college support for recent graduates. Oregon State now promises the college's support for teacher graduates who have difficulty adjusting to classroom stress or are required to confront subject matter they were not trained to teach. School principals are offered a variety of services if they hire Oregon State graduates, from on-site observation and comment by education professors to funds for substitute teachers so new staff members can attend workshops. If necessary, Oregon State will pay the teacher's tuition for an additional semester of college training.

An equally important trend is toward more accountability. In some of its application, this trend has had little to do with the emotional health of children — or, for that matter, of teachers. Albert Shanker, president of the American Federation of Teachers Union, told *U.S. News and World Report*: "Legislation has been adopted telling teachers what textbooks or exams to use and how many minutes to teach each course. Teachers are now being treated more like hired hands who are told what to do and not as professionals who exercise judgment. If we continue to do that, we're not going to attract people of high caliber into teaching.[20]

However, the creation of a national board to raise professional standards for teachers would be a step in the right direction. By raising teachers to a status closer to that of lawyers and doctors, respect and pay will likely follow as well as a more practical standard for removing bad teachers. (Today, without widely agreed-on standards, getting rid of a bad teacher is practically impossible. Sanford Dornbusch points out that, in California, firing a bad teacher costs a quarter of a million dollars in paperwork and appeals.) A national board to set standards, and a rigorous national proficiency exam for board-certified teachers — similar to the bar exam for lawyers — would help transform the isolated, powerless, and bitter atmosphere in which so many teachers work.

Reinforcing the Ethic of Caring

Shaping a good person is as important as shaping a good reader, according to Stanford professor Nel Nodding. She recommends that efforts to redesign schools and any move to professionalize teaching include what she calls the "ethic of caring," which should shape the size of a school, the way classrooms are arranged, the attitude of teachers. As she pointed out, the nineteenth-century concept of professionalism was wrapped in the idea of service and ethics. (Nursing, for example, is a field that over the years has developed an ethic of caring in tandem with a growing emphasis on professionalism.)

Dividing Big Schools into Clustered "Neighborhoods"

Schools of fifteen hundred to two thousand students have torn apart the idea of community; no one teacher is responsible for following an individual child's development over time. One goal should be that students spend a longer period of time, preferably spanning several school years, with mentor teachers who follow their development. Successful schools visited by the Carnegie Foundation "were true communities of learning, places where students are known and have ongoing contact with their teachers. They belong." The commission concluded that large schools should be divided into clusters with no more than 450 students each so that all students can be well known to each other, and to teachers. Large schools could have separate schools within schools. Each school would have its own director, its own team of teachers, and ideally its own counselors. Each cluster would, over time, build its own traditions and identity.[21]

The exceptions to the rule of anonymity are inspiring. At Mc-Donough 35 High School in New Orleans, where older students voluntarily adopt freshmen and take them under their wing, the academics are hard but social life flourishes. At Bret Harte Intermediate School in Los Angeles, students in the sixth and seventh grades are not sent to separate teachers for each subject. Instead, teams of two teachers teach all the subjects and build close rapport with students. Fremont High School in Los Angeles, with a 60 percent dropout rate, introduced an Adopt a Student program for 125 of its most at-risk pupils. Teachers, counselors, and other adults become surrogate parents to the students, helping them with homework, taking them on field trips. As a result, only 4 of the 125 dropped out.

Providing More Mental Health and Emotional Counseling in Schools

The preventive, whole-child, whole-school approach to counseling mentioned by the teachers I interviewed at the Van Asselt Early Learning Center is extremely rare in the nation's schools. Traditional guidance counseling is reactive and crisis-oriented, concentrating on the most troublesome or talented 10 or 15 percent of students. Much of a traditional counselor's time is spent on academic rather than emotional issues. School leaders "must see counseling as an integral part of the school curricula, not as an ancillary service provided to kids with problems," according to Nancy Hardy, president of the American School Counselor

Association. Along with teacher and counselor specialization "has come the creation of ad hoc programs to deal with the 'current' crisis, be it an outbreak of drinking or drug abuse, teen sex, dropping out, gang violence, or the like. Too often the result is Balkanization of social services in schools."

One reason for Balkanized services is, of course, funding. Another is the fear of malpractice lawsuits. Many schools see complex certification requirements for special kinds of counseling as a way to avoid litigation. The medical model of responding only to sickness limits the effectiveness of counselors, who should be proactive agents in the schools. Current counselor-to-student ratios are abysmal. In high schools there is one school counselor to every 350 or 450 students; in junior highs the ratio is 1 to 500. No national data exist on elementary schools since they have been virtually ignored by guidance counselors.[22] Educators agree that the earlier at-risk youngsters are identified, the better — and that the at-risk population grows exponentially as it ages. According to current estimates, about 10 percent of elementary school kids are at risk, and without early intervention that percentage doubles by the time the children reach junior high.

Ways to Increase the Schools' Connections to the Surrounding Community

Creating Satellite Schools

In a commuter society it would be a boon to many parents if their children's schools were on the way to work or even at work. As old, unsafe schools are closed, smaller facilities could be located in commercial buildings close to where students live or parents work. Like the Bankers Insurance satellite school in Miami, these schools would offer children more positive and frequent contact with their parents and other adults. But the best location for a community hub school is still within walking distance of the child's home. The revival of true neighborhood schools may gradually take place as the pressure to bus children recedes (either because of successful residential integration or political fatigue) and as more parents begin to work at home, thereby giving life to the neighborhoods. (One of the pleasures I find in being an at-home worker is that I am able to walk my son to school.)

Creating Hub Schools That Serve Adult Needs
as Well as Children's Needs

In San Diego one of the city's oldest high schools, Hoover High, is attempting to turn itself into a community center for the diverse, multicultural population surrounding it. In its community functions, it serves not only the children and parents of Hoover but also the students and parents of the seven elementary schools that feed into it. Principal Doris Alvarez says her long-range hope is to have Hoover become the hub for weekend sports and classes for adults and children in Spanish and French, clowning, computers, karate, gymnastics, even skateboarding. These classes will be taught by volunteer instructors — including high school students.

Connecting Higher Education
to the Web of Primary and Secondary Schools

In one city visited by the Carnegie Foundation, "the campuses of two universities could be seen from the local high school. Even though the institutions were within easy walking distance from each other, the principal reported that the school had no programs of any sort involving either institution." Colleges and universities could "adopt" elementary and secondary schools and, focusing on high-risk students, college students, faculty, and staff could mentor these youngsters.

Connecting Businesses to the Educational Web

In Houston, a program launched by Tenneco sends twenty-five employees to primarily Hispanic inner-city schools; Hughes Tool in Houston sends Hispanic and Vietnamese workers to tutor high school students of those ethnic groups. In Los Angeles, Atlantic Richfield employees are given time off to tutor Hispanic students in English usage and to counsel students with academic or personal problems. McDonnell-Douglas Corporation helps teachers renew their knowledge by opening its Employee Voluntary Improvement program to the staff at nearby Central High School at no charge; school administrators take management seminars, and teachers take courses in computer science, algebra, and trigonometry.[23]

But the most important way businesses can help to rebuild the web is to encourage parents to visit their own children's schools.

Linking the Retired and the Elderly to the Schools

As in Seattle and Miami, where senior citizens work directly with children in the classrooms, intergenerational programs in the schools could improve education, reduce teacher isolation, increase schools' ties to the community, and most important, reduce the isolation of children. As in Seattle, elder day-care centers could also be located at schools — particularly those with dwindling student enrollment.

Establishing Public Schools as a Primary Part of the Child-Care Network

Perhaps the best place for institutional day care is the public school. The brick and mortar already exists; the public school has a long tradition; we know where to find it; and, underutilized during much of the day, it needs the business. Parents already own the buildings, having paid taxes for them for years. Indeed, U.S. schools represent a $1 trillion investment; they ought to be used more efficiently.

"We can solve the child-care crisis by implementing a second system within existing elementary school buildings and create the school of the twenty-first century," says Edward Zigler. What Zigler proposes is, he believes, the synthesis of "everything we've learned in 25 years put into one system." Under his plan, on-site programs in school buildings would provide child care. These in-school programs would not offer formal schooling but rather quality day care. At age five, children would attend a half day of kindergarten in the same building. At noon, children who needed it would stay for a half day of child care. Older children, aged six to twelve, could receive child care at the school before and after school and during vacations.

Zigler believes that children should start formal schooling on a voluntary basis at age three — but only for day care, not for academic advancement. Trained teachers are too valuable and expensive to work in day cares, so Zigler suggests that child development associates, trained on the job to work with children, be the providers. What Zigler calls a "full-service school" could also train, oversee, and serve as a resource center for neighborhood in-home child-care providers — the largest and least monitored form of child care.[24] To pay for all this, Zigler suggests we raise taxes slightly. The various services would be offered on a sliding-scale fee system based on income. The federal government would provide subsidies only for the poor and for handicapped children. "Then we would have a complete child-care system. Parents would get excited

about having a good, safe place just down the street." Additional benefits of locating day care at public schools include the logistical — commuting time would be reduced for preschool and school-age children.
Most important, school-based day care would help create ongoing psychological hubs in the new family-friendly city.

Is such a massive effort practical? Between the fall of 1964 and the
summer of 1965, America managed to place 560,000 kids in Head Start.
Similar progress could be made in the nineties with day care, Zigler says,
if we take advantage of the public schools.[25]

Helping Parents Parent:
The Final Strand in the New School Web

The school should be the primary place where parents go to get help in
parenting; it should be, in short, a family support center, a place where
parents could meet with other parents. Programs such as Head Start
have already proven successful in helping children overcome many social, nutritional, and learning difficulties in the early years.

The full-service school, as envisioned in slightly different forms by
Zigler, Comer, and an increasing number of educators and parents, might
offer guidance and support for first-time parents. Beginning in the third
trimester of pregnancy, trained specialists would actually go into homes
and help teach mothers and fathers about parenting. Schools could also
provide an information referral system and resource center for parents,
and families could go to the school to find out about other local day
cares as well as additional family services. These school/family centers
could also be the distribution point for information about family rights
in the work place. Moreover, these centers, along with other hubs, could
offer inexpensive mediation services to help reduce the level of emotional and physical violence within neighborhoods. Not all of these roles
will be assumable by all schools, of course. One reason is budgetary;
family-friendly schools will not come cheap — but consider the eventual
price of not moving in this direction. Some initial resistance will come
from parents, who must be convinced that the purpose of these schools
is to support family life, not to replace it. Some resistance will come,
too, from teachers, who are already overburdened. Yet, when I have
spoken with teachers about the possibilities of the family-friendly city —
in which the school would be one hub among many — they often express enthusiasm, hope, idealism. One teacher told me, "If we know that
other institutions — businesses, libraries, churches, and the rest are giv-

ing more to children and families, then teachers will feel that they can give more too. It all comes down to knowing you're not alone."

Visualize, again, a great network, a supportive and intricate web.

One strand is the school system, another is the neighborhood, another is made of parents, and another is the work place and how it treats parents. As the web unravels the smallest bodies fall, and the safety net below cannot hold. At best, the bureaucratic child protection services, which are deluged and failing throughout the country, can catch only a few of these falling children. The ultimate answer is prevention.

Like the weather, everyone talks about prevention. Hardly anybody does anything about it.

Prevention is not very dramatic. Moreover, the experts and professionals most likely to travel to the state capitals or Washington or even the school boards and local governments are people who work for the protective children's services. Understandably, their first priorities are their own programs, and they may well fear that any money allocated for prevention will eventually be shifted out of their budgets.

"Child protective systems throughout the country are inefficient, expensive, and after-the-fact," said Dr. David Chadwick, director of the Center for Child Protection at Children's Hospital in San Diego and a nationally recognized expert on child abuse. One problem is that the studies of prevention techniques have been small and scarce. "Because we don't have the definitive statistics, it's tough to go into a state legislature and say, 'If you give me three million dollars in prevention services, I can save you thirty million in prisons in the next ten years." At minimum, he suggests, government ought to sponsor large-scale studies that would settle once and for all how to prevent child abuse, how to keep children from ending up in the protective system. "Then, I believe, we would have the arguments that we would need, how much money prevention can save in hospitalization, in learning disabilities, in the school dropout rate, and eventually in criminal behavior." Yet so many political decisions are made in this society with far less supporting evidence: witness how quickly cities, state legislatures, and even the White House moved to limit access to assault rifles after one lone gunman killed five children in Stockton, California.

While we wait for more studies, the web unravels a bit more.

In truth, sufficient evidence for prevention already exists. Good programs, though scattered and small, are on the ground, working now — and they, too, could be woven into the new web. At some hospitals around the country, for example, parents referred by child-abuse agencies may attend parenting classes and receive therapy, counseling, and contact with volunteer parent aides. In Seattle, Tacoma, and Spokane, Washington, Homebuilders provides in-home counseling and treatment to families in crisis, working with each family member at an average cost of $2,937 — compared with the average state price tag of $15,000 to place children in foster care.

But the most interesting, and potentially most powerful, approach is education for parents of infants and toddlers. Such education should be available for *any* family — not only those that have crossed the line into abuse.

This education should be offered gently — not as training, but as the provision of options and support by professionals, as well as contact with other new parents. The distribution points for that care could be the neighborhood schools.

One morning near the end of my journey, as I rode along with Diane Davis on her parent-education rounds in National City, California, I glimpsed a long-overdue future.

Davis is a parent-educator with the National City school district's Parents as Teachers program. Her job is to visit new parents once a month and to support them emotionally and educationally for the first three years of their babies' lives. These parents, who participate voluntarily, may have been referred by counselors or, responding to mailings or advertisements, may have contacted the school system directly.

Davis is an articulate and deeply committed woman who is eager to see this approach adopted throughout the country. "Parents are a child's first teachers. That's the key," she said as we walked up a flight of concrete and wrought iron steps and around the side of a plain stucco building to a two-bedroom apartment. Lonnie and Karen, waiting there with their small children, welcomed us inside.

Diane sat down on the worn carpet and pulled a coffee can filled with clothespins from her purse. The smallest child in the room reached in and took one out and began to pull at the spring.

"He's interested in taking things apart, isn't he?" asked Diane.

Karen, who was new to the program, put her hands up in frustration. "He's really a handful! He opens up the dressers, the trash, he's into everything!"

"That's because he's curious," Diane said gently. "He's not a trouble-maker. Could I suggest something? Make sure he can pull things out of one of the lower drawers in the kitchen. Make it his drawer." The little boy handed her a clothespin, and then the can. "He's a smart one, isn't he?" said Diane, and Karen smiled and sat up a little straighter.

"My parents thought good parenting was just providing food, a roof, and a ride to school," said Lonnie, one of the enrolled mothers. "And I thought that was all there was to parenting until Diane came."

The National City program teaches parents to seize the educational moment. If a child happens to be playing with blocks on the floor, for example, Diane might suggest that the parent get down on the floor and count the blocks or talk about the colors of the blocks rather than pulling the child away to read. She also suggests that, instead of buying expensive educational toys, parents make use of safe household utensils — plastic cups, wooden spoons, pots and pans.

She explains peekaboo as an educational game helpful in the development of short-term memory. And she tactfully discourages parents from using playpens to corral their kids for any length of time. "The idea is to encourage the child to learn to explore and maneuver," Diane explained later. "Many parents confine their children to playpens or walkers for long hours of the day. They think they're keeping their child safe — but in fact they're squashing their child's curiosity. If they're left in a restrictive environment long enough, they stop trying to find out about things. And by the time they get to school, their world is about the size of a playpen."

The National City program grew out of the nation's most ambitious early childhood education outreach program, the Parents as Teachers program in Missouri.

In 1981, the Missouri Department of Education hired child psychologist Burton White, author of *The First Three Years of Life*, whose work in the late sixties (which led to the establishment of Head Start) had shown that many children were already educationally disadvantaged by the time they entered kindergarten. White set up a model parent-education program in four school districts in Missouri representing a wide range of social and economic backgrounds and urban, suburban, small town, and rural settings. The pilot program continued for three years. Among its elements: monthly home visits by a parent-educator for the first three years of a child's life, group get-togethers for parents, a battery of monitoring procedures, and a referral service for parents to obtain help if any signs of educational difficulty appeared.

The verbal, videotaped, and written assistance given to parents in the private and group sessions was simple. The teachers outlined child development stages, but did not advocate high-pressure procedures designed to produce superbabies. (In White's opinion, such overstructured, high-pressure programs tend to discourage a child's interest in learning and creativity.) Instead of setting aside structured teaching times, parents were encouraged to set up interesting environments, to allow children to indulge their natural curiosity, and then to follow the children's leads. Parents were also taught how to set limits, and alternatives to spanking were suggested.

An independent organization evaluated the Missouri program's effectiveness and found that participating children scored significantly higher than average in intellectual and linguistic development. Surprisingly, the program worked about the same with children of parents with doctoral degrees and parents who were high school dropouts. The approach also worked about the same with black families and white families, teenage parents and parents in their thirties, married parents and single parents, families with an annual income of more than $40,000 and those below the poverty line. Though not all of the advice was followed by the parents, most of them were eager to get the help and the contact.

"But then, in eighty-five, the Missouri Legislature voted to make the program mandatory for schools to offer this to anyone raising babies," White explained to me one afternoon in his office in Newton, Massachusetts. In White's view, the state moved too fast; the average per-family expenditure was dropped from $800 to $165, and the number of in-home visits was cut from once each month to five a year. "So I quit the project. But the ingredients are there for anyone to do it right. I sit here pleased at the value of the work, but frustrated that nobody is doing it right."

The National City program, however, the only direct emulation of White's approach in the country, is determined to do it right — with monthly home visits and per-family expenditure of $600.

Now in its third year, the program is building a data base on participating children, and Davis and her fellow parent-educator, Linda Smith, intend to seek an outside agency to study the results. Meanwhile, in Missouri, the first children who participated in the Parents as Teachers program as infants are about to enter first grade, and researchers are planning to assess their intellectual and social skills. If the results of the studies are as encouraging as people involved in the program believe they will be, many school systems in the country could someday be sending out trained parent-educators to the homes of new infants.

Judging from the home environments I saw during my morning with Davis, such programs, well executed, could go a long way toward weaving the new web, toward nurturing a gentler new generation. One side effect of the program is that it could help prevent child abuse. For isolated, stressed-out parents, any kind of positive support from someone like Diane Davis could make all the difference.

And finally, at the end of my morning with Davis I met the remarkable Margaret Bridgewater, whose eloquence conveyed the essence of what I had come to learn about childhood's future, about the direction each of us must move, about the liberation that awaits those families who help weave the new web.

Margaret lives in National City in a tiny house that leans against itself. The old porch is covered with blooming bougainvillea, and a horseshoe hangs from an eave. The walls are clean but deeply stained from long years without fresh paint.

We sat in the living room, on very old couches covered in floral velvet. There was a ceramic statue of Christ on a table, and a television and video player.

Margaret is a large woman with deep beauty in her eyes and her voice and in the way she moves her hands. She is married to a pipe fitter, and they have three boys, aged two, seven, and nine, and a fifteen-year-old daughter.

Margaret told how she had called the school one day when she felt she could no longer stand the stress of child rearing, how on that day she was afraid of herself, fearful of what she might do. "I was afraid of losing control, and my children were out of control, and I had nobody telling me what I could do with my kids. There are no parenting-training classes in high school or the colleges to help you prepare for this, or to prevent this from happening. My children did not respect me. I didn't know how to get them to respect me. I would ask them, plead with them: 'Why don't you treat me with as much respect as you treat your teachers?' I was acting like a doormat. Maybe these things have gone on in my family two hundred years. These things went against what was morally inside me, but I did not know the alternatives.

"I was raised with an alcoholic father. It took me well into my thirties to recognize that I had feelings. We kids were told not to talk about feelings. My parents were indifferent. The opposite of love isn't hate, the opposite of love is indifference. I went within myself. I figured if I was a good girl I would wait in the corner. I wouldn't be a burden. But doing this went against what I really am. All along I went against my true nature. Looking within myself, I realized that there is no shame in asking for help.

"I found out about Diane through the school. She taught me about time-out, about mild disapproval — where your whole facial expression changes and you tell your kids exactly what you are upset about. I have found that consistency is what counts. Now I give them consistency. Time-out is one minute per year of their age: Kalen, who is two, gets two minutes, that's all; Max gets seven minutes. And I have set a few basic rules: no unacceptable language, no fighting, no hurting another person purposefully. And if I catch them being good . . ."

She looked over at Kevin, a clean-cut kid with a new haircut who had been sitting nearby, holding a book for Kalen but listening intently.

"I appreciate you reading to Kalen like that, and being quiet."

Kevin smiled.

"My husband has a temper," Margaret continued, "and I was worried he would go over the edge, too. He has a temper and he would hit them — not to the point of abuse, but he didn't see the connection, that by hitting them he was training them to hit their brothers and sisters. He's not the type to learn from books, or things like this program. So, instead of trying to change him, I changed my life, because I cannot change anybody but me. My husband resists the possibility that what he was taught was wrong. Discipline to him is like fear, but I know that discipline is like love. Allowing your children to talk about how they feel, that's a form of discipline. Sometimes I come up close to them when they act out and I say to them very quietly, 'Why are you feeling this way?' Now, with me as a role model, my husband is changing his behavior. And it's filtered out to the older kids. I have told them they are teachers, too, more than just role models."

The boys led me into the dark, sparse kitchen. They showed me their lighted terrarium, with long fence lizards and a turtle that their father had helped them catch. They were excited and proud.

On a little table in the kitchen was Margaret's electric typewriter. She said she planned to write a book someday. "All talent is is a lack of fear," she said.

Margaret is now PTA president at her children's elementary school, just down the street.

"It all correlates," she said softly but firmly. "Parents involved in school raise successful children. Sharing my time with the school makes my children care more about their school work. All my kids now are outstanding citizens and get high grades. My daughter is an honor student. It all correlates. I used to be a waitress, but now my job is my kids. We can do without. Children don't care about material things. They want love and nurturing. We rent this house and it isn't that great, but it's all we can afford, and they love it, it's their home. And it's a safe environment. I have it set up safe enough so they don't get hurt. I never forget how it was to be a kid. I remember that material things didn't matter, and how it was when my father didn't hug me."

Margaret Bridgewater has begun to weave her own strands in the web.

She pointed to the typewriter and her voice grew firmer still. "I wrote a letter to the governor. I told him if we catch children's problems at an early stage — like what Diane does — instead of waiting for junior high, then we have a chance. I told the governor this — I told him that the ultimate time-out is jail, which is something I say to my kids."

In 1988, California governor George Deukmejian vetoed an expansion of the Parents as Teachers program. The form letter sent to program administrators suggested that it was just another adult education program.

As we were turning to leave, I asked Margaret how she dealt with her fear, how she faced the bogeyman.

"Truth is the key. You have to be honest with your kids. There are bad things in the world. But I tell my children God is good. I tell them there are good things in the world too, and there is good in every tragedy. We have to learn from our mistakes. I guess I face the fear pretty much head-on. It helps my kids to understand that Mom cares enough to be with them. We have a safety committee at our PTA. We've gotten the police involved. I'll go down to the school grounds at drop-off time and at pick-up time and we give tickets to parents for speeding. So far it's been working. And it's not going to stop. One of my PTA newsletters asked parents, 'If you have older children, would they be willing to walk with the younger children?' So now we have groups of kids walking to school.

"I see a lot of parents hitting kids in public. It's not my business to tell them directly to stop, but sometimes at PTA conferences I speak about it. I get resistance. But unless we face what we are doing to kids, it will go on for generations.

"So that's the way it is. Every day I stand at the back of the school, and the principal stands in front, and I remind the little kids not to run up on the bank, to stay away from the curb, not to run across the street. We had one boy almost get hit by a car the other day. He was that close. I'm here, I'm not going to go away. It gets frustrating, but I refuse to let it frustrate me for very long because I have found that everything in life takes baby steps."

Postscript
Toward a Family Liberation Movement

●

The tools that have been described in this book are models only; many others like them are emerging. More important than specific programs, however, is the spirit that moves them.

Liberation is a never-ending process, not some final destination. The liberation movements of the past three decades have changed our lives, usually for the better, but now many of us find ourselves standing at the end of our liberation road, feeling strangely disconnected, even lonely, wondering what comes next. What's next is family liberation — the right of the family to be connected.

In this book I have offered a rough framework of what the shape of a family liberation movement might be. I have not invented this idea; it comes pushing outward from parents and children. The isolation of parents is ending — everywhere I went, parents were eager to talk about their roles and who they were and how their children were doing and the future that could be. Listening to parents, particularly those who came of age during the sixties, I often thought of the quotation from George Bernard Shaw paraphrased by Robert Kennedy at each campaign stop until the night he died: "Most men look at things as they are and wonder, Why? I dream of things that never were and ask, Why not?" A generation of parents, and other Americans as well, is about to collectively ask, "Why not?"

An evolving set of principles for this movement rises naturally from the voices of parents, children, and the professionals who work with children. Among the simple core ideas:

- None of us raises a child alone, even if we believe that we are alone.
- The nature of childhood is an environmental issue, not simply an educational one. Children and families are part of a larger ecosystem — a web.
- The concept of *family* must be defined as broadly as possible.
- The best way to decrease childhood isolation is to decrease the isolation of parents.
- The best way to deprogram our overscheduled children is to deprogram ourselves.
- We need to do everything possible to allow children to hang on to their childhood for as long as possible.
- The central goal of every private or public program involving children and families should be to increase positive contact between children and adults.
- In our institutions and in our families, we must continually reassess the balance between our children's autonomy and our parental and institutional control of them.
- Family fear and family time are interrelated: increase positive family time and we decrease fear in society, as well as some of the real reasons for our fear.
- Finding our place in time is as important as finding our place in our physical community.
- In addition to seeking mentoring parents for ourselves, we need to become mentoring parents to the next generation of parents, and thereby close the preparation gap.
- The emotional and spiritual life of children should be placed before talk of economic competitiveness. Kids are not capital.
- A truly family-friendly work place respects employees' needs for flexibility and time.
- A pro-family work place will be a more humane place to work for all employees, whether or not they have children of their own.
- A society that is pro-child and pro-family is a more humane and enjoyable society for all members, whether or not they have children of their own.
- Progress for children cannot be achieved politically if it is seen as simply pro-child. Rather than being exclusive or competitive with the needs of the elderly or of childless families, family liberation must be an inclusive movement.
- Family liberation should not become an exclusive benefit for upper-middle- and upper-class families, but should emanate outward from communities at all economic levels.

• Little meaningful political change will occur for children without grass-roots action beginning in the family and extending through neighborhoods, schools, and the work place.

The reshaping of childhood's future will not be easy to achieve.

We live in an age of accelerating marketplace competitiveness. In the near future Japan, the European Community, and the United States will place increasing pressure on families and children. In the work place, Americans will be asked to work even more hours. Children will be expected to spend more hours under mounting educational pressure. Further institutionalization and programming of childhood will be promoted in the name of economic competitiveness. For a time, those who push this philosophy may make it difficult for some of us to remember that the richness of life is found in slower moments, that the formation of creative young minds is accomplished not only by the hours spent in the classroom but also by watching tree branches move and the dust fall, and that love within families flourishes when there is time for love.

The withering of a people's creativity and joy, the submission of family life and childhood to the machine of international competition will guarantee our nation's decline, particularly if one measures progress not by the number of Cuisinarts sold but by the amount of laughter and love within the walls of home. But in time, the current definition of successful competition will change. In the long run, the nation that develops a balanced and humane system of cooperation between work and family is the nation that will win economically.

In America's state and national political bodies, children today carry virtually no political clout. Such power will not be gained by pitting one social or religious group against another, but rather will be based on the nearly untapped strength of our commonality. This strength will grow almost organically as thousands of individual heroes and warriors begin to take action; these new leaders will be community activists, teachers, parents, and hard-nosed business people, each of whom answers the call in his or her own way. I do not wish to imply that a "thousand points of light," as President Bush describes his ideal, will be enough. Such an image is a beginning, but not the final metaphor. Voluntarism does not necessarily bring about social change; change comes only when the points of light are connected politically and socially.

We should extend a challenge to one another — each family, each company, each school, each neighborhood, each city — to put together individual plans for childhood's future, sets of goals that can be achieved during the next one to five years.

In creating your own plan, some of the ideas within this book may be useful; but you may well have better ideas yourself. Assemble this plan soon. This week. This month. When enough plans are drawn up and have been acted on, political power on behalf of children and families will follow, and the new web will be rewoven.

This new web will come slowly, slower than it should, but it will come. We will reimagine our schools, and the daily structure of our family lives, and our cities and our neighborhoods, and it will come. While we work toward the creation of this new support system, we will make accommodations and more compromises than we would like — but we will do this in the belief that the new web will come. And we can see and feel and hear it coming. Although we can still hear the old web shredding, we can also hear the sounds of mending, of strands being pulled across, new strands being created, the strands of time and trust returning.

It would be inappropriate to end this book without giving some hint as to how my family and I were affected by the writing of it. Although we had always considered ourselves good parents, my wife, Kathy, and I realized how little focused time we spent with our children, how few activities we did as a whole family. Quite honestly, some of the time that was devoted to this book was stolen from family time. But we began to make changes. Fortunately, in my profession I am able to control the flexibility of my hours. I worked at home more (often with my older son playing or working beside me) and made a greater effort to involve myself in my sons' lives, my older son's school, and my younger son's cooperative day care. Kathy, a nurse practitioner, cut back to a sixteen-hour workweek and assumed a more traditional role at home. This decision was not easy for her, but it has worked out, and our current roles as father and mother are not cast in stone. Inspired by many of the people we encountered during the writing of this book, we are busy, too, devising our own family's plan for childhood's future.

Finally, I emerged from this three-year project more optimistic than when I began it. And I feel, in some way, that I have found my place in time.

One particularly hopeful and personal moment returns to me often: a walk I took with Tom Hilleary, at whose Kansas home one of the parent groups met. At dusk, before the group assembled, Tom and I, who grew up together, walked through his subdivision and across a highway. As when we were boys, we had no particular destination in mind.

We crossed a highway, its blacktop still sticky from the day's heat, to a vacant farmhouse. Its dark eyes looked out and its porch, its front steps gone, dipped like a grim, detached smile. Tom led the way. As curious as he had always been, he climbed up on the front porch. We poked around the old house, stepping across piles of fallen plaster. For a few moments we stood at a second-story window and looked out at the overgrown green fields and the fallen fences, and we wondered about the families that had lived here in the past, the children who had grown up in this house and run in the fields below.

We left the old house and walked farther, through other subdivisions. They were like the rings of a tree; their architecture revealed their age and the environmental conditions in which they had been built. The fifties neighborhood had small, boxy, conformist houses with large front picture windows. In the neighborhoods of the sixties and seventies the houses had grown larger and, gradually, had closed off, turned inward. The fronts of the houses were no longer designed in a way that revealed the shape of a human face: the smile of a porch, the eyes of windows. By the eighties, the faces of these houses were finally gone, turned away from the street and the neighborhood.

And then we came to another neighborhood, so new that the sod had just been laid down. The light was fading. A full moon was coming up above the far line of trees and suburban houses. No one had yet moved into this fresh new neighborhood. The lawns were dotted with FOR SALE and SOLD signs.

Looking at these houses, it suddenly occurred to me: they were *different*. They were surrounded by porches; their faces were inviting. Tom and I climbed the steps of one of the new houses and went inside. We walked through the rooms lit by moonlight. I paused, as I had at the old farmhouse, and looked out a window, and saw that the developer had left a small woods along a little creek. Lightning bugs were gracing the low branches now. I looked out at the other houses, arranged not in straight lines but in natural cul-de-sacs with dipping and sculpted land connecting them, arranged so that the people in them could watch their neighbors and their children play.

Standing at the window, I wondered about the generations of children who would grow up in this house and this neighborhood, and how it would be for them.

NOTES

BIBLIOGRAPHY

INDEX

NOTES

1. "I'll Play with You Tomorrow"

1. Ellen Goodman, "If We Could Only Bottle a Little Time," *San Diego Tribune*, December 1, 1989, sec. B.
2. "Parents Fight 'Time Famine' As Economic Pressures Increase," *Family Research Council*, March 13, 1990, 1; Priority Management Systems, *Agenda for the 1990s; An International Business Lifestyle Survey* (Irving, Calif.: Priority Management Systems, 1989).
3. "The Changing American Vacation," *Newsweek*, August 28, 1989.
4. "Average Income of Retirees Now Exceeds That of Middle-Aged Workers, Ricardo-Campbell Notes," Stanford University News Service, November 18, 1986. Ricardo-Campbell also reports that "with 70 percent of women in child-bearing years working, in large part because they and their husbands perceive that it is an economic necessity, fertility rates will remain below replacement."
5. Ruth Schwartz Cowan, *More Work for Mother* (New York: Basic Books, 1983). By 1980, the percentage of homes with air conditioners had quintupled, the percentage with two or more cars had tripled, and the percentage with dishwashers had increased by more than 700 percent.
6. Nickelodeon/USA Today/Yankelovich Youth Monitor results were based on twelve hundred in-person interviews conducted October through December 1986.
7. Sherrye Henry, "A Report from Mothers: 'If I Could Do It Over Again,'" *Woman's Day*, April 19, 1988, 66–69.

2. The Bogeyman

1. A black middle-class parent who works for the school district in San Diego told me: "Our larger institutions buy into this fear. For example, my office was charged with fingerprinting all kindergarten children. How many missing children have really been identified using fingerprints? So much of this

is crisis-oriented. We hear of a terrible case and everyone jumps at once. Rather than creating a national, ongoing plan, a policy, a direction, we jump on the bandwagon. There's no continuity, no consistency. In fact, we never found out where the fingerprints went. As far as I know it was all for show."

Initially, many of the private organizations and reporters concerned with missing children did not distinguish among runaways, children kidnaped by a noncustodial parent, and those abducted by strangers. One Chicago television station distributed a pamphlet that began: "Nearly 2 million children in this country disappear from their homes each year. Many end up raped, forced into prostitution and pornography. Many are never heard from again." These types of pamphlets and articles group the several categories into the general heading of "missing children," leading people to assume that abductions by strangers are far more commonplace than they are. The number of children kidnaped by strangers remains in dispute; however, the percentage is generally agreed to be much smaller than the earliest reports suggested. "In part, this reflects the secretive nature of crime," said Joel Best. "There is always a 'dark figure' of unreported offenses. We can never obtain a completely accurate count. More than anything else, the number of stranger abductions depends on one's definition of the crime."

2. Jim Jones, "Video, Film Violence Target of Campaign," *San Diego Tribune,* November 8, 1985, sec. C. Another study reveals our ambivalence about the amount of crime in our neighborhoods. Though 82 percent of adult Americans believe that crime is a serious problem, an even larger percentage said their neighborhoods were safe. Eighty-seven percent of the parents polled said their children's schools were safe. Sociologist David Altheide of the School of Justice Studies at Arizona State University comments in the survey report: "When thinking in general terms, people are saying, 'Yes, crime's a bad problem.' But for them personally, it isn't."

3. David Phillips, a professor at the University of California and the nation's leading expert on media-stimulated copycat suicides, worked as a consultant to the firm promoting the *Nightmare on Elm Street* movies. "I was called in because of a national rumor that the fictional Freddy was triggering a rash of teenage suicides," said Phillips. "It wasn't true. There were no suicides in the movie to mimic."

4. Richard J. Gelles and Murray A. Strauss, *Intimate Violence* (New York: Simon and Schuster, 1988). More than 2 million cases of child abuse were reported in 1986, compared with 669,000 in 1976; more than 1,200 children die each year through child abuse and neglect.

5. *Parents Magazine* news release, December 19, 1988.

6. Robert Barker, "Smoking Guns," *Barron's,* June 23, 1986, 43. According to the California Department of Education's third annual report on school crime for 1987–88, 789 guns were found on campuses — a 25 percent increase from the year before. Of the 8,539 weapons reported, most were knives (4,408) or explosives (2,216) ("Guns Said on Increase in Schools," *San Diego Union,* April 7, 1989, sec. A).

3. In Search of Beaver Cleaver

1. Barbara Whitehead, "Where Have All the Parents Gone?" *New Perspectives Quarterly* (Winter 1990), 30; idem, "Parents Get Lost in the Shuffle," *Boston Globe,* August 13, 1989, Focus section.

2. Basia Hellwig, "How Working Women Have Changed America: The Family," *Working Woman,* November 1986, 134–37; Peter Morrison, "Changing Family Structure: Who Cares for America's Dependents?" (report by the Rand Corporation, Santa Monica, Calif., December 1986).

3. Randolph E. Schmid, "Divorce Rate of 60% Seen for Over-30s," *San Diego Union,* April 5, 1986, sec. D.

4. Morrison, "Changing Family Structure," 1,3. Morrison projects that 56 percent of first marriages by women who were aged thirty-five to thirty-nine in 1985 will end in divorce. According to another study, two-thirds of all first marriages may eventually end in separation.

5. According to a study by scholars at the American Enterprise Institute, a conservative think tank: "Until recently, even broaching the subject [of the high out-of-wedlock birthrate among blacks] invited charges of racism. Ironically, now that it can be talked about freely, race has become a less important factor in illegitimacy rates. When income and education are taken into account, racial differences are cut in half" (Douglas Besharov, "A Portrait in Black and White: Out of Wedlock Birth," *Public Opinion,* May/June 1987, 43). Actually, the number of out-of-wedlock births is increasing more rapidly among whites than among blacks. Among blacks, the number has increased 85 percent; white numbers have increased 139 percent (*Vital Statistics of the United States: Natality* [Washington, D.C.: Government Printing Office, 1960–81]).

6. "Looking back at the generation of children born between 1950–54 (who are now adults in their mid-thirties), 19 percent of the whites and 48 percent of the blacks spent some part of their youth in a one-parent family," writes Morrison. "Those figures will be much higher for the generation born in 1980, assuming that current trends continue." In 1986, one American youngster in four lived with just one parent, more than two and a half times the proportion in 1960 ("Changing Family Structure," 6–7).

7. As recently as ten years ago, most Americans shared a pretty clear image of what life in the middle class looked like: Mom and Dad and Sis and Bud in a nice tract house on Elm Street, a Chevy or a Ford in the driveway, a barbecue in the back yard, a washer and dryer in the basement, and a street filled with kids. "If you tried to come up with an equally simple and widely accepted mental image today, you couldn't do it," said Whitehead. Middle-class life, of course, was never as simple as the media images made it seem, but here's a portrait of that same middle-class street today: At one end of Elm Street, in one of the new condos, lives an upscale family with a Porsche in the driveway, a big joint income, an equally large credit card debt, and their only child away at prep school. A few doors down lives a childless couple who work as a computer salesman and a clerk at a convenience mart. At the other end of the street lives a single mother who works as a middle-level bank manager. Next door is a family with a father who struggles along at an $8-an-hour blue-collar job; his wife works a few days a

week at the dime store; their American-made car is eight years old and the kids go to a public school where the broken windows don't get fixed as quickly as they used to. They're barely holding on. The economic and cultural changes in the middle class are part of something Whitehead calls the "new social ladder." At the top, just beneath the very rich, a new "overclass" commands the highest-level positions in media, advertising, real estate, finance, and politics. At the bottom of the ladder the poor have been joined by the underclass, people who are so far down that to call them poor is to overstate their well-being. But the middle class — the very core of American life — is where the most important and least understood changes are occurring. Whitehead classifies the old, expanding middle class of the fifties and sixties as being made up chiefly of white-collar and blue-collar workers. By contrast, what Whitehead sees as the new divergent middle class contains three main groups:

• *Bright collars.* The twenty million knowledge workers born since 1945: rising executives and mid-level administrators who earn their living by taking intellectual initiatives. Bright collars have eclipsed white collars. White collars believed in institutions; they were organization men and women. "The older white collars knew the rules and played by them, but bright collars can't be sure what the rules are and must think up their own," said Whitehead. Whereas three-quarters of managers and professionals of the fifties were men, today half are women. Bright collars make up a third of the baby-boom work force.
• *Blue collars.* The blue-collar work force is still with us, but it's shrinking. In 1960, almost 40 percent of the adult work force held blue-collar jobs; today less than 25 percent of baby boomers can be considered blue collar. "The blue-collar world is still a man's world," said Whitehead. Economically, blue collars are slipping fast.
• *New collars.* These workers, according to Whitehead, aren't managers or professionals, but they don't do physical labor either. They're secretaries, retail sales clerks, service workers. Two-thirds of the new collars are women. As the service-sector economy grows, this group is expanding quickly, but their income isn't.

The middle class has become the muddled class, spreading apart economically, but even further socially. On Elm Street during the fifties and mid-sixties, middle-class values were fairly monotone and in some ways stifling. Nevertheless, people shared a common vision of what they and their children could expect from American life — and most figured they would achieve this vision together. The folks who live on Elm Street today enjoy more personal freedom in what they think, feel, wear, and drive. But the sense of community that once existed on this street has faded like the color in an old photograph. These days, the people on Elm Street barely cross paths, let alone share their lives over the back yard barbecue. Such divergence makes it exceedingly difficult for politicians to champion the middle class. *Which middle class?*

8. Frank Levy and Richard C. Michel, "Are Baby Boomers Selfish?" *American*

Demographics, April 1985, 38; Laurent Belsie, "Family Income Level Stagnates," *Christian Science Monitor,* September 2, 1988.

9. Clifford M. Johnson, Andrew M. Sum, and James D. Weill, *Vanishing Dreams: The Growing Economic Plight of America's Young Families* (Washington, D.C.: Children's Defense Fund, 1988).

10. Levy and Michel, "Are Baby Boomers Selfish?" 38–41; Richard D. Lamm, "Children Are Gypped by Our Excesses," *San Diego Tribune,* July 10, 1985, sec. B; Craig D. Rose, "Economists Question Ortner's '600-a-Week' Job Report," *San Diego Union,* August 28, 1988, sec. I. Levy and Michel add: "One unavoidable problem for the baby boom [generation] stemmed from their sheer numbers. In the 1950s and 1960s, before the peak of the baby boom matured, the number of 25- to 34-year-old workers oscillated between 14 and 17 million persons. Since then, 25- to 34-year-old workers have exploded from 17 million in 1970 to over 30 million today. The huge number of new workers, all competing for advancement, meant that baby boomers would progress slowly even in a healthy economy." Lamm, the former governor of Colorado, puts mortgages in this perspective: "My generation made mortgage money available at subsidized rates and long payback periods to make it easy for us to buy homes. This helped cause the rapid inflation of the 1970s."

A proviso: Sylvia Nasar correctly points out that "most young buyers have forgotten how long it took their parents to land their first house. . . . Most boomers wouldn't be caught dead in their parents' first nests. Those Levittown dream houses were exactly half the size of today's new homes, and young families were a lot bigger. Building codes weren't what they are. The nearest equivalent today, quite literally, is a mobile home — the typical price of which is about half that of a Levittown econobox, not including its tiny plot of land" ("Do We Live as Well as We Used To?" *Fortune,* September 14, 1987, 32). Nasar neglects to point out, however, that moderately priced and downsized houses are not being built in any substantial number in many areas of the country. Condominiums are being built, but these are often architecturally inappropriate for growing families — and, too often, age-restricted.

11. "Women, Children Are Unintended Casualties of the No-Fault Divorce Revolution, Weitzman Says," Stanford University News Service, January 23, 1986. Moreover, the minimum wage did not keep up with inflation during the eighties.

12. "Hard Lesson in Economics: College Tuition to Rise 7%," *San Diego Tribune,* August 5, 1988, sec. A. At private four-year institutions, the average annual cost of going to college — including tuition, fees, room and board, and incidental expenses — hit $13,000 in 1988, up 9 percent from 1986–87. At public institutions, the average annual cost exceeded $6,000, up 5 percent.

A second characteristic of eduflation is that the more education Americans get, the less it seems to mean. Colleges spend an inordinate amount of time teaching kids what they should have learned in high school. A job that took a bachelor's or master's degree a few years ago now demands a doctorate. In addition to higher yearly expenses, parents or students end up paying for additional degrees just to keep up with the game. At many universities a bachelor's degree now takes an average of four and a half years to complete, and is heading for five years.

Marlys Harris, who is a contributing writer for *Money* magazine, suggested that parents with young children look at the problem this way: if parents are already accustomed to spending $2,000 to $4,000 a year on day care for one child, once their child heads for elementary school, they should be able to shift quite a bit of their child-care budget into savings for future education. "Save part of it for your kid's college, and spend the rest of it on yourself — as a reward for surviving the day-care years," said Harris. But what if a family has three kids? Or four? Then they'll be facing a bill of between $200,000 and $400,000. How, if wages and salaries do not keep up with inflation, do they save for that?

Will there be enough financial aid to go around? In 1960, only 4 percent of freshmen received institutional or government loans, grants, or work-study jobs; back then you asked your Uncle Irving for a loan if you needed it. Today half of all freshmen receive financial aid — but that aid is increasingly in the form of loans, not grants. The average student who graduates after four years in college begins a career $9,000 in debt. No wonder so many more college graduates opt for high-paying jobs and shun such professions as teaching and nursing. That debt is likely to increase. "Free money" is drying up. According to Dr. Kenneth C. Green, associate director of the Higher Education Research Institute at UCLA, "Many families who were eligible for [federal] grants in 1980 now find they cannot get assistance for their second or third child, even though their real [inflation-adjusted] income has not changed in six years." Colleges and universities are picking up much of the slack (though this expense is part of the reason for increased fees and tuition). And more financial help will come from local scholarship funds. The most important trend, however, is toward what Fred Morley, director of Partners in Education in Miami, calls "tuition futures," whereby parents bet that the returns from a special investment will outpace college inflation. Some private colleges are moving to set up such programs — invest now, send your child to that college later. But this approach has inherent problems. For example, what if the college doesn't accept the student? More promising is a move by a handful of states to adopt programs through which parents could deposit a few thousand dollars with the state, which would invest it for tax-free growth — guaranteeing the student a four-year education at a state school. The money, minus an administrative fee, would be refunded if the child did not attend college. Other suggested possibilities are a tax-free educational savings bond and a federally guaranteed student loan program that would permit students to repay bank loans through payroll deductions over their working lifetimes — unless the borrower elected to buy out the loan at a substantial penalty. The plan would essentially shift the burden of debt from parents to children. The problem with these proposals is that they fail to address the most essential issue: the need to cap the skyrocketing costs of higher education. Unless eduflation costs are capped, will new loan programs really help students — or will they simply drive this and the next generation further into debt, while fattening the industry of higher education?

Robert Iosue, president of York College of Pennsylvania, has been one of the few academic insiders to criticize the rising costs of education publicly. During the past decade, tuition at York College rose at a rate of only about two-thirds the average increase at all private schools, while its academic standing improved. York has no intercollegiate football team, only a small health clinic, a student-staffed security force, no phones in individual dorm rooms, and no academic vice president — which alone saves about $100,000 a year. The nation's entire educational system could benefit, Iosue said, "if colleges and universities got a little benign neglect by shifting some money from colleges to inner-city public schools and rural high schools. Indeed, unless we pay attention to the rudiments of education we are going to have two educational classes in this country. Business understands the problem, penal institutions understand the problem. Somehow, higher-education industry just doesn't get it."

13. T. C. Williams has set up a special endowment, the Scholarship Fund of Alexandria. The approach is similar to that taken by some schools for decades for their top athletes, but these endowments will be for nonathlete students. "We've decided that tenth grade is not soon enough to approach the parents," said McClure. "We're going to go into the junior high schools this year, and eventually we're going to get into our elementary schools, to show people they're going to have to plan ahead. That's what it's going to take."

14. Johnson, Sum, and Weill, *Vanishing Dreams*.

15. Karl Zinsmeister, "Family's Tie to the American Dream," *Public Opinion*, September/October 1986. Between 1968 and 1972 about 50 percent of male freshmen felt that being very well off financially was essential or very important in their lives. In the fall of 1973, however, as the economy was going sour, this proportion jumped to 62 percent, and reached 69 percent by the end of the decade. The number of freshman women who responded similarly jumped from 30 percent in 1972 to 46 percent in 1973 and up to 58 percent by the end of the decade (Levy and Michel, "Are Baby Boomers Selfish?").

16. John Sommerville, *The Rise and Fall of Childhood* (Beverly Hills: Sage, 1982), 20.

17. Mildred Hamilton, "As Our Society Ages, It'll Be 'In' to Be Old," *San Diego Tribune*, August 27, 1985, sec. E. Thirty years from now, the U.S. population will constitute one of the oldest societies in the world; more than half our adult population will be over fifty-five, eligible for membership in the American Association of Retired Persons. Ken Dychtwald, a psychologist and gerontologist at Berkeley and founder of the Institute of Aging, Health and Work, describes his vision of the future: "Society sculpts itself in the image of the people who make it up," and as the nation ages, all its institutions, from education to politics, all its physical properties, from stoplights to chair designs, will be changed to accommodate that population. He foresees a more "adult-focused society" with larger, easier-to-read books and periodicals, door levers instead of door knobs, bathtubs of soft material, and easy chairs that lift up to catch the person sitting down. "Gerontology and cosmetic surgery will boom. Shared and sheltered housing will be preferred addresses. Closed grammar schools will be converted to adult education centers" (ibid.).

18. "Average Income of Retirees Now Exceeds That of Middle-Aged Workers, Ricardo-Campbell Notes," *Stanford University News Service*, November 18, 1986. According to Ricardo-Campbell, during the past quarter century the proportion of the federal budget benefiting the aged has risen from 6 to 30 percent. The proportion of those aged sixty-five and higher has risen from 9 to 12 percent. Ricardo-Campbell charges that Social Security "absorbs about one-fourth of the U.S. budget" and "effectively transfers income from the working young to the non-working aged." Moreover, "more than half of all adults are paying more in Social Security taxes than in personal income tax." The *Washington Post* columnist George Will has also noted that "seventy percent of the budget consists of defense (declining), interest (soaring), Medicare and Social Security. Under Reagan, spending on Medicare and Social Security rose 115 and 67 percent, respectively" ("Just A-Feudin' and A-Duckin'," *San Diego Union*, February 25, 1988, sec. B).

19. TRB from Washington, "Blow Your House Down," *New Republic*, October 10, 1988, 4. For younger baby boomers, home ownership is a fading dream. On average, house payments in 1987 consumed almost 44 percent of the average thirty-year-old's income, whereas in 1960 they consumed only 16 percent of a worker's income. Among the elderly, 74 percent of all persons older than sixty-five own their homes — mostly free of mortgage.

20. Sommerville, *The Rise and Fall of Childhood*. The Judeo-Christian tradition introduced a revolutionary concept to the world, the ideal of service to one's neighbor — that service was more a mark of one's worth than dominance, and that this service should be extended to children. Of course, as Sommerville points out, "the notion of childhood innocence seems to conflict with another Christian teaching, the idea of infant depravity" — original sin. But the image of children took a sharp turn upward in the 1680s, when a group of Neo-Platonist philosophers at Cambridge University began to rethink the state of childhood, following Plato's teaching that souls are eternal, that children are born with certain inherent truths passed on from preexistence, and that growing up is, essentially, the loss of these eternal truths. During the Enlightenment, the new belief in the power of human reason contributed to an awareness of the child as a distinctive individual. The Victorians would later adopt the view that children were born as noble, unselfish beings until society crushed or corrupted their spirits. "It is also true that the Victorians who exalted the image of childhood innocence were, ironically, also guilty of raising repressiveness to something like record levels. It is important to note that whatever the prevailing view was of the child at the time did not always affect how they were treated — particularly children of the poor. . . ."

The Puritans, according to Sommerville, were the first modern parents: "Like many of us, they looked on their treatment of children as a test of their own self-control. . . . Being critics of their society, Puritans were among the first parents who felt they could not rely on their neighbors or existing social institutions to help them socialize their children. For they had rejected the manners and morals which prevailed and felt isolated in their task of child rearing. Some even determined to leave England to found their own communities, and these always remarked that their children had been a main motive for their move. Puritans resisted much that was traditional as well as their own impulses and thereby became conscious of just how problematical raisng children can be. . . . Puritans were to produce the first books written specifically for children and young people."

21. Helen Fisher and Kathleen McAuliffe, "A Primitive Prescription for Equality," *U.S. News and World Report*, August 8, 1988, 57.

22. Judith Wallerstein and Sandra Blakeslee, *Second Chances: Men, Women, and Children a Decade After Divorce* (New York: Ticknor & Fields, 1989). A cautionary note should be struck here: Wallerstein failed to survey a control group of children from intact families. How did the kids who remained in intact but troubled families fare? She readily admits this flaw, and points to other shorter-term studies done around the country which did compare both groups.

23. John G. Neihardt, *Black Elk Speaks: Being the Life Story of a Holy Man of the Oglala Sioux* (Lincoln: University of Nebraska Press, 1961), 43.

4. The Compassion of Children

1. Thomas J. Cottle, *Children's Secrets* (Garden City, N.Y.: Anchor, 1980). See also James Webb, "A Legacy for My Daughter," *Newsweek*, November 7, 1988.

5. The Children Who Own Themselves

1. Editorial, *Journal of Home Economics*, December 1941, 736.

2. Christopher Reynolds, "Who Is to Blame When Kids Drop Out?" *San Diego Union*, September 3, 1987, sec. C; "2 Million Children Stay Home Alone," *New York Times*, February 6, 1987; "Census Bureau Counts Latch-Key Kids," *Child Care Action News*, May/June 1987, 6. In questioning the numerical results of the Census Bureau study, *Child Care Action News* cites a United Way survey in Los Angeles which found that 24 percent of children aged seven to nine were without supervision after school. A similar study by the Working Parents Project in Kansas City found that 22 percent of school-age children were unsupervised. And in Mecklenburg County, North Carolina, 20 percent of school-age children were caring for themselves after school, and an additional 13 percent were being taken care of by siblings.

So far, few experts concerned with the problem are satisfied with the numbers. The Census Bureau admits several sources of possible error or bias that could affect the accuracy of its findings. Among them: parents answering surveys may have feared they were placing a child in jeopardy by disclosing that the child was alone or unsupervised after school, or they may have believed that doing so was socially unacceptable and they might be charged with child neglect.

3. Elizabeth Rhodes, "A Child Alone," *Seattle Times*, February 20, 1987, sec. B. Rhodes described a case in which a ten-year-old Seattle boy was discovered caring for his three- and six-year-old sisters and a disabled eighty-two-year-old man. No food was in the house, no money, and no father. The mother stayed away from home for days at a time. In another case, a ragged, hungry six-year-old and her four-year-old brother were found begging

for food at Seattle's Green Lake. Their mother dropped them off in the morning and picked them up at night.

4. Reynolds, "Who Is to Blame?"; J. L. Richardson et al., "Substance Use Among Eighth Graders Who Take Care of Themselves After School," *Pediatrics*, September 1989, 556; "Is Society Becoming 'Anti-child'?" *San Diego Tribune*, September 7, 1987, sec. C.

5. In the late seventies, David Elkind, professor of child study at Tufts University, began to chart the trend to push kids to take on the trappings of adulthood. His book *The Hurried Child: Growing Up Too Fast Too Soon* (Reading, Mass.: Addison-Wesley, 1981) warns that school failure, delinquency, drugs, and suicide are evidence of what Elkind calls the hurried child syndrome. Since the publication of the book, many of the young children Elkind wrote about have become harried teens, expected to assume all the normal pressures of adolescence but also to cook and shop and sometimes care for their families as well.

6. Kenneth Eskey, "Latchkey Kids May Be Fewer Than Was Thought," *San Diego Tribune*, February 6, 1987, sec. D. Teen-age Research Unlimited in Lake Forest, Illinois, estimates that, in 1988, children aged twelve to nineteen spent more than $31 billion of their own money and more than $47 million in family money.

7. *BSB Currents,* a publication of the New York advertising agency Backer Spielvogal Bates.

8. To attract and retain young employees, Burger King now offers college scholarships — teenagers can receive as much as $2,000 in tuition credits if they work at Burger King for two years. Some fast-food outlets organize softball games and parties. And an increasing number of companies offer youths more than the minimum wage.

Another paradox of the latchkey work force: the push toward child labor offers the possibility of escape for children of the underclass, for whom talk of the lost leisure of childhood is an academic exercise. During the next decade the nation has the potential to move millions of teenagers out of the underclass — out of the ghettos, off dope, away from illiteracy and hopelessness and into the economic mainstream. Such a window of opportunity has not existed for decades and may well disappear soon unless we move quickly. These future workers will enter an expanding service and information economy with a need for literacy and technological know-how greater than at any time in our history, and their skills are sorely lacking.

Along with the literacy gap comes the geographic mismatch between poor kids and jobs. John D. Kasarda, a sociologist at the University of North Carolina, said that economics and the population trends of American cities are on a collision course. Although most Americans have the ability to move to wherever there are jobs, the "new immobiles," as Kasarda described them, are locked into inner cities where blue-collar employment is disappearing. Nearly all manufacturing jobs have moved to the suburbs or beyond. "As a result of their isolation," he said, "it's difficult for these kids to get the kind of social experiences and role models they need to hold on to a job." A cynic would forecast that businesses won't touch the untouchables — underclass kids without adequate education and social skills — no matter how bad the shortage of workers becomes. Instead of adopting literacy programs, companies will "de-skill" jobs, using pictures instead of words on cash registers and so forth. (Will the nineties be known as the Decade of the Pictograph?) Businesses will also rely more on automation; robots, after all, don't smoke dope or show up late. In addition, companies will turn to older workers. And, of course, businesses could hire more illegal immigrants and push for relaxed immigration laws, leaving America's underprivileged kids outside the economic gates.

But what if the nation chooses a different course? "Among academics, there has been little talk of this as an opportunity," said Harley Shaiken, a labor expert at the University of California–San Diego. "But that could change." Some people are beginning to view the youth labor shortage as an opportunity. Assistant Secretary of Labor Roger Semerad said recently, "We're going to need these school dropouts, the functional illiterates, the welfare dependent, the pregnant teenagers, the drug abusers — but they have to be qualified to take the jobs coming down the road." Kasarda sees the possibility of pulling kids out of the inner cities, using expanded van-pooling services and housing vouchers (instead of building more low-income housing in ghettos) to encourage their families to live closer to where the jobs are. Another tool: stronger enforcement of fair-housing laws to enable minority families to move out of high-unemployment areas. In Boston, which has been hard hit by the youth worker shortage, the public/private Boston Compact promises kids jobs after high school graduation if they make decent grades. And there's renewed talk of a voluntary national youth service.

9. The legal definition of child labor exploitation depends on which government agency one believes. In San Diego, for example, child labor rules are set down by the federal and state departments of labor, the California Administrative Code, the California Education Code, state and federal labor codes, San Diego Unified School District procedures, and assorted city ordinances. The regulations are confusing at best, class-biased at worst. A thirteen-year-old flipping hamburgers is illegally employed; a five-year-old working as an actor is not. In California, the state education codes governing child labor consider seventeen-year-olds adults if they have graduated from high school, but not if they are high school dropouts, even if they are supporting families.

10. A startling 80 percent of high school seniors in the western United States hold jobs. John Orr, a professor at the University of Southern California, estimates that slightly less than half of these kids are working sixteen hours a week or more, 10 percent more than thirty hours weekly. See also Joan Libman, ". . . And Kids Do Too Much," *Washington Post,* September 19, 1988, Style section.

11. "The Perils of Teenage Employment," *U.S. News and World Report,* November 10, 1986, 94.

12. "Students Today: Conservative and Money-motivated," *USA Today,* May 1988.

13. Joan Libman, "Growing Up Too Fast," *Los Angeles Times,* San Diego County edition, August 9, 1988, sec. 5.

14. Kenneth B. Noble, "Library as Day Care: New Curbs and Concerns," *New York Times,* February 15, 1988.

15. Libman, "Growing Up Too Fast."

6. *If Day Care's the Answer, What's the Question?*

1. During the nineties, according to the Children's Defense Fund, the number of children younger than six needing child care will grow by more than 50 percent. "Of the 15.8 million mothers with children under 6, 56 percent were working or looking for work" (*A Vision for America's Future — An Agenda for the 1990s: A Children's Defense Budget* [Washington, D.C.: Children's Defense Fund, 1989]). See also "Labor Force Participation Unchanged Among Mothers of Young Children," *Bureau of Labor Statistics News,* September 7, 1988.

8. *Computers Can't Dance*

1. Vic Sussman, "Smart Toys: The Little Computers That Could," *Washington Post,* August 7, 1988, Book World section.

2. Peter H. Lewis, "Ex Machina: The Computer Revolution Revised," *New York Times,* August 7, 1988, sec. A. One major computer maker's advertisement depicts a classroom in which each child's desk is equipped with a computer, each running a different program, while the teacher reads to the students aloud from a book. Lewis, computer writer for the *New York Times,* observes, "Many teachers marveled at (a) the suggestion that 22 different children can be working placidly on their own individual projects while paying attention to a teacher reading aloud; (b) the realization that the money spent on the computers would probably equal the annual pay and benefits of three teachers; (c) the absence of space on the desk for a pencil and paper; and (d) the computers appeared to operate without any visible cables or power cords."

3. "High-Tech Teaching," *Los Angeles Times Magazine,* April 3, 1988, 22.

4. "Computer Is New Tool in Psychiatric Ward," *New York Times,* September 3, 1985, sec. C. Computers have also been shown to be useful in clinical treatment of the behaviorally disturbed.

5. Adeline Naiman, "Ed Tech — Computers in the Classroom," *Christian Science Monitor,* April 1, 1988. There are also scattered reports of computers being used successfully in accelerated programs. The Carlsbad, California, Unified School District, for instance, has reported that students undergoing computer-assisted instruction for the first time appear to progress at a rate of four years' growth for every year of work in language, and at a slightly slower rate in mathematics (Lola Sherman, "Computers Put Carlsbad Kids on Fast Track to Success," *San Diego Tribune,* March 19, 1987, sec. B). There are other bright spots: IBM has developed computer systems called Principles of the Alphabet Learning System (PALS), designed to help adult illiterates learn to read (in Atlanta, city employees have shown remarkable progress, sometimes progressing several levels in a few weeks), and Writing to Read, designed to help the teacher spend more time with individual students. In 1988, former secretary of education William J. Bennett praised seven schools as models for excellence in elementary education, including School No. 59, Science Magnet, in Buffalo, which has demonstrated the benefits of integrating computers into virtually every aspect of the curriculum. Computers are used to study languages, math, science, art, and mu-

sic — and even in exploring the grounds of the nearby zoo, where students use binoculars to observe animal behavior and characteristics and then come back to the classroom and enter that information into a data base. Computers are also used for publishing a student yearbook and the school newspaper, making report cards and keeping student records, and assisting in classroom preparation. Most important, classroom teachers are active and enthusiastic participants (Peter H. Lewis, "Personal Computers: 'Model' for U.S. Schools," *New York Times*, September 6, 1988).

6. Rhoda M. Galinsky, "Westchester Journal: Computer Network," *New York Times*, March 27, 1988, sec. WC.

7. Maria Shao, "Computers in School: A Loser? Or a Lost Opportunity?" *Business Week*, July 17, 1989, 109.

8. Among the other findings of the national survey: a much higher proportion of elementary school teachers use computers in the classroom (37 percent in the K–6 schools) than do secondary school teachers (15 percent). Gender news is mixed. Boys use school computers more than girls; girls constitute about half the students using computers for word processing and roughly half the students using computers overall. (Interestingly, girls play computer games as much as boys during elementary grades, but not in middle or high school.) The typical middle and high school reported that programming classes are about 45 percent female; that percentage was even higher in programming classes that require algebra or higher math as a prerequisite. For after-school use of computers, however, boys outnumber girls three to one — at the typical middle school, only 15 percent of the before- or after-school users are girls. Boys are much more likely than girls to play computer games or take elective programming activities in elementary school. And, just as in past decades when girls (preparing to be secretaries) took more typing credits than boys, high school girls outnumber boys in word processing. Another separator is differences in ability: higher-ability students are much more likely to use computers; students from the bottom third of their classes are well represented in elementary school, but by high school these pupils have fallen far behind in their computer use. This dropoff occurs even though the most frequently reported effect on lower-ability students is improved motivation, self-confidence, and self-discipline. Students in high-ability classes, as well as their teachers, are more likely to have a computer at home. In the long run, educators will lose faith in the value of computer-based instruction if objective evaluations begin to accumulate evidence that computers have made little difference in the education of most children and adolescents (Henry Jay Becker, "Using Computers for Instruction," *Byte*, February 1987, 149; Naiman, "Ed Tech").

9. "Don't Go Overboard Pushing Computer Education," *San Diego Union*, September 1, 1986, sec. AA. An extreme, isolated example was reported in a Danish medical journal: a young man "became so mesmerized by his computer that he was hospitalized with a 'computer syndrome' that made him unable to distinguish between the real world and computer programs." The report may be interpreted as alarmist or portentous. The journal said the unidentified eighteen-year-old had "contracted the new form of psychosis, called computer syndrome by three doctors at Copenhagen's Nordvang Hospital, after spending twelve to sixteen hours a day in front of his

computer. The doctors said the young man began to think in programming language, waking up in the middle of the night thinking, 'Line 10, go to the bathroom; Line 11 next.' " Furthermore, the young man told the doctors he "discovered that man is only a machine. There is no difference between the computer and man." One psychiatrist said the young man "merged with the computer and afforded it supernatural qualities." He suffered from insomnia and anxiety and had to be hospitalized. The doctors involved in the case said that children and youths may substitute computers for human contact because computers always respond rationally, but that the stress on logic can foster immaturity and emotional limitations (" 'Computer Syndrome' Afflicts Man," United Press International News Service, September 1, 1987).

9. The Thief of Time

1. Janet Sutter, "Alert Consumer" (column), San Diego Union, May 21, 1987, sec. E.
2. Joanmarie Kalter, "How TV Is Shaking Up the American Family," TV Guide, July 23, 1988, 5–11. "In family sitcoms a lot of the kids seem to be into themselves," Alvin Poussaint, a psychiatrist and consultant to the "Cosby Show," told Kalter. "Everybody is going in their own direction, doing their own thing. They flit in and flit out, giving their one-liners and disappearing. . . . There's a lot of emphasis on individual success and individual problems. The message is to pull together as a family, but they don't behave that way . . . the homes we see are entirely child-focused."
3. Gerbner elaborates on the mean-world syndrome in George Gerbner and Nancy Signorielli, Violence Profile: Enduring Patterns (Philadelphia: Annenberg School of Communications, 1990). Some of the overreaction to television violence borders on the ridiculous. In 1984, the National Coalition on Television Violence criticized the Disney Channel for being too violent. After monitoring the channel for two weeks, the watchdog organization declared that the channel carried an average of nine violent acts an hour on real-life programming and eighteen an hour on cartoons. Coalition chairman Thomas Radecki, a psychiatrist at the University of Illinois, claimed Disney violence could be harmful to children. Only 27 percent of the cartoons on the Disney network were rated "appropriate for children." The coalition criticized such scenes as one in which Donald Duck fastens his noisy nephews' bills shut with clothespins and another where the Three Little Pigs pour boiling water on the Big Bad Wolf. Disney officials responded: "The N.C.T.V. survey must be based on the assumption that the American public is totally oblivious to what is violent and what is not." Indeed, television's most perfidious trait may be that it reduces our ability to differentiate Porky Pig from Miami Vice ("Group Raps Disney Cartoon Violence," San Diego Tribune, April 24, 1984, sec. C).
4. In fairness, some programs do seem much better than shows were in the past. Watching children's shows with my son, I am impressed with some of the relatively intricate plots and characterizations on, say, the "Real Ghostbusters." And I was impressed that, rather than shooting human beings, the lead characters zap ghosts and demons, which seems to me to be a healthier

endeavor. (However, one fundamentalist family who visits from time to time is aghast that my wife and I would let our son watch such a corrupting show.) Yet even these more imaginative programs eventually go through the grinder. For example, Q5, a consulting company staffed by a team of psychologists, marketing specialists, and advertising professionals, advises children's show programmers to intensify what the organization calls "product payoff . . . the degree to which a product and its attributes match the needs and wants of the consumer." Employing computer data banks filled with standard psychological studies such as Stanford University's VALS (Value and Lifestyle), Q5 advises programmers at ABC as well as Hallmark, Marvel Productions, Twentieth Century Fox, Mattel, and Fisher-Price. Some children's television writers charge that Q5's influence is taking all the challenge out of children's television. "They aren't merely researching trends. They're trying to engage in social engineering," one former story editor told Diane Haithman of the Los Angeles Times. "There's absolutely no passion with these people. There is no sense of honor, of anger, of deep emotion, of love. They're bland-izers. They try to hammer out all of the high and low points of being a human being. I can see we're not doing Dostoevsky on Saturday morning, but there has to be some leeway to create characters who are free to express themselves." Michael Straczynski, a former story editor on the "Real Ghostbusters," said: "They [Q5] wanted us to knock off all the corners. Janine [the Ghostbuster's formerly wise-cracking secretary] was a strong, vibrant character. They wanted her to be more feminine, more maternal, more nurturing, like every other female on television. I think they reinforce stereotypes — sexist and racist. I think they are not helping television, they are diminishing it." Janine's new look was described by Q5 as "generally less harsh and 'slutty'. . . . she will have a warmer, more nurturing relationship with Slimer, the Ghostbusters' mascot ghost. The show was also stripped of much of its clever satire and relatively sophisticated verbal humor" (Haithman, "How Image Makers Shape Kids' TV," Los Angeles Times, September 3, 1987, sec. 6). About the time this happened, my older son, who was then six, lost much of his fascination with the show. In fact, we both lost interest in the show. He had loved the fact that I would sit with him and watch his show, and we would both laugh and talk about what we were seeing. Certainly not all children or parents share our tastes, but when I read about Q5 I realized why my son's favorite program no longer challenged him, and why that transition had occurred so suddenly. The good news was that he shifted his television-watching habits and began watching more science and nature documentaries on the Discovery Channel.

5. Keith Henderson, "Children, TV, and Creativity: Can They Mix?" Christian Science Monitor, April 20, 1987.

6. "TV Violence Changes Kid Play, Study Says," Los Angeles Times, March 29, 1987. The study has been published in book form: Nancy Carlsson-Paige and Diane E. Levin, The War Play Dilemma: Balancing Needs and Values in Early Childhood (New York: Columbia Teachers College Press, 1987).

7. Keith Henderson, "Studies Hint at Link Between TV, Creativity," Christian Science Monitor, April 20, 1987. The Notel study has been published in book form: Tannis MacBeth Williams, ed., The Impact of Television: A

Natural Experiment in Three Communities (Orlando, Fla.: Academic Press, 1986).

8. Henderson, "Studies Hint at Link Between TV, Creativity."

9. Janet Sutter, "Alert Consumer," May 21, 1987. Further findings of the survey: 36 percent allowed their children to select shows, but retained veto power; 30 percent told their children what to watch.

10. Eleanor Randolph, "For Children's TV, Increased Violence," *Washington Post*, January 29, 1990, sec. A.

11. Dorothy Singer's research does suggest that context counts — that an adult who watches television with a child, interpreting and discussing what appears on the screen, can improve the child's creativity.

10. The Children of Sex, Drugs, and Rock 'n' Roll

1. "Survey Finds More Teen-age Males Sexually Active, More of Them Using Condoms," *San Diego Union*, March 31, 1989, sec. F.

2. Barbara Kantrowitz et al., "Kids and Contraceptives," *Newsweek*, February 16, 1987, 56–57.

3. Charles Ballard, who runs the Teen Fathers Program in Cleveland, says he asked a group of fifteen boys how many were fathers. Only two raised their hands. When he asked how many had babies, fourteen hands went up. "They just don't think like fathers," Ballard says. "They don't connect pregnancy with marriage or husbanding or fatherhood." At least 65 percent of his clients never really knew their own fathers. "No man has ever touched their lives except a policeman," he says, "and he was approaching them with a gun or a billyclub in his hand" ("Kids and Contraceptives," *Newsweek*, February 16, 1987, 60). There is a growing awareness, as a Children's Defense Fund report points out, that males have been overlooked in pregnancy prevention efforts. The hope is that, if such efforts were made to reach teenage boys, not only would they father fewer children, but attitudes about sexuality learned early on could be carried into their twenties and beyond. Boys express more desire for access to sexuality information and counseling than do girls, yet girls have a better understanding of sexuality than do boys. "A major reason teen-age pregnancy prevention programs are not more effective is because instructors, counselors and other service providers often seem not to understand that when it comes to sex, boys and girls are different," according to the report. "Even co-educational sexuality programs typically are packaged for adolescent women rather than males, despite research suggesting girls already know more about sex than boys do. Educational efforts therefore may unconsciously reflect and even reinforce society's double standard of sexual behavior, which holds that boys who impregnate unintentionally are, at least, unwise. Rather than assume that since boys can't get pregnant they don't care, more attention should be paid to adolescent males attitudes toward employment and other 'manhood' perceptions increasingly seen as affecting male sexuality. While this 'whole adolescent' approach may be more important for boys than girls, current services tend to interpret 'whole adolescent' as 'whole girl.' These programs should be packaged differently to reach young men." Social response to unintended pregnancy for boys is much less critical and stigmatiz-

ing than it is for girls, and "societal definitions of responsible parenthood link responsibility to financial support for boys and to nurturing for girls, making it difficult for young men who do not have jobs or employment prospects to see themselves as 'responsible' parents either now or in the future." Adolescents with the most limited life options, including recreation, education and employment, are the most likely to become teenage parents, in part because the traditional message to adolescents to "wait until you are better off" makes little sense, as the Children's Defense Fund report points out, to an increasing segment of the population with diminishing prospects for economic security. "Given the societal emphasis on the father as provider, it is not surprising to hear some experts argue that, in many ways, improving young males' life options should be the first line of defense against teen-age pregnancy."

What should be done to help boys and young males delay sexual activity and pregnancy? The Children's Defense Fund suggests the following key points:

• Increase their knowledge about sexual activity and its possible consequences, as well as their knowledge about how to avoid these consequences.
• Increase their ability to make mature decisions about sexual behavior by providing general counseling services, including forums for male-only, coed, and parent-child discussions.
• Foster use of male contraceptive methods.
• Change the link between sex and manhood by showing positive alternative images of what it means to be a man. This can be done by providing positive role models, starting public education campaigns, changing current images in the media, and fostering concerted discussions and group counseling about alternative views of manhood.
• Strengthen the link between pregnancy and the responsibilities of parenthood. Specifically, improve the current legal systems for paternity establishment and child-support enforcement. In addition, "there is a need to help all young men, but particularly disadvantaged young men, have positive life options and a real sense of a future. This is important because it gives them clear and compelling reasons to delay parenthood. It also allows them to believe that if they delay parenthood now they will be able to be better parents in the future."

School-based clinics will be an important part of any program redirected to include males. Such clinics make up a small fraction of all adolescent health clinics, but in contrast to the general lack of male participation in traditional health settings, they have demonstrated that young men will use health-care services in schools. Of the more than fifty thousand students enrolled in school-based clinics in 1987, nearly four in ten were male (Karen J. Pittman et al., *What About the Boys? Teenage Pregnancy Prevention Strategies,* publication of the Adolescent Pregnancy Prevention Clearinghouse [Washington, D.C.: Children's Defense Fund, 1988]).

4. Erica E. Goode, "Telling '80s Kids About Sex," *U.S. News and World Report,* November 16, 1987, 83.
5. "Schools to Get Special Help on AIDS Instruction, Koop Says," *San Diego*

Union, July 27, 1987, sec. A; Mark Arner, "Curriculum on AIDS Unveiled by County," *San Diego Tribune,* July 27, 1988, sec. B.

6. Robert P. Hey, "U.S. Army Data Show AIDS Virus Is a Growing Teen-age Problem," *Christian Science Monitor,* May 2, 1988; "Scientists Trying to Find Why Teens Do Such Risky Things," *San Diego Union,* November 26, 1987, sec. A. The army tests also revealed a wide range of exposure to the virus. In some nonurban areas of the Midwest, as few as one in twenty thousand teenagers may have the virus, but in some cities, including New York and Baltimore, the rate may be as high as one in two hundred teenagers (Hey, "U.S. Army Data"). Cavalier recklessness and a disbelief in human mortality, combined with hormone-related thrill seeking, peak in the years between ten and the mid-twenties. Studies show that, when asked to anticipate which risks become more or less dangerous over time, teenagers see pregnancy from unprotected intercourse and drug use as becoming *less* dangerous over time. And the more times an adolescent does something risky, the less sense of risk the adolescent has ("Scientists Trying to Find Why"). Patricia Hersch, who conducted a study of homeless children, reports: "I talked to a guy, 25 years old, who'd been hustling since he was 14. He has AIDS, but he's going through denial and still doesn't use condoms. I asked him about the johns. Don't they want condoms? He answered, 'If they wanted safe sex, do you think they would be out on 42nd Street? They want fantasies. AIDS has no impact on what's going on in the streets.' " One young prostitute, Hersch writes, punched holes in the ends of condoms so they would not explode. For these children, sex has become a form of revenge ("Coming of Age on City Streets," *Psychology Today,* January 1988, 28).

7. Hersch, "Coming of Age." Some studies have suggested that youngsters who take courses in sex education are more likely to use contraceptives — and more likely to have sex. Other studies contest this claim.

8. "Kids and Contraceptives," *Newsweek,* February 16, 1987, 60. School-based clinics do more than counsel teens about birth control and pregnancy. One such school clinic, in the South Bronx, is part of an after-school program called the Hub, which includes aerobics and karate and computer lessons, in addition to group discussions about sex and contraceptives.

9. In Miami's poor Liberty City neighborhood, parents, community activists, and politicians overwhelmingly supported — and worked for two years to create — a clinic in a local high school to combat sexually transmitted diseases, drug and alcohol abuse, and unwanted pregnancies. After receiving a $600,000 grant for the proposed clinic, Republican governor Bob Martinez rejected the grant and killed the clinic. Though the clinic had strong parental support, Martinez's press secretary was quoted as saying: "We are philosophically opposed to clinics that also do sex counseling. When government steps in to do these kinds of things, it encourages parents to abdicate their responsibility." In a similar response, when the San Diego Board of Education created a task force to study the establishment of a health-care service on school campuses, the Catholic bishop of San Diego, Leo T. Maher, stated in the church newsletter: "It would appear that the principal reason [for the task force] is to find an apparently legitimized means of providing pregnancy counseling, contraceptives and abortion counseling for teen-age stu-

dents. . . . Offering contraceptives or abortions to school children is inherently evil, for it tacitly encourages them to act promiscuously. It clearly suggests to them that they are 'safe' to behave as though they were married adults, without any awareness of the responsibilities of adulthood or marriage. . . . It is anti-educational, for it discourages teen-agers from learning self-discipline and encourages them to act in a sexually irresponsible, self-indulgent and sinful fashion." And, he charged, "A principal underlying motivation for establishing these health centers is racist, namely, to deprive ethnic minorities of their right to have children." After listening to so many children describe their sexual environment, I find such moral posturing foolhardy at best.

10. One organization that helps schools set up health clinics, the Washington-based Center for Population Options, publishes a booklet that lists ten reasons not to have sex, including "You don't want to," "You're not ready," "You want to wait until you're in love or married," and "You're not using birth control." In 1988, the California Senate passed by a wide margin legislation that would require school sex education programs to emphasize abstinence and encourage students to make decisions based on ethical considerations. The bill was inspired by a program at San Marcos High School which had resulted in a drop in the number of pregnant girls from 147 in 1984–85 to 20 in 1986–87. The program emphasizes the importance of correct decision making regarding a variety of subjects, including sex and drugs. Under the bill, sex education programs are required to teach students how to communicate on a nonsexual level, how to reject sexual advances and "negative peer pressure," and that abstinence from sexual intercourse is the only completely effective protection against unwanted pregnancy. In addition, the bill requires sex education programs to discuss the fallibility of all contraceptives, the failure rate of condoms in preventing AIDS and other sexually transmitted diseases, the legal implications for minors of having sexual intercourse, and the financial responsibility of having children in or out of wedlock. But even this presentation drew opposition from some quarters, including one state senator, who argued, "We are asking schools to take over for mom and pop" (Michael Smolens, "State Senate OKs Sex Education Bill Pushing Abstinence," *San Diego Union*, May 13, 1988, sec. A).

11. Jane E. Brody, "Personal Health," *New York Times*, May 4, 1989, sec. B.

12. "Kids Who Take Drugs Pull Wool over Parents' Eyes," *San Diego Tribune*, November 3, 1988, sec. D.

13. "Teacher Poll Finds Most Battle Student Drinking," *San Diego Tribune*, September 22, 1989, sec. A. In 1989, the annual survey of teacher opinion by the Metropolitan Life Insurance Company found that the number of teachers in grades seven through twelve concerned about student drinking in their schools had increased from 66 percent in 1985 to 81 percent in the latest survey. Each day in America, about 1,000 people will die because of tobacco, 350 will die because of alcohol, and 35 will die because of illegal drug use. The total cost to society of alcohol abuse, including lost productivity in the work place, is about $115 billion. In comparison, the total cost of illegal drug abuse is about $60 billion.

14. *Weekly Reader Survey on Drugs and Drinking* (Middletown, Conn.: Field

Publications, 1987). Some of the material on alcohol abuse was provided by Bob Reynolds, former deputy director for alcohol services for the San Diego County Health Department and now an advocate for reform of alcohol-related laws in California.

15. "Looking to Social Setting for Crack Clues," *San Diego Union*, August 24, 1989, sec. A.

16. George Varga, music critic for the *San Diego Union*, contributed this idea.

11. Healing Emotions

1. "Up to 14 Million U.S. Kids Have Mental Disorders, Survey Says," *San Diego Tribune*, June 7, 1989, sec. A.

2. "Infant Killings, Suicides in 10–14 Age Group Rising," *San Diego Tribune*, February 28, 1989, sec. A; "One Out of Three Teens Has Considered Suicide," *San Diego Tribune*, March 10, 1989, sec. A.

3. Suzanne Fields, "Brain Sitters for Teens: New Psychiatric Pitch," *Washington Times*, August 1, 1989, sec. F.

4. House Select Committee on Children, Youth and Families, *No Place to Call Home: Discarded Children in America*, 101st Cong., 1st sess., 1989.

5. While the number of California juvenile arrests dropped 38 percent between 1975 and 1985, the number of juveniles on probation rose by 66 percent, the number of adolescents in county detention centers, camps, and ranches grew by 24 percent, and the juvenile population in the California Youth Authority (the agency that runs the state's detention facilities for youth) grew by 66 percent. These findings are reported by Thomas David of the James Irvine Foundation and Marc Ventresca, a sociology and education graduate student at Stanford, in a report entitled "Children, Delinquency and the Legal System." The report, which was issued in February 1989, is part of a larger study, "Conditions of Children in California," a groundbreaking, comprehensive look at children in the state conducted by Policy Analysis for California Education (PACE). Michael Kirst, professor of education at Stanford and the co-director of PACE, oversaw the study, which included the work of twenty-six researchers around the state.

6. Carl M. Cannon, "High Schools Turn Peer Pressure Against Drugs," *San Diego Union*, December 17, 1989, sec. A.

7. Mona Charren, "What's Happening to Our Kids?" *San Diego Union*, May 13, 1990, sec. C; "Infant Killings, Suicides in 10–14 Age Group Rising," *San Diego Tribune*, February 28, 1989, sec. A.

12. The Nature of Childhood

1. At the Nature Company, a California chain of stores originally targeted at children but now focused on their parents, nature is both whimsical and antiseptic; see, for example, "The Nature Company Presents: Nature," on audio tape and compact disk. And for your video player, there are "mood tapes" such as "Tranquility," a forty-seven-minute musically scored video that the Nature Company catalogue describes as a "deeply calming, beautiful study in the shapes and colors of clouds, waves, unfolding blossoms and light."

2. Brian Sutton-Smith, "The Child at Play," *Psychology Today*, October 1985, 64–65.

Weaving

1. "Kids Face More Problems Today, U.S. Adults Say," *San Diego Union*, September 24, 1986, sec. C.

14. Reweaving the Family

1. Betty Friedan, *The Second Stage* (New York: Summit, 1981).

15. The Weaving of New Parent Networks

1. John Sommerville, *The Rise and Fall of Childhood* (Beverly Hills: Sage, 1982).
2. A theme common to much of the current advice is that neither authoritarian nor permissive parenting works particularly well, and a mid-course approach is probably best. But two other popular themes are not so wise. One promotes a kind of time-oriented, work-centered parenting in a system of applying "one-minute scoldings." The second trend is reminiscent of both the behavioralism of the twenties and the turn-of-the-century eugenics movement: the belief that parents can create perfect children through genetic tricks performed in the womb, or enrolling them in special classes, or clothing them in the right labels. Though few parents or experts have access to the tools of genetic manipulation, they do have the tools to attempt psychological or material perfection. One researcher in infant behavior I spoke with described the "epoxy theory" of early emotional development — the new emphasis on bonding in the delivery room or before. This idea isn't bad, she said, but its interpretation by vulnerable parents is sometimes carried to an extreme: if the baby hasn't bonded perfectly, it's not considered a perfect baby.
3. Welcome to the new eugenics, says Garland Allen, a biologist at Washington University in St. Louis, where some of the most important genetic science is being conducted. Allen, who specializes in the history and philosophy of biosciences, is highly critical of some of his fellow scientists. "Some genetic researchers are too willing to oversimplify their findings, and so are some of the reporters who cover them," he said. "Story after story is attributing to genetic causes such characteristics as criminality, antisocial behavior, and even the willingness to take risks. Ideas of fifty or sixty years ago — about how we're shaped — are resurfacing." In the United States and Western Europe between 1900 and 1940, people who subscribed to this quasi-scientific philosophy claimed that many social, personality, and mental traits were hereditary. (The word *eugenics* was coined by a cousin of Charles Darwin's from a Greek root word meaning "good birth.") Charles B. Davenport, an American geneticist and early advocate of eugenics, classified problems such as feeble-mindedness, unemployment, alcoholism, prostitution, and unruliness as products of specific genes. Davenport even suggested that such traits as nomadism and thalassophilia — love of the

sea — were inherited. He argued that love of the sea was determined by a sex-linked recessive gene that was passed by mothers to half of their sons. Eugenicists believed that society should encourage its healthy, productive, smart, and sober members to reproduce, and should discourage everyone else. Eventually, their theories helped produce the Immigration Restriction Act of 1924, which limited immigration from central European and Mediterranean countries, whose people were of "inferior biological stock." Eugenics also helped shape compulsory sterilization laws in more than thirty states. In the thirties, nearly ten thousand forced sterilizations were performed in California. And in Europe, the emphasis on better human breeding and racial purity helped plunge Europe into World War II.

Surely, one might ask, we're beyond such nonsense? Not according to Allen. Many adoption boards, he said, tend to place children in families with socioeconomic environments similar to those of the natural parents. Furthermore, few of the genetic predisposition studies delve into actual biological parameters. They simply trace histories, behavior, and statistics. The eugenics debate is likely to continue on several fronts. Researchers are looking at the possible link between specific genes and criminal behavior, for example, and genetic research is already producing some stunning medical breakthroughs as well as new eugenics issues: proposals for sperm banking by Nobel prize–winning intellectuals and for using embryonic biopsy to create "perfect" children.

4. Sanford M. Dornbusch et al., "Single Parents, Extended Households, and the Control of Adolescents," *Child Development* 56 (1985): 326–41.

5. At a San Fernando single-parents group, "members are discouraged from voicing 'pig messages' about themselves, like 'I don't deserve to have fun. I should only work.' A joke-store aerosol can of 'Guilt Spray,' which sprays a rose-colored mist, is kept on a wicker table at the center of the group circle. If someone gives a 'pig message,' another group member will reach for the bottle and give the offending member a dose. . . . Perhaps the most important [positive message] is that the single-parent family is not a 'broken home.' " The group offers more than group therapy: members trade babysitting services, haircuts, and motor oil changes, and many of them participate in the network for years. (Kathy Seal, "Single-Parent Connection Provides Lessons in Self-Esteem," *Los Angeles Times,* San Diego County edition, January 15, 1987, sec. 5.) Of course, single-parent families need more than oil changes and haircuts. College financial aid would be one way of decreasing isolation. Most universities treat single-parent students like everybody else. Changing that policy would raise questions about the equity of financial help, but current policy should be challenged. Given the logistical and financial difficulties of being a single parent, and considering the ongoing cost to society if single parents remain minimum-wage earners or on welfare, helping them with higher education would help pull single parents out of their isolation. This help could come in the form of extended and adequate day care, which most colleges and universities do not offer, or in the form of financial aid. The nation has supported such financial programs for decades for minority students. Why not bring impoverished single parents into the social and economic web?

6. Marilou Regan, "Extended Family at the Y Reaching Out to Community," *Philadelphia Inquirer,* April 19, 1987.

7. Anita Shreve, *Remaking Motherhood* (New York: Viking, 1987).
8. Mike Barnicle, "Beyond the Evening News," *Boston Globe,* May 28, 1989, Metro/Region section; Bob Sipchen, "Call of the Wild," *Los Angeles Times,* June 25, 1989, sec. 6.

16. Toward Fourth-Wave Child Care

1. Rena Cheskis-Gold, "Child Care: What Parents Want," *American Demographics,* February 1988, 46.
2. Fern Schumer Chapman and Susan Caminiti, "Who's Taking Care of the Children?" *Fortune,* February 16, 1987.
3. "Kinder-Care on Business Week Top 1000 List," *Exchange,* July 1987, 9. See also Dan Bellm, "The McChild-Care Empire," *Mother Jones,* April 1987, 32.
4. "Study Finds Low Wages in Child-Care Jobs," *San Diego Union,* January 2, 1988, sec. A.
5. "Competitive, Learning-Intensive Programs Harmful to Preschoolers, Expert Says," Stanford University News Service, November 9, 1984.
6. The National Association for the Education of Young Children, seeking to accredit programs that meet a long list of criteria, says there should be at least one adult for every four infants; for every five children twelve to twenty-four months old; for every six children two to three years old; and for every nine preschoolers (Karen Berney, "Recognizing Quality Child Care," *Nation's Business,* May 1988, 20).
7. Robert J. Trotter, "Project Day-Care," *Psychology Today,* December 1987, 36.
8. Elizabeth Janeway, "Child Care Inc.," *World Monitor,* October 1988, 68. Are we moving toward Sovietized day care? Hardly. Some Russians, for their part, are headed the other way. "Upwardly mobile Muscovites tend to look for alternatives to nurseries and kindergartens for their young children these days, and the perception seems to be widespread that children need more stimulation and individual attention than they get in institutionalized child care. Acceptance of day care for very young children is still far from the norm in rural areas of the Soviet Union, where the standard of care is thought to be low" (Sophie Quinn-Judge, "Kindergarten No. 1069," *Christian Science Monitor,* September 7, 1988).

17. The Family-Friendly Work Place

1. "Frustration on the Job: Workers Less Trusting of Management, Survey Claims," *San Diego Tribune,* June 1, 1989, sec. A; Randolph E. Schmid, "Guilt Wracks Dads, Too: Devotion to Family Duels with Career," *San Diego Union,* June 17, 1989, sec. C; Roger Thompson, "Caring for the Children," *Nation's Business,* May 1988, 18.
2. Kathleen Mackay, "Corporate Orphans," *California Business,* April 1987, 45.
3. Maria Padilla, "Statistics Attest That Top Business Leaders Just Don't Understand," *Orange County Register,* April 19, 1987, sec. C. The article reports on a study by Korn/Ferry International.
4. Mackay, "Corporate Orphans."

5. Patricia McCormack, "Workplace Day-Care Could Help Prevent Abuse of Children," *San Diego Union*, July 31, 1985, sec. D. Levi Strauss and Company found that its home-office employees, when surveyed, didn't want an on-site center: they didn't want to drive their children from their suburban homes to the company office in downtown San Francisco; instead, they wanted their children to be cared for in their communities, where they could make friends close to home.

6. David Bloom and Todd Steen, "Why Child Care Is Good for Business," *American Demographics*, August 1988, 22–27, 58–59.

7. Mark Satin, ed., "Support Parental Leave," *New Options*, September 30, 1987.

8. Julie Devaud and Jonathan Kronstadt, "Family Leave in U.S.: Its Time Has Come," *Graduate Woman*, March/April 1987; Ken Marshall, "Most Working Women Don't Have Maternity Leave" (graphic), *San Diego Union*, June 20, 1988, sec. C.

9. Edward F. Zigler, "For Many, Father's Day Is No Field Day," *New York Times*, June 14, 1986, sec. I.

10. "Congress Takes Up Parental Leave," *Child Care Action News*, 1988.

11. Laura Fraser, "Parental Leave Policies: A Global Review," *Parenting*, August 1987. Some other examples of leave policies:

• *Argentina:* Eight to twelve weeks' paid maternity leave before childbirth, and six weeks' paid leave afterward.
• *Austria:* Eight weeks' paid maternity leave both before and after delivery, and a one-year unpaid leave option.
• *Egypt:* Married women get twelve weeks' paid leave after childbirth, and up to two years' unpaid leave; single mothers get no leave.
• *France:* Mothers get eighteen weeks' paid leave (ten of which are compulsory); fathers receive three days' paid leave.
• *Italy:* Eight weeks' paid maternity leave before childbirth, and twelve weeks' paid leave after childbirth, both at 80 percent salary, with a one-year optional leave at 30 percent salary.

12. "Administration Opposes Extended Birth, Sick Leave Proposal," *San Diego Union*, October 30, 1987, sec. A. U.S. families are losing at least $607 million a year because of the lack of legislation guaranteeing workers unpaid leave to care for young children or sick parents, according to the Women's Legal Defense Fund. The report "Unnecessary Losses," for the Family and Medical Leave Act Coalition, was based on a survey of seven thousand families conducted by the Institute for Social Research at the University of Michigan in 1988. According to the analysis, family losses represent "the additional earnings lost by new mothers who return to work, but are unable to return to their former jobs because their employers don't have parental leave policies in place."

13. Kerry Elizabeth Knobelsdorff, "Congress Enters Debate over Time Off for Family Care," *Christian Science Monitor*, August 5, 1987.

14. Marilyn Gardner, "Family-Friendly Corporations: They Help Balance Demands of Home and Work," *Christian Science Monitor*, June 30, 1988.

15. Margaret Meiers, "Parental Leave and the Bottom Line," *Personnel Jour-*

nal, September 1988; Toni A. Campbell and David E. Campbell, "71% of Employers Say They Could Be Part of the Child Care Solution," *Personnel Journal*, April 1988. Among other recommendations to make parental leave a right rather than the privilege of a few:

- Extend state disability legislation (which now exists only in five states) to all states.
- Extend public programs to ensure health insurance coverage of physician and hospital costs for those whose employers do not provide insurance and who are not dependents under another plan.
- Extend disability benefits now provided by employers to include a "child" component, increasing the permitted leave to at least fourteen weeks.
- Supplement available disability benefits with a six-month parenting or child-care leave that would allow either parent to take an unpaid but job-protected leave to devote time to child rearing.
- Make part-time work and phased-in return more available to new parents who would like to make a greater investment in child rearing while continuing their investment in their jobs.
- Develop insurance "pools" to make it easier for employers to purchase disability insurance that they could not afford otherwise.

Rather than taking a monolithic approach, these proposals aim for choice and flexibility.

16. Marilyn Gardner, "Home with the Kids — Job Break Without Penalty," *Christian Science Monitor*, June 9, 1988.
17. David Blankenhorn, "Wanted: Bosses Who Care About Families," *Baltimore Sun*, September 1, 1986.
18. Felice N. Schwartz, "Management Women and the New Facts of Life," *Harvard Business Review*, January/February 1989.
19. Jim Schachter, "The Daddy Track," *Los Angeles Times Magazine*, October 1, 1989, 7–16.
20. Evan Thomas et al., "The Reluctant Father," *Newsweek*, December 19, 1988, 64; "Forget the Mommy Track: Make Room for Daddy," *Glamour*, June 1989, 156.
21. Arlie Hochschild and Anne Machung, *The Second Shift: Working Parents and the Revolution at Home* (New York: Viking, 1989).

18. Heading Home

1. How radically and rapidly our opinions on staying home have changed, and then changed again. Author Joel Garreau told me this tale: "A few years ago my wife, Adrienne, who considers herself a feminist, decided that she wanted me to make as much money as I could so she could stay home to raise our child. Now, suddenly, we've realized that having a parent staying home with kids gets you status points on the party circuit. Five years ago, if you told someone at a cocktail party that you were a housewife staying home, people would think, Isn't that unfortunate, and start looking over your shoulder for someone else to talk to. But now it gets you points because it's a sign of affluence, like owning a BMW! This is especially true

if the woman staying home is making money over the modem — like Adrienne, who writes a gardening column from home. Then you've really broken the code."

2. William R. Beer, *Househusbands* (South Hadley, Mass.: Bergin, 1983).
3. Carole Gould, "Mom Suits Up Daily for an Endless Marathon," *Wall Street Journal*, January 13, 1987.
4. Bureau of Labor Statistics, "Labor Force Participation Unchanged among Mothers with Young Children," United States Department of Labor News, September 7, 1988.

19. The Global Child

1. Leon F. Bouvier and Robert W. Gardner, "Immigration to the U.S.: The Unfinished Story" (report by the Population Reference Bureau, Washington, D.C., November 1986).
2. Social Research Services, "New Immigrants, New Minorities" (Trend Analysis Program) report by the American Council of Life Insurance, Washington, D.C., 1986), 4–5. The fertility of Hispanic women as a group, according to the report, is 60 percent higher than the U.S. average. And although Asians constitute less than 2 percent of the population, they're the fastest-growing ethnic group in America. Asian-Americans are increasing their number at a rate fourteen times greater than that of the general population, and their total number will triple by the year 2000. Such figures suggest a fascinating possibility. If a higher birthrate becomes a national priority (as it already has in West Germany, Sweden, and France), the United States may be forced to choose between encouraging native-born Americans to have more children or depending on young, prolific immigrants.
3. Joseph Thesken, "Minority Kids Shortchanged, Educator Says," *San Diego Union,* June 19, 1987, sec. A. In most states, the study found that while black students have managed to hold on to the early gains in desegregation, Hispanic students are becoming increasingly isolated. According to Fillmore, the University of California system will face serious problems in educating the growing number of minority children in California if reforms are not made among teachers at the elementary level (Thesken, "Minority Kids Shortchanged").
4. Thomas Wayr, *Hispanic U.S.A.: Breaking the Melting Pot* (New York: Harper & Row, 1988). Wayr predicts that by the year 2000 as many people in the United States will be speaking Spanish as they will English.
5. Some of the linguistic permutations of the multicultural generation are counterintuitive. According to a Stanford study, among Asians, Hispanics, foreign-born blacks, and foreign-born Anglos, "where a foreign language is spoken at home, the kids are doing better in school. This could mean that adolescents who become assimilated to American educational norms, speaking only one language, may work less hard in school" ("Speaking Two Languages at Home Associated with Better Grades in High School, Stanford Study Shows," Stanford University News Service, February 11, 1986).
6. Cultural and linguistic ignorance is currently tripping even the most muscular of corporations. For instance, a slight mispronunciation in Spanish commercials for the Chevrolet Nova changed "Nova" to "doesn't go." Coca-

Cola Company changed the name of its soft drink in China after discovering that the words mean "bite the wax tadpole" in Chinese. (Columnist Dave Barry thinks changing the name was crazy: " 'Bite the Wax Tadpole' is the best name I ever heard for a soft drink.") My personal favorite is Pepsi-Cola's slogan, "Come alive, you're in the Pepsi Generation," which in Thai translates: "Pepsi brings your ancestors back from the dead." ("And you know, it does," says Barry, "which is why so many people switch.") Still, we're learning.

7. The California State University system required all entering freshmen in 1988 to have taken two years of foreign language. But New York State will require all ninth-grade students to have taken two years of foreign language by 1995, and Louisiana has ordered compulsory foreign language instruction for at least thirty minutes a day beginning in the fourth grade. Yet California school officials continue budget cuts in the second-language programs. "California is riding high and doesn't see the need to change," said Jon Strolle, dean of languages and humanities at Monterey Institute of International Studies. "We live in a multicultural state, but instead of talking about how to preserve and expand the state's linguistic abilities, the voters want to make English the official language."

8. Ironically, criticism of the Spanish immersion program comes from some Mexican-American educators. They contend that money allocated for the program would be better spent on more traditional bilingual education, which focuses on students whose first language is Spanish. Richard Pacheco, director of elementary bilingual teacher training at San Diego State University, worries that some people will use the success of the immersion technique as an argument against bilingual education. The argument could go like this: if immersing English-speaking kids in Spanish works so well, why not just immerse Spanish-speaking kids in English (the pull-yourself-up-by-your-adverbs approach)? "If that happens, Spanish-speaking children will leave their native language behind," said Pacheco, who as a child was punished for speaking Spanish in his grade school. "If you take a child whose parents and grandparents are illiterate, then immerse them in English and in unfamiliar concepts, you'll have a 75 percent dropout rate." Pacheco places student teachers in bilingual programs. A few years ago, he stopped sending them to Longfellow. "We have trouble getting qualified teachers," admitted Adel Nadeau, the principal at Longfellow, but she refused to criticize Pacheco. "His position is a valid one. In fact, I have recommended that we open this program up to Spanish-speaking children as well."

20. Bringing the Generations Together

1. Andrew J. Cherlin and Frank F. Furstenberg, Jr., *The New American Grandparent: A Place in the Family, A Life Apart* (New York: Basic Books, 1986), 24–26. Only about 37 percent of all males and 42 percent of all females born in 1870 survived to age sixty-five. But for people born in 1930, 63 percent of males and 77 percent of females survived to 65 (pp. 27, 34, 36). Cherlin and Furstenberg base these statistics on studies by Peter Uhlenberg ("Demographic Change and the Problems of the Aged," in *Aging from Birth to Death*, ed. Matilda White Riley [Boulder, Colo.: West-

view, 1979], 153–66; "Death and the Family," *Journal of Family History* 5 [Fall 1980]: 313–20). Even as demographic changes make it more likely for children to gain positive adult contact from the elderly, other winds are blowing. Cherlin and Furstenberg write: "State legislators who worked for grandparents' rights undoubtedly were motivated by the increasing proportion of older voters. When Grandparents Day legislation reached the House floor in 1978, only eight representatives opposed it. Voting against grandparents is political suicide. The renewed attention to grandparents also comes at a time when cost-conscious policy makers are searching for ways to substitute family support for government assistance programs. In 1985, for example, the state of Wisconsin enacted a law that requires parents of teenaged sons and daughters to support any grandchildren until the unwed teenaged parents reach age eighteen."

2. Phillip Longman, *Born to Pay: The New Politics of Aging in America* (Boston: Houghton Mifflin, 1987).

3. Kenneth Eskey, "Generation Gap Is Shrinking; Prosperity Gap Widens — Study," *San Diego Tribune*, February 11, 1987, sec. C. Indeed, a survey conducted for the American Association of Retired Persons by the Daniel Yankelovich Group included group discussions with Americans of various ages and income levels in Atlanta, Kansas City, Los Angeles, and New York. Tension between the old and the young is mostly a myth, says the report. It found few signs of tension between generations, despite allegations by "some in the news media and governmental circles" that old-age programs such as Social Security are a burden on the young. In fact, says the report, young adults are concerned about the health problems of the elderly, the elderly are concerned about the financial problems of the young, and both are concerned about the large number of children — one in four — living in poverty. Only 13 percent of young adults interviewed believe older workers should be encouraged to retire early to make room for the young. And 77 percent favor expanding Medicare to help cover the cost of long-term health care that otherwise would be borne by the family. The report suggests that the most dangerous tension is not between the old and the young, but between the poor young and every other group — that poor, badly educated people tend to harbor resentments against any group, including the elderly, who seem to be "better off or better taken care of." "Anti-elderly values that do exist are tied to lower income and most significantly, educational status — not age."

Yet a telephone survey of 2,000 adults found that older Americans often help foster such attitudes by opposing more money for elementary schools, secondary schools, and higher education. "This may reflect concerns about property taxes, or criticism of current educational methods, or may be a function of their own relatively lower level of education," the report points out. "It is possible that as succeeding, better-educated generations age, support for education funds may improve."

4. "Reversing Roles: Taking Care of Our Parents," *Christian Science Monitor*, February 1987.

5. Robert E. Tomasson, "At Hospice, Preschoolers Reach Out to the Dying," *New York Times*, December 27, 1987. Ken Dychtwald of the Institute on Aging, Health and Work at Berkeley wants to create an "Elder Corps," groups of older people who will assist the aging. He noted that one retire-

ment community in Arizona has about 2,000 volunteers working at its hospital, and suggests that an Elder Corps would succeed because older Americans "want to work to put their experience and good will to public good." But why should such an Elder Corps focus only on the problems of the elderly? Why not unleash older volunteers to work on the problems of children?

6. In my own city of San Diego, one political consultant has advised the school board not to bother trying to court the senior vote for school boards — an attitude far too common among school officials and politicians.

21. Creating the Family-Friendly City

1. Sir Banister Fletcher, *A History of Architecture*, 19th ed. (London: Butterworth, 1987).
2. Neal Peirce, "Seattle Places 'Kids First,' " *San Dego Union*, 1980.
3. Jacquie Swaback, *Planning Sacramento: Views of Students and Parents* (Sacramento, Calif.: Urban Interdependence, 1986).
4. Clare Cooper Marcus and Wendy Sarkissian, *Housing as If People Mattered* (Berkeley: University of California Press, 1986), 109–110, 136. Sometimes new condo communities include pre-fab play areas but, as Marcus and Sarkissian point out, "providing play areas alone will not fulfill children's needs." Children need to explore and discover the whole site or neighborhood, to interact with adults in their daily activities. "We cannot buy off our children by merely providing playgrounds. Children are more deeply affected by the environment than any other age group" and can be physiologically and psychologically harmed by constant restrictions on their play. "Children learn from the environment what society values," write Marcus and Sarkissian, "for the environment itself is a potent communication medium. . . . If a housing environment implies that kids are low-priority users, they will decode the message as 'we do not count.' Vandalism could be looked on as a form of nonverbal protest against environments that are hostile to the young. Three principal factors render an environment suitable for child rearing: (1) direct access to private open space for easily supervised outdoor play by small children, (2) direct, safe access to an area for communal outdoor play for school-age and older children, and (3) reasonable auditory and visual privacy so that children's daytime noise and prying eyes or infants' nighttime cries do not disturb the neighbors. One study indicates that children in above-ground (walk-up) apartments went outside less than those in nearby row houses and therefore suffered higher rates of diseases caused by lack of vitamin D. Their mothers suffered higher rates of psychoneurotic complaints. . . . Another study, by a doctor with a practice in a Liverpool estate, reveals that mothers isolated in five- to eight-story deck-access blocks exhibit relatively high rates of psychiatric disturbance and that their children ten to suffer from respiratory ailments caused in part by lack of fresh air and sun. These mothers fear to let their children out to play on vandalized decks, stairways, and elevators. . . . Several studies show that lack of auditory privacy causes parents to restrict children's indoor play severely. This may limit outlets for aggression and creativity, lead to tension between children and irritable adults, and encourage sedentary, passive activities such as TV viewing."

The word *recreation* comes from the words that mean "to make over." We should make over our concepts of children's recreation. The first step could be to determine what recreational facilities kids are *not* using — and why. In a survey of New York City's playgrounds, the *New York Times* found playgrounds in Brooklyn and the Bronx which had been without swings so long that parents said they could not remember when there had been any (Jo Thomas, "On City's Playgrounds, Both Joy and Danger," *New York Times*, August 11, 1986, sec. A). But drugs aren't the only reason for the non-use of urban — and suburban — parks. In recent decades, park designers produced thousands of boring flat green deserts for adults and children. Recreation experts marvel at how children often avoid these parks, but play on raw hillsides and in streets next to the parks. In their overprogrammed lives, many children have little chance to experience risk, to test their environment. Part of the cause of such boring designs for playgrounds and parks is municipal fear of legal liability. In San Diego, playground injuries result in the highest number of lawsuits directed against the city park and recreation department. (The people involved aren't always kids. In one case, a two-hundred-pound woman sat in a tot swing and crashed to the ground. She sued the city for $15,000 and won.) "Most public playgrounds are absolutely lousy environments for everybody, able-bodied or not," according to Robin C. Moore, vice president of the International Association for the Child's Right to Play, in *Childhood's Domain: and Place in Child Development* (London and Dover, N.H.: Croom Helm, 1986). The average public playground, Moore says, "is blacktop from end to end with a couple of pieces of old equipment. With luck, the swings still have seats. But the place is dangerous, boring, and not used." Some commercial playground and park developers are creating "holistic parks" for the whole child, incorporating areas for creativity — playing games, drawing, using computers — and the means for exercise — tunnels made of cargo netting where kids climb and scramble and other well-padded (and supervised) exercise facilities.

5. Philip Langdon, "A Good Place to Live," *Atlantic Monthly*, March 1988, 39.
6. Ralph Keyes, "Cutting Childhood Short," *Family Weekly*, February 17, 1985, 4.
7. Linda Crismond, "The Future of Public Library Services," *Library Journal*, November 15, 1986, 42.
8. Ron Chepesiuk, "Reaching Out: The Greenville County Library's Latchkey Kids Program," *Library Journal*, March 1, 1987, 46.
9. Crismond, "The Future of Public Library Services."
10. Bill Lohmann, "New-Style Maternity Homes Offer Religion with Prenatal Care," United Press International News Service, December 17, 1987.

22. Schools and the Reweaving of Time

1. Carnegie Foundation for the Advancement of Teaching, *An Imperiled Generation: Saving Urban Schools* (Princeton, N.J.: Carnegie Foundation for the Advancement of Teaching, 1988).
2. John J. Goldman and Eileen V. Quigley, "N.Y. Schools: Islands of Excellence, Sea of Trouble," *Los Angeles Times*, May 14, 1988, sec. 1.
3. Robert Marquand, "Reform Movement Cries for Ideas — Substance Before Skills," *Christian Science Monitor*, August 28, 1987.

4. Edward B. Fiske, "Schools' Back-to-Basic Drive Producing Gains in Arithmetic," *New York Times,* June 8, 1988, sec. A.

5. The Scholastic Aptitude Test (SAT), the most commonly used measure, was never intended to be the ultimate barometer of educational quality. As Terry Hartle reports, "The results from the SAT are undeniably grim: between 1960 and 1980, the average scores on the verbal and math section fell by 95 points. Since 1980, however, the total scores have risen 16 points, placing them at 1975 levels. No one knows if this slight increase reflects better education of the test takers or simply more widespread use of coaching to help students prepare for the test" ("Education Reform: We Have a Lot to Learn," *Public Opinion,* September/October 1987, 48). Thomas C. Collins has pointed out that in 1985 Ohio spent two and a half times as much per pupil in real dollars as it did in 1960. Yet it is difficult to be sure improvement occurred. "There are no measures that any of us can have confidence in. We don't know how Ohio's pupils are achieving compared to the past. We don't know how Ohio's pupils are achieving compared to pupils in other states. And, we don't know how Ohio's pupils are achieving right now in each of the state's 614 school districts. Thus, there is no basis for analysis which could provide state policy makers with insight on which program factors are associated with high pupil achievement" ("Why Shouldn't Our Schools Compete?" *Vital Speeches of the Day,* December 15, 1986, 154).

6. Robert Marquand, "Students Head Back to Class — and to Better Schools," *Christian Science Monitor,* September 8, 1987.

7. "School Test Results Said Misleading," *San Diego Union,* November 28, 1987, sec. A; John Gaines, "School in El Cajon Is Accused of Cheating on Skills Test," *San Diego Union,* October 8, 1988, sec. B. The national survey, which was conducted by mail and telephone in August 1987 by a seven-hundred-member watchdog group in West Virginia called Friends for Education, found that "no state is below average at elementary level on any of the six major nationally normed, commercially available tests."

8. Carnegie Foundation, *An Imperiled Generation.*

9. Jim Bencivenga, "Summer Work-Study Program Gives At-Risk Teens a STEP Up," *Christian Science Monitor,* August 28, 1987, sec. B; "High School Drop Outs Back in Focus," *Issues Management Letter,* June 4, 1987, 3.

10. National Commission on Excellence in Education, *A Nation at Risk: The Imperative for Education Reform* (Washington, D.C.: National Commission on Excellence in Education, 1983).

11. In Boston in 1986, fifty-five students were expelled from public schools for carrying guns (Alexander Reid, "Pupil Alleged to Have Gun, 8th-Grader Arrested at School," *Boston Globe,* September 12, 1987, Metro/Region section). California's Little Hoover Commission reported at least seventy thousand cases of violent crimes on California campuses during the 1986–87 school year ("Violent Crime Plaguing Schools, State Panel Says," *San Diego Tribune,* December 22, 1988, sec. A.). The Chicago school board banned personal beepers in schools because so many students were using them to stay in touch with drug buyers, or to arrange for prostitution ("Beepers Banned in Schools," *New York Times,* December 16, 1988).

12. John J. Goldman and Eileen V. Quigley, "N.Y. Schools: Islands of Excellence, Sea of Trouble," *Los Angeles Times,* sec. 1. "At one school in Queens, when some teachers tried to get in before classes started, the custodian re-

taliated by locking doors and the electrical box so the lights could not be switched on." To raise money for music and library services not provided by the board of education, one Manhattan parent-teacher organization collected $161,000 using the school cafeteria for Saturday fund-raising benefits. But it had to pay $40,000 of the total to the custodians to keep the cafeteria open on weekends.

13. "Action Urged to Cut Teacher Dropout Rate," *San Diego Union,* March 17, 1987, sec. A.

14. Carnegie Foundation, *An Imperiled Generation.*

15. Ivan Illich, "The Ritual Power of Daily Humdrum," *Utne Reader,* November/December 1987, 75. This article incorporates material that originally appeared in Illich's *Deschooling Society* (New York: Harper & Row, 1970). In a classic critique of the role of schools in society, Illich writes: "The school system today performs the threefold function common to powerful churches throughout history. It is simultaneously the repository of society's myth, the institutionalization of that myth's contradictions, and the locus of the ritual that reproduces and veils the disparities between myth and reality. . . . Of course, school is not by any means the only modern institution whose primary purpose is shaping our vision of reality. The hidden curriculum of family life, health care, so-called professionalism, or the media play an important part in the institutional manipulation of man's world — vision, language. And demands. But school enslaves more profoundly and more systematically, since only school is credited with the principal function of forming critical judgment, and, paradoxically, tries to do so by making learning about oneself, about others, and about nature depend on a prepackaged process. School touches us so intimately that none of us can expect to be liberated from it by something else. As long as we are not aware of the ritual through which school shapes the progressive consumer — the economy's major resource — we cannot break the spell of this economy and shape a new one."

16. Carnegie Foundation, *An Imperiled Generation,* 43.

17. Robert Marquand, "Parents Want More Say-So in How Schools Operate," *Christian Science Monitor,* August 31, 1987.

18. Joyce L. Epstein, "When School and Family Partnerships Work: Implications for Changing the Role of Teachers" (paper presented at a meeting of the American Educational Research Association, Chicago, April 1985).

19. George J. McKenna III, "Parents and Business — a Partnership," *Los Angeles Times,* June 1, 1986, sec. 5.

20. "We Must Reorganize Schools," *U.S. News and World Report,* May 26, 1986, 57.

21. Robert Marquand, "Filling the School 'Values Vacuum,' " *Christian Science Monitor,* June 17, 1988; Carnegie Foundation, *An Imperiled Generation.*

22. Jim Bencivenga, "School Counselors Face Up to New Challenges," *Christian Science Monitor,* January 22, 1988.

23. Carnegie Foundation, *An Imperiled Generation.*

24. Nadine Brozan, "Mapping Future of Child Care," *New York Times,* October 5, 1987.

25. Robert J. Trotter, "Project Day-Care," *Psychology Today,* December 1987, 32–38.

BIBLIOGRAPHY

Beer, William R. *Househusbands*. South Hadley, Mass.: Bergin, 1983.
Bellah, Robert N., et al. *Habits of the Heart: Individualism and Commitment in American Life*. Berkeley: University of California Press, 1985.
Bettelheim, Bruno. *A Good Enough Parent*. New York: Knopf, 1987.
Carnegie Foundation for the Advancement of Teaching. *An Imperiled Generation: Saving Urban Schools*. Princeton, N.J.: Carnegie Foundation for the Advancement of Teaching, 1988.
Cherlin, Andrew J., and Frank F. Furstenberg, Jr. *The New American Grandparent: A Place in the Family, a Life Apart*. New York: Basic Books, 1986.
Children's Defense Fund. *A Vision for America's Future — An Agenda for the 1990s: A Children's Defense Budget*. Washington, D.C.: Children's Defense Fund, 1989.
Coles, Robert. *The Moral Life of Children*. Boston: Atlantic Monthly Press, 1986.
——. *The Political Life of Children*. Boston: Atlantic Monthly Press, 1986.
Cowan, Ruth Schwartz. *More Work for Mother*. New York: Basic Books, 1983.
Dillard, Annie. *An American Childhood*. New York: Harper and Row, 1987.
Elkind, David. *The Hurried Child: Growing Up Too Fast Too Soon*. Reading, Mass.: Addison-Wesley, 1981.
Erikson, Erik H. *The Life Cycle Completed*. New York: Norton, 1985.
Gelles, Richard J., and Murray A. Straus. *Intimate Violence*. New York: Simon and Schuster, 1988.
Greer, Germaine. *Sex and Destiny: The Politics of Human Fertility*. New York: Harper and Row, 1984.
Hewlett, Sylvia Ann. *A Lesser Life: The Myth of Women's Liberation in America*. New York: Warner Books, 1987.
Hughes, Dana, et al. *The Health of America's Children: Maternal and Child Health Data Book*. Washington, D.C.: Children's Defense Fund, 1987.
Johnson, Clifford M., Andrew M. Sum, and James D. Weill. *Vanishing Dreams: The Growing Economic Plight of America's Young Families*. Washington, D.C.: Children's Defense Fund, 1988.

Kozol, Jonathan. *Rachel and Her Children: Homeless Families in America.* New York: Crown, 1988.

Longman, Phillip. *Born to Pay: The New Politics of Aging in America.* Boston: Houghton Mifflin, 1987.

Marcus, Clare Cooper, and Wendy Sarkissian. *Housing as If People Mattered.* Berkeley: University of California Press, 1986.

Meyrowitz, Joshua. *No Sense of Place.* New York: Oxford University Press, 1985.

Morrison, Peter A. "Changing Family Structure: Who Cares for America's Dependents?" Report by the Rand Corporation, Santa Monica, Calif., December 1986.

Moskos, Charles C. *A Call to Civic Service: National Service for Country and Community.* New York: Free Press, 1988.

Moynihan, Daniel Patrick. *Family and Nation.* San Diego: Harcourt Brace Jovanovich, 1987.

National Commission on Excellence in Education. *A Nation at Risk: The Imperative for Educational Reform: A Report to the Nation and the Secretary of Education, United States Department of Education.* Washington, D.C.: National Commission on Excellence in Education, 1983.

Phillips, David P. "The Found Experiment: A New Technique for Assessing the Impact of Mass Media Violence on Real-World Aggressive Behavior," *Public Communication and Behavior* 1 (1986): 256–306.

Rutkowska, Julie C., and Charles Crook, eds. *Computers, Cognition and Development: Issues for Psychology and Education.* New York: Wiley, 1987.

Snyder, Tom, and Jane Palmer. *In Search of the Most Amazing Thing: Children, Education, and Computers.* Reading, Mass.: Addison-Wesley, 1986.

Sommerville, John. *The Rise and Fall of Childhood.* Beverly Hills: Sage, 1982.

Swaback, Jacquie. *Planning Sacramento: Views of Students and Parents.* Sacramento, Calif.: Urban Interdependencies, 1986.

U.S. Congress. House Select Committee on Children, Youth and Families. *No Place to Call Home: Discarded Children in America.* 101st Cong., 1st sess., 1989.

Wallerstein, Judith, and Sandra Blakeslee. *Second Chances: Men, Women, and Children a Decade After Divorce.* New York: Ticknor and Fields, 1989.

Welsh, Patrick. *Tales Out of School: A Teacher's Candid Account from the Front Lines of the American High School Today.* New York: Viking, 1986.

INDEX

Abortion, 60, 155, 157, 330
Action for Children's Television, 134
Adam, 29
African-Americans. *See* Minority groups
"After School Care of Children," 84
AIDS, 28, 136, 143, 149, 150, 151, 152,
    155, 156, 157, 175, 213, 394n.6
Aid to Families with Dependent Children
    (AFDC), 97
Alcohol and alcoholism, 82, 89, 92, 143,
    150, 159, 160, 168, 169, 199, 333,
    359
Aldrich, Robert, 312, 313, 314, 316, 324,
    332
Allen, Garland, 397n.3
Altheide, David, 378n.2
Alvarez, Doris, 360
American Childhood, An, 13
American Council of Life Insurance, 286,
    287, 293
American Demographics, 239
American Federation of Teachers, 335,
    357
American Ninja, 135
American School Counselor Association,
    358–59
Americans for Generational Equity (AGE),
    300
Anderson, Gary, 251, 252
Annenberg School for Communication, 31,
    138
Asians. *See* Minority groups
AT&T, 255, 270, 273
Atlantic Monthly, 319
Au pairs, 257
Autobiography of Malcolm X, The, 163

Baby and Child Care, 219
Backer Spielvogal Bates agency, 90
"Back to basics," 125, 335, 343, 351
Back to the Beach, 135
Baez, Joan, 164
Baldi Middle School (Philadelphia), 19, 53,
    77, 161, 162
Ballinger, Charles, 346, 347
Bankers Insurance Group, 258, 259, 261,
    275, 276, 359
Bank Street College of Education, 255
Barnicle, Mike, 233
Barr Films (Pasadena), 92–93
Batman, 115, 116
Beaman, Tom, 144
Bearss, Kathryn A., 250–51
Beatles, 162, 163
Bell High School (Watts, Calif.), 291
Bell Junior High School (San Diego), 72,
    168, 169
Bender, Sheila Mae, 338, 343, 349, 355
Bennett, William, 160, 339
Best, Joel, 29, 32
Better Baby Institute (Philadelphia), 219
Big City Project, 230
Bilingual education, 287, 288, 289, 339;
    language immersion, 288, 289, 290,
    403n.8
"Birth, School, Work, Death," 20
Blacks. *See* Minority groups
Blackwell, Dana, 324
Blaine Elementary School (Philadelphia),
    135–36, 137
Blakeslee, Sandra, 59
Bloody Valentine, 131
Bloom, Allan, 335

Bloom, David, 261
Boosman, Frank, 128–29
Born to Pay: The New Politics of Aging in America, 300
Boston Globe, 233
Boy Scouts, 329
Brandeis University, 149
Brazelton, Dr. T. Berry, 265
Bret Harte Intermediate School (Los Angeles), 358
Bridgewater, Kalen, 367
Bridgewater, Kevin, 368
Bridgewater, Margaret, 367, 368, 369
Bridgewater, Max, 367
"Bumper," 308, 309, 310
Burger King, 386n.8
Bush, President George, 372
Bush Center in Child Development and Social Policy, 245, 265, 268
Business Week, 128, 244
Busing, 345, 346, 354

Cable television. *See* Television viewing
California Achievement Test, 351
California Assessment Program, 336
California Business, 256
California Department of Education, 35
California State Library, 326
Camper, Ken, 305, 306
Carleton, Pam, 290
Carnegie Foundation for the Advancement of Teaching, 333, 334–35, 337, 344, 352, 353, 358
Carrington, Loye, 305
Cartwright, Madeline, 135, 136, 194–97, 200–206, 209, 336, 350
Cartwright, Tyrone, 197
Catalyst (company), 267
Center for Child Protection (San Diego), 363
Center for Labor Market Studies, Northeastern University, 48
Center for Research on the Influence of Television on Children, 141
Centers for Disease Control, 166
Chadwick, Dr. David, 363
Charlotte's Web, 135
Charren, Peggy, 134, 142
Cherlin, Andrew J., 192, 297, 298
Chesterton Elementary School (San Diego), 130–33
Child care. *See* Day care
Child Care Action Committee, 94, 257
"Child Care: An Idea Whose Time Has Come," 244
Child Education Center (Irvine, Calif.), 243
Childhood, 3; dangers of, 25, 26; defined, 17; holding on to, 113–16; institutionalization of, 96; isolation of, 73, 74, 371; mythology of, 12; reshaping the future of, 370–74. *See also* Children
Child labor laws, 91
Childlessness, 58
Children: abuse of, 32, 38, 82, 170, 189, 219, 253, 363; and "adopted grandparents," 309; and AIDS, 156; bilingual, 339; and books, 139; choices for, 13, 14; compassion of, 70–82, 165; and computers, 117–29; and creativity, 140–41, 186; and day care, 96, 102–108; and depression, 50, 59, 165; and divorce, 60; drug and alcohol abuse among, 158, 395n.13; emotional health of, 70, 173, 337; fears of, 27, 28, 71, 132, 138; gifted, 118; and grandparents, 296–310; heroes of, 146, 230–37; and ideas for cities, 314–16; income of, 92; isolation of, 123, 125, 126, 127, 128, 160, 163, 180, 311, 340, 361, 371; latchkey, 83–95; loss of freedom by, 33–34; and malls, 323–25, 326; memories of, 11–13, 43, 70, 77; and mental illness, 166, 167; missing and runaway, 2, 29–30, 39, 90, 377nn.1; multicultural influences on, 286–95; murder of, 30; and nature, 173–78; on parenting, 106, 107, 108; openness of, 77–82, 165; pressures on, 19, 111, 150; and programmed time, 109, 110–11; and public schools, 333–69; and quality time, 17–24; and self-care, 86–88; self-esteem of, 39; self-reliance and autonomy of, 37, 83–95, 110, 371; and stay-at-home parents, 277, 278; and suicide, 166, 167, 169, 171; and teenage pregnancy, 149, 152–55, 157, 330, 341, 392n.3; television viewing by, 130–47; and violence, 130, 131, 132; working, 91–92, 96, 386n.8, 387n.9
Children's Defense Fund, 48, 50
Children's Hospital (Los Angeles), 156
Child support payments, 49–50, 226
China, 288, 314
Christiansen, Niels, 286–87
Churches, 6, 110, 113, 157, 236, 237, 329, 330
Cities: exodus from, 312; and family, 311–32
Clapton, Eric, 162
Clark, Joe, 350
Clark, Kenneth B., 227
Clark, Laura Beth, 32, 32–33, 176, 177
Clark, Steve, 32
Closing of the American Mind, The, 335
Cobb, Nancy, 282
Cody-Fuller, Carolyn, 327, 328
Coles, Robert, 67

Columbia Point Elementary School (Landover, Md.), 351
Columbia University, 141
Comer, James, 6, 350, 351, 362
Communities, 7, 36; and schools, 348–51
Community Y (Lansdowne, Pa.), 226, 227
Companies: on-site day care at, 255–65, 269; and parental leave, 265–69; and public schools, 258–61
CompuServe, 283, 284
Computers, 135, 140, 148; bulletin board systems, 117–19, 228, 229, 232, 283, 284; and children, 179; games, 122, 123, 126; and homework, 119; in schools, 124–27, 388n.5, 389n.8; word processors, 128
Condry, John, 133
Congressional Budget Office study, 336
"Consumer culture," 42
Contraception, 150–51, 152, 156, 157, 330, 392n.3, 394n.6
Cornell University, 133
Corning Glass Works, 270, 274
Coronado Touring Company, 282
Corporate Child Development Fund, 269
Cosby, Bill, 233
"Cosby Show," 135, 154
Cottle, Tom, 79
Counseling, 166, 358–59
Cowan, Don, 251–52
Cowan, Ruth Schwartz, 16
Crawford High School (San Diego), 72, 73, 74, 86, 105
Creativity, 139, 140, 141, 147, 186
Crime and violence, 26, 30–31, 35, 37, 55, 130, 131, 132, 170, 235; and drugs, 236; gang, 359; and nature, 183; neighborhood, 362; on TV, 4, 133, 134, 136, 137, 138, 390nn.3, 4; and schools, 349, 350; and teachers, 338, 339
Crismond, Linda, 326, 328
Cross, Kathy, 250
Cultural literacy, 290, 335
Curriculum: open-ended, 335; reform, 333, 335, 336, 338, 348

Dade County school district (Fla.), 258, 259, 306
Daniel Yankelovich Group, 62, 404n.3
Davis, Deborah, 240, 241
Davis, Diane, 364, 365, 366, 367, 369
Davis, Robert S., 319, 320
Dawson, Deborah, 282
Day care, 5, 21, 23, 43, 49, 56, 84, 96–108, 155, 211, 331, 332, 333, 334; afterschool, 247; children's feelings about, 102–8; cooperative, 248; costs of, 97,

207, 241, 252; dissatisfaction with, 255; employer costs of, 256; employer-sponsored, 239, 240, 241, 244, 250, 251, 252, 253; family centers, 246, 246–49; funding of, 245–46, 247; 278, 279; by government, 61, 98, 108; government regulations for, 256, 257; in-home, 207, 239–53, 361; licensing of, 249; nannies, 240–43; on-site, 112, 232, 244, 255–65, 269; parental leave, 246, 247, 249, 250; providers of, 98, 99, 102, 273, 276, 302; quality of, 98, 245, 246; by schools, 361, 362; and single parents, 215–16; and year-round schools, 347; YMCA-sponsored, 227
Denmark, 318
DePinto, Rose, 294
Depression, economic, 47–54, 59. See also Economic factors
Desegregation, 287, 402n.3
Deukmejian, George, 369
Devin, Justin, 25
Dewey Elementary School (San Diego), 21, 49, 118–20; child-care center, 216; and single parents, 215–16; and video games, 179
Dillard, Annie, 13
Dillman, Richard, 308, 309, 310
Disney Channel, 134, 135
Divorce, 43, 44, 46, 47, 59, 60, 61, 62, 72, 73, 75, 78, 82, 114, 192; role of grandparents after, 297
Dodge, Michelle, 37–38, 282
Donahue, Phil, 219
"Donna Reed Show," 45
Donovan, Christina, 280, 281, 282
"Door-key children." See Latchkey children
Dornbusch, Sanford M., 90, 337, 340, 357
"Double Dare," 143, 144, 145
Drescher, Jon, 73, 125, 140
Drugs, 14, 26, 29, 31, 34, 35, 37, 71, 89, 90, 92, 148, 150, 156, 158–61, 165, 168, 169, 170, 196, 197, 198, 199, 200, 206, 336, 350, 359; among the poor, 158; dealers, 233; war on, 235
Du Pont Corporation, 273, 274
Duschene, Kathleen, 20–21
Dutton, Leslie, 290
Dychtwald, Ken, 383n.17
Dyer, Lucinda, 276

Early Childhood Resource and Information Center (New York), 227
East Harlem Performing Arts School, 73, 125, 140, 339
Eastside High School (Paterson, N.J.), 350

Eaton, Paul, 304
Economic factors, 21–22, 31, 35, 51, 55, 213; of aged, 301, 302; anxieties about money, 72; child support, 226; child tax exemptions, 279; college costs, 50, 51, 52, 381n.12; counseling, 359; and day care, 97, 207, 244, 250, 256, 269, 270, 271; of family-friendly cities, 331–32; health costs, 56; income, 21, 23, 48, 49, 53, 57–58, 61, 84, 92, 97; income for women, 254; for middle class, 47, 48; nursing home costs, 302; parental and maternal leave, 266, 267, 268; poverty, 17, 48, 57, 75; retirement income, 287, 384n.18; in single-parent families, 224; tax credits, 355; and teenage pregnancy, 154–55
Educational Coalition (Boston), 337
Edwards, Dr. J. David, 288
Edwards, Paul, 283
Edwards, Sarah, 283, 284
Ehrlich, Max, 77
Elder care, 249, 250, 252, 253, 261, 287; centers, 361; by children, 293, 301–3
England: Return to Work plan, 268
Epstein, Joyce L., 352–53
Erikson, Erik, 6, 7
Espenshade, Thomas, 192
Ethnic groups. See Minority groups
Eugenics, 397n.3
Even, William, 267

Falwell, Jerry, 62, 330
Families: activities of, 41; centers for, 322, 323, 331; counseling for, 363, 364; defining, 5, 43, 44; and exodus from cities, 312; extended, 6, 350; fears of, 36, 42; liberation of, 4, 5, 192, 193, 334; nuclear, 44, 47; and quality time, 17–24; single-parent, 89, 398n.5; stepfamilies, 45, 46; stresses on, 43; and time, 14, 15, 36, 39, 96; values of, 7, 13, 255, 292–95
Family and Medical Leave Act, 266
"Family Double Dare," 144
Family Protection, 29–30
Family Resource Coalition, 226
Family Television Research and Consultation Center, 140
"Family Ties" Proposal, 249–53, 354
Farson, Richard, 35, 219, 220
"Father Knows Best," 43
Fathers: balancing work and family, 255, 273, 274; and development of infants, 265; househusbands, 278, 279. See also Parenting; Parents
Femiano, Robert, 339, 342
Feminine Mystique, The, 211

Feminism, 23, 60, 62, 193, 211, 231, 275, 277, 278, 330; and poverty, 272
Field Guide to Western Reptiles and Amphibians, A, 174
Fillmore, Lily Wong, 287
Finklehor, David, 30, 39
First Three Years of Life, The, 365
Fisher, Helen, 59
Fitzsimons, Beth, 25, 148, 155, 161, 206–9, 212, 213, 214, 222, 223, 224
Fitzsimons, Devin, 25, 206, 207
Fitzsimons, Elizabeth ("Biz"), 25, 149, 206, 208
Fitzsimons, Justin, 25, 148–49, 161, 206, 208, 209, 212
Fitzsimons, Tom, 25, 26, 98, 148, 155, 161, 206–9, 213, 214, 222, 223
Fortune, 242, 300
Foster, Ezola, 290, 291, 292
France, day care in, 246
Frank, Judy, 123
Franklin High School (Seattle), 34, 46, 72, 75, 292, 293, 340
Fremont High School (Los Angeles), 358
Friday the Thirteenth, 31, 131, 134
Friedan, Betty, 211
Friedman, Leah, 301
Frischman, Ramona, 307, 310
Fritz, Bobby Jo, 30
Fuchs, Lawrence H., 293
Furstenberg, Frank F., Jr., 297, 298

Gallup, George, 15, 236
"Garbage Pail Kids," 142
Gardner, Marilyn, 268
Garfield High School (San Diego), 152
Garfield Pregnant Minors Program, 154
Garreau, Joel, 401n.1
Gebner, George, 31
Generational factors, 6, 55–59, 298–310; multicultural, 5, 286–95
George Washington Preparatory High School (Los Angeles), 354
Germany, parental leave in, 266
Gerontology Education and Training Center, 301
Girardi, Pat, 227
Girl Scouts, 329
Golden Child, The, 135
Goldman, Charlene, 147
Gomez, Amanda, 249
Goodkin, Sanford, 324, 325
Goodman, Paul, 64
"Grandpa and Grandma's Place," 302
Grandparents, 23, 57, 75, 76, 77, 98, 133, 183, 199; and child care, 247, 248; "fos-

ter," 302, 309; and grandchildren, 296–310; and single-parent families, 224; and teenage pregnancy, 155; and war on drugs, 235
Gray Panthers, 307
Greeks. *See* Minority groups
Green, Dr. Kenneth C., 382n.12
Greenberger, Ellen, 91–92
Greenville County Library (S.C.), 327, 328
Grossmont Community College (San Diego), 99–100
Guggenheimer, Ellen, 94
Guns, 26, 27, 28, 36. *See also* Crime and violence
Gutierrez, Manola, 260, 261

Haithman, Diane, 391n.4
Halloween sadist, 28, 29, 31, 32
Hamilton Middle School (Seattle), 51, 95
Hardy, Nancy, 358, 359
Harris, Louis, 15, 84, 149, 158
Harris, Marlys, 382n.12
Harrison, Bennett, 49
Hartman, Bob, 107
Harvard Business Review, 271, 272
Harvard Medical School, 265
HBO channel, 135, 136
Head Start, 245, 306, 362, 365
Hecht-Nielson, Robert, 128
Hendrix, Jimi, 162
Heroes, 230–37, 372
"Heroes of Young America" survey, 233
Hersch, Patricia, 394n.6
Hewlett-Packard, 270, 271, 332
Higher Education Research Institute (UCLA), 382n.12
Hill, Dona, 288, 289, 290
Hill, Joanne, 216
Hilleary, Sherry, 112
Hilleary, Tom, 55, 112, 373, 374
Hines, Chezar, 288, 289, 290
Hirsch, E. D., 335
Hispanics. *See* Minority groups
History of Architecture, A, 311
Hochschild, Arlie, 274
Hocker Grove Middle School (Shawnee Mission, Kans.), 20, 103–104, 106, 345
Holland, 318
"Home Alone: You're in Charge," 93
Home schooling, 217, 218, 222, 232
Homicides. *See* Crime and violence
Hoover, Linda, 40
Hoover High School (San Diego), 360
Hoover Institution, 16
Horsey, David, 272–73
Housing, 318, 319

Housing as If People Mattered, 318, 405n.4
How-to-parent books, 4, 218, 219, 220, 225, 232
Hubbard, Mary, 134
Hughes, Bev, 177
Hughes, Jack, 32, 80, 112, 177
Hughes Tool, 360
Hunter, Robert, 355, 356
"Hurried Child, The," 111

Illich, Ivan, 408n.15
Illiteracy, 341, 342
Imperiled Generation, An, 334–35, 358
Income. *See* Economic factors
Infant Care, 218
In Search of the Most Amazing Thing, 126
International Nanny Conference, 240, 241
"In the News," 142
"Introduction to the Latchkey Program," 328
Iosue, Robert, 382–83n.12
Italians. *See* Minority groups
It's Alive, 58

Jabocowski, Gerald, 294
Jackson, Jesse, 233, 234
Jackson, Michael, 169
James, Fern, 236, 237
James G. Blaine Public School (Philadelphia), 194–96
Janeway, Elizabeth, 399n.8
Japan, 266, 288, 314, 348, 372
Jerabek Elementary School (San Diego), 45, 102–3, 110, 134, 135
J. K. Communications, 90
Johns Hopkins University, 166, 170, 192
Johnson & Johnson, 267, 271
Joint National Committee for Languages, 288
Jordan, Odaris, 292
Jordan High School (Watts, Calif.), 291, 292

Kaagan, Lawrence, 62
Kafka, Ben, 120, 121
Kafka, Simon, 121
Kafka, Tina, 11–12, 113, 121
Kalter, Joanmarie, 134
Kansas Children's Service League (Wichita), 96, 107, 329
Kasarda, John D., 386n.8
Katherine Brennan Elementary School (New Haven), 351
Katz, Lillian, 245
Kay, Alan, 127
Keen, Sam, 264
Keiser, Roberta, 259

Kenwood Elementary School (Miami), 72, 88, 111, 180
Keyes, David, 173, 279, 280
Keyes, Muriel, 279, 280
Keyes, Ralph, 99, 173, 174, 279, 280
Keyes, Scott, 279, 280
KidsPlace, 313–16, 318, 324, 332
Kinder-Care Learning Centers, 244
Kinderfeindlichkeit, 58
King, Joan, 90
King, Martin Luther, 198, 234, 291
King's Ranch (Ala.), 330
Kirsten, Judy, 154, 157
Kiwanis Club, 171, 172
Kleber, Dr. Herbert, 160
Klinghoffer, Mike, 144–45
Koop, C. Everett, 156, 157–58
Koreans. *See* Minority groups
Kwiat, Dorothy, 237
Kyes, Kris, 284–85

Lamm, Richard D., 381n.10
Lanez, Jim, 166–67
Langdon, Philip, 319, 321
Language-immersion programs, 288, 289, 290, 403n.8. *See also* Bilingual education
La Petite Academy (Kansas City), 244
Latchkey children, 3, 83–95, 327, 328, 347, 385nn.2, 3
Laybourne, Gerry, 143
"Leave It to Beaver," 9, 43, 46, 47, 62, 78, 318
Leon, Julia, 259–60
Levin, Henry M., 125
Levine, James, 255
Levi Strauss and Company, 269, 270
Lewis, Katharine, 212
Lewis, Richard, 272
Lewis, Shari, 145
Liberation of families, 4, 5, 370–74
Libraries, 85–86, 93, 139, 146, 222, 227, 304, 305, 318, 331; as family hubs, 325–28
Library Journal, 328
Lipman, Myra, 227
Lolita, 58
Lombard North Central (Company), 268
Longman, Phillip, 300
Los Angeles Times, 233, 354
Louv, Jason, 109
Louv, Kathy, 373
Lovelace, Valeria, 44, 146, 147

MacCartee, Gerry, 282
McClure, Jim, 50

McDonnell-Douglas Corp., 360
McDonough 35 High School (New Orleans), 358
Machung, Anne, 274
McKenna, George J., III, 354, 355
Magnet schools, 288, 317, 318
Malcolm X, 234
Malls, 323–25, 326, 331
Malueg, Sally, 288
"Management Women and the New Facts of Life," 271
Marcus, Clare Cooper, 318, 405n.4
Martin, Jeanne, 256–57
Martinez, Bob, 394n.9
Maude Carpenter Children's Home (Wichita), 166
Mechanic Arts High School (St. Paul), 156–57
Medicare, 300, 404n.3
Meeks, Brock, 217
Meeks, Sandy, 217
Mental health, 358–59
Mental illness, 82, 170, 171, 213
"Mentor houses," 204
Merck and Company, 267, 269, 270, 274
Metropolitan Life Foundation, 158
Metropolitan Reading Test, 346
Miami Agricultural School, 308
Miami University of Ohio, 267
Middle class, 13, 14, 47, 48, 53, 64, 379n.7
Millison, Martin, 324
Minority groups, 17, 34, 36, 44, 130, 134, 137, 153, 230, 234, 339; black schools, 350; and day care, 257; and illegitimacy rates, 379n.5; multicultural and multiracial influences, 286–87; racism, 70, 71; teachers, 341; and teenage pregnancy, 155; tutoring of, 360
Missouri Department of Education, 365
"Mister Rogers' Neighborhood," 140, 141, 316
Mitchell, Don, 356
Mitterrand, François, 321
Modernists, 61, 62
Mommy Track, 271, 272, 273, 274, 278
Mondot, Juliette, 121–22
Mondot, Misha, 121, 122
More Work for Mother, 16
Morley, Fred, 382n.12
Morrison, Jim, 162, 163
Morrison, Peter, 15, 16, 44
Mothers: and Mommy Track, 278; stay-at-home, 275–85. *See also* Parenting; Parents
Mothers at Home More, 38, 262
Mothers First, 263

Movies, 31, 32, 36, 53, 58, 134, 278, 378n.3; on TV, 135; and sex, 136; and violence, 131, 132
Mr. Mom, 278
MTV channel, 135
Murphy, Eddie, 233
Music, 19, 161, 162; and computers, 122; rock 'n' roll, 163

Nagely, Richard, 34, 78, 293
Nannies, 101, 107, 240–43, 250; costs, 241; Nanny Company, 242
Nasar, Sylvia, 381n.10
National Academy of Sciences' Institute of Medicine, 165
National Association for Year-Round Education, 346
National Association of Working Women, 265
National Council on Alcoholism and Drug Dependence, 160
"National Geographic Explorer," 183
National High School Senior Drug Abuse Survey, 158
National Incidents Study of Missing Children, 30
National Survey of Instructional Uses of School Computers, 124–25
Nation at Risk, A, 338
Nature, 173–78
Neighborhoods, 4, 6, 12, 14, 36; magnet, 331; safety of, 405n.4; schools, 345; and shaping of children, 317; and violence, 26, 362
Nelson, Eric, 243, 244
Networking, 215–37, 238; for single parents, 224–26
New Options, 264
Nickelodeon, 134, 135, 143
Nickelodeon/Yankelovich Youth Monitor study, 18
Nightmare on Elm Street, 31, 32, 36, 131, 378n.3
1990s Father: Balancing Work and Family Concerns, 255
Nodding, Nel, 357
No One Here Gets Out Alive, 163
Norris, Bob, 291

O'Connor, Mayor Maureen, 236
Office of Child Development, 245
Olberson, Mary, 149–50, 168
O'Neil, Harold F., 123
O'Neill, Mary Grassa, 346
Oregon State University, 288, 357
Osuna, Magdalena, 235

Otero, Trish, 259, 260
Overland Park (Kans.), 28, 32, 80, 81, 112, 176, 177, 178, 210
Over the Top, 135

Pacheco, Laraine, 293, 294
Page, Jimmy, 162
Parenting, 42, 51; abandonment of, 37; bonding, 397n.2; books on, 4, 218, 219, 220, 225, 232; centers for, 226; classes in, 215, 216, 227, 228, 362, 363, 364, 367; and day care, 100, 101; devaluing of, 109; "good" and "bad," 223; school programs for, 33; by teenagers, 155; time restraints in, 220–24; USENET, 228, 229. *See also* Parents
Parents: abuse of children by, 219; at-home, 263, 275–85; and buddy system, 227; and care of elderly parents, 293, 301–303; classes, for, 365–67; and computers, 121, 127; counseling for, 363, 364; and day care, 98–99, 104; divorced, 61, 72, 73, 75, 114; emotional health of, 70; fears of, 3, 4, 14, 25, 27, 28, 31; home schooling by, 217, 218, 222; housing services for, 318, 319; isolation of, 216, 256, 311, 340, 370; memories of, 57, 58, 77, 187, 188; networking by, 215–37, 238; and openness, 80–82; parental leave for, 12, 13, 232, 246, 247, 249, 250, 261, 265–69, 400nn.11, 12, 15; and programmed time, 111–13; and public schools, 333–69; and quality time, 17–24, 101; and responsibility, 192; as school volunteers, 351–56, 364, 372; and self-care by children, 88–89; and sex issues, 150, 155, 156; single, 44, 49, 89, 215–16, 225, 237, 398n.5; stepparents, 44, 114; support groups for, 262; and television viewing, 131, 141–47; values of, 80; and war on drugs, 235, 236; and work, 19, 20, 21, 87, 232, 255; work-at-home, 280–85
Parents as Teachers, 364, 365, 366, 369
Parents League, 227
Parents' League of New York, 111
Parents magazine, 142
Parent-Teacher Association (PTA), 229, 230, 231, 232, 307, 341
Parent-Teacher Organization (PTO), 204, 230
Park Center (Bethesda, Md.), 123
Parrish, Michael, 311
Partners in Education (Miami), 382n.12
Pavlov, Ivan, 218
Payzant, Tom, 13, 14
Peer programs, 168, 169

Permissiveness, 62
Personnel Journal, 267
Pets, 12, 26
Pham, Kim, 247, 248
Pharmaceuticals, 160
Philadelphia Inquirer, 201
Phillips, David, 139, 378n.3
Phillips, J. Douglas, 267
Phoenix, 322, 323
Pittsburgh Priority Management Company, 15
Planned Parenthood, 149
Please Touch Museum, 179
Point Loma High School (San Diego), 162
Political Life of Children, The, 67
Population factors, 15, 16
Pornography, 62, 136
Potter, Maria, 289
Poverty, 17, 48, 75, 206, 339, 343; feminization of, 272; in north Philadelphia, 194–205; and welfare, 196. *See also* Economic factors
Pregnancy, teenage, 149, 152–55, 341
Prenatal University (Fremont, Calif.), 219
"Pressured Parent, The," 111
Principle of the Alphabet Learning System (PALS), 388n.5
Project Promise (Boston), 346
Project Self-Sufficiency, 225
Psychology Today, 264
Psychotherapists for Social Responsibility, 264

Racial factors. *See* Minority groups
Rand Corporation, 340, 356, 357; Population Research Center, 15, 16, 44
Reading with a Friend, 304
Reagan, Ronald, 142
Reisman, Barbara, 257–58
Remaking Motherhood, 231
Retail Advertising Conference, 90
Rhodes, Elizabeth, 85, 385–86n.3
Ricardo-Campbell, Rita, 16, 384n.18
"Ritual Power of Daily Humdrum," 408n.15
Riverview Plaza (Sacramento), 302
Roberts, Monica, 140, 303, 304, 305
Robertson, Pat, 60, 219
Rocky IV, 135
Rodgers, Fran, 255, 272
Roommates for Today's Family, 224
Rose, Craig D., 381n.10
Rouse, James, 325
Rubenfeld, Frank, 264

Safety issues, 37
Salaries. *See* Economic factors

San Diego City Schools Psychologists Association, 170
San Diego County Department of Social Services, 249
San Diego High School, 18, 151, 158
San Diego Organizing Project (SDOP), 235, 236
San Diego Unified School District, 13, 156, 171
San Diego Union, 250, 317
San Jose State University, 301
Sarkissian, Wendy, 318, 405n.4
Scanlon, Matt, 291
Schlafly, Phyllis, 60
Schmitt, Paul, 251, 252
School Programs Involving City Elderly (SPICE), 305, 306
Schools, 6, 7, 64; and academic achievement, 347; and adult needs, 360; and community, 348–51; counseling in, 358–59; curriculum reform by, 333, 335, 336, 338; and day care, 361, 362; intergenerational programs in, 361; longer hours in, 346, 347, 348, 352, 372; magnet, 317, 318; neighborhood, 357, 359; parental involvement in, 351–56; private, 64, 111; as refuge, 349, 350; satellite, 359; tax credits for, 355; and testing, 336, 337; and violence, 349
Schwartz, Felice N., 271–72
Schwarzenegger, Arnold, 233
Seal, Kathy, 398n.5
Seaside, Fla., 319, 320, 321
Seattle Post-Intelligencer, 273
Seattle Times, 85
Second Chances: Men, Women, and Children a Decade after Divorce, 59
Second Shift: Working Parents and the Revolution at Home, 274
Segregation, 345, 346
Select Commission on Immigration and Refugee Policy, 293
Self-care. *See* Children; Latchkey children; Parents
Semerad, Roger, 386–87n.8
"Sesame Street," 44, 146, 162
Sesma, Mary Ann, 291
7-Eleven, 252, 326, 346
Sex issues, 5, 19, 31, 35, 82, 118, 137, 138, 148, 149–58, 169; in education, 149, 156, 395n.10; equal pay, 61; gender roles, 210; and movies, 136; on TV, 134, 135; for teenagers, 359; teenage pregnancy, 392n.3
Shaiken, Harley, 386n.8
Shanker, Albert, 335, 357
Sharkey, Phil, 259

Shaw, George Bernard, 370
Shawnee Mission North High School (Kans.), 39–40, 296
Shelburne, Nancy, 74
Shelby, Karen, 100, 101–2, 247
Shreve, Anita, 230–37, 232
Shuston, Aletha, 141
Singer, Dorothy, 140–41
Skippies, 90
Skolnick, Art, 312, 317
Sloan School of Management, MIT, 49
Smith, Linda, 366
Smoking, 90, 160
Smythe, Robert, 144
Snyder, Tom, 125–26, 127
"Soapbox," 79
Social Security, 300, 302, 404n.3
Societal factors, 13, 31, 58. *See also* Minority groups
Sommerville, John, 56, 58, 218, 384n.20
Southland Corporation, 251, 252, 253
Southwood Elementary School (Raytown, Mo.), 79, 182
Space Balls, 135
Speak and Spell, 122, 123
Spock, Dr. Benjamin, 218, 219, 222, 225, 227
Stanfield, Grace, 304
Stanford Center of Family, Children and Youth, 90
Stanford University, 124, 125, 224, 337, 340, 357
Stanley, Sydney, 327
"Star Trek," 183
Star Wars, 129
Stebbins, Robert, 174, 175
Steelcase (company), 270
Steen, Todd, 261
Stein, Steve, 22
Steinberg, Laurence, 92
Stillman, Amy, 38, 39, 262, 263–64
Straczynski, Michael, 391n.4
Strong, Gary, 326, 327
Suicide, 166, 167, 169
Summerville, Lara, 290
"Super Baby Grows Up," 111
Surveys and polls, 16, 84, 92, 124–25, 149, 158, 170, 191, 254, 276; on child care, 210; on heroes, 233; on libraries, 326; on part-time work by parents, 273, 274; on teacher demand, 340, 341; on work issues, 255; of teacher skills, 352; of television viewing, 142; of working mothers, 281
Sussman, Vic, 122
Sutton-Smith, Brian, 179–80
Swaback, Jacquie, 97, 269, 331, 332

Swarthmore, Pa., 25, 27, 98, 99, 173, 206, 209
Swayze, Patrick, 233
Sweden: day care, 246–47; parental leave, 266, 279

Tales Out of School, 341
Tanelian, Katherine, 270, 271
T. C. Williams High School (Alexandria, Va.), 50, 53, 78, 106, 107, 111, 150, 341
Teachers, 3, 34, 338–43; interviews with, 14; isolation of, 356, 357, 361; morale among, 342; professional standards for, 357; skills of, 352; and violence, 338, 339
Teachers College Press, 141
Teenage Research Unlimited, 90
Television viewing, 15, 18, 28, 91, 92, 106, 117, 130–37, 148, 176, 350; frequency of, 31; and loss of creativity, 139, 140; and video games, 178; and violence, 4, 133, 134, 138, 142, 146, 147, 390nn.3, 4
Tenneco, 360
Tests, 23, 336; achievement, 333, 336, 337, 351; college entrance, 111, 280; and computer use, 125; reading, 346; SAT, 335, 336, 407n.5; teacher proficiency, 357
Texas Instruments, 122
Thigpen, Willie, 176
"Thirty Minutes," 142
Thomas, Norman, 229–30
"Three o'clock syndrome," 94
Thumm, Francis, 162, 163, 164
Thurow, Lester, 49
Time, 39, 42, 55; as a resource, 82; constraints, 22; family, 14, 36; and intergenerational issues, 298; leisure, 15; parenting tricks, 220–24; programmed, 109–13; quality, 17–24, 40, 56
Time, Inc., 268
Timilty Middle School (Boston), 346
TRAC, 337
Trend Facts, 324
Trends in Learning, 337
Trinity School (New York), 52
Trump, Donald, 234, 235
Tuel, Kathy, 177, 178, 220
Tuel, Mike, 28, 32, 177, 220
TV Guide, 134
Tyson, Mike, 233

Unions, 270
United Federation of Teachers, 294
University of British Columbia, 141
University of California, 139
University of California, Berkeley, 287
University of California, Irvine, 91
University of California, San Diego, 311

University of Illinois, 245
University of Kansas, 141
University of Massachusetts, 47–48, 238
University of Miami, 22
University of Michigan, 92, 166
University of Pennsylvania, 138
University of San Diego, 220
University of Southern California, 123
University of Wisconsin, 92
Urban Institute, 192
U.S. Census Bureau, 273
U.S. Chamber of Commerce, 266, 267
USENET, 228, 229
U.S. News and World Report, 59, 357

Van Asselt Early Childhood Center (Seattle),
    17, 338, 342, 349, 355, 356, 358
Videocassettes. See Television viewing
Village Homes (Davis, Calif.), 320, 321
Violence. See Crime and violence
Visconti, Robin, 73

Waits, Tom, 162
Wallerstein, Judith, 59, 60
Wall Street, 53
Wall Street Journal, 280
"Waltons, The," 297
Watson, John B., 218
Weekly Reader, 160
Weingartner, Ed, 251
Weitzman, Lenore, 49
Welsh, Pat, 53, 78, 111, 150, 341, 342
Western Behavorial Sciences Institute (La
    Jolla), 35, 219
Westinghouse Science Talent Search, 294
Westview Elementary School (Miami), 307
"What's It All About," 142
Wheaton College, 149
White, Burton, 365, 366
Whitehead, Barbara, 42, 218, 238, 239,
    379n.7

Whitehead, Ralph, 47–48, 238, 239
Whittier Elementary School (Seattle), 303,
    304, 305
Whittier Senior Reading Partners, 304
Wichita Collegiate School, 52, 104
William Cullen Bryant High School (New
    York), 293, 294
Williams, Ned, 345
Wilson, Laval, 345
Wilson, Wesley, 307, 308
Winfrey, Oprah, 137, 219, 233, 234
Woman's Day, 23
Woman's Workshop Quarterly, 281, 282
Women, 50; divorced, 49; maternity leave
    for, 265, 266; and Mommy Track, 271,
    272, 273, 274; salaries of, 254; and
    "transitional stress," 255. See also Moth-
    ers; Parents
Women's movement. See Feminism
Work and workplace, 6, 7, 39, 53, 72, 87,
    216; at-home, 359, 401n.1; family-
    friendly, 254–74, 371; flex-time and job
    sharing, 261, 270; on-site day care, 255–
    65, 269; parental leave, 265–69
Work/Family Directions, 255, 272
Worthington, Dr. Barry, 170, 171
Wuerthner, J. J., 300, 302
Wunderlich, Judith, 283, 284
Wyche, Freeman, 306, 307
Wyrich, Paul, 60

Xandor Xet, 118
Xerox Corporation, 277

Yale Child Study Center, 6, 350
Yale University, 140, 239
Yates, Gary, 156
YMCA, 284, 328
YWCA, 329

Zigler, Edward F., 245, 265–66, 361, 362
Zinsmeister, Karl, 50